WHERE AMERICA STANDS 1997

M‍ICHAEL G‍OLAY

F‍OREWORD B‍Y J‍UDY W‍OODRUFF,
C‍O-HOST OF CNN'‍S "I‍NSIDE P‍OLITICS"

A N‍EW E‍NGLAND P‍UBLISHING
A‍SSOCIATES B‍OOK

Robinson Public Library District
606 North Jefferson Street
Robinson, IL 62454-2699

John Wiley & Sons, Inc.
New York • Chichester • Weinheim • Brisbane • Singapore • Toronto

This text is printed on acid-free paper.

Copyright © 1997 by John Wiley & Sons, Inc.

Published by John Wiley & Sons, Inc.

All rights reserved. Published simultaneously in Canada.

Reproduction or translation of any part of this work beyond that permitted by Section 107 or 108 of the 1976 United States Copyright Act without the permission of the copyright owner is unlawful. Requests for permission or further information should be addressed to the Permissions Department, John Wiley & Sons, Inc.

This publication is designed to provide accurate and authoritative information in regard to the subject matter covered. It is sold with the understanding that the publisher is not engaged in rendering legal, accounting, or other professional services. If legal advice or other expert assistance is required, the services of a competent professional person should be sought.

NEW ENGLAND
PUBLISHING
ASSOCIATES

Produced by New England Publishing Associates, Inc.
Editor: Edward W. Knappman
Illustration and Design: Ron Formica
Copyediting: Toni Rachiele
Indexing: Roberta J. Buland
Editorial Administration: Ron Formica

ISBN 0-471-16183-7

Printed in the United States of America

10 9 8 7 6 5 4 3 2 1

CONTENTS

FOREWORD
vii

PREFACE: HOW POLLS ARE CONDUCTED
ix

1 Gay Rights
Is Tolerance or Affirmation the Issue?
1

2 Gambling
A Risky Business—for the Customers
19

3 Smoking and Drinking
How Far Should Government Go to Break Our Bad Habits?
39

4 The War on Drugs
The Strategy Debate Never Ends
59

5 Abortion and Euthanasia
Controversy over the Beginning and End of Life
77

6 Education Reform
Do America's Schools Make the Grade?
101

CONTENTS

7 Immigration
Should America Leave the Welcome Mat Out?
125

8 Crime and Punishment
Anxiety Up, Crime Down
145

9 Welfare Reform
Will It Break the Dependency Cycle?
167

10 Affirmative Action
Does It Widen or Narrow the Racial Divide?
187

11 Israel, the Arabs, and the U.S.
Americans Give Israel Cautious Support
205

12 Campaign Reform
Can We Cut Spending Without Curbing Free Speech?
221

13 The 1996 Election
Americans Stay the Course
243

INDEX
263

FOREWORD

by Judy Woodruff
Co-host, CNN's
"Inside Politics"

The hallmark of a democracy is that citizens drive the agenda, setting the course for government. Elites, especially political leaders and the news media, can and frequently do shape the dialogue that helps determine that agenda. But, ultimately, the citizens decide.

The past three elections in the United States are forceful reminders of this simple truth. In 1992, voters decided to throw out a Republican president who they felt was out of touch with their concerns; two years later they sent a message in reaction to what they viewed as the ineptitude of the man they had elected president instead, by giving Republicans full control of Congress for the first time in four decades. Then, last year, in 1996, ignoring the wisdom of some pundits, voters signaled that they believed the president had learned from that experience: they re-elected Bill Clinton by a comfortable majority.

The way the issues shaped how voters make those and other decisions is the centerpiece of the valuable and insightful second annual edition of *Where America Stands*. This book is based on the work of the prestigious Gallup Organization, the nation's oldest public opinion firm. Public opinion on every major event or issue raised over the past year—affirmative action, immigration, education reform, and gay rights to cite just a few—is carefully traced and analyzed here. It is a road map to what transpired and why. It also examines public views on some enduring public policy issues such as crime, smoking, and abortion.

This book, and Gallup, are special to CNN, my professional home for almost four years. We do regular polls with Gallup and USA Today, which have much better enabled us to follow many of the shifts in public attitudes as they unfolded. And this notion of the body politic, as well as market economies, being driven from the bottom up, epitomizes the origin and the success of CNN over its 17-year history.

This is not to suggest that either politics or journalism should be driven primarily by public opinion polls: not infrequently they are overused or misused. Moreover, some public perceptions are simply wrong, such as the persistent notion that the government spends a big chunk of the budget on foreign aid. But used and analyzed correctly, polls can give politicians and journalists a genuine feel for where the country stands at a given time and why. That doesn't always produce good policy or good news stories. But there is a better chance of producing both with that knowledge than without it, or, even worse, with erroneous or merely anecdotal information about public opinion. In addition, this knowledge enables CNN to perform two important roles: as reporter of news "from the top down," but also as reporter of public opinion "from the bottom up."

This book is not about dry numbers: it is well written and aided by easy-to-understand charts and graphs. Behind it all is a look at what makes America tick.

Preface: How Polls Are Conducted

by
Frank Newport, Lydia Saad,
and David W. Moore
Editors, The Gallup Poll

Public opinion polls would have less value in a democracy if the public—the very people whose views are represented by the polls—didn't have confidence in the results. This confidence does not come easily. The process of polling is often mysterious, particularly to those who don't see how the views of 1,000 people can represent those of hundreds of millions. Many Americans contact the Gallup Organization each year (1) to ask how our results can differ so much from their own, personal impressions of what people think, (2) to learn how we go about selecting people for inclusion in our polls, and (3) to find out why they have never been interviewed. The public's questions indicate a healthy dose of skepticism about polling. Their questions, however, are usually accompanied by a strong and sincere desire to find out what's going on under Gallup's hood.

It turns out that the callers who reach Gallup's switchboard may be just the tip of the iceberg of those who are curious about the polls. Survey researchers have actually conducted public opinion polls to find out how much confidence Americans have in polls—and have discovered an interesting paradox: People generally believe the results of polls, but they do not believe in the scientific principles on which polls are based. In a recent Gallup "poll on polls," respondents said that polls generally do a good job of forecasting elections and are accurate when measuring public opinion on other issues. Yet when asked about the scientific sampling foundation on which all polls are based, Americans were skeptical. Most said that a survey of 1,500 to 2,000 respondents—a larger-than-average sample size for national polls—cannot truly represent the views of all Americans.

In addition to these questions about sampling validity, the public often asks questions about the questions themselves—that is, who decides what questions to ask the public, and how those looking at poll results can be sure that the answers reflect the public's true opinion about the issues at hand.

The Sampling Issue

Probability sampling is the fundamental basis for all survey research. The basic principle: A randomly selected, small percentage of a population of people can represent the attitudes, opinions, or projected behavior of all the people, if the sample is selected correctly.

The fundamental goal of a survey is to come up with the same results that would have been obtained had every single member of a population been interviewed. For national Gallup polls, in other words, the objective is to present the opinions of a sample of people that are exactly the same opinions that would have been obtained had it been possible to interview all adult Americans in the country.

The key to reaching this goal is a fundamental principle called equal probability of selection, which states that if every member of a population has an equal probability of being selected in a sample, then that sample will be representative of the population. It's that straightforward.

Thus, it is Gallup's goal in selecting samples to allow every adult American an equal chance of falling into the sample. How that is done, of course, is the key to the success or failure of the process.

> "The fundamental goal of a survey is to come up with the same results that would have been obtained had every single member of a population been interviewed."

Selecting a Random Sample

The first 1,000 people streaming out of a Yankees game in the Bronx clearly aren't representative of all Americans. Now consider a group compiled by selecting 1,000 people coming out of a Major League Baseball game from the 28 Major League ballparks—28,000 people! We now have a much larger group, but we are still no closer to representing the views of all Americans than we were in the Bronx. We have a lot of baseball fans, but depending on the circumstances, these 28,000 people may not even be a good representative sample of all baseball fans in the country—much less all Americans, baseball fans or not.

When setting out to conduct a national opinion poll, the first thing Gallup does is select a place where all or most Americans are equally likely to be found. That wouldn't be a shopping mall, a grocery store, an office building, a hotel, or a baseball game. The place nearly all adult Americans are most likely to be found is in their home. So reaching people at home is the starting place for almost all national surveys.

By necessity, the earliest polls were conducted in person, with Gallup interviewers fanning out across the country, knocking on Americans' doors. This was the standard method of interviewing for nearly fifty years, from about 1935 to the mid-1980s, and it was a demonstrably reliable method. Gallup polls across twelve presidential and thirteen midterm congressional elections between 1936 and 1984 were highly accurate, with the average error in Gallup's final prediction of national support for the winning candidate or political party being only 2.2 percentage points. (The average error since 1984 has also been 2.2 points.)

By 1986, enough American households had at least one telephone to make telephone interviewing a viable and substantially less expensive alternative to the in-person method. And by the end of the 1980s, the vast majority of Gallup's national surveys were being conducted by telephone. Today, approximately 95 percent of all households have a telephone, and every survey reported in this book is based on

"**Reaching people at home is the starting place for almost all national surveys.**"

Gallup Poll vs. Final Election Results: 1936–1996

Since Gallup began polling voters for presidential elections, the percentages for the winning candidates have been within an average of 2.73 percentage points of those for the final election results. Here is a look at how Gallup's final polling numbers compare with the election results in presidential elections since 1936.

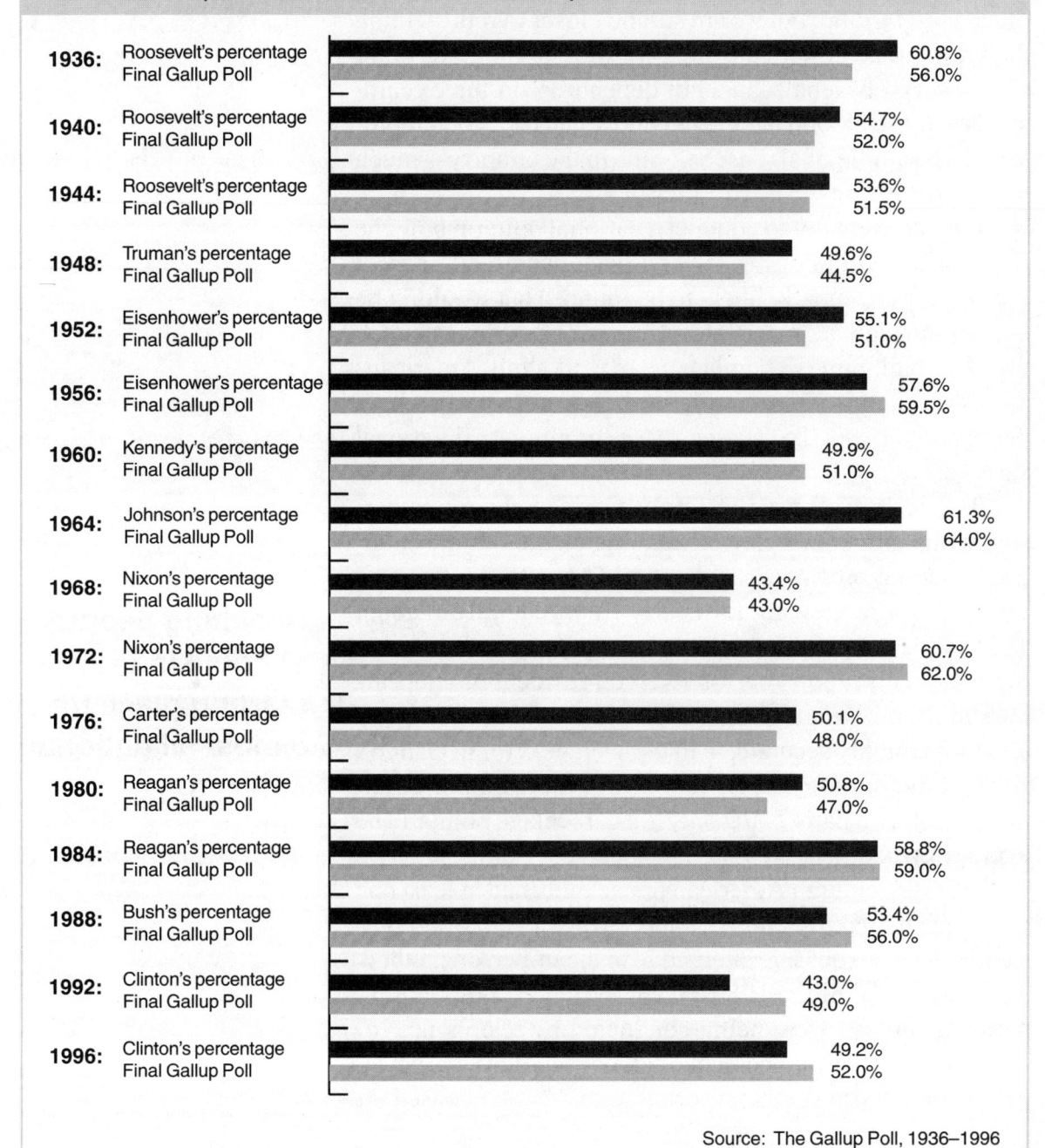

Year		Percentage	Final Gallup Poll
1936:	Roosevelt	60.8%	56.0%
1940:	Roosevelt	54.7%	52.0%
1944:	Roosevelt	53.6%	51.5%
1948:	Truman	49.6%	44.5%
1952:	Eisenhower	55.1%	51.0%
1956:	Eisenhower	57.6%	59.5%
1960:	Kennedy	49.9%	51.0%
1964:	Johnson	61.3%	64.0%
1968:	Nixon	43.4%	43.0%
1972:	Nixon	60.7%	62.0%
1976:	Carter	50.1%	48.0%
1980:	Reagan	50.8%	47.0%
1984:	Reagan	58.8%	59.0%
1988:	Bush	53.4%	56.0%
1992:	Clinton	43.0%	49.0%
1996:	Clinton	49.2%	52.0%

Source: The Gallup Poll, 1936–1996

interviews conducted by telephone.

Gallup proceeds with several steps in putting together its poll, with the objective of letting every American household, and every American adult, have an equal chance of falling into the sample.

1. *First, we clearly identify and describe the population that a given poll is attempting to represent.* If we were doing a poll about baseball fans on behalf of the sports page of a major newspaper, the target population might simply be all Americans aged eighteen and older who say they are fans of the sport of baseball. If the poll were being conducted on behalf of Major League Baseball, however, the target audience required by the client might be more specific, such as people aged twelve and older who watch at least five hours' worth of major league baseball games on television, or in person, each week.

In the case of Gallup polls that track the election and the major political, social, and economic questions of the day, the target audience consists of those generally referred to as "national adults." Strictly speaking, the target audience is all adults, aged eighteen and over, living in telephone households within the continental United States. In effect, it is the civilian, noninstitutionalized population. On campus college students, armed forces personnel living on military bases, prisoners, hospital patients and others living in group institutions are not represented in Gallup's "sampling frame." Clearly these exclusions represent some diminishment in the coverage of the population, but because of the practical difficulties involved in attempting to reach the institutionalized population, it is a compromise Gallup usually needs to make.

2. *Next, we choose or design a method that will enable us to sample our target population randomly.* In the case of the Gallup poll, we start with a list of all household telephone numbers in the continental United States. This complicated process really starts with a computerized list of all telephone exchanges in America, along with estimates of

> **" Gallup proceeds with several steps in putting together its poll. "**

> "How many interviews does it take to provide an adequate cross section of Americans?"

the number of residential households those exchanges have attached to them. The computer, using a procedure called random digit dialing (RDD), actually creates phone numbers from those exchanges, then generates telephone samples from those. In essence, this procedure creates a list of all possible household phone numbers in America and then selects a subset of numbers from that list for Gallup to call.

It's important to go through this complicated procedure, because estimates are that about 30 percent of American residential phones are unlisted. Although it would be a lot simpler if we used phone books to obtain all listed phone numbers in America and sampled from them (much as you would if you simply took every thirty-eighth number from your local phone book), we would miss out on unlisted phone numbers and introduce a possible bias into the sample.

The Number of Interviews Required

One key question faced by Gallup statisticians: How many interviews does it take to provide an adequate cross section of Americans? The answer is, not many—that is, if the respondents to be interviewed are selected entirely at random, giving every adult American an equal probability of falling into the sample. The current U.S. adult population in the continental United States is 187 million. The typical sample size for a Gallup poll that is designed to represent this general population is 1,000 national adults.

The actual number of people that are interviewed for a given sample is to some degree less important than the soundness of the fundamental principle of equal-probability-of-selection. If respondents are not selected randomly, we could have a poll with a million people and still be significantly less likely to represent the views of all Americans than a much smaller sample of just 1,000 people if that sample is selected randomly. This is something many people find hard to believe, but it is true.

To be sure, there is some gain in sampling accuracy from increasing sample sizes. Common sense—and sampling theory—tell us that a sample of 1,000 people probably is going to be more accurate than a sample of 20. Surprisingly, however, once the survey sample gets to a size of 500, 600, 700, or more, there is a smaller and smaller accuracy gain from increasing the sample size. Gallup and other major organizations use sample sizes of between 1,000 and 1,500 because they provide a solid balance of accuracy against the increased economic cost of larger and larger samples. If Gallup were to—quite expensively—use a sample of 4,000 randomly selected adults each time it did its poll, the increase in accuracy over and beyond a well-done sample of 1,000 would be minimal and, generally speaking, would not justify the nearly fourfold increase in cost.

Statisticians over the years have developed quite specific ways of measuring the accuracy of samples, as long as the fundamental principle of equal probability of selection is applied to when the sample is drawn.

For example, with a sample size of 1,000 national adults (derived using careful random selection procedures), the results are highly likely to be accurate within a margin of error of plus or minus 3 percentage points. Thus, if we find in a given poll that President Clinton's approval rating is 50 percent, the margin of error indicates that the true rating is very likely to be between 53 and 47 percent. It is very unlikely to be higher or lower than that.

To be more specific, the laws of probability say that if we were to conduct the same survey a hundred times, asking people in each survey to rate the job Bill Clinton is doing as president, in ninety-five out of those one hundred polls, we would find his rating to be between 47 and 53 percent. In only five of those surveys would we expect his rating to be higher or lower than that because of chance error.

As discussed above, if we increase the sample size to 2,000 rather than 1,000 for a Gallup poll, we would find that the results would be accurate within plus or minus 2 percent of the underlying population value, a gain of 1 percent in terms of accuracy, but with a 100 percent increase in

> **Once the survey sample gets to a size of 500, 600, 700, or more, there is a smaller and smaller accuracy gain from increasing the sample size.**

the cost of conducting the survey. These are the cost-value decisions that Gallup and other survey organizations make when they decide on sample sizes for their surveys.

The Interview Itself

Once the computer has selected a phone number for inclusion in the sample, Gallup goes to extensive lengths to make contact with an adult American living in that household. In many instances, there is no answer or the number is busy on the first call. Instead of forgetting that number and going on to the next, Gallup typically stores the number in the computer, where it comes back up to be recalled a few hours later, and then if there is still no contact, the number will be recalled again on subsequent nights of the survey period. This procedure corrects for a possible bias that could occur if we included interviews only with people who answered the phone the first time we called their numbers. For example, people who are less likely to be at home,

American Opinion

Do you think a sample of 1,500 or 2,000 people can accurately reflect the views of the nation's population?

Source: The Gallup Poll 1996

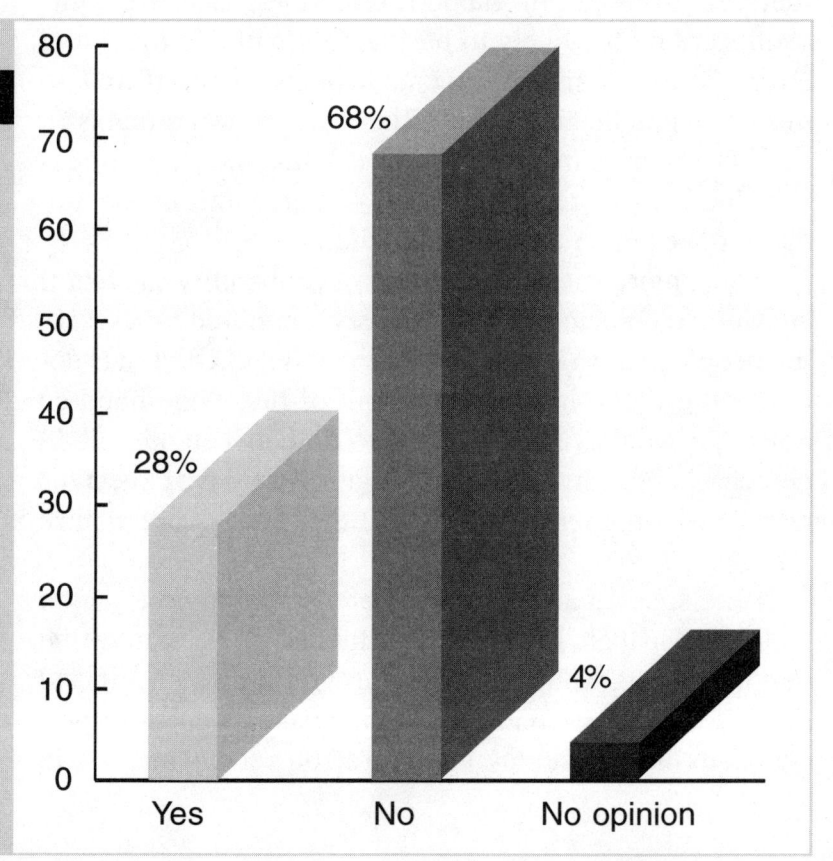

Response	Percentage
Yes	28%
No	68%
No opinion	4%

such as young single adults, or people who spend a lot of time on the phone, would have a lower probability of falling into the sample than an adult American who was always at home and rarely talked on his or her phone.

For those households that include more than one adult, Gallup also attempts to ensure that an individual within that household is selected randomly. There are several different procedures that Gallup has used through the years for this within-household selection process. Gallup sometimes uses a shorthand method of asking for the adult with the latest birthday. In other surveys, Gallup asks the individual who answers the phone to list all adults in the home based on their age and gender, and Gallup randomly selects one of those adults to be interviewed. If the randomly selected adult is not home, Gallup tells the person on the phone that Gallup will need to call back and try to reach that individual at another time.

These procedures, while expensive and while not always possible in polls conducted in very short time periods, help to ensure that every adult American has an equal probability of falling into the sample.

The Questions

The technical aspects of data collection are critically important, and if done poorly, can undermine the reliability of even a perfectly worded question. When it comes to modern-day attitude surveys conducted by most of the major national polling organizations, however, question wording is probably the greatest source of bias and error in the data, followed by question order. Writing a clear, unbiased question takes great care and discipline, as well as extensive knowledge about public opinion.

Even such a seemingly simple thing as asking Americans whom they are going to vote for in a forthcoming election can be dependent on how the question is framed. For example, in a presidential race, the survey researcher can include the name of the vice presidential candidates along with the presidential candidates, or the researcher can just

> **"Question wording is probably the greatest source of bias and error in the data."**

> **Questions about policy issues have an even greater range of wording options.**

mention the presidential candidates' names. One can remind respondents of the party affiliation of each candidate when the question is read, or one can mention the names of the candidates without any indication of their party. Gallup's rule in this situation is to ask the question in a way that mimics the voting experience as much as possible. We read the names of the presidential and vice presidential candidates, and mention the name of the party line on which they are running. All of this is information the voter would normally see when reading the ballot in the voting booth.

Questions about policy issues have an even greater range of wording options. Should we describe programs like food stamps and Section 8 housing grants as "welfare" or as "programs for the poor" when asking whether the public favors or opposes them? Should we identify proposed health care legislation as health care "reform" or as "an overhaul of the health care system"? When measuring support for the U.S. military presence in Bosnia, should we say the United States is "sending" troops or "contributing" troops to the UN-sponsored mission there? Any of these wording choices could have a substantial impact on the levels of support recorded in the poll.

For many of the public opinion areas covered in this book, Gallup is in the fortunate position of having a historical track record. Gallup has been conducting public opinion polls on public policy, presidential approval, approval of Congress, and key issues such as the death penalty, abortion, and gun control for many years. This gives Gallup the advantage of continuing a question in exactly the same way that it has been asked historically, which in turn provides a very precise measurement of trends. If the exact wording of a question is held constant from year to year, then substantial changes in how the American public responds to that question usually represent an underlying change in attitude.

For new questions, which don't have an exact analogue in history, Gallup has to be more creative. In many instances, even though the question is not exactly the same, Gallup can follow the format it has used for previous questions that seemed to produce accurate results. For instance, when

Gallup was formulating the questions we asked the public about the Persian Gulf War in 1990 and 1991, we were able to go back to questions we asked during the Vietnam War and borrow their basic construction. Similarly, even though the issues and personalities change on the national political scene, we can apply the same question formats used for previous presidents and political leaders to measure support for current leaders.

One of the oldest question wordings Gallup has in its inventory concerns presidential job approval. Since the days of Franklin Roosevelt, Gallup has been asking, "Do you approve or disapprove of the job [blank] is doing as president?" That wording has stayed constant over the years, and provides a very reliable trend line for how Americans are reacting to their presidents.

For brand-new question areas, Gallup will often test several different wordings. Additionally, Gallup may ask several different questions about a content area of interest. Then in the interpretation phase of a given survey, Gallup analysts can make note of the way Americans respond to different question wordings, presenting a more complete

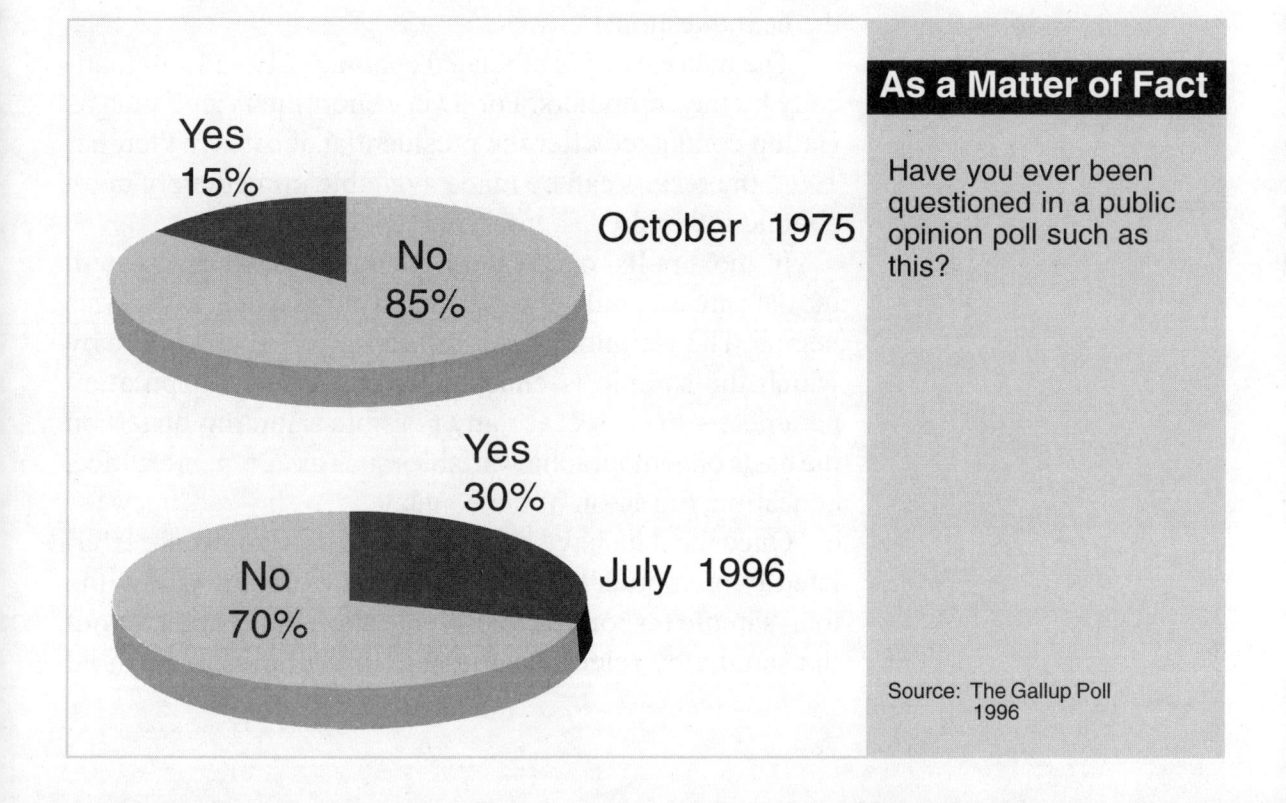

October 1975
- Yes 15%
- No 85%

July 1996
- Yes 30%
- No 70%

As a Matter of Fact

Have you ever been questioned in a public opinion poll such as this?

Source: The Gallup Poll 1996

picture of the population's underlying attitudes.

Through the years, Gallup has often used a split-sample technique to measure the impact of different question wordings. A randomly selected half of a given survey is administered one wording of a question, while the other half is administered the other wording. This allows Gallup to compare the impact of differences in the wording of questions, and often to report the results of both wordings, allowing those looking at the results of the poll to see the impact of nuances in patterns of public opinion.

Conducting the Interview

Most Gallup interviews are conducted by telephone from Gallup's regional interviewing centers around the country. Trained interviewers use computer-assisted telephone interviewing (CATI) technology, which brings the survey questions up on a computer monitor and allows questionnaires to be tailored to the specific responses given by the individual being interviewed. (If you answer "yes" to a question about whether you like pizza, the computer might be programmed to read, "What is your favorite topping?" as the next question.)

The interviews are tabulated continuously and automatically by the computers. For a very short interview, such as Gallup conducted after the presidential debates in October 1996, the results can be made available immediately upon completion of the last interview.

In most polls, once interviewing has been completed, the data are carefully checked and weighted before analysis begins. The weighting process is a statistical procedure by which the sample is checked against known population parameters to correct for any possible sampling biases on the basis of demographic variables such as age, gender, race, education, or region of the country.

Once the data have been weighted, the results are tabulated by computer programs that show not only how the total sample responded to each question but also break out the sample by relevant variables. In Gallup's presidential

> "Most Gallup interviews are conducted by telephone from Gallup's regional interviewing centers around the country."

polling in 1996, for example, answers to the presidential vote question were broken out by political party, age, gender, race, region of the country, religious affiliation, and other variables.

Interpreting the Results

There are several standard caveats to observe when interpreting poll results. Primary among these are issues discussed in this chapter: question wording, question order, the sample population, the sample size, the random selection technique used in creating a sampling frame, the execution of the sample (including the number of people called back and the length of the polling period), and the method of interviewing (in person versus telephone versus mail).

Anyone using Gallup poll results can do so with assurance that the data were obtained with extremely careful and reliable sampling and interviewing methods. Gallup's intent is always to be fair and objective when writing questions and constructing questionnaires. The original mission of polling was to amplify the voice of the public, not distort it, and we continue to be inspired by that mission.

With those assurances in mind, the outside observer or researcher should dive into poll data with a critical mind. Interpretation of survey research results is most heavily dependent on context. What the American public may say about an issue is most valuable when it can be compared with other current questions or with similar questions asked across time. Where trend data exist, one should also look at changes over time and determine whether these changes are significant and important. Let's say, for example, that Bill Clinton has a job approval rating of 48 percent. Is this a good rating or a poor rating? The best way to tell is to look at history for context: Compare it with Clinton's ratings throughout the rest of his presidency, then compare it with approval ratings for previous presidents. Did previous presidents with this rating at the equivalent point in time tend to get re-elected or not? Then it can be compared with approval ratings of Congress and of the Republican and the

> **Gallup's intent is always to be fair and objective when writing questions and constructing questionnaires.**

Democratic congressional leaders.

Gallup generally provides written analysis of its own polling data. But we also provide ample opportunity for the press, other pollsters, students, professors, and the general public to draw their own conclusions about what the data mean. The results of all Gallup surveys are in the public domain—that is, once they have been publicly released by us, anyone who chooses can pick up the information and write about it themselves. The survey results are regularly published in the major media, in the *Gallup Poll Monthly*, and through several electronic information services such as the Roper Center at the University of Connecticut and on the Internet. We also make the raw data available to researchers who want to perform more complex statistical analysis. In addition to the exact question wordings and current results, Gallup provides the historical results to all questions that have been asked previously, so that even the casual observer can review the current results in context with public opinion in the past and follow the trends.

The key concept to bear in mind when analyzing poll data is that public opinion on a given topic cannot be understood by using only a single poll question asked a single time. It is necessary to measure opinion along several different dimensions, to review attitudes based on a variety of different wordings, to verify findings on the basis of multiple askings, and to pay attention to changes in opinion over time.

This is good advice to bear in mind as you work your way through the topics presented in *Where America Stands, 1997*.

Gay Rights
1 Is Tolerance or Affirmation the Issue?

The Gallup Organization has charted a steady, if slow rise in the theoretical acceptance of homosexuals in American society. Yet on many of the practical issues of the gay rights agenda, opinion remains sharply divided and sometimes contradictory. And around half of those queried in Gallup surveys in 1996 said they do not regard homosexuality as an acceptable way to live.

Eighty-four percent of respondents in a 1996 poll favored equal job opportunities for homosexuals, a rise from the 59 percent of eleven years earlier. But in a 1994 survey, only 39 percent supported the formal extension of civil rights protection to gays and lesbians. In the same poll, a majority, 56 percent, said gay rights leaders were too aggressive in pursuit of their goals. And in a 1996 sample, fully two-thirds opposed granting legal recognition to same-sex marriages.

Such attitudes reflect the gulf between tolerance and approval of gays and lesbians, between evenhanded treatment on the job and full social acceptance. Many people draw a distinction between, say, workplace guarantees and the institution of marriage.

"I think when people think of marriage, they think of sex," observed Brigid Quinn, a federal employee from Washington, D.C., and a lesbian. "When people think gay and sex in the same phrase, it just unnerves them. But when you think of the workplace, they think of colleagues, people doing the same thing they do. And they think, 'Why shouldn't Brigid be protected the same way I'm protected?' "[1]

> "Many people draw a distinction between, say, workplace guarantees and the institution of marriage."

> "In some respects, Americans are little more accepting of homosexuality today than they were a decade or two ago."

In some respects, Americans are little more accepting of homosexuality today than they were a decade or two ago. In the 1994 survey, more than a third thought homosexuals ought to "stay in the closet," presumably so gay issues would simply disappear from public view.

That seems unlikely to happen. Same-sex marriage; discrimination in public life; homosexuals in the military, the clergy, and the schools; and responses to the AIDS epidemic doubtless will continue to be hotly debated.

For those most closely engaged—gay rights advocates on one side, religious and cultural conservatives on the other—the issues are tightly bound up in the question of whether or not homosexuality is a choice. After all, if being gay is involuntary and therefore blameless, how can such people be denied the protection of civil rights laws that assure no one is penalized because of conditions of birth? On the other hand, if it is a question of morality and a matter of choice and homosexuals could change their behavior if they wished, mainstream society has a right to regard the choice as immoral.

Writes Andrew Sullivan in *Virtually Normal: An Argument About Homosexuality*: "There's a lamentable tendency to try to find some definitive solution to human predicaments—in a string of DNA, in a conclusive psychological survey, in a verse of the Bible—in order to cut the argument short. But none of these things can replace the political and moral argument about how a society should deal with the

American Opinion

Over the past decade, there has been a steady but slow rise in the acceptance of homosexuals in American society. Today, a vast majority of Americans favor equal job opportunities for homosexuals.

Source: The Gallup Poll 1982, 1996

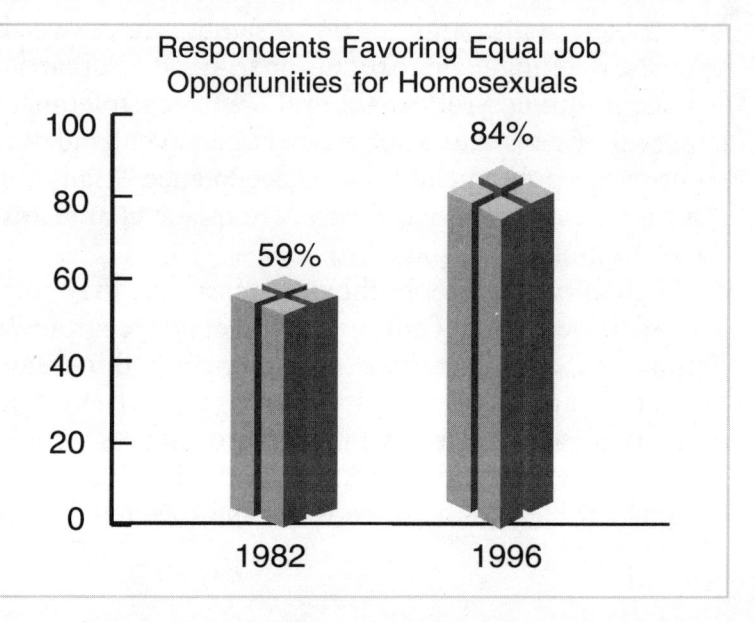

Respondents Favoring Equal Job Opportunities for Homosexuals

Year	Percentage
1982	59%
1996	84%

presence of homosexuals in its midst."[2]

In the broad, generally tolerant middle range, people are accepting of homosexuals as private persons, largely persuaded that sexual inversion is more an orientation than a lifestyle choice, less than enthusiastic about formal legal recognition of gay rights, and disinclined to debate the matter openly and at length.

Equal Rights or Special Rights?

Ending job discrimination on the basis of sexual orientation—discrimination is legal in forty-one states—has long been a key element of the gay rights agenda. The movement enlisted President Clinton's support in 1996 for a bill that would have banned workplace discrimination against homosexuals. In a September 1996 Senate roll call, the measure failed by only one vote—a surprising near triumph for the gay rights lobby.

In *Virtually Normal*, Sullivan calls for an end to all public, state-sponsored discrimination against homosexuals. He would strike sodomy laws, where they exist, off the books. He favors the teaching of facts about homosexuality in public school sex-education classes. He would ban discrimination in any government agency, including the military. And he supports the legal recognition of same-sex marriages. Sullivan would extend to homosexuals all the rights and responsibilities that heterosexuals take for granted as public citizens.

Gallup findings suggest Americans have become more doubtful about across-the-board protection for gays and lesbians as discussion of the issue has intensified. In an April 1993 poll, 46 percent favored extending to homosexuals the same civil rights laws that now apply to blacks, other minorities, and women, while 48 percent were opposed.

In September 1994, in the aftermath of the controversy over the Clinton administration's effort to lift the ban on gays in the military, only 39 percent were in favor of extending civil rights protection to homosexuals. Fifty-eight percent were opposed, and 3 percent had no opinion.

Breaking down opinion in the 1994 survey, Gallup found women (45 percent) more likely than men (32 percent) to favor extending rights to gays. People aged eighteen to

"
Gallup findings suggest Americans have become more doubtful about across-the-board protection for gays and lesbians.
"

twenty-nine (46 percent) were more favorable than people older than fifty (34 percent). Easterners (46 percent) were more likely to favor civil rights for homosexuals than Westerners (38 percent), Midwesterners (38 percent), or Southerners (35 percent). Racial minorities (49 percent) were more in favor than whites (37 percent).

The 1996 antidiscrimination vote turned out to be closer than expected, buoying gay rights activists, who pledged to press for congressional action on the issue in 1997. "When you look at where we started and then to come within a breath of victory, this is a powerful movement in terms of the overall civil rights movement for all gay Americans," said Elizabeth Birch, executive director of the Human Rights Campaign, an advocacy group for homosexuals.[3]

A High-Court Affirmation

In a split decision with a vigorous dissent, the United States Supreme Court ruled in favor of homosexual rights in 1996. Voting 6 to 3, the high court struck down a 1992 Colorado constitutional clause that voided civil rights protection for gays and barred the adoption of new antidiscrimination laws. The court did not, however, require Colorado to offer new rights protection to homosexuals.

In the majority opinion, Justice Anthony M. Kennedy suggested that "animus" alone could explain Colorado's action in nullifying local gay rights ordinances in Aspen, Boulder, and Denver.

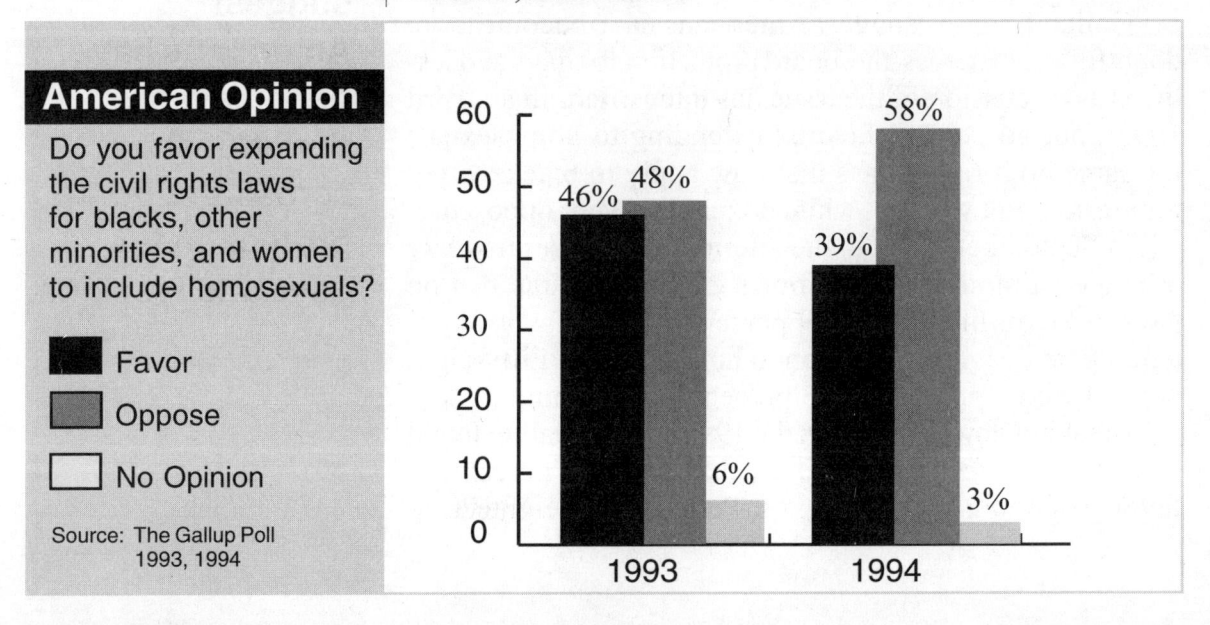

American Opinion

Do you favor expanding the civil rights laws for blacks, other minorities, and women to include homosexuals?

- ■ Favor
- ▨ Oppose
- ☐ No Opinion

Source: The Gallup Poll 1993, 1994

Year	Favor	Oppose	No Opinion
1993	46%	48%	6%
1994	39%	58%	3%

"A state cannot so deem a class of persons a stranger to its laws," wrote Kennedy, a 1988 appointee of former president Ronald Reagan. "It is not within our constitutional tradition to enact laws of this sort."[4]

In a minority opinion, Justice Antonin Scalia accused the majority of choosing sides in the "culture wars." He noted, too, that Colorado voters had approved the provision, known as Amendment 2, in a statewide referendum. Fifty-three percent of those voting favored the measure.

Chief Justice William H. Rehnquist, also in dissent, characterized Amendment 2 as a reasonable means of slowing the "piecemeal deterioration of the sexual morality favored by a majority of Coloradans."[5] Lawyers for Colorado argued that the amendment merely removed special protections local advocacy groups had written into the laws of the three Colorado cities.

Wrote Kennedy: "We find nothing special in the protections Amendment 2 withholds. These are protections taken for granted by most people either because they already have them or don't need them; these are protections against exclusion from an almost limitless number of transactions and endeavors that constitute ordinary civil life in a free society."[6]

Gay rights activists hailed the ruling in that case, *Romer v. Evans*, as a significant victory. "I don't want to exaggerate, but I believe it is the capping of our liberation," said longtime Los Angeles gay leader Morris Kight.[7]

> **In a minority opinion, Justice Antonin Scalia accused the majority of choosing sides in the 'culture wars.'**

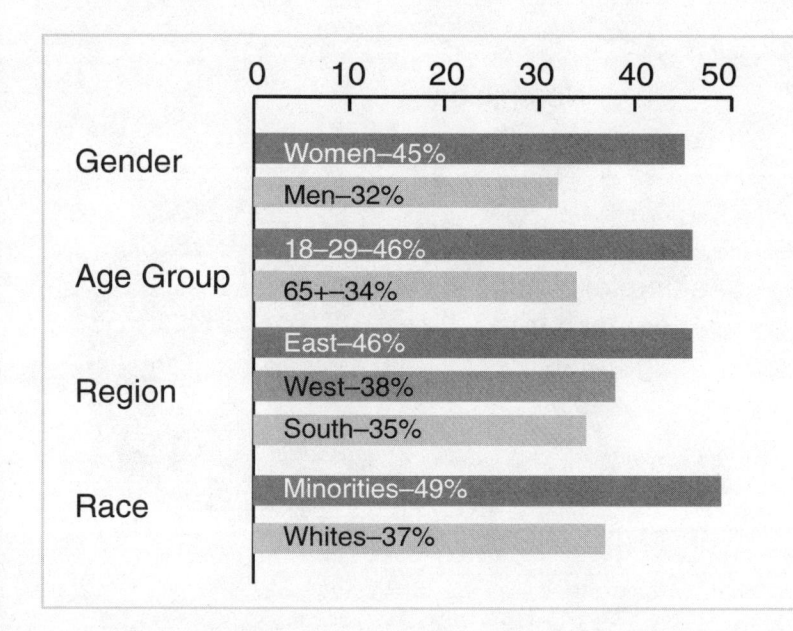

American Opinion

According to gender, age, region of America, and race, here is the support for extending civil rights to gays.

Category	Group	Percent
Gender	Women	45%
	Men	32%
Age Group	18–29	46%
	65+	34%
Region	East	46%
	West	38%
	South	35%
Race	Minorities	49%
	Whites	37%

Source: The Gallup Poll 1994

> "Gay rights activists hailed the ruling as a significant victory."

In Colorado Springs, where the referendum initiative began, some gays thought Amendment 2 actually advanced their cause. "It forced us to become more visible, to show people that we do not have three heads and three arms," Regina DiPadova said.[8]

On the other side, some commentators argued the Supreme Court had confused affirmation with tolerance. "The case arose when various Colorado cities chose not to remain neutral, but to give 'sexual orientation' (the code word for homosexuality) an exalted place under the law," wrote Douglas W. Kmiec, a professor of law at University of Notre Dame.[9]

Gallup surveys suggest that people divide about evenly on the question of whether homosexuals are seeking special rights for themselves or are asking only for rights and protections others take for granted. In a 1993 poll, 44 percent thought gays and lesbians sought special rights; 49 percent said gays and lesbians wanted the same rights others claim.

It should be noted, too, that in America the question is perhaps more a matter of degree than of kind. Gays enjoy broad rights of free speech and association. There are even gay and lesbian clubs in some American high schools. Such a degree of acceptance would be unthinkable in many parts of the world. In the southern African nation of Zimbabwe, for example, the government in 1995 and 1996 barred a gay group from setting up an exhibit in the annual Interna-

American Opinion

Are gays seeking special rights for themselves or are they asking only for the rights and protections others take for granted?

- No opinion: 7%
- Seeking special rights: 44%
- Asking for rights others take for granted: 49%

Source: The Gallup Poll 1993

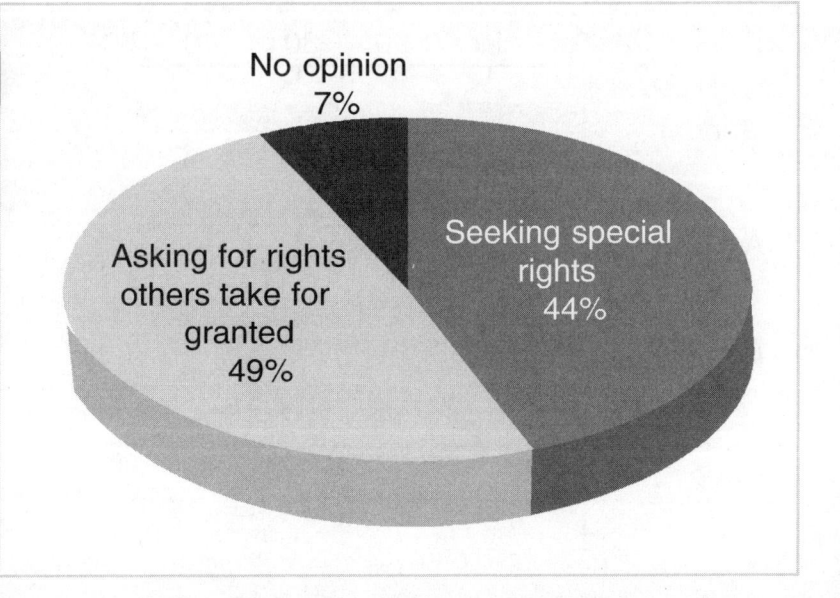

tional Book Fair in Harare, the capital. Zimbabwean citizens regard homosexuality as "moral repulsiveness," the government said.[10]

The Pulpit and the Barracks

The presence of open, practicing homosexuals in the clergy and the military has become a flash point for controversy. Gallup has found that survey respondents are considerably more tolerant of gays in some fields than in others.

In a 1996 survey, 65 percent thought it all right for gays to serve in the military; 29 percent disapproved. Fifty-three percent approved of gays in the clergy; 40 percent disapproved. Fifty-five percent approved of gay men and lesbians teaching in the elementary schools while 40 percent disapproved.

The debate over gay clergy has caused deep pain in America's churches and synagogues. "Homosexuality is one of the hottest and most divisive issues in many denominations—and people are being forced to deal with it whether they want to or not," said Keith Hartman, an Atlanta journalist and the author of *Congregations in Conflict: The Battle over Homosexuality*.[11]

In just one four-month span during 1996, three large denominations were embroiled in controversies over homosexuality.

"
Gallup has found that survey respondents are considerably more tolerant of gays in some fields than in others.
"

Do You Approve or Disapprove of:

	Gays in the military	Gays as doctors	Gays in the clergy	Gays as teachers
Disapprove	29%	25%	40%	40%
Approve	65%	69%	53%	55%

American Opinion

Gallup polls show that Americans approve of gays in a variety of professions.

■ Approve
▨ Disapprove
☐ No Opinion

Source: The Gallup Poll 1996

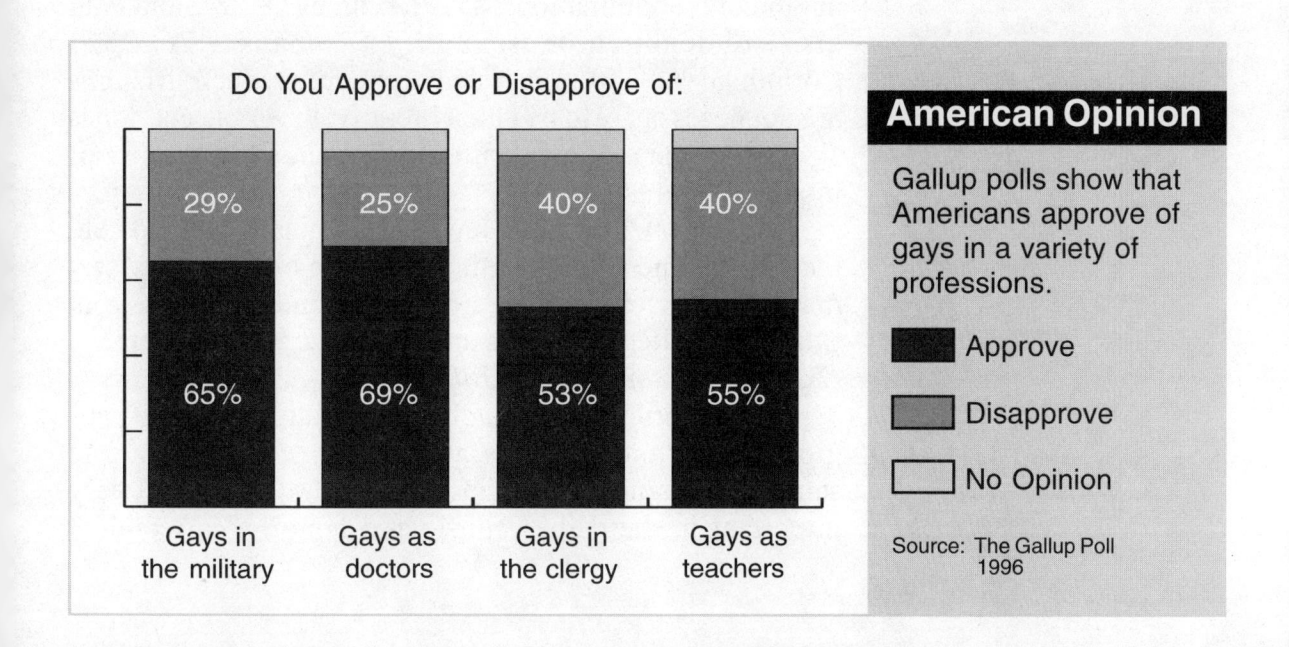

> "For fundamentalist Christians, the scriptures settle all questions."

- In April 1996, the quadrennial conference of the 8.6-million-member United Methodist Church upheld a church policy that declares homosexuality incompatible with Christian teaching.

- Ten bishops of the Episcopal Church brought heresy charges against a bishop who had ordained a gay man as a deacon, the rank just below priest. The charges were dismissed against Bishop Walter C. Righter in May 1996, after an ecclesiastical court ruled the church had no core doctrine barring the ordination of a noncelibate homosexual in a stable relationship with a person of the same sex. All the same, the ten bishops said they would lobby the 2.5-million-member church's General Convention to enact a law obligating members of the clergy to be celibate outside marriage. The convention, the Episcopalians' legislature, next meets in July 1997.

- In July 1996, the Presbyterian Church (USA) voted to deny practicing homosexuals ordination as pastor, elder, or deacon. "Our congregations will neither respect nor follow persons who flaunt their failures at sexual self-control," asserted the conservative church newspaper the *Presbyterian Layman*.[12]

For fundamentalist Christians, the scriptures settle all questions. "Thou shalt not lie with mankind, as with womankind: it is abomination," says Leviticus 18:22. Saint Paul also condemns homosexuality (Romans 1:26–27, I Corinthians 6:9–10). Liberal interpreters say such strictures are not necessarily to be taken literally; the Bible condones slavery, so the argument runs, and abjures the lending of money at interest.

"No major Christian or Jewish denomination would hold that all statements in the Bible ought to be observed," remarked Michael Coogan, a religious-studies professor at Stonehill College in Massachusetts and co-editor of *The Oxford Companion to the Bible*.[13]

Gallup surveys show a clear connection between religious belief and attitudes about homosexuality. In one sample, three-quarters of those who regard religion as very important in their lives considered homosexual conduct immoral. Fewer than a third for whom religion is only somewhat important or is not at all important viewed gay sexual activity as immoral.

The United Church of Christ is the only major Protestant denomination to allow the ordination of gays. The UCC urges individual congregations not to deny the pastorate to homosexuals, though it leaves the final decision up to church regional associations. The Unitarian-Universalist Association and the Reform branch of Judaism also permit the ordination of open homosexuals.

Ordination of gay clergy has not become a major issue in the Roman Catholic Church, in which the priesthood is sworn to celibacy. Catholic doctrine recognizes a homosexual *condition* as unchangeable and blameless for some people. Yet Catholic teaching describes homosexual *acts* as wrong in all circumstances.[14]

President Clinton's "don't ask, don't tell" policy sought a compromise that would allow gays and lesbians to serve in the armed forces as long as they did not make their sexual orientation public or engage in homosexual acts. The military, in turn, would stop its purges of gay personnel.

This tortured policy—which prescribed, for example, that a soldier or sailor could patronize a gay bar but could not write a love letter to a same-sex friend—satisfied neither the services nor gay-rights advocates. "The final military policy was not about excluding gays from the military; it was about keeping their mouths shut," Sullivan wrote.[15] Clinton had vowed to lift the ban, and some gay activists considered the compromise as a retrograde step.

As the debate intensified, Gallup surveys found sharp but roughly even divisions over the issue. A series of polls showed slight majorities in favor of retaining the ban on gays in the military. Most respondents rejected the civil rights argument; in January 1993, only around a third said they equated gays in the military with blacks' struggles to serve in the 1940s. The Clinton compromise took effect in July 1993. By January 1994, 50 percent supported "don't ask, don't tell"; 47 percent were opposed.

A federal judge struck down the Clinton policy in March 1995, dismissing the government's argument that military performance would suffer if openly homosexual men and women were allowed to serve. The ruling, in Federal Dis-

> **" Ordination of gay clergy has not been a major issue in the Roman Catholic church, in which the priesthood is sworn to celibacy. "**

trict Court in Brooklyn, New York, applied only to the six military personnel who brought the lawsuit.

In October 1996, the Supreme Court rejected the first Costitutional challenge to the "don't ask, don't tell" policy. The Court declined to overturn a lower court ruling that let stand the Navy's discharge of a flyer who announced his homosexuality.[16]

The Matter of Wedlock

By Gallup's measure, public opinion tilts strongly against granting legal recognition to marriages between homosexual couples. In an April 1996 survey, two-thirds of respondents said they opposed a law that would grant recognition to same-sex unions. Only 28 percent favored such a law.

Older people are less likely than younger ones to support gay marriage, according to Gallup. Women are somewhat more favorable to the notion than men, Democrats more favorable than Republicans. Self-described liberals are about evenly divided.

As of late 1996, same-sex marriages were nowhere legally binding in the United States. The Federal Defense of Marriage Act of 1996 denied recognition of such unions and excused states from having to recognize same-sex marriages performed elsewhere. President Clinton signed the bill on September 21, 1996. Fifteen states had laws banning gay marriages on the books, with others considering

"
As of late 1996, same-sex marriages were nowhere legally binding in the United States.
"

American Opinion

No state in America legally recognizes same-sex marriages. Two-thirds of the American public opposes any legislature that would grant legality to such unions.

Source: The Gallup Poll 1996

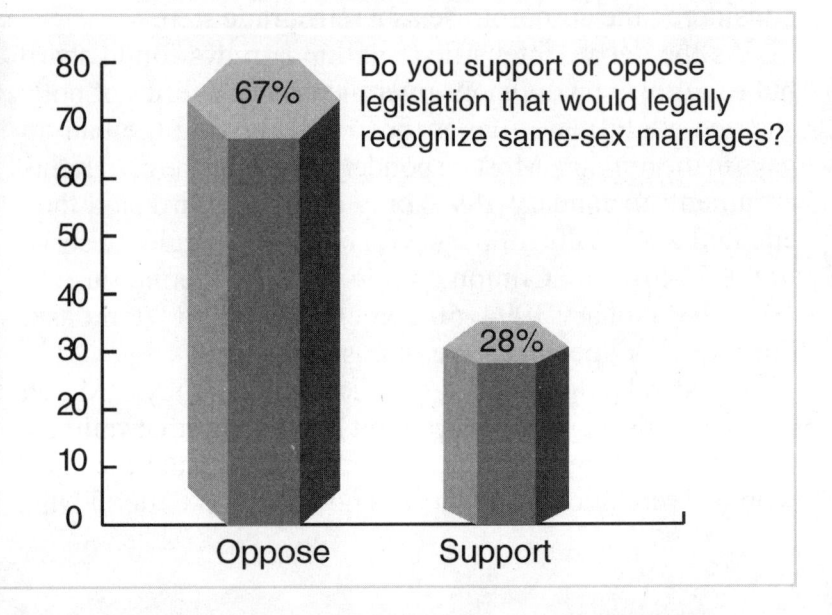

Do you support or oppose legislation that would legally recognize same-sex marriages?

- Oppose: 67%
- Support: 28%

AIDS: Progress at a Price

Researchers report progress in the fight against AIDS, but combinations of drugs that reduce the level of the virus are so costly that they may be beyond the reach of many people.

An estimated 50 percent of all U.S. AIDS cases are gay men, and increasing federal support for research into causes and potential cures of the virus has been a key element of the gay rights agenda.

Researchers say a new group of antiviral drugs known as protease inhibitors could, in combination with other drugs, reduce the human immunodeficiency virus (HIV), which causes AIDS. Their findings suggest AIDS might become a manageable and treatable, if chronic, condition.

The problem with the new drug therapies is cost—as much as $20,000 a year in the United States. In response to the potential treatment breakthrough, the Clinton administration in 1996 allocated an additional $65 million to the states for their AIDS Drug Assistance Programs, bringing the total allocation for the year to $195 million.

The state programs, which rely on federal funds for about two-thirds of their budgets, assist some 69,000 people with HIV and AIDS who cannot afford prescription drugs.

"With a lot of the new drugs that have become available, the demands have vastly outstripped the available resources," said Derek Link of the Gay Men's Health Crisis in New York City, a private AIDS service organization.[1]

such statutes. In 1996, Mississippi became the first state to ban gay unions by executive order.

A number of liberal religious groups sanction same-sex marriages. In 1995, the Central Conference of American Rabbis endorsed government recognition of gay unions but left the decision whether to bless them to individual rabbis. The United Congregational Church and some Quaker meetings bless homosexual marriages. On the other hand, Christian fundamentalists condemn homosexual partnerships as well as marriages. In June 1996, the Southern Baptist Convention voted to boycott the Walt Disney Company for giving health benefits to same-sex domestic partners.

The Defense of Marriage Act does not outlaw homosexual unions. For the first time, though, it codifies a federal definition of marriage as between one man and one woman, and it decrees that a "spouse" is a person of the opposite sex who is a husband or a wife.

For a brief time, the issue became caught in the coils of presidential election-year politics. The Christian Coalition, a powerful political-action group that claims 1.7 million members, lobbied hard for the Defense of Marriage Act. The Republican nominee, Robert Dole, sponsored the legislation. President Clinton said he accepted its basic premise, though in a gesture to homosexuals he called the measure unnecessary and accused its backers of "gay baiting."

The issue inflamed passions on both sides of the aisle.

"America will not be the first country in the world that throws the concept of marriage out the window and for the very first time in the history of civilization says that homosexual marriages are as important as, and rise to the level of, the legal and moral equivalency of heterosexual marriage," said Representative Bob Barr, a Georgia Republican and the bill's author.[17]

Patricia Schroeder, a Democratic congresswoman from Colorado, retorted, "If you think there isn't enough hate and polarization in America, you're going to love this bill."[18]

A Hawaii court's anticipated ruling that the state must recognize same-sex marriages spurred the swift passage of the Defense of Marriage Act. Supporters argued that gay and lesbian couples would descend on Hawaii, tie the knot there, and return to the mainland to claim all the rights, privileges, and benefits of civil marriage under the constitution's "full faith and credit clause"—the principle that states must acknowledge each other's public acts, records, and judicial proceedings. A Honolulu judge did in fact declare Hawaii's ban on gay couples unconstitutional. Lawyers for the state won a stay of the December 3, 1996, ruling pending a Hawaii Supreme Court appeal.[19]

Though formal sanction eluded them, some gay couples in 1996 achieved tangible benefits of marriage. The Denver City Council voted to extend health insurance to gay partners of city employees. An Oregon judge ordered a public agency there to offer homosexual couples the same medical, life, and dental insurance benefits that married couples receive. IBM, the nation's sixth-largest corporation, said it would give health care coverage and other benefits to partners of gay and lesbian employees.

Some gay rights leaders were dismayed that the marriage issue boiled up during an election year—"an out-of-control freight train," David M. Smith, a spokesman for the Human Rights Campaign, called it. Presidential politics

> "'If you think there isn't enough hate and polarization in America, you're going to love this bill.'"

aside, gay groups are far from a consensus about same-sex marriages anyway. Some argue there are more important issues: job discrimination, violence against homosexuals, and increased government support for promising AIDS research that has begun to offer hope that the disease may be manageable.

Some radical homosexuals view marriage, whether gay or straight, as imprisoning and oppressive. Comedian Kate Clinton diagnosed the drive for recognition of gay and lesbian unions as mad vow disease. "The freedom not to marry was always one of the things I enjoyed about being gay," she said in *The Progressive* magazine.[20]

Andrew Sullivan argues forcefully for equal access to marriage as the most important step of all for gay rights. "Denying it to homosexuals is the most public affront possible to their public equality," he wrote.

"Until gay marriage is legalized, [a] fundamental element of personal dignity will be denied a whole segment of humanity. No other change can achieve it. If nothing else were done at all, and gay marriage were legalized, ninety percent of the political work necessary to achieve gay and lesbian equality would have been achieved. It is ultimately the only reform that truly matters."[21]

Opponents agree at least in asserting the basic importance of the question. "Recognizing the legal union of gay and lesbian couples would represent a profound change in the meaning and definition of marriage," wrote William J. Bennett, co-director of Empower America. "It would be the most radical step ever taken in the deconstruction of society's most important institution.

"It is exceedingly imprudent to conduct an untested and inherently flawed social experiment on an institution that is the keystone in the arch of civilization," Bennett went on. "That we have to debate this issue at all tells us that the arch has slipped."[22]

Finally, there is this prospect: If same-sex marriages become a norm, same-sex divorces surely will soon follow. When New York City social worker Kathy Duggan and her partner split up, she found herself in a void. Having taken wedding vows, she keenly felt the absence of a ritual that would undo the ceremony. "I sometimes jokingly refer to Mary as my first wife," Duggan wrote. "I hope to marry

> **Some radical homosexuals view marriage, whether gay or straight, as imprisoning and oppressive.**

> "Until fairly recently, homosexuality had been the subject of only the most cursory scientific study."

again and I hope that by the time I do, my partner and I will be able to do it legally. Right now, though, I want a divorce."[23]

Nature and Nurture

"We do not even in the least know the final cause of sexuality," Charles Darwin wrote in 1862. "The whole subject is hidden in darkness."[24]

Until fairly recently, homosexuality had been the subject of only the most cursory scientific study. The term itself is of comparatively recent origin, common English usage dating only from 1897, according to the *Oxford English Dictionary*. It probably entered the language as a clinical substitute for "pederasty" (in its most exact definition, sex between males, but especially between a man and a boy, according to Webster's) and for the somewhat cruder and more general "sodomy" (any sexual intercourse held to be abnormal, also according to Webster's).

For many years, psychologists treated homosexuality as a mental disorder, a disease, most probably the result of an improper or misguided upbringing. Sigmund Freud regarded homosexuality as a state of arrested development. In males, an inability to break the sexual bond with a dominant mother led to sexual inversion. Freud's notions lent scientific weight to the theory that homosexuals were ill and that they could be cured. Some religious conservatives accept this. They

American Opinion

For years, the "cause" of homosexuality has been debated. Up until 1974, the American Psychiatric Association defined homosexuality as a mental illness. Americans are increasingly likely to believe it is nature rather than nurture.

Source: The Gallup Poll 1996

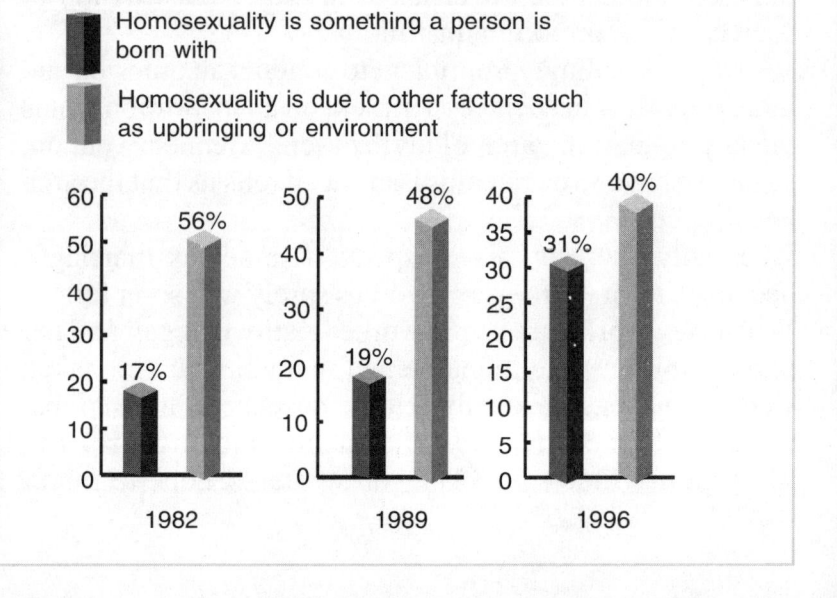

- Homosexuality is something a person is born with
- Homosexuality is due to other factors such as upbringing or environment

Year	Born with	Other factors
1982	17%	56%
1989	19%	48%
1996	31%	40%

believe homosexuals are aberrant, sinful persons who can and should control their urges and correct their behavior.

The American Psychiatric Association removed homosexuality from its list of mental illnesses in 1974. And most scientists believe that the causes of homosexuality, though mysterious, are most probably a blend of genetic factors and very early childhood development, and that for most adult gays the condition is involuntary.

"It is neither a sickness nor a sin, but the natural predisposition of a minority of human beings," rights advocates Michael Nava and Robert Dawidoff assert.[25]

For many homosexuals, the answer is instinctive. Writes Sullivan: "I was once asked at a conservative think tank what evidence I had that homosexuality was far more of an orientation than a choice, and I was forced to reply quite simply: my life."[26]

For a team of National Cancer Institute geneticists, a tentative explanation emerged from scientific inquiry. In July 1993, Dean Hamer and his colleagues published results of their two-year study that claimed a genetic link to homosexuality—evidence that the condition is at least partly inherited.[27]

Hamer, who cautioned that his work did not isolate a so-called gay gene but only detected a linkage, studied forty pairs of homosexual brothers and found that thirty-three of the forty had identical genetic markers on a small area near the tip of the X chromosome. This suggested that the men's sexual orientation was influenced genetically. Previous studies had shown a greater likelihood of identical twins, who share the same genes, being homosexual than fraternal twins, whose genes are different.[28]

One's view of gay rights issues seem to flow naturally from one's notion of the origins of homosexuality. By Gallup's measure, people are as divided on the conundrum of cause as on practical questions involving homosexuals in society.

In the April 1993 poll, around a third, 31 percent, thought homosexuality is caused by "something that people are born with." And this third invariably showed stronger support for issues on the gay rights agenda. Fourteen percent thought homosexual behavior develops "because of the way people are brought up"—the Freudian view, more or less. And

> **By Gallup's measure, people are as divided on the conundrum of cause as on practical questions involving homosexuals in society.**

another third, 35 percent, said that homosexuality was a choice, that it was just the way some people prefer to live.

Still, choice or compulsion, most people are moving slowly, if they are moving at all, from private toleration to public affirmation. Only a minority would abolish all distinctions in law, society, and culture between homosexuality and heterosexuality.

Notes: **Gay Rights** Is Tolerance or Affirmation the Issue?

1. Steven A. Holmes, "Civil Rights Dance Lesson: The Tiny Step Forward," *The New York Times,* Week in Review, September 15, 1996, 1.
2. Andrew Sullivan, *Virtually Normal: An Argument About Homosexuality* (New York: Alfred A. Knopf, 1995), 16.
3. John E. Yang, "Senate Passes Bill Against Same-Sex Marriages," *The Washington Post*, September 11, 1996, 1.
4. Linda Greenhouse, "Gay Rights Laws Can't Be Banned, High Court Rules," *The New York Times*, May 21, 1996, 1.
5. Greenhouse, "Gay Rights Laws Can't Be Banned."
6. Greenhouse, "Gay Rights Laws Can't Be Banned."
7. Adam Nagourney, "Affirmed by the Supreme Court," *The New York Times*, Week in Review, May 26, 1996, 4.
8. James Brooke, "Gay Life Thrives Where Ballot Fight Began," *The New York Times*, May 29, 1996, 12.
9. Douglas W. Kmiec, "Affirmation and Tolerance Are Not the Same," op-ed, *The Philadelphia Inquirer*, May 29, 1996.
10. "In Reversal, Zimbabwe Bans Gay Rights Exhibit," Associated Press report in *The New York Times*, July 25, 1996, 6.
11. Diego Ribadeneira, "Debate on Gays Divides Religious," *The Boston Globe*, July 16, 1996, B1.
12. Ribadeneira, "Debate on Gays Divides Religious."
13. Ribadeneira, "Debate on Gays Divides Religious."
14. Sullivan, *Virtually Normal*, 36.
15. Sullivan, *Virtually Normal*, 128.
16. Linda Greenhouse, "High Court Rejects Challenge to Military's Gay Policy," *The New York Times*, October 22, 1996.
17. Jerry Gray, "House Passes Bar to U.S. Sanction of Gay Marriage," *The New York Times,* July 13, 1996, 1.
18. Gray, "House Passes Bar."
19. Carey Goldberg, "Hawaii Judge Ends Gay-Marriage Ban," *The New York Times,* December 4, 1996.
20. David W. Dunlap, "Some Gay Rights Advocates Question Effort to Defend Same-Sex Marriage," *The New York Times,* June 7, 1996, 7.
21. Sullivan, *Virtually Normal*, 179; 184.
22. William J. Bennett, "Homosexual Marriage Is Not a Very Good Idea," *The Boston Globe*, op-ed, June 10, 1996.
23. Kathy Duggan, "I Earned This Divorce," op-ed, *The New York Times*, July 25, 1996.
24. Quoted as epigraph in Dean Hamer and Peter Copeland, *The Science of Desire: The Search for the Gay Gene and the Biology of Behavior* (New York: Simon & Schuster, 1994), 11.
25. Michael Nava and Robert Dawidoff, *Created Equal: Why Gay Rights Matter to America* (New York: St. Martin's Press, 1994), xii.

26. Sullivan, *Virtually Normal*, 15-16.
27. Hamer and Copeland, *The Science of Desire*, 17–18.
28. Hamer and Copeland, *The Science of Desire*, 217.
29. William F. Allman, "The Biology-Behavior Conundrum," *U.S. News & World Report*, July 26, 1993, 6–7.

Notes: AIDS: Progress at a Price

1. David W. Dunlap, "Clinton Seeks $65 Million for State AIDS Programs," *The New York Times*, July 24, 1996, 16.

Gambling
2 A Risky Business—for the Customers

State lotteries, Las Vegas fantasylands, Indian casinos, blackjack boats afloat in Rust Belt backwaters: legal gambling has grown explosively since the 1970s. Promoters, Wall Street investors, and re-formed Indian tribes grow rich. State and local governments rake in revenues from gambling's voluntary tax. Gambling ventures have transformed communities—some for the better, others arguably for the worse.

Still, a backlash may be building in gambling America. Voters in six states defeated wagering proposals in November 1996. Legislatures in five other states turned back gambling initiatives in 1995 and 1996.

Most Americans wager in one form or another, according to Gallup Organization surveys, but they also recognize the risks of expanded legal gambling. In a 1996 poll, more than half the respondents said they'd bought at least one lottery ticket within the past year, and a quarter said they'd visited a casino. At the same time, public opinion seems tepid toward two of the fastest-growing forms of gambling, casinos and high-tech video games. And set against new jobs in casino country are rising crime rates, choking traffic, and a siphoning off of sales (and sales tax revenues) from other businesses. Studies suggest that in some circumstances, gambling is a net loss for a community.

Casinos take in 70 percent of their revenues from high-odds slot machines, but all casino games give the house a mathematical edge. And in any game of pure chance—such

> "**Most Americans wager in one form or another.**"

> "At $40 billion a year and rising, gambling may soon overtake tobacco as America's most profitable addiction."

as roulette, craps, or slots—a player will lose in the long run. The longer he gambles, the longer the odds against him. "If you wanna make money in a casino, own one," advises Arnold Snyder, editor of the *Blackjack Forum* newsletter.[1]

At $40 billion a year and rising, gambling may soon overtake tobacco, at $45 billion, as —in commentator Frank Rich's phrase—America's most profitable addiction. Anyone who has ever stood interminably in a convenience store line behind a player calling out serial strings of numbers can testify to the appeal of the lottery, now available in thirty-seven states and the District of Columbia. Casinos operate in twenty-five states. Casino wagering alone is at $15 billion a year and climbing. Las Vegas is the fastest-growing city in the United States.

All the same, there are indications that gambling's growth may be slowing.

- In the face of an intense lobbying effort from the powerful American Gaming Association, Congress in mid-1996 established a national commission to undertake a two-year study of the costs, consequences, and benefits of gambling. President Clinton signed the bill on August 3.
- In some places, casinos have been a bust. At least seven venues that opened in Mississippi in the early 1990s had closed by the end of 1995. Riverboat gambling enterprises in Illinois and Iowa sank without a trace. In New Orleans in late 1995, Harrah's suspended construction on an $850 million casino after a temporary gambling hall generated only half the projected revenue.
- In April 1996, in a case involving a Florida Seminole tribe, the U.S. Supreme Court ruled Indians could not sue the states to allow gambling. The decision emboldened antigambling governors to lobby Congress to curb reservation gambling.
- Indian casino gambling seemed to be on a fast track in Massachusetts. Then, in the autumn of 1995, casinos went down in four of five referendum votes—in the worn, exhausted industrial towns of Chicopee, Springfield, Lawrence, and Methuen.
- At the same time, Massachusetts' Democratic legisla-

ture blocked a deal between Republican Governor William Weld and the Wampanoag Indian tribe to build a casino on a municipal golf course in the old whaling port of New Bedford.

"There's a possibility that the public appetite for casinos has peaked," Massachusetts House Speaker Thomas Finneran observed. "Somehow or other, this in the eyes of most people goes to a quality-of-life issue, and I'm not sure people want to see the face or the nature of Massachusetts transformed into the Las Vegas of the East."[2]

Gambling America

Fully six of every ten Americans gamble, according to Gallup surveys of the 1990s. Young people are more likely to gamble than their elders. Men are more approving than women. More than three-quarters believe organized crime has infiltrated casino gambling. Few believe, though, that gambling is immoral.

Most say they prefer gambling enterprises to set up somewhere over the horizon. Even the American Gaming Association's Frank Fahrenkopf acknowledges that. "The overwhelming majority of Americans really see nothing wrong with gaming," said Fahrenkopf, a former Republican national chairman. "But that does not necessarily mean they want a riverboat parked down the street from them."[3]

> "
> **'There's a possibility that the public appetite for casinos has peaked.'**
> "

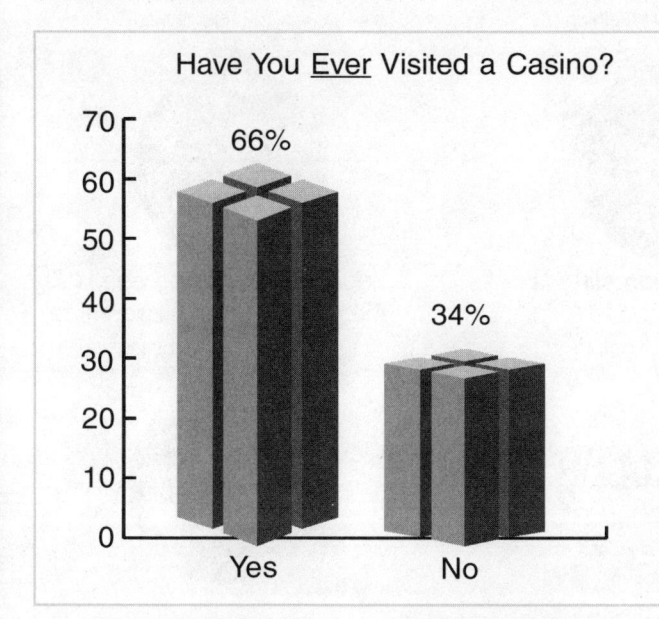

Have You Ever Visited a Casino?

- Yes: 66%
- No: 34%

As a Matter of Fact

With the proliferation of casino gambling in America over the past two decades, two-thirds of all Americans have now been to a casino.

Source: The Gallup Poll 1996

"
'Casinos strike many Americans as a dangerous playground that should not be located too close to home.'
"

This reluctance to share the neighborhood applies equally to land-based gambling palaces. "Casinos strike many Americans as a dangerous playground that should not be located too close to home," wrote Gallup analysts Larry Hugick and Lydia Saad.[4]

In a June 1996 Gallup sample, 57 percent said they had bought a lottery ticket within the past twelve months; 23 percent had taken part in an office pool; 17 percent had played video poker; and 9 percent had played bingo for money. More than a quarter, 27 percent, had visited a casino within the past year, more than double the 12 percent who had done so in 1982, before the spread of casino gambling far beyond Atlantic City and Las Vegas. Two-thirds, 67 percent, said they had visited a casino at some point.

Respondents were more accepting of some forms of gambling than others. In the 1996 poll, 77 percent approved of lotteries and bingo as a means of providing revenue for their state. Two-thirds, 68 percent, supported resort casino gambling as a revenue raiser; 63 percent were in favor of riverboat casinos. Gallup found less support for casino gambling on Indian reservations (57 percent) and in major cities (55 percent); for off-track betting on horse races (55

American Opinion

How Americans view legalized gambling.

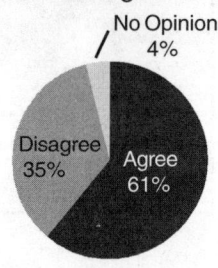

Source: The Gallup Poll 1996

Legalized gambling encourages people who can least afford it
- No Opinion 2%
- Disagree 31%
- Agree 67%

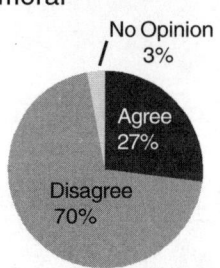

Legalized gambling can make compulsive gamblers out of people who would never participate in illegal gambling
- No Opinion 3%
- Disagree 36%
- Agree 61%

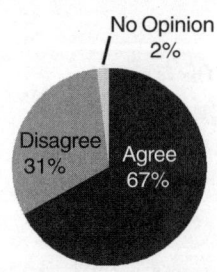

Legalized gambling is immoral
- No Opinion 3%
- Agree 27%
- Disagree 70%

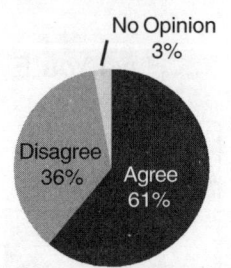

Legalized gambling opens the door for organized crime
- No Opinion 4%
- Disagree 35%
- Agree 61%

American Opinion

Do you approve or disapprove of the following types of gambling as a way for your state to raise revenue?

		Approve	Disapprove	No Opinion
Bingo for cash prizes:	1992	72%	25%	3%
	1996	72%	25%	3%
Lotteries for cash prizes	1992	75%	24%	1%
	1996	77%	22%	1%
Off-track betting on horse races	1992	49%	47%	4%
	1996	55%	41%	4%
Betting on professional sports	1992	33%	65%	2%
	1996	40%	58%	2%
Video poker machines at local establishments	1992	38%	52%	10%
	1996	37%	59%	4%

Source: The Gallup Poll, 1992, 1996

percent); for betting on sporting events (40 percent); and for video poker (only 37 percent).

Though they endorse state-run lotteries and bingo, many respondents showed a fair degree of skepticism about arguments for state-endorsed gambling. A bare majority, 51 percent, accepted the notion that gambling revenues support education and social programs for old people. Only a third believed that state involvement tends to keep organized crime out of gambling.

Close to two-thirds, however, credited the claim that gambling creates jobs and stimulates the local economy. And around six of every ten agreed that since people will gamble anyway, the state might as well take a slice of the earnings.

Only around a quarter of respondents, 27 percent, accepted the argument that states ought to stay out of the gambling business because it's immoral. Two-thirds, though, thought gambling encourages people who can least afford it to squander their money. Sixty-one percent believed legal gambling can make compulsive gamblers out of people who would never gamble illegally.

Few in the 1996 sample said gambling had led to trouble in their lives. Only 7 percent admitted that they sometimes gamble more than they should. Only 5 percent said gambling had ever been a source of problems in their family.

From Colonial Lotteries to Video Poker

Lotteries helped fund American colonial governments. By the turn of the eighteenth century, casino gambling was flourishing in French New Orleans, soon to become American New Orleans, in 1803. But America's founders recognized the dangers of this form of revenue raising.

No less an authority than George Washington stigmatized gambling as "the child of avarice, the brother of iniquity, and the father of mischief."[5] During much of the nineteenth century, Americans associated gambling with flashy riverboat sharps and the rough, ready, and corrupt amusements of the western frontier. By century's end, it was illegal in most places.

Not that people backed away from laying the odd bet, then or later. In 1938, when Gallup first asked the question, more than half the respondents said they'd done some form of gambling within the past twelve months.

Much of that action doubtless was illegal. In 1931, Nevada had become the first state to lift bans on most forms of gambling. The industry took wing there after World War II. Mobster Bugsy Siegel opened the first big postwar casino, the Flamingo, in Las Vegas in 1946.

In a 1950 survey, 59 percent of Gallup's sample reported having gambled. Support for legalized gambling lagged, however. In a 1951 poll, fewer than four in every ten favored legalized betting on horses, lotteries, or the numbers.

A generation later, the middle-class tax revolt fueled the expansion of state-sponsored gambling. New Hampshire introduced the first modern state lottery in 1964. New York followed three years later. In 1989, more than half of Gallup respondents, 54 percent, reported having bought lottery tickets within the past year.

Lotteries pump $11 billion a year into state treasuries. Government sponsorship and promotion of lotteries helped dissolve most of what remained of Americans' squeamishness about gambling. Along the way, too, most churches withdrew their longstanding moral objections. Some wanted to preserve their bingo and Las Vegas Night

> "Lotteries pump $11 billion a year into state treasuries."

fund-raisers. Others turned to what their communicants regarded as more imperative issues, such as abortion or school prayer.

Casino gambling came to the fading oceanfront resort of Atlantic City, New Jersey, in 1978. In 1987, the U.S. Supreme Court became the catalyst for the casino boom. In *California v. the Cabazon Band of Mission Indians*, the Court ruled that if a state allowed a form of gambling, such as blackjack at a charity event, a tribe could offer the form on its reserved lands—and offer it all the time, free of state control.

Congress passed the Indian Gaming Regulatory Act in 1988. The measure aimed to promote tribal economic self-sufficiency. In some instances, it has done that. The 300-member Mashantucket Pequot tribe of Connecticut operates the largest and most profitable casino in the Western Hemisphere, and Pequots have become rich beyond calculation. The law had the unintended consequence of spreading casino gambling, Indian and otherwise, from one end of America to the other.

"What does this mean for American civilization?" asked columnist Frank Rich. "No one is sure. . . . The stench of influence peddling suffuses some state governments where gambling rules. In the Midwest, riverboat casinos can be an economic boon but sometimes suck local retail businesses dry. Statistics suggest that crime, domestic abuse and alcoholism rise in gambling's wake—while the poor get most conspicuously poorer."[6]

Costs vs. Benefits

The gambling lobby uses the term "gaming," connoting sport and play, rather than gambling, with its suggestion of risk and the potential for ruin. The industry's trade group styles itself the American Gaming Association.

The AGA's Fahrenkopf—offering Joliet, Illinois, and other 1990s gambling centers as examples—argues broadly that gambling revitalizes communities, lowers tax rates, creates jobs with good pay and benefits, and produces revenue for local and state governments. Casinos, the AGA notes, paid out some $2 billion to state and local governments in 1995.

> 'Statistics suggest that crime, domestic abuse and alcoholism rise in gambling's wake.'

Critics say the gains are illusory.

"Let's strip away the political cover and let's call gambling gambling," said the Reverend Tom Grey, a Methodist minister who heads the National Coalition Against Legalized Gambling, not "benign entertainment, or economic development, or a painless tax."[7]

In many places, in fact, the weight of evidence suggests that gambling chiefly benefits promoters and those who work for them. Central City, Colorado, found casino developers' promises of an economic El Dorado to be exaggerated. Central City used to be known as a Rocky Mountain cultural center. The casinos came in 1990.

"Despite the crowds," travel writer Peter Hellman observed, "culture hasn't thrived. Central City's opera attendance has fallen. The town's jazz festival was canceled one year. The new crowd wants just to gamble."[8]

The industry has worked diligently to overcome the perception that gambling is a backstreet, mob-ridden hustle that lures and then fleeces the credulous. The big casinos promote themselves as "family entertainment," some with

American Opinion

In just the past four years, Americans have grown increasingly more approving of various types of casino gambling.

Source: The Gallup Poll 1992, 1996

Percentage of Respondents Who Approve of the Following in Their State

Casino gambling at resort areas: 1992: 51%, 1996: 68%

Casino gambling in a major city: 1992: 40%, 1996: 55%

Casino gambling on Indian reservations: 1992: 42%, 1996: 57%

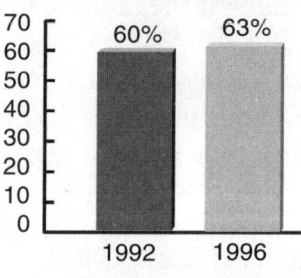

Casino gambling on "River Boats": 1992: 60%, 1996: 63%

gaudy theme parks on the premises, most with gymnasium-scale playrooms where children amuse themselves while their parents pull the slots.

"Gambling's something you used to do on the other side of the tracks until they 'main-streeted' it, or tried to," Grey said. "What we're doing is kicking it back to the other side of the tracks."[9]

Critics are scathing about the family themes that are the casino fashion of the moment. They emphasize, too, the ironic overtones of the name of one of the glitziest of gambling resorts, Stephen Wynn's Mirage in Las Vegas.

"When you bring in the casinos, whether you like it or not, you're going to have increased crime, increased prostitution, increased corruption," observed Representative Frank Wolf, a Virginia Republican who co-sponsored the legislation establishing the National Gambling Study commission.[10]

The social cost of out-of-control gambling is difficult to quantify, though supporters and critics alike generally accept that 4 to 6 percent of all players are potentially compulsive.

Casino operating procedures encourage patrons to keep playing, whether they can afford to or not. Some places pipe in a pleasant-smelling scent called Odorant 1, which is thought to subtly influence gamblers to increase their bets. Research suggests players respond favorably to black, purple, and blue, so slot machines are tricked out in dark

> "Casino operating procedures encourage patrons to keep playing, whether they can afford to or not."

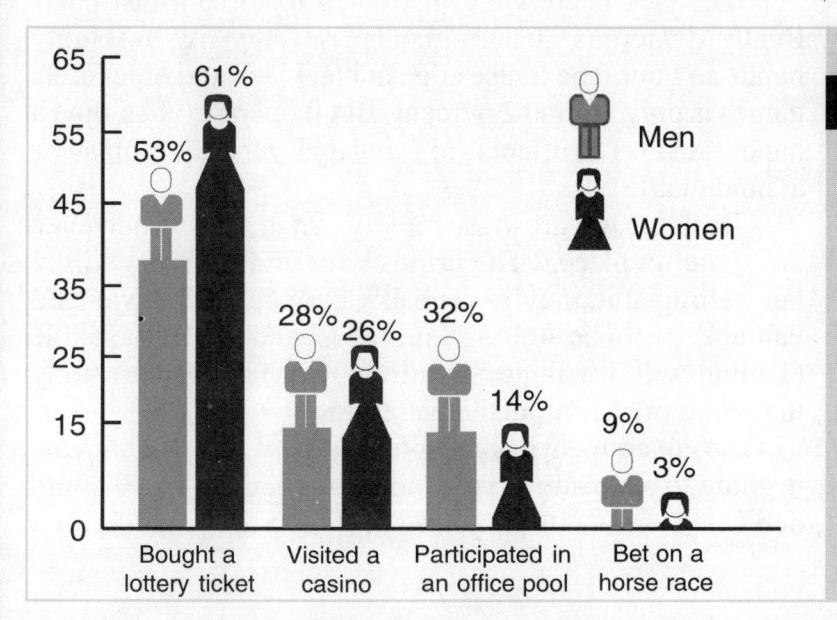

American Opinion

In the past 12 months have you done any of the following?

Activity	Men	Women
Bought a lottery ticket	53%	61%
Visited a casino	28%	26%
Participated in an office pool	32%	14%
Bet on a horse race	9%	3%

Source: The Gallup Poll 1996

Indians and States Clash over Reservation Gambling

A 1987 U.S. Supreme Court ruling brought slots, blackjack, and roulette to America's Indian reservations. A 1996 Court "correction" could slow gambling's spread.

The earlier decision, *California v. the Cabazon Band of Mission Indians*, led to 1988 federal legislation that encouraged large-scale casino development on tribal trust lands. Since then, tribes and state governments have clashed over gambling in Connecticut, Rhode Island, New Mexico, and other states.

The 1996 decision, *Seminole Tribe of Florida v. Florida*, the Court ruled tribes can't sue states to allow gambling, a strong affirmation of state's rights. Indian tribes, claiming sovereignty, argue the states have no right to bar or even restrict gambling on reservations.

In some cases, the ruling has been interpreted as relieving states of the obligation, explicit in the 1988 law, to negotiate gambling deals with tribes. Rhode Island Gov. Lincoln Almond, for example, rejected his predecessor's agreement with the Narragansett tribe and has given no indication he intends to work out a new one.[1]

Rhode Island Sen. John Chafee introduced legislation in September 1996 to restore a 1978 state-tribe agreement in which the Narragansett Indians were

(Continued on page 29)

---

colors. Many casinos distribute only low-denomination chips, figuring gamblers might be reluctant, after a string of losses, to hazard higher denominations but will keep playing with $5 chips.[11]

Blackjack dealers are instructed to force a fast pace. Really dexterous dealers manage seventy-five to eighty hands an hour. The house edge at blackjack and other table games is only around 2 percent. But it operates each time a hand is dealt. The effect is to grind a player's bankroll away at predictable rates.[12]

Gambling has grown so rapidly that there is no adequate safety net in place. "The critics who said we were a little late getting at it, they're probably correct," acknowledged Fahrenkopf.[13] The AGA's National Center for Responsible Gaming will distribute $2 million over ten years to study the problem of compulsive gambling.

The government has a responsibility as well. "If the state is going to advocate a risky business, then the state should dedicate some of its gambling profits to the rehabilitation

granted reservation lands in Charlestown, Rhode Island, with the restriction that all state and local civil, criminal, and regulatory law would remain in effect. This likely would doom the tribe's plans to open a casino in the state.

In New Mexico, the state Supreme Court in 1996 overturned gambling compacts between Gov. Gary Johnson and six Indian pueblos on grounds the state legislature had not approved them. The casinos, which generate $200 million a year for the tribes, continued to operate despite the ruling.

Gambling opponents have found unlikely allies in Donald Trump, of the Taj Mahal in Atlantic City, and other promoters who claim the government has given Indians unfair competitive advantages.

"We are the most heavily regulated gaming industry in America, and they're the least regulated," Trump said.[2]

In the wake of the high court ruling, the federal Department of the Interior will decide eventually how state and tribal conflicts are to be resolved. The department oversees all Indian affairs in the U.S.

and study" of addicted gamblers, said Sirgay Sanger, a psychiatrist and former president of the National Council on Problem Gambling.[14]

Success, at a Price

The gambling industry answers critics with apparent success stories such as that of Joliet, a northern Illinois city of 83,000, a declining farm-equipment and steel-manufacturing center with recent history of high unemployment. For one month in 1983, the jobless rate in Will County, Illinois, had reached an astonishing 27.6 percent. Joliet's four riverboat casinos have helped drive the rate down to around 5 percent. They are now the city's biggest employer, bigger than the 3,500-worker Caterpillar tractor plant.

Harrah's operates two boats; a local venture, the Empress River Casino Corp., operates the other two. The boats run twenty-two hours a day, making short cruises on the Des Plaines River and an old industrial canal. Together they

> "Gambling advocates say crime rates in casino country are no higher than in other tourist centers."

employ 4,000 people, 90 percent of them full-time. Casino workers earn above-average wages, around $24,000 a year, plus employer-funded health insurance and other benefits.

"Workers are buying things they never had, getting medical attention they never had," said Teri Shannon, a Joliet union organizer. "They're buying cars and motorcycles. Single mothers without college educations are doing a lot better than they ever could have without the riverboats."[15]

The casinos have netted Joliet more than $60 million in tax revenues since 1992, according to the AGA. The city has cut property taxes, revitalized downtown, and built a new police headquarters. "Joliet's been an amazing success," Fahrenkopf said.[16]

The city will need the police building, critics say. William Thompson, a public administration professor at the University of Nevada at Las Vegas, suspects the casinos are draining money from locals who can ill afford the loss, not out-of-towners. Joliet pays a price in local retail sales, social problems, and crime, said Thompson.[17]

Thompson's research suggests a casino needs to draw at least 50 percent of its business from out of town for a community to benefit. When too many of the customers are local people, the bet is misplaced. The locals stay, and their problems stay with them. In some Illinois towns with riverboat casinos, close to two-thirds of the customers are locals.[18]

Blackjack dealer Jan Craven serves out the cards aboard one of Harrah's Joliet riverboats. Sometimes, not infrequently, she accepts the bets of a gambler's last chips, then sweeps them up after an unlucky fall of the cards.

"Sometimes they have days where they lose all they've won," Ms. Craven said. "We just shuffle the cards. They make the decisions. When they lose like that, they're not happy, and you can't make them happy. It kind of brings down the whole table. It brings you down, too."[19]

Ten casinos have opened since 1992 in Tunica County, Mississippi, south of Memphis. Gambling has brought a flood of money into Tunica, once one of America's poorest counties. In 1991, a fifth of the county's people were on welfare, and half received food stamps. Four years later, the percentage on food stamps had fallen to about one-third. The welfare caseload had declined to around 10 percent.

The effects on unemployment have been mixed, however. At around 13 percent in 1990, the jobless rate fell below 9 percent for a time before climbing upward again, reaching 12.9 percent in 1995. The casinos created jobs, but evidently not enough jobs to go around. And they spawned few spinoff enterprises. "Except for a boom in hotel construction, development is nonexistent," wrote James Thomas Snyder of the *Daily News* in Memphis.[20]

At the same time, there is evidence that a crime wave has rolled over Tunica County. The AGA vigorously disputes claims that casinos breed crime. Gambling advocates say crime rates in casino country are no higher than in other tourist centers such as Orlando, Florida, and Anaheim, California.

"Explain that to the court workers in Tunica County, who have faced at least a tenfold increase in their caseload—1,200 filings to 12,000—since the casinos opened," Snyder countered. "Felony indictments increased from 13 in 1992 to 172 in 1995."[21]

The Las Vegas Boom

In Las Vegas, six major casinos were under construction in mid-1996, part of a building boom that began in 1989. All are designed to be full-service resorts that attract families.

New York, New York replicates America's largest city, with a stylized Manhattan skyline and a copy of the Cyclone roller coaster at Coney Island in Brooklyn. At MGM Grand's Emerald City, Dorothy, the Tin Man, and the others travel the Yellow Brick Road. The Luxor has talking camels. Wynn's 3,000-room Mirage—with its mechanical volcano, patch of tropical forest, and dolphin pool—is meant to conjure up a "South Seas oasis in the desert."[22]

"Look, it's life," a Californian touring one of the "theme" resorts with her children told *The Christian Science Monitor*. "They might as well be with you when they're exposed to it. My husband and I aren't really gamblers. I think we've pulled one slot machine since we've been here."[23]

Some 30 million people visit Las Vegas a year. Ninety percent of casino patrons are from out of town. Proceeds

> **Gambling on Indian reservations has become a $6-billion-a-year business, and it is growing.**

> "Estimates are that Foxwoods does in excess of $1 billion in gambling business a year."

from the influx keep the tax rate low and employment high. "Las Vegas is the quintessence of what casinos can do—the big splash," said John Smith, a Nevada journalist. "All you have to do is give a community fifty years and a steady stream of income."[24]

The Foxwoods Phenomenon

In southeastern Connecticut, the Indian Gaming Regulatory Act revived two moribund Indian tribes, the Mashantucket Pequots and the Mohegans. Their casino ventures are turning a corner of Connecticut into one of the nation's busiest gambling centers.

Nationally, 150 tribes have negotiated gambling compacts with states since 1988. Gambling on Indian reservations has become a $6-billion-a-year business, and it is growing.

Almost overnight, the Foxwoods Casino on Mashantucket Pequot reservation land in suburban and semirural Ledyard, Connecticut, altered the social fabric of Ledyard and the neighboring towns of Preston and North Stonington. It has raised questions, too, about the purpose and effects of the Indian gaming act and about the regulation of gambling operations of largely autonomous tribes.

Foxwoods' tribal owners do not release income figures, but estimates are that Foxwoods does in excess of $1 billion in gambling business a year. By terms of its compact with Connecticut, Foxwoods turns over 25 percent of its annual slot machine revenues to the state—around $115 million in 1995. On the busiest days, 50,000 people try their luck there.

The Pequots were virtually annihilated in a 1637 massacre near Mystic, Connecticut. Some of the few survivors were absorbed into the neighboring Narragansett tribe; others were sold into slavery. In 1667, the Connecticut colonial government established a 2,000-acre reservation in what today is Ledyard.

Over time, the reservation contracted around the remnant of the tribe, dwindling to fewer than 200 acres by the late 1970s. By then, only a single elderly woman, Elizabeth George by name, remained on the reservation, and Connecticut moved to take over the tribal lands for a state park.

Elizabeth George's grandson decided to move onto the reservation and keep the tribe alive. Skip Hayward recruited a few dozen men and women with some Pequot ancestry and successfully obtained federal recognition. With a foreign loan drained of risk by virtue of a federal Bureau of Indian Affairs guarantee, the Pequots, over strong state opposition, opened a high-stakes bingo hall on reservation land in 1986. The Foxwoods casino opened six years later. It hasn't closed since.

The goal of tribal self-sufficiency has been achieved—and assured for generations, given prudent management. The tribe has financed nongambling ventures, purchased hundreds of acres of land in the region (some of which it is trying to add to the reservation), and established comprehensive social, educational, and health programs for its members.

The costs for the larger community are mounting, however. Traffic clogs the two-lane roads leading to Foxwoods. Crime, drugs, and prostitution are on the rise. There were allegations of New England mob involvement in game fixing at Foxwoods in 1996. Swarms of gamblers have brought unwanted development in their train—road widening, vast areas of woodland and pasture paved over for parking lots, commercial strips of gas stations and fast-food restaurants.

Foxwoods' neighbors are deeply resentful. The towns have challenged the Pequots' plans to annex to the reservation land purchased with gambling income, a legal device

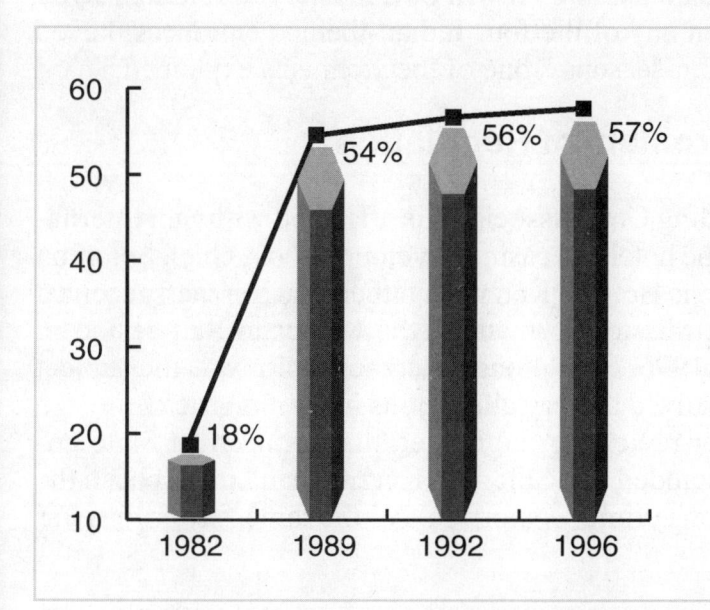

As a Matter of Fact

Have you bought a state lottery ticket within the past 12 months?

Year	Percentage
1982	18%
1989	54%
1992	56%
1996	57%

Source: The Gallup Poll 1982, 1989, 1992, 1996

that would remove property from the tax rolls and exempt the tribe from local zoning and other regulations.

Ledyard and neighboring towns have moved to adopt ordinances restricting such enterprises as adults-only bookstores, massage parlors, and nightclubs.

"Our region is changing quickly, and we've lost control of a lot of our land because of federal mandates regarding Indian reservations," said Cynthia Brewster, a Ledyard councilor who helped draft a town antipornography ordinance. "This is an attempt to regain some of that control."[25]

A second large casino opened in October 1996 in Montville, Connecticut, only ten miles from Foxwoods, under the aegis of another recently reestablished tribe, the Mohegans. In September 1995, the federal Department of the Interior declared a 240-acre former industrial complex the Mohegans' aboriginal reservation. The $300 million Mohegan Sun casino there has 180 gaming tables, 3,000 slot machines, shops, restaurants and—in keeping with the family theme—a large children's play area. "Our focus is the whole experience," said Howard Kerzner, a principal in Trading Cove Associates, the firm that manages the casino for the Mohegans. "We do not build gambling halls—we build recreational experiences for families."[26]

The main part of the casino is the old United Nuclear Corp. plant. The architects used extensive plantings of conifers, laurel, and birch to screen the unlovely building, a *trompe l'oeil* intended to suggest the environs of a woodland Indian habitat. "It will be a mystery unfolding as you approach any of the four Indian-themed entrances, keyed to the four seasons," one of the architects explained.[27]

The Problem of Regulation

Trading Cove Associates is affiliated with Sun International, the hotel and casino developer whose chief, Solomon Kerzner, is Howard Kerzner's father. The Kerzners received final permission to manage the Mohegan Sun casino in August 1996, even though Kerzner senior was the subject of unresolved bribery allegations in South Africa.

After reviewing the matter, the Connecticut State Police concluded that Solomon Kerzner had himself been the victim of a crime—extortion. All the same, say critics, the case raised questions about the substantially self-regulated business of Indian gambling.

The National Indian Gaming Commission is the federal authority responsible for regulating casino operations on reservations. Its chairman is Harold Monteau. He grew up on a Chippewa reservation in Montana and, as a tribal attorney and advocate for Indian gambling, lobbied against any federal regulation of reservation enterprises.

Critics contend Monteau has a clear conflict of interest. And in general, they say, the patchwork of state, federal, and tribal regulations has too few safeguards, making Indian gambling a major scandal in waiting.

In the early 1990s, Solomon Kerzner spent millions to assemble a team of lawyers and anthropologists to put together a case for federal recognition of the defunct Mohegans. When recognition came, it made the tribe eligible for Indian gambling. Notwithstanding the bribery allegations, Monteau swiftly approved Solomon Kerzner's application to manage the Mohegan casino, according to *The Wall Street Journal*. In return, the Mohegans agreed to give 40 percent of net revenues to the manager of the casino, Trading Cove Associates. The industry standard, *The Journal* reported, is 30 percent.

"It was the tribe's call to make," Monteau said of the Mohegans' deal with Kerzner.

"My integrity and the integrity of this tribe should never be doubted," tribal chairman Ralph Sturges told Monteau, as if that guarantee closed the matter.[28]

"It's not a system that inspires confidence," countered Bernard Horn, the political director of the National Coalition Against Legalized Gambling. "Why don't we just ask Steve Wynn to regulate himself?"[29]

What's to Come?

Gambling and the revenue stream it feeds exert a hypnotic fascination on politicians of both parties. "The state is a compulsive gambler; it's addicted to money," noted Tom Grey.[30] Republicans and Democrats alike regard casino development as an engine for providing jobs and keeping tax rates within bounds.

Not incidentally, they also appreciate the gambling

"
Critics say the patchwork of state, federal, and tribal regulations has too few safeguards, making Indian gambling a major scandal in waiting.

"

lobby's largesse. Since 1993, the industry has given more than $3 million to the major political parties. Promoter Wynn raised nearly $500,000 in 1995 for Bob Dole's presidential campaign. The Connecticut Pequots have given tens of thousands to Democratic candidates and causes.

New York governor George Pataki, a Republican, favors the legalization of casino gambling in the state. A Pataki commission reported in August 1996 that gambling could bring $2.6 billion in new business to the state and create 38,000 jobs.

The report claims New York casinos would capture money now flowing to Atlantic City and southeastern Connecticut. "I think the most important thing is to stop losing billions of dollars to surrounding states," Pataki said. Those billions, the governor's commission estimated, would yield the state some $278 million a year.[31]

By contrast, Rhode Island and Massachusetts have had second thoughts about large-scale gambling ventures. Rhode Island's Republican governor rejected his Democratic predecessor's casino deal with the Narragansett tribe. In Massachusetts, the Democratic legislature has held up the Republican governor's agreement with the Wampanoags.

In economic terms, critics see gambling as a large-scale transfer of resources from the poor-to-middling to the rich, producing little or nothing of permanent value. Advocates portray gambling as another, and an increasingly popular, form of entertainment, like professional sports events or rounds of golf or a day at an amusement park. And while money spent on other forms of leisure is irrecoverable, gamblers at least have a chance to recoup.

Observers of casino crowds wonder how entertaining gambling really is for most people. Excitement, a tingling of the nerves, the illusion of living large, doubtless, but enjoyment? After all, the house always wins in the end.

"At Foxwoods," commentator Jon Keller wrote, "it's easier to spot the despondent expressions of patrons cleaned out by the house's onerous odds and antes than it is to find happy faces."[32]

Notes: Gambling A Risky Business—for the Customers

1. James Popkin, "Tricks of the Trade," *U.S. News & World Report*, March 14, 1994.
2. Jon Keller, "Snake eyes for casinos," op-ed, *The Boston Globe*, July 29, 1996.
3. Patricia Edmonds, "Gambling's backers find it isn't a sure bet," *USA Today*, December 29, 1995, 1.
4. Larry Hugick and Lydia Saad, "America's Gambling Boom," *The Public Perspective*, January/February 1994, 8.
5. Richard Worsnop, "Gambling Boom," reprinted from *CQ Researcher*, March 18, 1994, in Andrew Riconda, ed., *Gambling* (New York, H.H. Wilson, 1995), 20.
6. Frank Rich, "Loving Las Vegas," op-ed, *The New York Times*, May 8, 1996.
7. Edmonds, "Gambling's backers find it isn't a sure bet."
8. Peter Hellman, "Casino Craze," reprinted from *Travel Holiday*, March 1994, in Riconda, ed., *Gambling*, 41.
9. Alexandra Marks, "Gambling Surges, and Backlash Grows," *The Christian Science Monitor*, June 3, 1996, 1.
10. Edmonds, "Gambling's backers find it isn't a sure bet."
11. Popkin, "Tricks of the Trade."
12. Vicki Abt, James F. Smith and Eugene M. Christiansen, *The Business of Risk: Commercial Gambling in Mainstream America* (Lawrence, Kan.: University Press of Kansas, 1985), 72.
13. Marks, "Gambling Surges."
14. Worsnop, "Gambling Boom."
15. Peter T. Kilborn, "Portrait from New Era of Nation's Gambling," *The New York Times,* February 28, 1996, 10.
16. Marks, "Gambling Surges."
17. Marks, "Gambling Surges."
18. Marks, "Gambling Surges."
19. Kilborn, "Portrait from New Era of Nation's Gambling."
20. James Thomas Snyder, "Casino County," op-ed, *The New York Times*, July 24, 1996,
21. Snyder, "Casino County."
22. Marks, Gambling Surges."
23. Marks, "Gambling Surges."
24. Marks, "Gambling Surges."
25. Robert A. Hamilton, "Can Towns Control Gaming's Downside?" *The New York Times*, Connecticut Weekly section, April 28, 1996, 1.
26. Eleanor Charles, "Just 10 Miles from Foxwoods, A 2nd Indian Casino," *The New York Times*, Real Estate section, February 11, 1996, 11.
27. Charles, "Just 10 Miles from Foxwoods."
28. Bruce Orwall, "The Federal Regulator of Indian Gambling Is Also Part Advocate," *The Wall Street Journal*, July 22, 1996, 1.
29. David Collins, "Potential conflicts abound at Foxwoods, but many cite regulatory system as tough," *The Day*, New London, Conn., August 18, 1996, 1.
30. Marks, "Gambling Surges."

31. Raymond Hernandez, "Pataki Panel Says Casinos Could Bring in $2.6 Billion," *The New York Times*, August 31, 1996, 1.
32. Keller, "Snake eyes for casinos."

Notes: Indians and States Clash Over Reservation Gambling

1. John Mulligan, "Chafee Amendment Could Kill Casino," *The Providence Sunday Journal,* September 8, 1996, A8.
2. Hellman, "Casino Craze."

3 Smoking and Drinking
How Far Should Government Go to Break Our Bad Habits?

Smoking and excessive drinking may be unhealthful and wasteful. Yet as long as Americans have their way, these indulgences will remain legal. There is no consensus for direct government action to change the nation's habits, still less for outright bans of tobacco and alcohol.

Three-fifths of Americans drink; around a quarter smoke. Personal habits aside, Gallup Organization surveys suggest that most people believe smoking and drinking are matters of personal choice. For most, a stubborn desire to preserve freedom of choice outweighs concerns about social costs and consequences.

All the same, patterns of tobacco and alcohol use have changed. Smoking is banned or restricted in most public places and in many shops, factories, and offices. At break time, workers pour outdoors to gather under a nimbus of tobacco smoke. The venerable urban institution of the corner bar is slowly disappearing. Some law-enforcement authorities see a connection between the decline of neighborhood drinking places and a sharp drop in the adult murder rate, which has fallen by fully half since 1981.

Americans clearly recognize the dangers of tobacco. Only around half the respondents in a 1957 Gallup survey believed smoking could cause lung cancer; only a third thought it could contribute to heart disease. Today, three-quarters say even secondhand smoke is harmful.

Surveys show a strong recognition, too, of the high cost

"
Americans clearly recognize the dangers of tobacco.

"

of alcohol abuse. In a 1994 poll, two-thirds of the respondents graded excessive drinking a major national problem. More than 80 percent believed pregnant women should keep off alcohol entirely.

Tobacco Trends

Cigarette makers find themselves increasingly under siege. Tobacco is said to kill 400,000 Americans a year. State and federal government agencies are stepping up the pressure to regulate cigarettes and to collect reimbursements for health costs associated with smoking. At the same time, the cigarette business is thriving, especially among young Americans and overseas among Africans, Asians, and eastern Europeans of all ages.

The numbers have declined steadily since 1950, when nearly half of all adults smoked. By 1996, the percentage had fallen to a quarter—some 50 million people. Those who do smoke were smoking more, though—an average of 27 cigarettes, close to a pack and a half, a day.[1]

In a May 1996 poll, 27 percent of respondents told Gallup they had smoked cigarettes within the past week. More than half the smokers, 54 percent, admitted to going through at least a pack a day. Men and women were about equally likely to smoke cigarettes. Men accounted for most of the cigars, pipe tobacco, and chewing tobacco sold in America. Younger smokers tended to be lighter smokers than their elders. Women smoked less than men.

Nearly seven of every ten smokers said they had taken up the habit by the time they were eighteen years old. Someone once observed that tobacco is the only industry that kills off its customers. Cigarette makers thus have become adept at rebuilding their sales base. Advertising campaigns such as those featuring the R. J. Reynolds Company's Marlboro Man and, more recently, the cartoonish bon vivant "Joe Camel" are controversial because they appear to be deliberately aimed at young people. And cigarette use among the young is on the rise. The federal Food and Drug Administration says one million children take up smoking each year. The FDA adds that a third of these will die eventually from tobacco-related illnesses.

In a 1995 Federal Centers for Disease Control survey,

> "Tobacco is said to kill 400,000 Americans a year."

35 percent of high school students seventeen or younger said they had smoked in the previous month, up from around 27 percent in 1991. Sixteen percent said they had smoked a pack or more during the month, according to the survey of 11,000 students. While it's illegal to sell cigarettes to people younger than eighteen, three-quarters of the young smokers in the CDC survey said they had not been asked to show proof of age.[2]

The tobacco industry, which spends $5 billion a year on advertising and promotion, has fiercely resisted FDA calls for stricter regulations on the marketing, distribution, and sale of cigarettes. The Tobacco Institute, a trade group, says manufacturers' voluntary initiatives—among them a program that trains store clerks to card young people before they ring up a sale—are sufficient.

"This is not an isolated phenomenon, and has to be considered along with things like rising drug use," Tobacco Institute spokesman Walker Merryman said of the increase in young smokers. "It is part of the social fabric going awry."[3]

In August 1996, the Clinton administration authorized the FDA to impose new curbs on appeals to children, the first significant restrictions since cigarette ads were banned from television in 1971. They included tougher enforcement of the sales ban and limits on billboard, magazine, and newspaper advertising. Also prohibited were cigarette-brand sponsorship of sporting events and giveaways of promotional items such as T-shirts and gym bags.

> **The federal Food and Drug Administration says one million children take up smoking each year.**

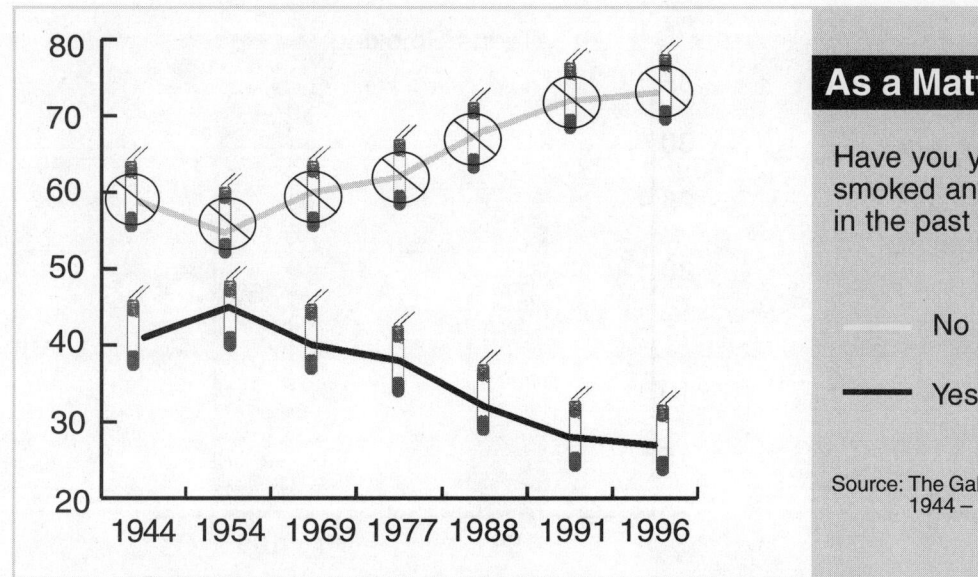

As a Matter of Fact

Have you yourself smoked any cigarettes in the past week?

— No
— Yes

Source: The Gallup Poll
1944 – 1996

"This epidemic is not an accident," Clinton spokesman Joe Lockhart said. "Children are bombarded daily by massive campaigns that play on their vulnerabilities, their insecurities, their longings to be something in the world. Joe Camel promises that smoking will make you cool. Virginia Slims models whisper that smoking will help you stay thin."[4]

The tobacco and advertising industries immediately challenged the new rules. Cigarette makers claimed the FDA had no authority to regulate tobacco. Advertisers challenged the restriction on grounds of free speech. The litigation is expected to drag on for years.

"The rule opens a Pandora's box of regulation that tramples on the Constitution and the rights of millions of adult Americans," the cigarette maker Philip Morris said. "We will stand by those adults who choose to smoke."[5]

The Rise of the Cigarette

Native Americans cultivated *Nicotiana tabacum*, crumbling and smoking the leaves ritualistically in pipes and smoking or chewing it for medicinal purposes or simply for pleasure. Columbus's crews took to tobacco at once and carried it home to Europe. Within a century or so of Columbus's first voyage of New World exploration, the plant, native to the Western Hemisphere, had spread around the world.

Cigarettes are of comparatively recent origin. French

As a Matter of Fact

The number of teens seventeen or younger who have smoked cigarettes in the past month.

Source: Federal Centers for Disease Control, 1996

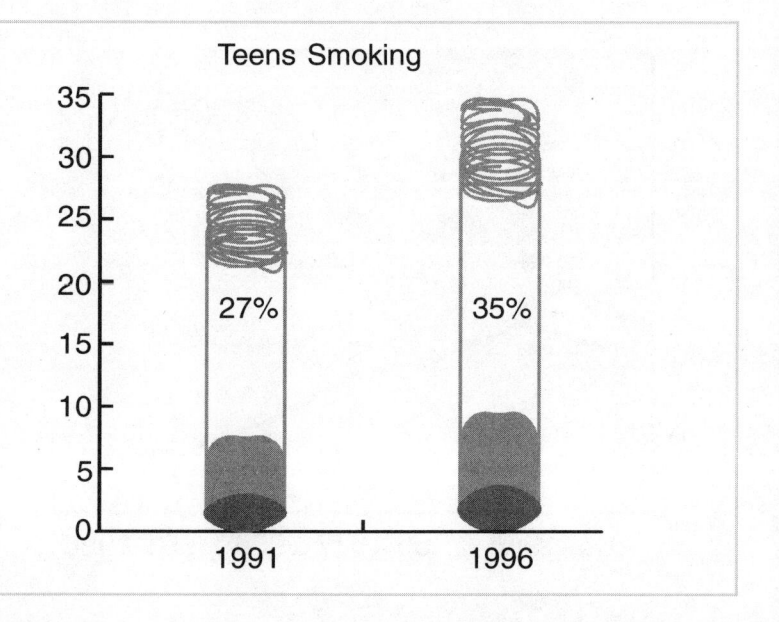

Teens Smoking

Year	Percent
1991	27%
1996	35%

soldiers introduced this form of smoking to their British allies during the Crimean War in the 1850s. A London tobacconist named Philip Morris is credited with building a wider English market for cigarettes. In America, widespread cigarette smoking dates from the Civil War: Soldiers in the field found cigarettes handier and more portable than pipe tobacco.

Cigarettes gradually gained on cigars and pipes as the smoke of choice in the decades following the war. For a generation or more, most cigarette smokers rolled their own, though as early as 1880 some 500 million ready-made cigarettes were being sold annually. By 1889, W. Duke & Sons of Durham, North Carolina, from small beginnings with a tobacco brand called Pro Bono Publico, had become America's leading cigarette maker, claiming 40 percent of the market. In 1889–90, Duke and several competitors combined to form the American Tobacco Company, with James Buchanan Duke, a son of the founder, as president.[6]

Soon dozens of competing brands with catchy names and logos were available. By the 1920s, women were smoking in increasing numbers. Tobacco companies touted the relaxing, stress-relieving, and healthful qualities of cigarettes with aggressive marketing. During World War II, packs of cigarettes formed an essential part of a soldier's kit. Today cigarettes account for 90 percent of the tobacco industry's revenues.

Public Wary of Legal Curbs

The average cigarette smoker loses seven or eight years of his life. The most widely quoted figures for the number of tobacco-related deaths each year, 400,000 to 420,000, sound like a gross exaggeration but in fact are generally accepted as accurate. It is a wonderment, then, that there is not a groundswell for stricter regulation or even an outright ban on cigarettes. Richard Kluger, whose book *Ashes to Ashes* (1996) is an indictment of the industry, has a partial explanation.

"The smoker's death is banal, private, noticed only by family and friends, and, in the final analysis, self-inflicted," he writes.[7]

For many people, the government went as far as it needed

"
The average cigarette smoker loses seven or eight years of his life.
"

> "As a drug-delivery device, the government says, tobacco thus falls under FDA jurisdiction."

to go in 1964, when the surgeon general documented tobacco's health risks in a landmark report. "There's a strong strain in American culture that says that's the limit of regulation," observed Allan Brandt, a professor of the history of medicine at Harvard. For good or ill, smoking is a private matter.[8]

In the 1996 Gallup survey, only 11 percent of respondents thought smoking should be declared illegal. Fewer than half, 45 percent, thought government should ban all cigarette advertising. And fewer than four in every ten, 38 percent, thought the government should classify tobacco (specifically, its nicotine component) as a drug and regulate its sale and use accordingly. A solid majority, 57 percent, said they favored no change in tobacco regulation and use.

All the same, the government persisted. The FDA declared nicotine an addictive drug in 1996, following the surgeon general's 1988 lead. Tobacco leaves are rich in nicotine, which can be lethal in large doses. (It is named for Jean Nicot, who introduced tobacco to French court circles in the mid-sixteenth century.) As a drug-delivery device, the government says, tobacco thus falls under FDA jurisdiction.

Scientific consensus overwhelmingly supports the FDA. In a 1996 study, scientists at Italy's University of Cagliari found that nicotine targets the same "reward system" in the brain as cocaine, amphetamines, and morphine. It also triggers the brain's release of dopamine, a chemical messenger

American Opinion

Which comes closer to your view concerning U.S. government tobacco policy?

- The government should classify tobacco as a drug: 38%
- The government should NOT classify tobacco as a drug: 57%
- No opinion: 5%

Source: The Gallup Poll 1996

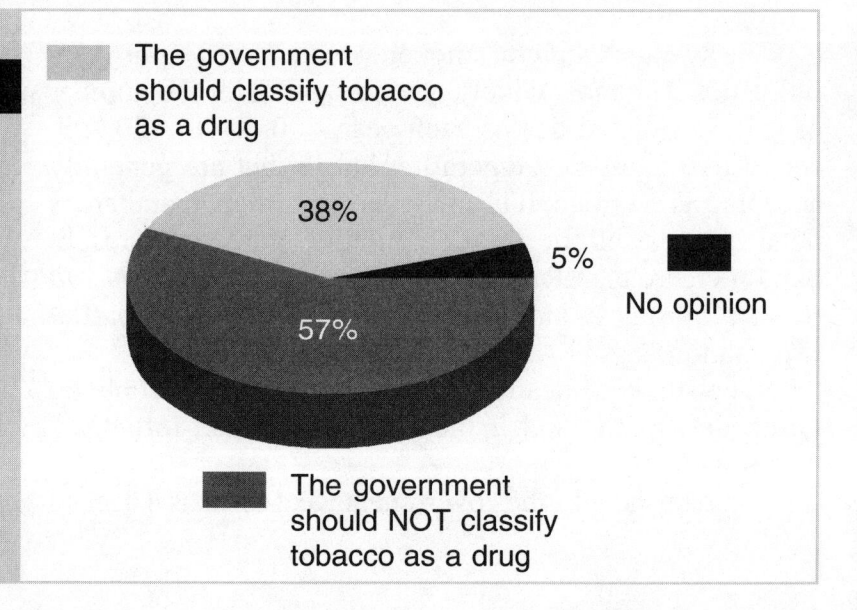

that has been linked to the addictive effects of other drugs.[9]

Smokers themselves freely acknowledge they are addicted—nearly seven of every ten told Gallup so in 1994. And three-quarters said they would like to break the habit but can't—the addiction is too powerful a thing to subdue.

In the same poll, more than half the respondents sympathized with the smoker's plight precisely because of nicotine's ensnaring properties. Sixty-one percent said they're sympathetic because they know smokers are addicted and would find it difficult to stop even if they wanted to.

There are, of course, many reasons to light up. Smoking used to be associated with political back rooms, card games, cocktail parties, good times in cafés and bars. Addicted or not, a smoker could still crave a cigarette. "People don't smoke just for nicotine," writes commentator John Leo. "They smoke for a great array of nonchemical reasons, from depression and peer pressure to a courting of danger, or a belief that smoking equals liberation. Or because lighting up has become embedded in day-to-day life as a ritual, a way of punctuating a phone call, the end of a meal, the start of a difficult project."[10]

Who Should Pay for Damages?

Smoking's link to cancers, heart disease, emphysema, and other diseases has been proved beyond doubt. As a consequence, groups of smokers and, now, state government

> "
> **Addicted or not, a smoker could still crave a cigarette.**
> "

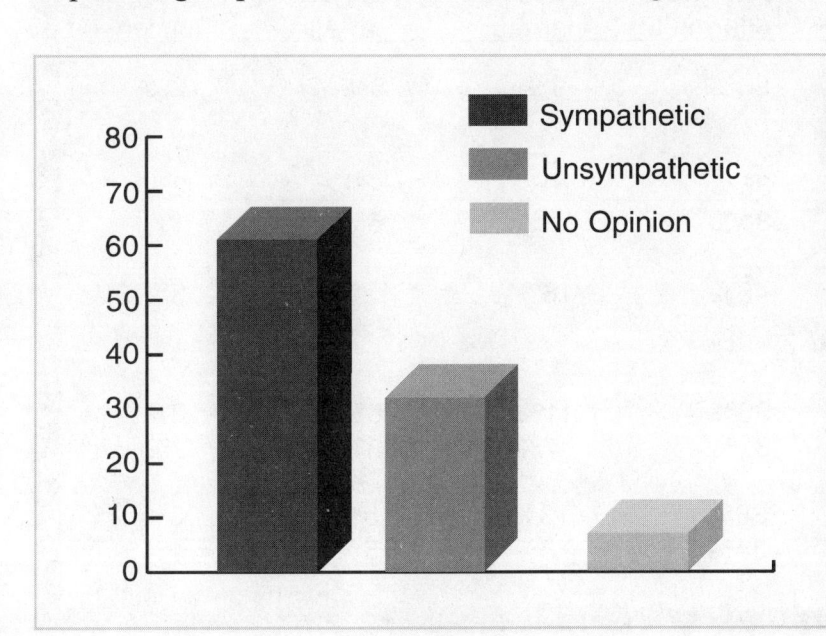

American Opinion

Most Americans are sympathetic to smokers "because they know that smokers are addicted to cigarettes and have a difficult time trying to quit the habit."

Source: The Gallup Poll 1996

> "'Many smokers bear a measure of blame for their woes, particularly those who picked up a pack after the health peril became obvious.'"

agencies have pursued the tobacco companies in the courts for damages and reimbursements for the cost of treating people with smoking-related illnesses. "Many smokers bear a measure of blame for their woes, particularly those who picked up a pack after the health peril became obvious," *The St. Petersburg Times* commented. "But the industry carries a heavy burden for promoting smoking as glamorous and invigorating, while knowing it can be the ticket to an early grave."[11]

According to Gallup, fewer than a third of survey respondents, 30 percent, agree the tobacco companies should be held responsible for smoking-related deaths. A slight majority, 51 percent, believe the warning notice on cigarette packs absolves the companies of responsibility.

In 1996, for the first time in forty years of tobacco litigation, a cigarette maker volunteered to pay health claims for smoking-related illnesses. To free itself from a major nationwide class-action lawsuit, the Liggett Group, the smallest of the major tobacco companies, also offered to reimburse five states a portion of their Medicaid costs.

As it turned out, the first round in that legal battle went to the tobacco companies. In May 1996, a federal appeals panel in New Orleans dismissed the omnibus suit against

American Opinion

In general, how harmful do you feel second hand smoke is to adults?

	Very Harmful	Somewhat Harmful	Not too Harmful	Not Harmful at All	No Opinion
OVERALL	48%	36%	9%	5%	2%
REGION					
East	50%	36%	10%	2%	2%
West	54%	31%	8%	6%	1%
SMOKERS	22%	46%	16%	12%	3%
IDEOLOGY					
Liberal	45%	36%	11%	6%	2%
Conservative	51%	37%	7%	3%	2%
MALE	41%	38%	13%	5%	3%
FEMALE	55%	34%	5%	5%	1%

Source: The Gallup Poll, 1996

the companies on behalf of millions of smokers.

The action, known as the Castano case, named for the smoker's widow who brought it in 1994, accused the tobacco companies and their lobby arm, the Tobacco Institute, of concealing evidence that nicotine is addictive and of manipulating nicotine levels in cigarettes.[12] The tobacco industry argued successfully that the suit, which potentially could have included fifty million smokers, would have been too large and clumsy to manage. The plaintiffs' lawyers countered that they would file individual suits in all fifty states.

The New Orleans ruling did not affect other legal challenges. At least nine states have sued the tobacco companies to recoup tobacco-related Medicaid costs, and more are considering such action. (The nine are Mississippi, Florida, Minnesota, West Virginia, Massachusetts, Texas, Louisiana, Maryland, and Connecticut.)

In August 1996, a Florida jury ruled the Brown & Williamson Tobacco Corp. had to pay $750,000 to a longtime smoker suffering from lung cancer, only the second time the industry has been ordered to pay damages in a liability case. A Brown & Williamson lawyer, Bruce Sheffler, argued that Grady Carter, sixty-six, a smoker since 1947, had known all along about the risks of cigarettes. "He continued smoking Lucky Strikes because he liked them," Sheffler said.[13]

Brown & Williamson said it would appeal the State Circuit Court ruling. All together, there have been about twenty liability cases, but the tobacco companies have yet to pay out any money for damages. A New Jersey woman won $400,000 in a 1988 case, but a higher court overturned the award, and the plaintiff eventually dropped the matter.

In a gruesome Swiftian response, some economists argue smokers have already covered anticipated medical costs by paying the 50 cent-a-pack tax on cigarettes—and by dying early, before they can collect the health and retirement benefits due them. One study estimated the yearly pension savings alone at $30 billion. "Killing yourself by smoking incurs costs, which for yourself are horrendous and miserable, and for everyone else include higher insurance costs," said Peter W. Huber, an analyst at the Manhattan Institute for Policy Research. "But there are offsets. It's quite pos-

> **At least nine states have sued the tobacco companies to recoup tobacco-related Medicaid costs, and more are considering such action.**

sible that smokers are doing us a small favor. It's a ghoulish argument—it's horrible—but if you're going to have an economic case, you've got to use economics. You can't use sentiment."[14]

Duke University economist W. Kip Viscusi put it baldly: "Social Security would go bankrupt if nobody smoked," he said. "We'd all have to work to age eighty."[15]

Other studies, including those of the federal CDC, peg smoking/health costs much higher. And human lives count more than healthy Social Security account balances. All the same, the economists, substituting aging smokers for poor children in their own "modest proposal," have a point.

"The alternative to death from a smoking-related illness is not immortality and perfect health—it is later death, and perhaps from a more costly illness," Congressional Research Service economists Jane Gravelle and Dennis Zimmerman wrote in the *Washington Post*.[16]

Tobacco Politics

The tobacco industry has long occupied a powerful position in American life. James Buchanan Duke, the nineteenth-century cigarette entrepreneur, supplied the money that established eponymous Duke University in Durham, North Carolina. Duke's generosity benefited hospitals, Methodist churches, and orphans, too.

Cigarette makers support—and influence—politicians with massive doses of money in the form of campaign contributions. Like robber barons endowing the church with their lands, they fund arts groups, symphony orchestras, and other cultural institutions. They sponsor such mass-appeal events as car racing.

Tobacco influence has been a drag on government efforts to regulate the industry. The tobacco lobby fought hard to counter the effects of the 1964 surgeon general's report that directly linked smoking to cancer and suggested a strong link to heart disease. In a nod to the industry, the report also acknowledged that smoking had laxative effects, kept smokers' weight down, and acted as a tranquilizer.

Pressure continued to build throughout the 1960s and '70s. The government stopped telling "both sides" of the health story. Beginning in 1966, warning labels were re-

> " 'Social Security would go bankrupt if nobody smoked.' "

quired on cigarette packs. Cigarette advertising was banned from television. The secretary of Health, Education and Welfare stigmatized smoking as "Pubic Health Enemy No. 1."

Today, according to Gallup, opinion surveys suggest Americans favor suasion over regulation, "Thank you for not smoking" signs over outright bans.

Around half the respondents in a 1994 Gallup poll said they would grant a smoker's request to light up at the next table in a restaurant. Close to half said they would tell a smoker they'd prefer he didn't smoke. Only 1 percent said they would withhold permission.

Strong majorities favor set-aside smoking areas in public places—68 percent in hotels, 63 percent in workplaces, 57 percent in restaurants. There is far less support for outright bans—20 percent in hotels, 32 percent in workplaces, 38 percent in restaurants.

State and federal agencies continue to pursue regulatory solutions. In mid-1996, Massachusetts became the first state to force cigarette makers to disclose all the ingredients in their products. Among other things, the measure required precise information on nicotine levels in each brand.

As always, the industry reacted aggressively, claiming the law violated a federal statute governing trade secrets. "You [could] put any consumer product under a microscope," Tobacco Institute spokesman Thomas Lauria said. "There are a hundred ingredients in a charcoal-grilled

"
Beginning in 1966, warning labels were required on cigarette packs.
"

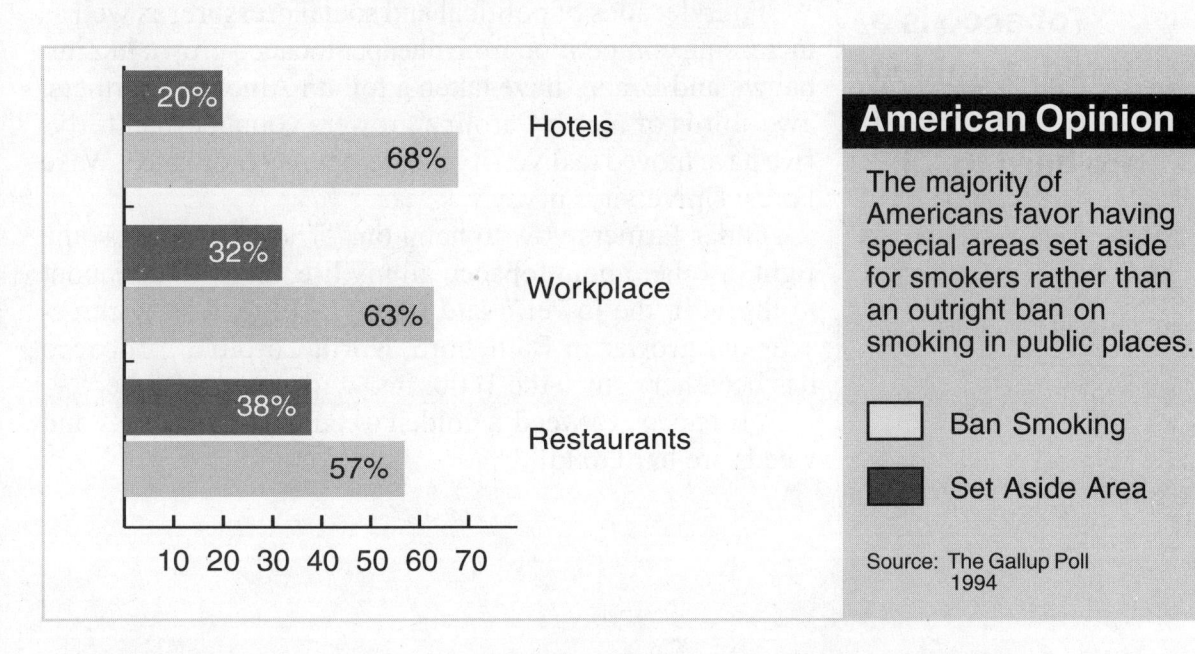

American Opinion

The majority of Americans favor having special areas set aside for smokers rather than an outright ban on smoking in public places.

☐ Ban Smoking
■ Set Aside Area

Source: The Gallup Poll 1994

Hotels: 20% / 68%
Workplace: 32% / 63%
Restaurants: 38% / 57%

steak."[17] Within a few days of the bill's passage, the industry sought an injunction blocking it until a federal court could consider the matter.

Down on the Farm

Price supports for the American South's growers of bright-leaf tobacco were a staple of New Deal political and social policy. To relieve Depression-era distress, the government agreed to buy surplus tobacco if farmers would limit their production—that is, accept quotas. Over the next half century the price-support program benefited 500,000 farm families and kept cigarette makers supplied with what experts still regard as the world's finest tobacco.[18]

In the past quarter century, though, U.S. tobacco production has declined steadily, from around 20 percent of the world's supply in 1970 to less than 10 percent in 1995. Tobacco used to be grown widely throughout the upper South. Today North Carolina produces two-thirds of the U.S. crop of flue-cured bright-leaf tobacco.

Tobacco remains a lucrative cash crop, pumping $1 billion a year into the North Carolina economy. Tobacco profits approached $1,000 an acre in 1995, compared with $150 an acre for corn. But it is a difficult, labor-intensive plant to cultivate. Even with the most modern equipment, notes Richard Kluger, it still takes roughly 200 hours of work to bring one acre of tobacco to market.

Four decades of political and social pressure, as well as increasing competition from cheaper tobacco grown in Zimbabwe and Brazil, have taken a toll on American farmers. Two-thirds of North Carolina growers younger than forty-five have moved to diversify their crops, according to a Wake Forest University survey.

Older farmers vow to hang on. "There has been some fight or other about tobacco all my life, and I'm not about to throw in the towel," said Bruce L. Flye, a sixty-three-year-old grower in Battleboro, North Carolina. "Tobacco has been here since the 1600s and will continue to be."

"Tobacco is a weed, a golden weed," Flye went on, "and weeds are hard to kill."[19]

> "
> 'Tobacco is a weed, a golden weed, and weeds are hard to kill.'
> "

Beer, Wine, Spirits

The number of people identifying themselves as drinkers has changed little over Gallup's fifty-five-year history of polling on alcohol habits. The most recent surveys suggest that around six of every ten adults drink, consistent with Gallup's long-term 55 to 65 percent range. More men drink than women; more younger people drink than older.

In recent years, though, surveys seem to show that Americans who do drink are drinking less. In a 1994 poll, 41 percent of the sample said their alcohol consumption had gone down during the previous five years. Only 7 percent said they were drinking more. And only 25 percent admitted they sometimes drink more than they should.

Drink is indissolubly associated with conviviality, celebration, fellowship, roistering. Quoth Byron's Don Juan:

> Man, being reasonable, must get drunk;
> The best of life is but intoxication:
> Glory, the grape, love, gold, in these are sunk
> The hopes of all men, and of every nation.

Social pressures have curbed Americans' drinking in recent years. More people are health-conscious. State dramshop laws—which impose liability on the seller of liquor when someone is injured—and campaigns against drunk

> " **Social pressures have curbed Americans' drinking in recent years.** "

Percentage of Americans Who Drink: 1939–1996

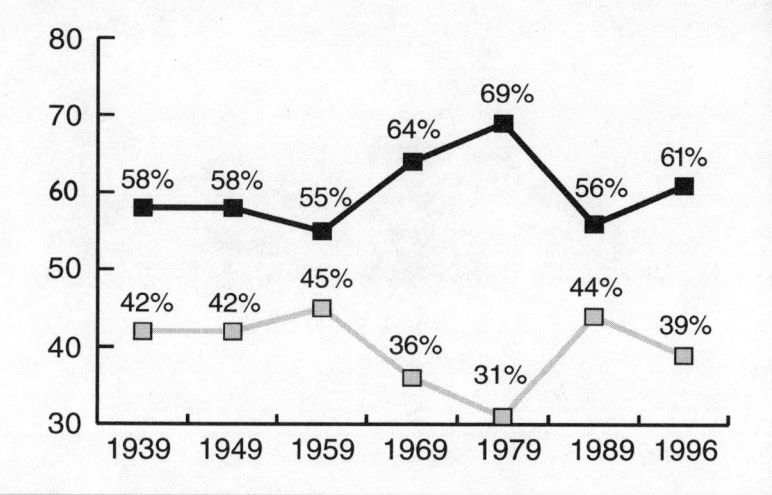

Year	Use	Abstain
1939	58%	42%
1949	58%	42%
1959	55%	45%
1969	64%	36%
1979	69%	31%
1989	56%	44%
1996	61%	39%

As a Matter of Fact

Do you have occasion to use alcoholic beverages such as liquor, wine, or beer, or are you a total abstainer?

— Use
— Abstain

Source: The Gallup Poll 1939–1996

> "By international standards, Americans are a temperate race, well down on the list in alcohol consumption."

driving, including stiff penalties for drivers who test over the limit, are slowly changing people's habits. Since 1992, several states—among them Georgia, Massachusetts, Nebraska, New Hampshire, Ohio, and Texas—have passed laws that automatically revoke the licenses of drivers who fail or refuse to submit to an alcohol breath test.

By international standards, Americans are a temperate race, well down on the list in alcohol consumption. Luxembourgers lead the world, with an annual per person intake of 13 quarts of pure alcohol, the equivalent of three beers a day for every man, woman, and child in the country. Beer is the beverage of choice for nearly half of America's drinkers. Wine, the choice of around a quarter of Gallup's sample, is the next most popular drink. Liquor is third, at 20 percent.

Beer is more popular with men than with women; women prefer wine over beer. Younger people are more likely than older people to drink beer; wine gains steadily as a preference as the age of the sample increases.

Specialty beers are the fastest-growing alcohol market in the United States. Microbrewery production has increased 40 percent a year during the 1990s; more than 300 small breweries are now in operation, turning out modest quantities of quality beers with evocative brand names such as Catamount (Vermont), Tun Tavern (Pennsylvania), Legacy (Illinois), and Dixie (Louisiana).

"It is the most exciting part of the alcohol beverage

As a Matter of Fact

Do you most often drink liquor, wine, or beer? (Asked of people who said they had a drink in the past seven days.)

Source: The Gallup Poll June 1996

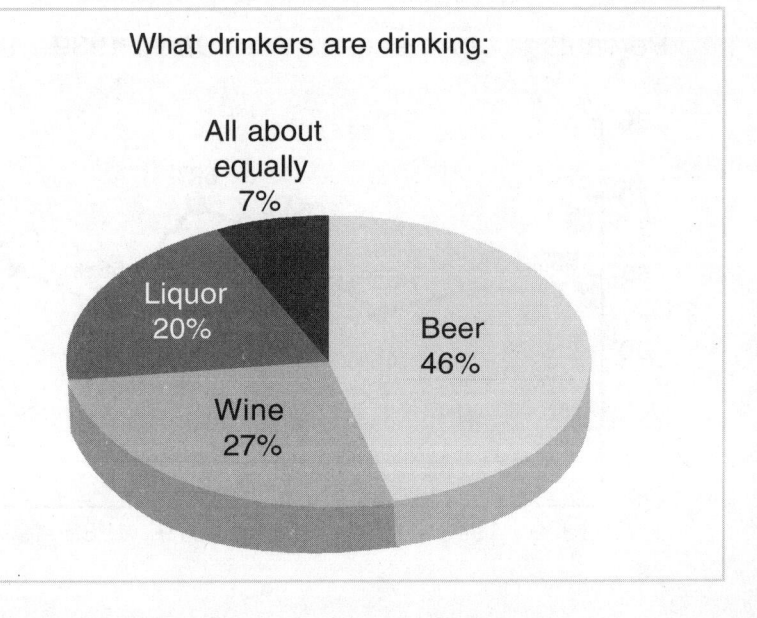

What drinkers are drinking:

- All about equally 7%
- Liquor 20%
- Beer 46%
- Wine 27%

In Sonoma, Vines to Hops

The 36,000 acres of grapevines in Sonoma County, Calif., produce an annual wine-grape crop valued at $160 million. Now one major Sonoma vintner has pulled up some of its merlot vines to plant hops instead.

The Benziger Family Winery of Glen Ellen, Calif., plans to capture a share of the fastest-growing alcoholic beverage market in the United States—high quality specialty beers. Gallup surveys show that while wine is gaining ground, beer remains the beverage of choice for nearly half of America's drinkers.

The Benzigers' Sonoma Mountain Brewing Company occupies 20 acres in the heart of Sonoma wine country. The company is the first in Sonoma to plant hop gardens on a large scale.

Hops, whose aromatic buds are a key ingredient in beer, were an important crop in Sonoma County until the 1950s. Now most U.S. hops are grown in the Yakima Valley of Washington.

The Benzigers expect to produce around 100,000 cases annually, using a variety of hops "that will give us a distinct Sonoma County taste, a flavor that will distinguish our beer," said Mike Benziger, who heads the family's enterprises

market right now," said Tim Wallace of the Benziger Family Winery of California, which planned to open its own microbrewery to produce 100,000 cases of pilsner and lager beers annually.[20]

The Case for Prohibition

Drunkenness and its chronic form, alcoholism, have destroyed families, wrecked careers, and contributed to the carnage on America's highways.

Around a quarter of the sample in Gallup's 1994 poll, 27 percent, acknowledged alcohol as a "cause of trouble" in their families—the highest figure the polltakers had yet recorded. When Gallup first asked the question in 1950, only 14 percent identified alcohol as a problem. And exactly two-thirds of respondents in the 1994 survey characterized alcohol abuse as a major national problem.

Ironically, Gallup found greater support (17 percent) for banning alcohol, which in moderation is beneficial to health and quality of life, than tobacco (11 percent), which is dangerous beyond a doubt. Not surprisingly, those who said they had endured drinking problems in their families were

> "Gallup surveys suggest religious beliefs strongly color people's attitudes toward alcohol."

more likely to favor prohibition (23 percent) than those who had no such troubles (18 percent). Women were more likely to favor an alcohol ban than men; and Southerners were more prohibitionist than Midwesterners, Easterners, and Westerners.

Close to half the sample in the 1996 poll supported a ban on beer and wine advertising on TV. Nearly two-thirds thought ads for hard liquor (whiskey, vodka, and gin) should be kept off the air. The leading U.S. liquor trade association moved in 1996 to end the decades-long ban on broadcast liquor advertising anyway, following Seagram's decision to begin airing ads for products in some markets.

Gallup surveys suggest religious beliefs strongly color people's attitudes toward alcohol. A majority (53 percent) of Gallup respondents who say religion is highly important in their lives claim to be teetotalers. "Born again" Christians are less likely still to drink. Neither group, however, favors a return to prohibition.

Temperance has a long and colorful history in America. A Saratoga County, New York, physician founded the country's first formal temperance society in 1808. The charter members pledged to "use no rum, gin, whiskey, wine or any distilled spirits except by advice of a physician, or in case of actual disease." With a strong push from the Protestant clergy, the movement slowly gained hold in New York and New England. By the middle of the notoriously hard-drinking 1830s, a million Americans had taken the pledge.[21]

American Opinion

A surprising 17 percent of Americans favor banning the sale of beer, wine, and liquor. Here is the breakdown according to gender, race, and region of America.

Source: The Gallup Poll 1996

- Total — 17%
- Women — 20%
- Men — 14%
- White — 16%
- Black — 31%
- South — 22%
- East — 15%
- West — 13%
- Mid-West — 17%

American Opinion

Advertising Beer: Approval by Subgroups

	Allow	Ban	No Opinion
SEX:			
Men	57%	40%	3%
Women	41%	57%	2%
RACE:			
White	49%	49%	2%
Black	49%	49%	2%
POLITICS:			
Republican	46%	52%	2%
Democrat	53%	45%	2%
Independent	47%	50%	3%

Source: The Gallup Poll, 1996

Over time, temperance evolved into prohibition—a different matter entirely. In 1919, Anti-Saloon League agitation resulted in the ratification of the 18th Amendment to the U.S. Constitution, which banned the manufacture, sale, import, and export of alcoholic beverages. The amendment, impossible to enforce, led to the proliferation of speakeasies, the distilling of oceans of bathtub gin, and a boom in employment, wages, and benefits for gangsters.

The 21st Amendment repealed Prohibition in 1933. By the mid-1960s, there were no statewide prohibition laws in the United States, though local option kept many towns and counties dry, especially in the South and West. Prohibition sentiment persists in some places. In Alaska, some eighty villages have gone dry since the 1980s. Others have gone "damp"—meaning bars and liquor stores are shut down but people can still import liquor to drink at home.

The citizens of Barrow, Alaska, the northernmost town in the United States, voted in a total alcohol ban in October 1994. When the ban took effect, the nearest drink was 250 miles to the south. In the first year, the police reported fewer complaints and made many fewer drunk-driving arrests, and there were fewer visits to the hospital emergency room.[22]

Rockport, Massachusetts, one of twenty-three dry towns

> "The beneficial effects of moderate drinking have been recognized since Biblical times."

in the Bay State, voted to stay that way after a lively repeal campaign in 1996. Rockport voted by a two-to-one ratio against a proposal to allow beer and wine sales in restaurants.

The town's prohibition law dates from 1856. On July 8 of that year, temperance crusader Hannah Jumper led 200 hatchet-wielding women on a five-hour romp through Rockport that sent some 250 gallons of spirits, mostly rum, spilling into the streets.

Rockport divided into wet and dry camps in 1996, just as it had done 140 years before. Prohibitionists felt bound to appease Mrs. Jumper's shade.

"We live in what was once Hannah Jumper's home," dry advocate Peggy Russell said. "I can't in good conscience cross her spirit."[23]

The Healthful Grape

Heavy drinking is clearly harmful, physically and emotionally destructive. Overuse of alcohol can cause liver diseases such as cirrhosis. Drunks are more likely to injure or kill themselves in a fall, a car wreck, or some other accident. And hardly anyone doubts that pregnant women should keep off alcohol entirely, because of the potential for birth defects.

The beneficial effects of moderate drinking have been recognized since Biblical times. "Drink no longer water,

American Opinion

While most Americans want television advertising for hard liquor banned, the country is almost evenly split when it comes to allowing television advertisements for beer and wine.

Source: The Gallup Poll 1996

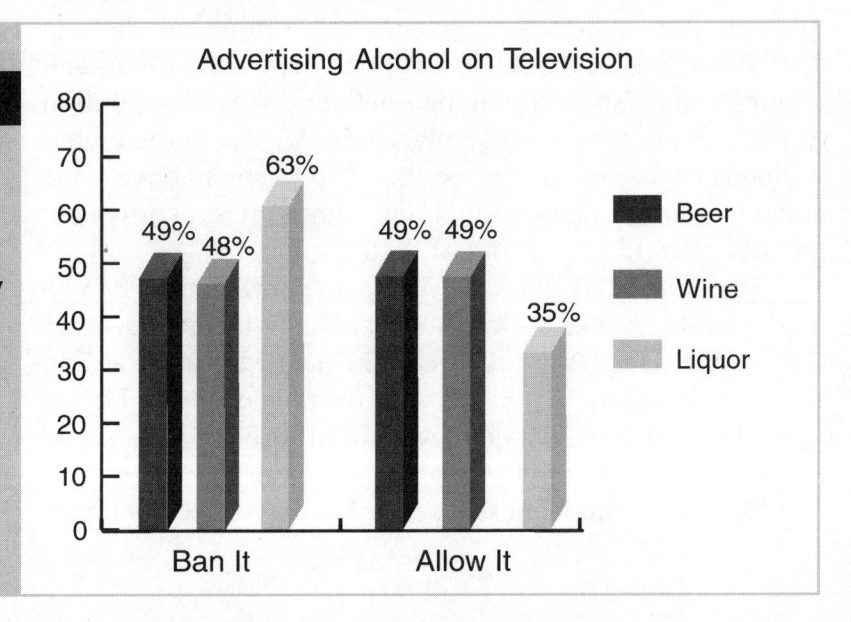

Advertising Alcohol on Television

	Ban It	Allow It
Beer	49%	49%
Wine	48%	49%
Liquor	63%	35%

but use a little wine for thy stomach's sake and thine often infirmities," Saint Paul advises.

Today a growing body of scientific evidence suggests that in moderate doses drinking—unlike smoking—can be actively salutary. Those who take a drink or two a day, studies show, are half as likely to have heart disease as teetotalers.

A number of studies have established that red wine can be beneficial to the heart, in part because of the antioxidants it contains. A Harvard Medical School researcher's study suggested that moderate use of beer or liquor could be as effective as wine. Alcohol, said Dr. J. Michael Gaziano, produces so-called "good cholesterol," which keeps arteries clear of dangerous buildups. "People who drink two martinis at dinner are no different from those who drink two glasses of red wine," Gaziano said.[24]

If a little wine is good, could, say, a bottle a day be better? The Copenhagen Heart Study, a twelve-year study of 13,000 Danish men and women, claimed that only wine, and not beer or alcohol, can prolong life, and that the greatest benefits accrued to people who drank not a glass or two but three to five glasses of wine a day. Such people had a substantially decreased risk of dying of coronary heart disease or a stroke, according to this study.[25]

Skeptics pointed out, though, that the Danish study reported only deaths from cardiovascular causes. Other international studies have suggested that death rates— especially for cancer, cirrhosis, and traffic mishaps—climb when consumption rises above two drinks a day. Dr. Michael Criqui of the medical school at the University of California, San Diego, said it's not clear why the study showed increased benefits from higher levels of wine consumption.

"Maybe it has to do with differences in genetics, social support, medical care or maybe they have straighter roads," he said.[26]

"
A Harvard Medical School researcher's study suggested that moderate use of beer or liquor could be as effective as wine.
"

Notes: Smoking and Drinking How Far Should Government Go To Break Our Bad Habits?

1. Richard Kluger, *Ashes to Ashes: America's Hundred-Year Cigarette War, the Public Health, and the Unabashed Triumph of Philip Morris* (New York: Alfred A. Knopf, 1996), xii.
2. Barnaby J. Feder, "Increase in Teen-Age Smoking Sharpest Among Black Males," *The New York Times*, May 24, 1996, 20.
3. Feder, "Increase in Teen-Age Smoking."
4. Peter T. Kilborn, "Clinton Approves a Series of Curbs on Cigarette Ads," *The New York Times*, August 24, 1996, 1.
5. Kilborn, "Clinton Approves a Series of Curbs."
6. Kluger, *Ashes to Ashes*, 18 – 26.
7. Kluger, *Ashes to Ashes*, xii.
8. Laura Mansnerus, "Don't Smoke. Please. Pretty Please," *The New York Times*, The Week in Review, September 15, 1996, 4.
9. Richard Saltus, "Authors Say New Study Confirms Nicotine's Addictive Properties," *The Boston Globe*, July 18, 1996, A4.
10. John Leo, "Thank You For Not Smoking," *U.S. News & World Report*, July 15/July 22, 1996, 18.
11. Editorial, *The St. Petersburg Times*, March 18, 1996.
12. Glenn Collins, "Huge Tobacco Lawsuit Is Thrown Out on Appeal," *The New York Times*, May 24, 1996, 1.
13. "Stricken Smoker Awarded $750,000," Associated Press report in *The New York Times*, August 10, 1996, 1.
14. Laura Mansnerus, "Making a Case for Death," *The New York Times*, May 5, 1996, The Week in Review, 1.
15. Mansnerus, "Making a Case for Death."
16. Quoted in Mansnerus, "Making a Case for Death."
17. Frank Phillips, "Cigarette bill passes," *The Boston Globe*, July 25, 1996, 1.
18. Kluger, *Ashes to Ashes*, 85; 550.
19. Glenn Collins, "On Tobacco Road, A Generation Gap," *The New York Times*, May 30, 1996, D1.
20. Tim Tesconi, "Tearing Out Vines to Plant Hops," *The New York Times*, May 29, 1996, C4.
21. John A. Krout, "Temperance Movement," *Dictionary of American History*, Vol. 7 (New York: Charles Scribner's Sons, 1976), 22.
22. "Alaska Town Rethinks Ban on Alcohol," Associated Press report in *The New York Times*, September 10, 1995, 35.
23. David Arnold, "Last call, 1856," *The Boston Globe,* August 21, 1996, 1.
24. "Any Alcohol Will Suffice to Aid Heart," Associated Press report in *The New York Times*, November 17, 1995, 26.
25. Jane E. Brody, "Danish Study Shows Wine Aiding Longevity," *The New York Times*, May 5, 1995, 18.
26. Brody, "Danish Study Shows Wine Aiding Longevity."

4 The War on Drugs
The Strategy Debate Never Ends

Illicit drugs make an attractive target for politicians as election dates near. No candidate for high office has yet been known to come out in favor of cocaine. Because solutions, such as they are, can only be partial at best, no officeholder's record is attack-proof. For shattered families, though, and for the police, courts, toxicologists, and social workers, the problem remains, intractable as ever, long after the political caravan moves on.

Opinion polls continue to show that drug abuse ranks as one of the national problems that most agitate Americans. In an extensive Gallup Organization survey in 1995, more than 90 percent of the sample rated illegal drugs as a "crisis" or a "serious problem." Still, respondents regarded illicit drugs as a distant problem, far more serious nationally than in their home communities. In some polls in recent years, drugs rank just behind crime—and well ahead of health care, welfare, and other issues—on the list of matters of highest concern. Twenty percent of Gallup respondents acknowledged that drugs had caused trouble in their own families. The surveys show support for a broad range of anti-drug programs, but almost nobody favors the legalization of drugs as a remedy.

With reports that drug use among adolescents had begun to rise again after some years of decline, drug issues made a fleeting appearance in the 1996 presidential campaign. As it happens, most analysts regard America's drug problem as serious but not critical. Overall, drug use in the

"
Opinion polls continue to show that drug abuse ranks as one of the national problems that most agitate Americans.

"

> "There are an estimated 2.7 million hard-core drug addicts in America."

mid-1990s falls far short of the levels reached during the epidemic years of the late 1970s.

The government's National Household Survey on Drug Abuse reported in August 1996 that 12.8 million Americans had used illegal drugs at least once a month during the previous year—about the same number as in 1994, but a sharp drop from 23.3 million users in 1985. Three quarters were marijuana smokers.[1]

Still, drugs are dangerous, corrosive, and socially expensive. The crack blight has nearly destroyed some inner-city communities. U.S. prisons bulge with convicts serving tough mandatory sentences for drug possession or sales. There are an estimated 2.7 million hard-core drug addicts in America. The government says drug abuse kills 20,000 people a year and costs the country $67 billion a year.[2]

More troubling in 1996 were reports of an upswing in teenagers' experimentation with illicit drugs. One survey suggested teen drug use had doubled, from 5.3 percent to 10.9 percent, between 1992 and 1995.[3]

The public appeared to take note of the trend in 1996—if not on its own merits, then perhaps as a result of Bob Dole's focus on the issue in the campaign. In 1995, most respondents, 68 percent, thought the nation had either "stood still" or "made some progress" in the war on drugs over the previous year or two. But by November 1996, only 52 percent agreed the problem had not grown worse.

American Opinion

How would you describe the problem of drug abuse <u>in your neighborhood</u>, including the local schools?
("No opinion" omitted)

Response	Percent
Crisis	10%
Serious problem	44%
Minor problem	37%
Not a problem	6%

Source: The Gallup Poll 1995

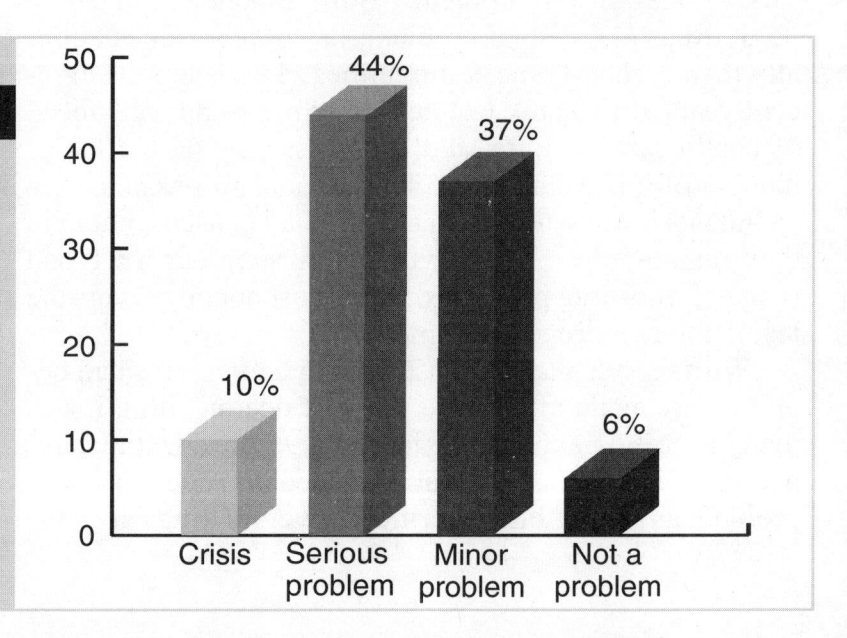

The Political Angle

Republicans accuse Democrats of being soft on drugs. Conservatives such as William Bennett call for an expanded military response to drug smuggling and for the use of troops to disrupt sources of supply. Democrats accuse Republicans of choking off funds for drug prevention and treatment programs while ignoring the social ills that contribute to the problem.

Bush administration drug officials had targeted so-called recreational users on the theory that scaring them off would damage the drug business, cut into dealers' profits, and eventually reduce the pool of addicts. In a policy shift, the Clinton administration in 1993 decided to redirect emphasis from "casual" drug users to hard-core addicts. Even the top Clinton drug official conceded the shift may have contributed to the rise in adolescent drug use.

"We took our eye off the ball," said Barry McCaffrey, the retired army general named to head the White House Office of National Drug Control Policy early in 1996. "We stopped talking about it. Our kids went back to using drugs."[4]

On the other hand, Republicans in Congress starved drug programs of funds. Budget cuts in 1995 and 1996 forced the dismantling of 79 drug prevention programs and 33 treatment programs around the country. Clinton used the veto to restore the more than $200 million (half the total) Congress

> **" The Clinton administration in 1993 decided to redirect emphasis from "casual" drug users to hard-core addicts. "**

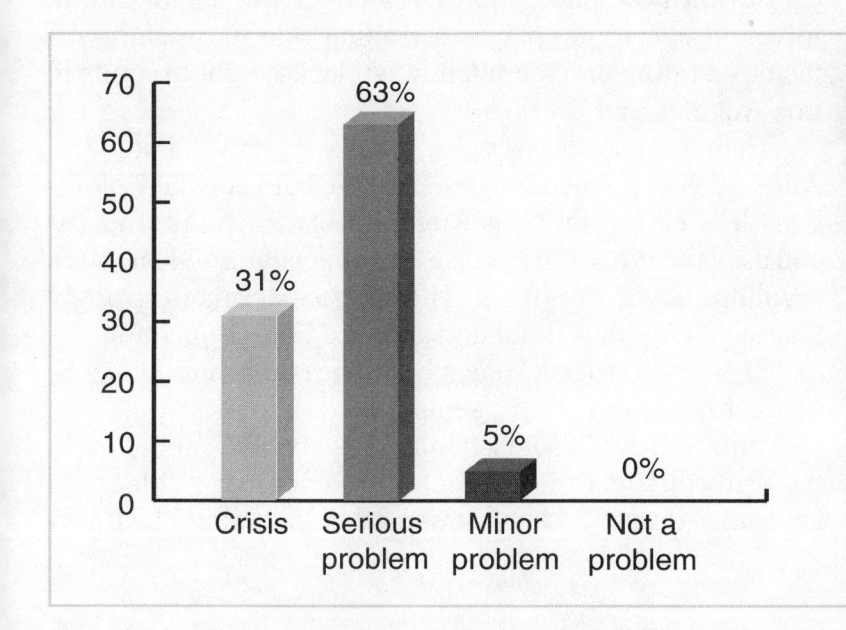

American Opinion

How would you describe the problem of drug abuse <u>across the country</u>? Is it a crisis, a serious problem, a minor problem, or not a problem?
("No opinion" omitted)

- Crisis: 31%
- Serious problem: 63%
- Minor problem: 5%
- Not a problem: 0%

Source: The Gallup Poll 1995

> 'The Clinton Administration has taken the Republican drug war to soaring new heights of Draconian ineffectiveness.'

sought to cut from the Safe and Drug Free Schools Act.[5]

The commentator Joshua Wolf Shenk saw ample fault on both sides. Neither party seems willing to act on the generally accepted notion that the problem is demand rather than supply. Only around a third of the Clinton administration's record $15 billion 1997 budget for control of illegal drugs goes for prevention and treatment—programs that potentially can reduce demand.

Accusing the Democrats of being soft on drugs is silly, he suggested. "In fact," wrote Shenk, who is a correspondent for the magazine *The Economist*, "the Clinton Administration has taken the Republican drug war to soaring new heights of Draconian ineffectiveness."[6]

Whoever's to blame, reports of increasing adolescent drug use concern the experts. The increase corresponds with a steep upward spike in the teenage population. By 2010, demographers project there will be more adolescents than ever before in American history, and adolescents are the group regarded as most at risk of taking drugs.

"The problem is getting worse and doing so sharply, and we need to attend to it, but I don't think we need to exaggerate it," said Lloyd Johnson, a University of Michigan social scientist who has tracked drug use among teenagers since the 1970s.[7]

Has the government actually contributed to the drug problem? On the drug issue, distrust of government built a receptive audience for an explosive series of articles in a California newspaper that claimed U.S.-backed Contra forces in Nicaragua played a leading role in touching off the devastating crack epidemic in black neighborhoods in Los Angeles in the 1980s.

The Contras, the *San Jose Mercury-News* charged in August 1996, opened the first pipeline between the Colombian drug cartels and Los Angeles's black neighborhoods, and used the profits to finance their war against Nicaragua's revolutionary government. The newspaper hinted strongly that the CIA knew about and approved the connection.

CIA director John Deutsch said he had no credible evidence that government agents fueled the epidemic. "The CIA fights drugs," Deutsch told a largely black audience in the Watts district of Los Angeles in November. "It does not encourage drugs."[8] Major newspapers, including *The Wash-*

ington Post and the *Los Angeles Times*, debunked the *Mercury-News* series, titled "Dark Alliance."[9]

The View from Gallup

Law enforcement authorities tend to believe that drug prevention and treatment programs work better than police sweeps. Most Americans agree on the importance of prevention, according to Gallup opinion surveys. Asked to rate different measures according to their effectiveness and cost efficiency in keeping drugs under control, respondents in the 1995 poll rated education ahead of reducing supply and punishing drug offenders. Few, however, believed drug-treatment programs were effective.

Generally, respondents favored a comprehensive approach that included elements of interdiction, punishment, and prevention. They showed broad support for the concept of reducing the drug supply. Two-thirds said the government needs to do a lot more in this area, and six in every 10 cited interdiction as a highly effective antidrug strategy. But they were less than enthusiastic about aggressive interdiction proposals: Only 50 percent, for example, favored using U.S. forces abroad to search out and arrest drug traffickers, and a majority opposed increasing foreign aid to support overseas antidrug operations.

While support for antidrug activities abroad is soft, strong majorities favor domestic efforts. The 1995 poll showed overwhelming support for specific law-enforcement initiatives against drug sellers and users, including increased funding for police, harsher penalties for drug offenders, and the use of U.S. troops in American cities to enforce drug laws.

Experts emphasize the importance of education in deflecting the young from drugs. Gallup respondents wholly supported that view. An overwhelming 93 percent favored more drug education in the public schools; 85 percent supported increased funding for community antidrug education efforts; and 64 percent believed education is a highly effective strategy.

Many respondents believed the entertainment industry encouraged lax attitudes toward drugs that contributed to the problem, especially among young people. Only the pres-

> **"Generally, respondents favored a comprehensive approach that included elements of interdiction, punishment, and prevention."**

> "America is self-sufficient in the nation's drug of choice, marijuana."

sure of their peers, the poll suggested, had more influence on adolescent notions than television, movies, music, and other forms of entertainment.

Some analysts agree. They say, too, that the entertainment industry can have the reverse effect. "When mass media outlets focused on the country's drug problem during the late 1980s, something profound happened," James Burke, chairman of the advocacy group Partnership for a Drug-Free America, told Gallup. "Public attitudes about drugs changed dramatically and drug use plummeted."[10]

The Problem of Imports

America is self-sufficient in the nation's drug of choice, marijuana. Most of the crop is cultivated domestically. The great drug import is cocaine. Coca is grown almost exclusively in the Andean nations of Bolivia, Peru, and Colombia; the giant illegal Colombian cartels collect, process, and ship 70 percent of the world supply. Finished cocaine is smuggled into the U.S. by jet aircraft, by sea in large ships or overland through Mexico in cars and trucks.

The Colombian gangs, at one time the leading suppliers of marijuana to the U.S. market, diversified into the more profitable cocaine in the mid-1970s. The Colombians both responded to and helped create the demand for cocaine in the United States. As early as 1974, the Household Survey reported 5.4 million Americans had tried cocaine at least once.

With their contacts with the Andean growers at one end and establishment of their own distribution networks in major American cities at the other, the Medellin-based gangs dominated the trade. By the early 1980s, cocaine use in America had reached epidemic proportions. The Colombians opened up an enormous new market in 1985 with the introduction of cheap, smokable, and highly addictive crack cocaine. Almost overnight, crack became the hit of choice for America's urban poor.[11]

The government estimates it seizes a consistent one-third of the annual cocaine crop. But stable prices in major markets suggest the proportion of drugs confiscated to drugs produced holds roughly steady, analysts say.[12] And supply continues to exceed U.S. demand: the financial rewards are

American Opinion

How much influence do you think each of the following currently has over the attitudes of children and teenagers toward the use of drugs:

	Great deal	Moderate amount	Only a little	No influence	No opinion
School-based prevention and education programs	30%	50%	16%	2%	2%
Public service advertising on television and radio against drug use	26%	44%	24%	5%	1%
The entertainment industry, including television, movies, and music	63%	24%	8%	4%	1%
Organized religion	31%	39%	20%	7%	3%
Parents	58%	28%	11%	2%	1%
Other children and teenagers	74%	20%	4%	1%	1%
Professional athletes	51%	34%	10%	4%	1%

Source: The Gallup Poll, 1995

> "Traffic in cocaine, heroin, and marijuana is estimated to be a $122 billion annual business in the United States and western Europe."

so great that suppliers can afford 33 percent wastage. Americans consume around 300 tons of cocaine a year—about 300 million one-gram packets.

Despite stepped-up seizures, crop eradication, and arrests of leading drug kingpins, the cocaine trade is fabulously profitable for the great cartels—one of the most lucrative businesses in the world. Traffic in cocaine, heroin, and marijuana is estimated to be a $122 billion annual business in the United States and western Europe. The annual income of the Cali (Colombia) cocaine cartel, whose senior managers today run the business from prison, is estimated at $7 billion.[13]

The cartels reinvest in legitimate businesses (two of Cali's managers own a large Colombian drugstore chain), which provide a steady stream of income to reinvest in every phase of the drug operation, from planting coca seedlings in Andean clearings to bribing top officials at the Ministry of Justice in Bogotá.

An estimated 70 percent of cocaine imports are channeled through Mexico, which shares a 2,000-mile frontier and a free-trade agreement with the United States. Once safely in the country, cocaine enters the national distribution system, along with marijuana and other drugs, and largely disappears from the view of law-enforcement agents.

Increasingly, traffickers are turning to one of the oldest of federal government agencies, the U.S. Postal Service, to ship their products. Postal officials say there has been a steady increase in the use of the mails, especially Express Mail and overnight delivery, to move drugs. They report a substantial rise in seizures and arrests—and broad suspicions that they are intercepting only a small portion of the trade.

Postal inspectors arrested more than 3,700 suspects in 1995 and 1996 and confiscated more than 18 tons of marijuana, 1,500 pounds of cocaine, thousands of hits of other drugs, and $20 million in cash. One investigation alone yielded arrests of six suspects accused of mailing 1,200 pounds of marijuana from Los Angeles to addresses in Detroit, Philadelphia, New York City, and other locations. In another, police charged a Maryland man with accepting delivery of 42 pounds of cocaine with a street value of $2 million.[14]

Marijuana as Medicine

Voters in two states in 1996 approved the use of marijuana for medical purposes. One advocate of liberalized drug laws hailed the initiatives in California and Arizona as the first rollback of controlled-substance laws since the repeal of Prohibition.

"The public is increasingly cynical and jaundiced about drug war politicking," said Ethan Nadelmann, director of the Lindesmith Center, a New York City institute that favors loosening the laws on drugs.[1]

The referendum votes may spur campaigns in other states to make some illicit drugs legal in certain circumstances. Californians voted by 56 to 44 percent to allow the use of marijuana on a physician's recommendation. By 65 to 35 percent, Arizonans approved a broader law allowing any prohibited drug to be prescribed so long as two doctors concur.

Initiative supporters based their case on compassionate grounds, saying marijuana ought to be allowed where it would ease the pain of chronically or terminally ill patients. Opponents called the medical argument disingenuous.

"They're using the AIDS victims and terminally ill as props to promote the use of marijuana," said James E. Copple, president of Community Anti-Drug Coalitions of America. "It's a brilliant diversionary tactic, but we're going to oppose it, punch through it."[2]

The coalitions are moving to try to block similar campaigns in other states. In a 1995 Gallup survey, more than eight of every ten respondents said they opposed the legalization of marijuana and other psychoactive drugs.

Federal officials suggested the state initiatives are in conflict with federal law. In any case, the issue is likely to end up in court, supporters and opponents say.

"It's going to be a disaster," said General Barry R. McCaffrey, the retired soldier who heads the White House Office of Drug Control Policy. "It violates federal law, and it sends the wrong message to young people."[3]

The Arizona referendum also requires probation and treatment rather than jail for violators of drug-possession laws. Second offenders are to be released to education programs. Third offenders will continue to be subject to tough existing sentencing guidelines for drug offenses.

Zeroing in on suspicious packages is a hit-or-miss proposition, however. The nation's 30,000 post offices handle a billion parcels a year. The closer the postal service's 2,200 inspectors look, though, the more contraband they expect to find. "It is a viable method of moving drugs," acknowledged James McGivney, a spokesman for the federal Drug Enforcement Agency.[15]

Who is buying hard drugs? In the standard image, cocaine has a double market: in the cheap form of crack, desperately addicted inner-city denizens; as a finer and more expensive powder, the young, spoiled, educated, affluent middle classes. The experts say persons on bail, probation, or parole buy 60 percent of the cocaine and heroin sold in the United States.[16]

Most of America's regular drug users—three-quarters, according to the government's Household Survey—smoke marijuana. It is cheap, readily available, and, according to popular wisdom, comparatively benign—no more dangerous than alcohol. Although recent studies show a strong link between marijuana use and lung disease, a Gloucester, Massachusetts, teenager expressed the popular opinion this way:

"People say, 'Why smoke cigarettes and get cancer when you can smoke weed and just lose a few brain cells?' "[17]

Paratroops and Prisons

Most drug authorities and experts call for a comprehensive approach: prevention, enforcement, treatment. That is the general view. In detail, approaches to the antidrug cam-

American Opinion

Thinking in terms of how much each proposal might cost, and how effective you feel it would be, do you strongly favor, favor, oppose, or strongly oppose these proposals to combat the drug problem in America?

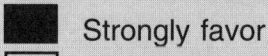

- ■ Strongly favor
- □ Favor
- ■ Strongly oppose
- ■ Oppose
- □ No opinion

Source: The Gallup Poll 1995

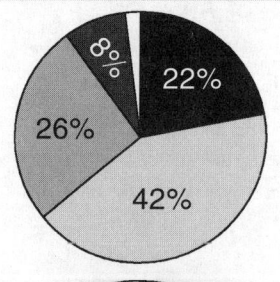

Use of U.S. military and drug-enforcement advisers in foreign countries to help fight and arrest drug traffickers: 22%, 42%, 26%, 8%

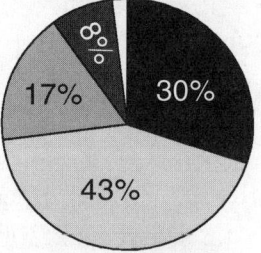

Use of the U.S. military in U.S. cities and on the U.S. border to reduce the sale and use of drugs: 30%, 43%, 17%, 8%

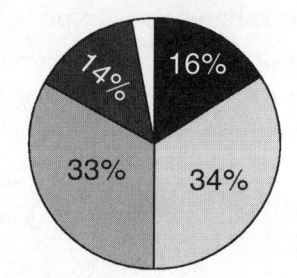

Use of U.S. military forces inside other countries to help fight or arrest drug traffickers: 16%, 34%, 33%, 14%

paign break down broadly along liberal and conservative lines.

Liberals tend to regard drug abuse as a mental illness or as a despairing response to poverty and want. They emphasize treatment, counseling, and prevention. Conservatives tend to view drug taking as an indulgence, the outward sign of an inward failing. So they call for correction: stiffer sentences for drug offenders, more prisons.

Some years ago, in an appearance on a television talk show, William Bennett, the Bush administration "drug czar," nodded in agreement when a phone-in participant proposed beheading for drug dealers. "One of the things that I think is a problem is that we are not doing enough that is morally proportional to the nature of the offense," Bennett said on *Larry King Live*, the CNN program. "I mean, what the caller suggests is morally plausible. Legally, it's difficult."[18]

President Clinton has called for the death penalty for drug dealers, though not by guillotine or scimitar. And as noted, the Clinton administration spends $2 to stop the drug supply to every $1 for programs that suppress demand. The result: enough drug offenders in America's prisons to please even the most tough-minded moral crusader. Drug offenders with no history of violence and with no prior criminal conviction made up more than 20 percent of the federal prison population in the mid-1990s.[19]

Politicians and the press speak routinely of fighting a "drug war"—an unfortunate choice of metaphor, mislead-

> "The Clinton administration spends $2 to stop the drug supply to every $1 for programs that suppress demand."

American Opinion

Do you strongly favor, favor, oppose, or strongly oppose the legalization of all drugs as a way to end the drug problem in this country?

Response	Percent
Strongly favor	5%
Favor	9%
Oppose	31%
Strongly oppose	54%

Source: The Gallup Poll 1995

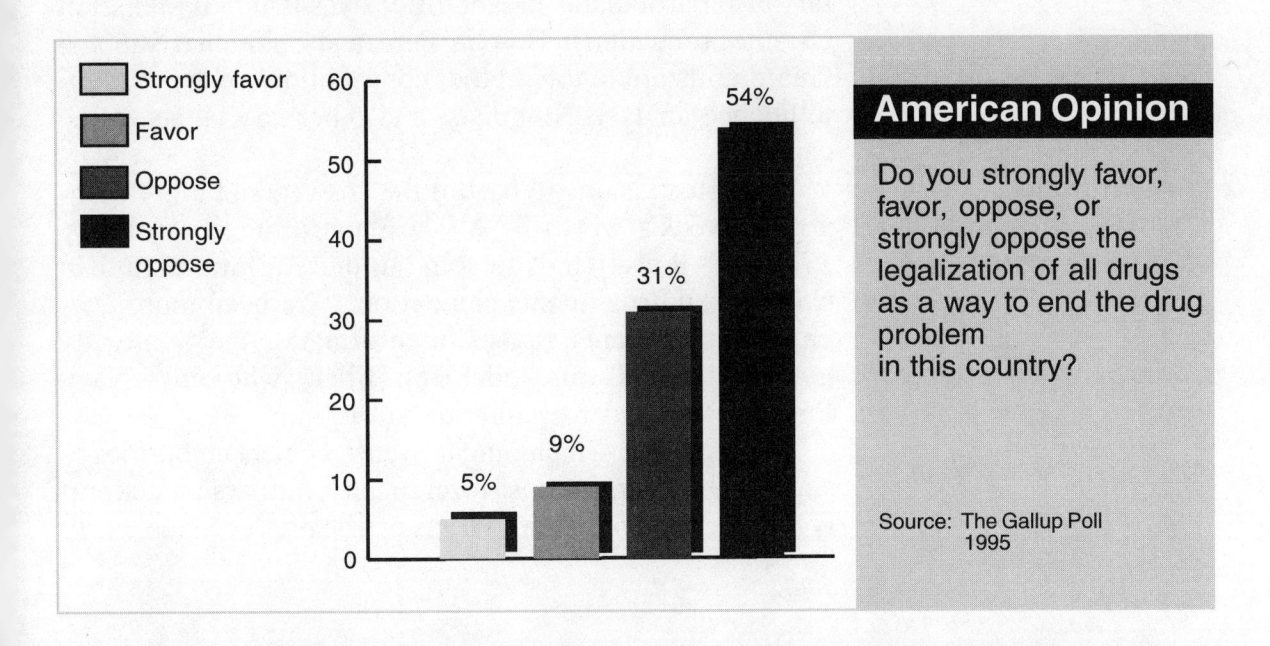

ing and harmful, according to those on the front lines.

"The victims of drug abuse are not our enemies," said McCaffrey, the former soldier who runs Clinton's antidrug effort. "They're our relatives, co-workers, and classmates. There is no surprise attack that will yield a quick victory. We must instead care for the victims of drug abuse, address its multiple causes, and use scientific knowledge, compassion, and legal remedies to develop effective preventive programs."[20]

In recent years, U.S. military forces have provided the scientific and technical expertise to which McCaffrey referred. Everyone agrees that America's long borders make an absolute halt in smuggling an impossibility. However, advocates of aggressive interdiction claim it works. Bennett, for example, says Bush administration offensives against smugglers led to a doubling, and in some cases a tripling, of cocaine prices in some U.S. cities in 1990.[21]

Some analysts suggest, however, that military operations achieve few lasting results. In 1989, U.S. forces invaded Panama to snatch Panamanian President Manuel Noriega, suspected of complicity in the cocaine trade. According to Paul B. Stares of the Brookings Institution, drug trafficking and money laundering quickly recovered in Panama, soon reaching and eventually exceeding pre-invasion levels.[22]

To track airborne smuggling, the U.S. uses high-tech surveillance, including Air Force early-warning (AWACS) aircraft and Navy long-distance ground radars. The military also participates in land offensives that aim to disrupt cocaine production in Bolivia, Peru, and Colombia. National Guard units are involved too, contributing some 3,000 intelligence analysts, linguists, and other specialists to the cause.

High-tech is only a part of the answer, and it is expensive: a week's worth of AWACS patroling costs nearly $700,000. It also tends to spin out more information than overworked drug agents can act on. "We need more law-enforcement agents, to use the information we've already got," explained Commander Bob Hillery, who runs a Navy long-distance radar installation in Virginia.[23]

Most experts—including law-enforcement authorities— suggest that wars against foreign coca farmers and export tycoons are unwinnable. "Drugs can be produced too easily

American Opinion

For each of the following, do you think a lot more should be done, somewhat more should be done, or enough is being done by the U.S.?

	A lot more	Somewhat more	Doing enough	No opinion
Education and prevention programs to keep young people off illegal drugs	54%	31%	14%	1%
Treatment programs to help drug addicts get off illegal drugs	43%	34%	20%	3%
Law-enforcement efforts to punish and convict people for the use and sale of illegal drugs	58%	25%	14%	3%
Government efforts to reduce the supply of drugs coming into the United States	66%	22%	10%	2%

Source: The Gallup Poll, 1996

in too many places," Stares noted. "Likewise, drugs can be smuggled too easily in too many ways for interdiction efforts to have any sustained or significant effect on market availability." Stares calls for more emphasis on education, prevention, and treatment programs that could reduce demand.[24]

For William Bennett, who believes the drug problem is "fundamentally a crisis of social and moral authority," the first priority is to stanch the flow of drugs and to track, catch, and punish drug traffickers.

"The most immediate need is not to teach fire prevention, but to put out the fire," Bennett said. "Something is wrong when law-enforcement officers start sounding like sociologists and when their leaders want to spend more time psychoanalyzing a drug dealer's behavior rather than getting their men to arrest him."[25]

> "The Clinton administration stepped up the campaign against illicit drugs in 1996."

Education, Treatment, Prevention

The Clinton administration stepped up the campaign against illicit drugs in 1996, partly in response to Republican challenges on the issue. Among other initiatives, the president sought to make federal aid for prison construction contingent on each state's adopting comprehensive testing and treatment programs for inmates and parolees.

Clinton, however, failed to deliver on his 1992 promise of treatment on demand for hard-core addicts. A Democratic Congress cut deeply into his funding request for treatment programs, and he did not fight hard to restore the money. As a consequence, an estimated 1 million of 2.7 million addicts were not being served in 1996—a record only marginally better than that of the Bush administration.[26]

In any case, the experts report mixed success for most treatment programs. Some studies of cocaine addicts suggest that only around half are drug-free one to two years after treatment. Experts are skeptical, too, about the effectiveness of the leading national drug education program, Drug Abuse Resistance Education, known by its acronym, DARE.

Specially trained police officers teach DARE, which is in use in three-quarters of the nation's public schools. The schools like it because it costs them nothing; cities pay the salaries of the police officers who do the teaching. Researchers say, however, that there is scant evidence that DARE has lasting effects on young people's attitudes about drugs, and that DARE is better at marketing its program than influencing behavior.

"The DARE evaluations did not show behavioral change" in smoking, drinking, or trying drugs, said Mathea Falco, whose Drug Strategies organization has reviewed a number of analyses of DARE and other programs. Another authority, Dr. Gilbert J. Botvin, of Cornell, has questioned whether police officers, as authority figures, are the right people to teach adolescents about the dangers of drugs.[27]

For most children, parents outrank police officers and teachers as figures of influence. That is why many analysts found a 1996 survey on parents' attitudes toward drugs so discouraging. The Columbia University Center on Addiction and Substance Abuse reported that two-thirds of Baby

Boomer parents who had experimented with marijuana expected their own children to do the same, and that they felt powerless to stop them. Close to half the parents in the Columbia University survey said they had smoked marijuana. Of the overall sample, 46 percent expected their teenagers to try drugs.

"That the baby boomers appear to be so ambivalent and so resigned to drug use by their kids is very disturbing," said Joseph A. Califano, of the Columbia center. "They should be mad as hell. Instead, they're saying there's nothing we can do about it."[28]

The Republican charge against Clinton turned on the president's alleged ambivalence about drugs—he once admitted to trying marijuana as a graduate student, though he said, famously, that he had not inhaled. Later, during an MTV appearance, he joked that he regretted his inability to inhale. To Clinton's opponents, his flippancy about the issue made him unfit to lead an attack on drug use among teens.

It's anyone's guess how great an influence national leaders actually command on such matters, especially with young people.

"I think the notion that high school kids do what the president wants them to do is pretty silly," said Mark A. R. Kleiman, a drug-policy authority at the University of California at Los Angeles.[29]

Kleiman and others agree, though, that the president can establish the agenda for an effective campaign against illegal drugs, and that he can further it effectively from the bully pulpit.

"Occupants of the White House can't do the work of prosecutors and police chiefs," *The Christian Science Monitor* observed in an editorial. "They can help set a tone for society and devise policies that steer local initiatives."[30]

Notes: The War on Drugs The Strategy Debate Never Ends

1. Christopher S. Wren, "U.S. Drug Policy Surges as an Issue in Election-Year Give and Take," *The New York Times*, September 17, 1996, 1.
2. Barry McCaffrey, "Stopping the Flow of Drugs," op-ed, *The Christian Science Monitor*, September 13, 1996.
3. Wren, "U.S. Drug Policy Surges as Issue."
4. Michael Kranish, "Snagged Plans Put Clinton on Defensive," *The Boston Globe*, September 16, 1996, 1.
5. Wren, "U.S. Drug Policy Surges as Issue."
6. Joshua Wolf Shenk, "Baring Teeth in the Drug War," op-ed, *The New York Times*, October 30, 1996.
7. Wren, U.S. Drug Policy Surges as Issue."
8. B. Drummond Ayres Jr., "C.I.A.'s Director Goes to Watts to Deny the Rumors of a Crack Conspiracy," *The New York Times*, November 16, 1996, 9.
9. Mark Jurkowitz, "The Payoff in the CIA-Crack Controversy," *The Boston Globe*, November 13, 1996, F1.
10. The Gallup Organization, "A 1995 View of the Drug Problem in America" (Princeton, N.J., 1995), 6.
11. Paul B. Stares, *Global Habit: The Drug Problem in a Borderless World* (Washington, D.C.: The Brookings Institution, 1996), 29-32.
12. Stares, *Global Habit*, 2.
13. Stares, *Global Habit*, 1.
    Howard LaFranchi, "Cali Drug Cartel Stretches Out Tentacles," *The Christian Science Monitor*, February 8, 1996, 1.
14. Pierre Thomas, "Drug Dealers Employ U.S. Mail as Carrier," *The Washington Post*, November 4, 1996, A1.
15. Thomas, "Drug Dealers Employ U.S. Mail."
16. Wren, "U.S. Drug Policy Surges as Issue."
17. Christopher S. Wren, "Teen-Agers Find Drugs Easy to Obtain and Warnings Easy to Ignore," *The New York Times*, October 10, 1996, 20.
18. William J. Bennett, *The De-Valuing of America* (New York: Summit Books, 1992), 116.
19. Marshall Ingwerson, "Small-Time Drug Dealers Crowd Nation's Prisons," *The Christian Science Monitor*, February 18, 1994, 1.
20. McCaffrey, "Stopping the Flow of Drugs."
21. Bennett, *The De-Valuing of America*, 114.
22. Stares, *Global Habit*, 34.
23. Richard J. Newman, "Unwinnable War," *U.S. News & World Report*, November 4, 1996, 41.
24. Stares, *Global Habit*, 13.
25. Bennett, *The De-Valuing of America*, 133–34.
26. Kranish, "Snagged Plans Put Clinton on Defensive."
27. Gina Kolata, "Experts Are at Odds on How Best to Tackle Rise in Teen-Agers' Drug Use," *The New York Times*, September 18, 1996, B7.

28. Lauran Neergaard, "Study: Parents Expect Teenagers to Try Drugs," Associated Press report in *The Boston Globe*, September 10, 1996, A3.
29. Wren, "U.S. Drug Policy Surges as Issue."
30. "Crime, Drugs, and Politics," editorial, *The Christian Science Monitor*, September 23, 1996.

Notes: Marijuana as Medicine

1. Christopher S. Wren "Votes on Marijuana Are Stirring Debate," *The New York Times*, November 17, 1996, 16.
2. Wren, "Votes on Marijuana Are Stirring Debate."
3. William Raspberry, "Quandary About Drugs," *The Washington Post*, November 1, 1996

5 Abortion and Euthanasia
Controversy over the Beginning and End of Life

At the near edge of life, abortion—the deliberate destruction of a developing human being—has tormented a generation of Americans. At the far edge of life, euthanasia—the deliberate destruction of the terminally ill—is potentially an agony as great. No moral or legal consensus appears to be at hand on these vexed questions.

Is abortion a matter preeminently for a woman to negotiate with her conscience, or does it have a broader moral significance? To many abortion-rights supporters, an embryo is no more a child than an acorn is an oak. Government has no more right to lay down the law on abortion, to ban or even closely regulate it, than to order women to attend church on Sundays, abortion-rights supporters believe.

For opponents, abortion is the unconscionable taking of human life. "Abortion stops a beating heart," runs the famous—and unassailably true—pro-life slogan. Government must protect the unborn living just as it protects others who are weak or helpless.

"It is a question of primitive conviction," writes the legal scholar and philosopher Ronald Dworkin.[1]

Is euthanasia—the supposedly merciful killing of the terminally ill—an act of generosity or an act of murder? What about assisted suicide? Is it a mercy to permit dying people a measure of control over the time and manner of their end? Or would it harden Americans' attitudes toward death and raise the potential for abuse of the poor, the old, the sick, the demented, the unwanted?

In Dworkin's phrase, the abortion battle is "America's new version of the terrible seventeenth-century European civil wars of religion."[2] The issue—with the Roman Catholic Church and some conservative Protestant denominations at one extreme and an absolute abortion-rights movement at the other—has caused conflict and anguish since the U.S. Supreme Court ruled in *Roe v. Wade* in 1973 that a pregnant woman has a constitutional right to an abortion.

Almost immediately, abortion became widely available. In the mid-1990s, one of every four pregnancies terminated in abortion in the United States. The procedure ends more than 1.5 million embryonic lives each year.

Judicial decree, not legislation, made abortion legal in America. And it appears possible that the courts, not Congress or the states, will also decide the questions at the far edge of life. The Supreme Court heard arguments in 1997 on whether the Constitution gives the terminally ill the right to a doctor's assistance in hastening death.

Physician-assisted suicide is nowhere legal in America, though federal appellate courts in two cases have struck down state laws barring it. The issue gained urgency in part because of the challenge of Jack Kevorkian. In defiance of the law, Dr. Kevorkian, a retired Michigan pathologist, helped at least forty-six patients to an early grave between 1990 and 1996.[3]

The Abortion Paradox

While ideologues of the right and left fight in the front lines of the abortion wars, most Americans fall somewhere in the ambivalent middle, Gallup Organization surveys suggest. They are noncombatants, or perhaps conscientious objectors: they favor choice on abortion, but also express a certain moral queasiness about it. For such people, the abortion-rights movement's incantatory invocation of reproductive rights is not persuasive.

Yet they do not care to substantially abridge abortion rights. Many doubtless would agree with the feminist legal scholar Robin West, who in a 1990 essay titled "Taking Freedom Seriously" advised the pro-choice movement to supplement the privacy right affirmed in the *Roe v. Wade* ruling with a theory of moral responsibility.

> "While ideologues of the right and left fight in the front lines of the abortion wars, most Americans fall somewhere in the ambivalent middle."

"Women need the freedom to make reproductive decisions not merely to vindicate the right to be left alone, but often to strengthen their ties to others: to plan responsibly and have a family for which they can provide, to pursue professional or work commitments made to the outside world, or to continue supporting their families or communities," West wrote.

"At other times the decision to abort is necessitated, not by some murderous urge to end life, but by the harsh reality of a financially irresponsible partner, a society indifferent to the care of children, and a workplace incapable of accommodating or supporting the needs of working parents," West went on. "When made for any of these reasons, the decision to abort is not one made in an egoistic private vacuum. Whatever the reason, the decision to abort is almost invariably made within a web of interlocking, competing, and often irreconcilable responsibilities and commitments."[4]

A solid majority in a 1996 Gallup survey, 58 percent, believed abortion should be legal under certain circumstances. Only 25 percent said it should be legal under any circumstances. And only 15 percent believed abortion should be illegal in all circumstances.

Among those who said abortion should be legal in certain circumstances, a Gallup follow-up question found that fewer than a quarter, 23 percent, believed abortion should be permitted in "most" circumstances. Nearly three-quar-

> **A solid majority in a 1996 Gallup survey, 58 percent, believed abortion should be legal under certain circumstances.**

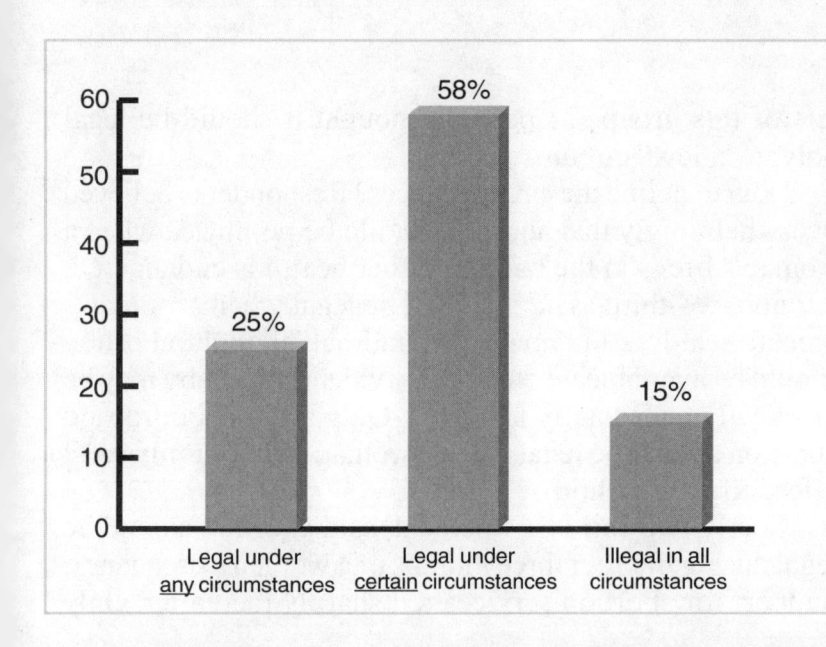

American Opinion

Do you think abortions should be legal under any circumstances, legal only under certain circumstances, or illegal in all circumstances?

("No opinion" omitted)

Source: The Gallup Poll 1996

- Legal under any circumstances: 25%
- Legal under certain circumstances: 58%
- Illegal in all circumstances: 15%

American Opinion

In the following situations, abortion:	Should be legal	Should be illegal	Refused/ No opinion
When the woman's life is endangered:	88%	7%	5%
When the woman's physical health is endangered:	82%	11%	7%
When the woman's mental health is endangered:	66%	27%	7%
When there is evidence that the baby may be physically impaired:	53%	37%	10%
When there is evidence that the baby may be mentally impaired:	54%	36%	10%
When the pregnancy was caused by rape or incest:	77%	18%	5%
When the woman or family can't afford to raise the child:	32%	62%	6%

Source: The Gallup Poll 1996

ters of this group, 74 percent, thought it should be legal only in "a few" circumstances.

How to define the circumstances? Respondents believed overwhelmingly that abortion should be permitted when a woman's life is in the balance or her health is endangered. Around two-thirds said it should be legal when a woman's mental health is in danger. Around half thought abortion should be available when there is evidence the baby may be physically or mentally impaired. Only around a third said abortion should be legal when a woman or her family can't afford to raise a child.

Nearly two-thirds, 64 percent, said abortion should be legal during the first three months of a women's pregnancy. Support for abortion services fell sharply thereafter. Only

26 percent believed it should be legal during the second three months, and only 13 percent during the final three months, according to the 1996 survey.

Support for an absolute right to abortion fell somewhat in 1996, perhaps as a result of the pro-life movement's campaign against partial birth abortions. Between 1990 and 1995, a consistent one-third of Gallup respondents said abortion should be legal in all circumstances, with the highest figure, 34 percent, recorded in June 1992. In July 1996, however, only 25 percent supported abortion rights in all circumstances.

In response to a different question in a 1996 poll, around half the respondents, 48 percent, said they regarded themselves as "pro-choice." Forty percent were "pro-life." Of those who described themselves as pro-choice, 54 percent felt that way very strongly; 27 percent felt somewhat strongly. Of pro-lifers, 61 percent held their beliefs very strongly and 29 percent somewhat strongly.

Gallup's 1996 polling found broad support for a set of mildly restrictive measures that draw vigorous opposition from abortion-rights activists.

- More than seven of every ten respondents, 74 percent, supported a law that would require a woman to wait 24

" Support for an absolute right to abortion fell somewhat in 1996. "

American Opinion

Do you think abortion should be generally legal or generally illegal during each of the three stages of pregnancy?

- Legal
- Illegal
- Refused/No opinion

In the first three months of pregnancy.
- 64%
- 30%
- 6%

In the second three months of pregnancy.
- 65%
- 26%
- 9%

In the last three months of pregnancy.
- 82%
- 13%
- 5%

Source: The Gallup Poll 1996

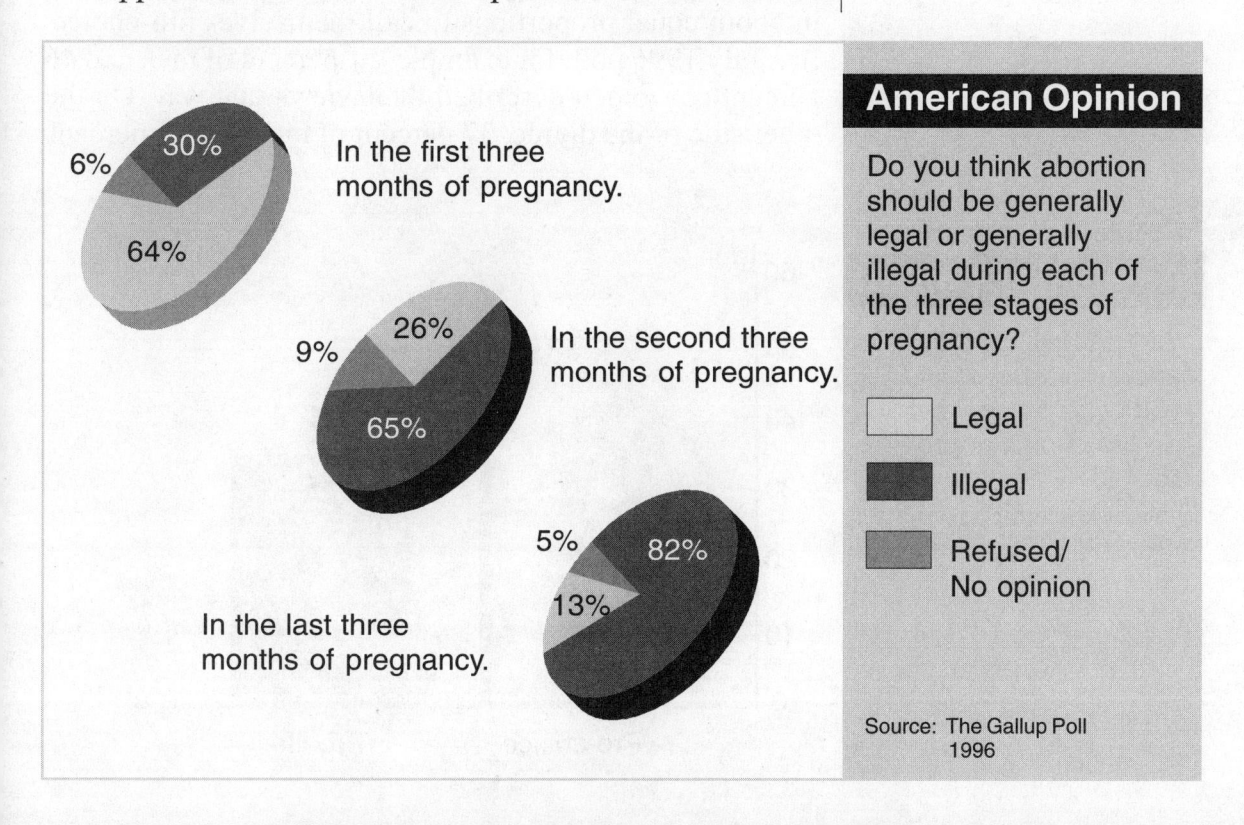

hours for an abortion. Only 22 percent were opposed. More than eight of every ten, 86 percent, favored a law requiring doctors to inform patients about alternatives to abortion before performing one. Only 11 percent opposed this measure.
- Nearly three-quarters, 74 percent, supported a law requiring women younger than eighteen to obtain their parents' consent for an abortion. Twenty-three percent were opposed.
- Seventy percent of the sample favored a law requiring a woman's husband to be notified if she decides on an abortion. Around a quarter, 26 percent, were opposed.

Surveys show a close connection between religious beliefs and views on abortion, with deeply religious respondents more troubled about the issues than others. In a 1995 Gallup poll, around one-third of respondents said religion is not of great importance in their lives. Of this group, close to half said abortion should be legal in all circumstances. By contrast, those who described themselves as "born-again" Christians were twice as likely as other groups to believe abortion should be completely outlawed.

Gallup surveys suggest that men and women are likely in about equal proportions to call themselves pro-choice. In a July 1996 poll, for example, 51 percent of men and 46 percent of women described their views that way. On the other side of the divide, 37 percent of men and 43 percent

American Opinion

With respect to the abortion issue, would you consider yourself to be pro-choice or pro-life?

("No opinion" omitted)

Pro-choice: 53%
Pro-life: 36%

Source: The Gallup Poll 1996

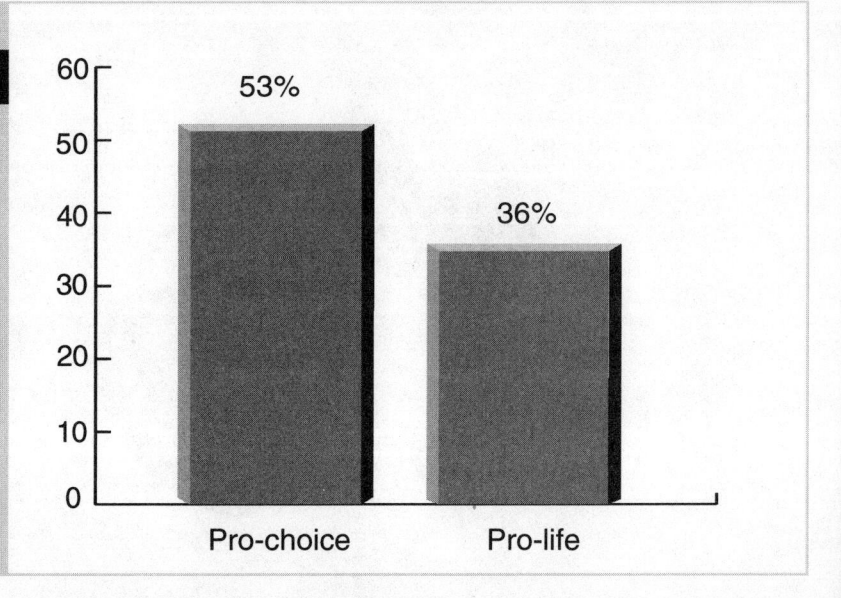

of women said they were "pro-life."

Women appear, however, to hold their views more intensely than men. Pro-choice women are more likely than pro-choice men to say they feel very strongly about the matter. Similarly, pro-life women feel more strongly about abortion than pro-life men.

Education, age, and income also influence attitudes toward abortion. In the 1996 sample, Gallup tracked how support for abortion rights rose as income and educational levels rose.

Around one-third of those with college or post graduate degrees favored legal abortion in all circumstances. Among respondents with less formal education, 22 percent of females supported abortion in all circumstances. Thirty-one percent of those with annual incomes of $75,000 or more endorsed legal abortion in all circumstances, compared with only 16 percent among those with incomes of $20,000 or less.

To some analysts, the polls reveal a paradox. Consistent majorities say they want to preserve abortion as a legal right. At the same time, even larger majorities favor what the abortion-rights movement regards as unacceptably burdensome restrictions.

The feminist author Naomi Wolf argues that the pro-choice movement's refusal to recognize the moral gravity of abortion has helped create the paradox. Reliance on euphemism and circumlocution—"on a political rhetoric in

> **Women appear to hold their views more intensely than men.**

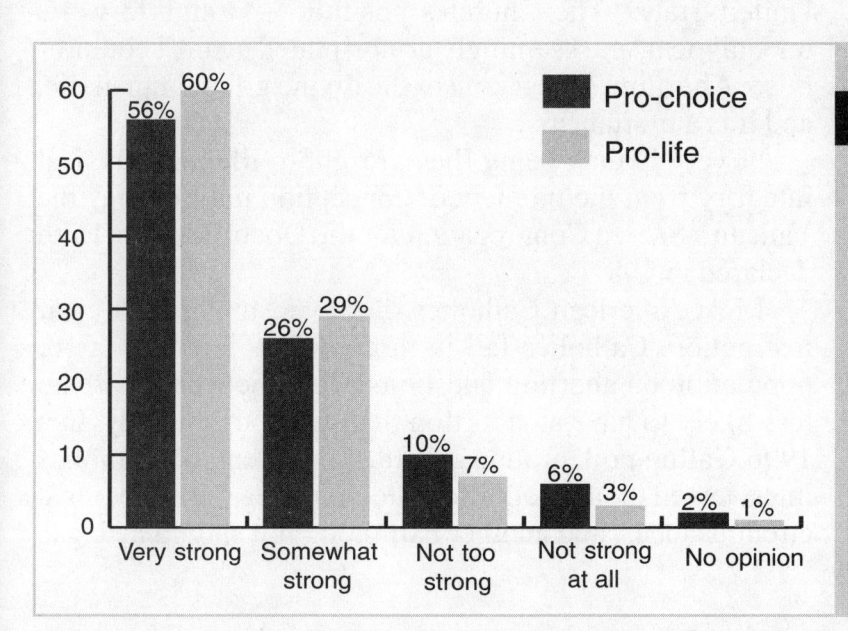

American Opinion

How strongly do you feel about your position on abortion: very strong, somewhat strong, not too strong, or not strong at all?

Response	Pro-choice	Pro-life
Very strong	56%	60%
Somewhat strong	26%	29%
Not too strong	10%	7%
Not strong at all	6%	3%
No opinion	2%	1%

Source: The Gallup Poll 1996

which the fetus means nothing," in which it is sometimes described as "tissue" or even as a "mass of dependent protoplasm"—has cost the movement political support and undermined its legitimacy, says Wolf.[5]

"Clinging to a rhetoric about abortion in which there is no life and no death, we entangle our beliefs in a series of self-delusions, fibs, and evasions," Wolf wrote. "And we risk becoming precisely what our critics charge us with being: callous, selfish, and casually destructive men and women who share a cheapened view of human life."[6]

As an example of what she regards as hard-hearted, amoral rhetoric, Wolf cited former U.S. Surgeon General Joycelyn Elders' much-quoted offhand defense of abortion: "We really need to get over this love affair with the fetus." Drawing a parallel with euthanasia, Wolf imagined the outrage that would confront a movement that spoke of getting over our love affair with the terminally ill.[7]

"What Americans want and deserve is an abortion-rights movement willing publicly to mourn the evil—necessary evil though it may be—that is abortion," Wolf wrote. "We must have a movement that acts with moral accountability and without euphemism."[8]

The Absolutes of Dispute

The Roman Catholic Church has provided the main organizational leadership of the pro-life movement in the United States. The Church's position is straightforward, unequivocal, and seemingly armor-plated against compromise: Abortion is the taking of the divine gift of human life, and it is a mortal sin.

"Every human being [has a] right to life and physical integrity from the moment of conception until death," the Vatican's Sacred Congregation for the Doctrine of the Faith declared in 1987.[9]

Most American Catholics, however, ignore this clear instruction. Catholics fall in more or less with the larger population on abortion questions; Catholic women are no less likely to have an abortion than women generally. In a 1996 Gallup poll, around a third, 31 percent, of Catholics interviewed thought abortion should be legal in all or most circumstances, and another half thought it should be legal

> " 'Clinging to a rhetoric about abortion in which there is no life and no death, we entangle our beliefs in a series of self-delusions, fibs, and evasions.' "

in rare circumstances. Only 17 percent thought abortion should be illegal in all circumstances.

The absolutist wing of the pro-life movement has carried out an intermittent, sometimes violent campaign of blockade and harassment at abortion clinics. Hooded guerrillas operating in darkness glue shut the locks of clinics. Zealots picket the homes of physicians who perform abortions, flash gruesome enlarged photographs of aborted fetuses, and display fetuses preserved in spirits. Many wear gold lapel pins with the tiny, though recognizably human, feet of a ten week-old fetus.

Abortion protest crossed the well-marked boundary into terrorism in two murder cases and in other violent incidents in the mid-1990s. In Pensacola, Florida, Paul Hill claimed to be saving unborn children when he killed an abortion-clinic doctor and his bodyguard. John Salvi opened fire at an abortion clinic in Brookline, Massachusetts, killing two women and wounding five others. Both men eventually were convicted of murder. (Salvi died in prison in November 1996, an apparent suicide.)[10]

Abortion-rights groups also reported increases in bomb threats, stalkings, arsons, and other forms of violence. Such incidents have a chilling effect, pro-choice forces say. "What we have seen is women being more hesitant and more scared about having an abortion," observed Priscilla Smith, an attorney for the Center for Reproductive Law and Policy in New York.[11]

At the same time, though, blockades of abortion clinics showed a dramatic decrease, largely because of a 1994 law that makes obstructing clinic entrances a federal crime. The National Abortion Federation reported fewer than 400 incidents of violence and disruption during the first nine months of 1996, down from more than 3,400 in all of 1993. There are fewer blockades and less picketing, the group said.[12]

Abortion opponents claim the law breaches the free-speech rights of protesters, who fear arrest and prosecution for engaging in what they regard as missionary work. "They're afraid to even offer alternatives to women considering abortion because they fear that such sidewalk counseling will be construed as an attempt to intimidate women," said Catherine W. Short, the legal director of the Life Legal

"
The absolutist wing of the pro-life movement has carried out an intermittent, sometimes violent campaign of blockade and harassment at abortion clinics.
"

The Abortion Pill

A French abortion drug that abortion-rights supporters hail as safe and protest-proof and that opponents regard as anathema made its long-delayed way through the U.S. regulatory process in 1996.

The U.S. Food and Drug Administration certified the pill, introduced in Europe as RU-486, as safe and effective in July 1996 and issued a conditional approval in September. But legal wrangling over manufacturing and distribution rights between the American licensee, the nonprofit Population Council, and the council's business partner held up introduction of the drug, known as mifepristone. It wasn't likely to become available before the end of 1997, if then.[1]

Proponents say the pill, which can induce abortion during the first seven

(Continued on page 87)

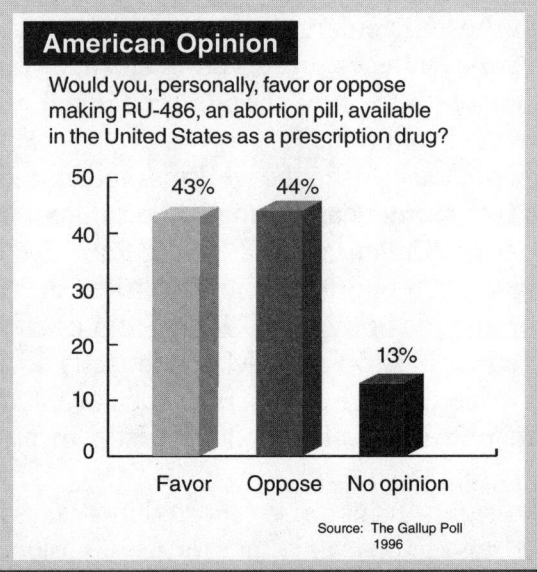

American Opinion

Would you, personally, favor or oppose making RU-486, an abortion pill, available in the United States as a prescription drug?

- Favor: 43%
- Oppose: 44%
- No opinion: 13%

Source: The Gallup Poll 1996

Defense Foundation of Napa, California.[13]

At the other end of the spectrum, the absolutist view of abortion rights challenges any restrictions, even those—such as a 1996 measure to ban partial-birth abortions—that draw strong support from people who say they favor choice.

C. Everett Koop, one of Joycelyn Elders' predecessors, likened the abortion-rights movement's reflexive and unbending opposition to restrictions that most people find reasonable to the gun lobby's response to any measure, however modest, to regulate firearms.

"Neither AK-47s nor partial-birth abortions have a place in civil society," said Koop, surgeon general from 1981 to 1989.[14]

Roe v. Wade, and After

In a 7-to-2 vote in *Roe v. Wade*, the Supreme Court struck down a Texas law that made abortion a crime except when performed to save a mother's life. Citing a woman's gen-

weeks of pregnancy, gives women an option that does not require an invasive medical procedure. Moreover, private physicians would dispense it, allowing women to avoid the leafleters and sidewalk counselors that often swirl around abortion clinics.

Philosophical questions apart, pro-life groups argued RU-486 had not been adequately tested in the United States. It has been in use in France since 1988 and is reported to be effective 95 percent of the time.[2]

In a 1996 Gallup survey, close to two-thirds of the respondents, 65 percent, said they had heard of RU-486. They divided evenly, though, over whether it should be made available as a prescription drug to American women. Forty-three percent favored making the abortion pill available; 44 percent were opposed.

eral right to privacy, the court declared unconstitutional any state law that forbade abortion within the first two trimesters of pregnancy.

The ruling touched off a quarter century of conflict. As Dworkin has suggested, it choked off debate, blocking normal political channels through which some compromise might have been worked out. At the time of *Roe*, legal scholars Elizabeth Mensch and Alan Freeman note, sixteen states, with 40 percent of the U.S. population, had liberalized their abortion laws, and other states were taking up the question. The court's simple, flawed rationale of privacy rights, Mensch and Freeman argue, "dismissed as legally irrelevant a continued ethical, theological, and political debate."[15]

In many states, legislatures moved cautiously to test the limits of *Roe v. Wade*, imposing restrictions such as a wait period or a requirement to accept counseling. Congress entered the dispute in the mid-1970s, enacting a law that barred the use of federal Medicaid funds for abortion.

In 1992, in *Planned Parenthood v. Casey*, the high court

> "Gallup surveys showed strong support for a limited ban on partial-birth abortion."

upheld a set of mild restrictions on abortion access written into the Pennsylvania state statutes, including informed consent, a 24-hour waiting period with counseling, parental consent for minors, and mandatory record-keeping and reporting. At the same time, though, the court in a 5 to 4 vote reaffirmed the central tenet of *Roe v. Wade*: that a woman has a constitutional right to an abortion. And later in the year, the court refused to review a lower-court decision that struck down a strict anti-abortion measure in the U.S. Pacific territory of Guam.

The congressional effort to ban partial-birth abortion injected the issue into the 1996 presidential campaign. The procedure, which doctors term "intact dilation and extraction," is one of several used to abort a fetus after twenty weeks. Congress approved the ban in the spring of 1996. President Clinton swiftly vetoed it, saying the practice should be preserved for women whose health is in jeopardy.

In a partial-birth abortion, the fetus is partially extracted, feet first, until the head is lodged in the birth canal. Then the brain and spinal fluid are suctioned out so the skull can be collapsed, making extraction possible.

The ban's opponents argued it is rarely used, and then only in extreme circumstances when the mother's life is imperiled. Supporters said, however, that partial-birth abortion is performed regularly and capriciously, in most cases involving a healthy woman and a normal fetus. The numbers are in dispute. Early in the debate, ban opponents claimed only around 500 partial-birth abortions were done a year. Later reports indicated as many as 1,500 may be performed annually in one New Jersey clinic alone.[16]

Gallup surveys showed strong support for a limited ban on partial-birth abortion. Seventy-one percent in a 1996 sample said the procedure should be barred except in the case of a threat to the life of the mother. Twenty-three percent opposed a ban.

To Koop, the former surgeon general, the dispute revealed "a deep national uneasiness" about abortion. During the Senate attempt to override the president's veto, even some long-time supporters of choice recoiled from its implications.

Senator Daniel Patrick Moynihan, a Democrat from New York, who believes abortion is a constitutionally protected matter of freedom of conscience, suggested the partial-birth procedure is "close to infanticide." Pro-choice Senator Arlen Specter, a Pennsylvania Republican, agreed. "The line is really drawn between infanticide and the right to choose when the child is partway out of the womb," Specter said.[17]

Although the House was able to muster the necessary vote for an override of the veto, in September 1996, the Senate fell eight votes short of an override of the veto of the ban on partial-birth abortion.

Bridging the Divide

The abortion debate has turned on stark biological and legal issues: When does life begin? Is a fetus a person under the law, with a person's rights and interests—above all with the right to life?

In *Roe v. Wade*, the Supreme Court ruled a fetus is not a person under the Constitution. Biologists agree that a human embryo is a living organism by the time it is implanted in the womb—that is to say, within fourteen days or so after conception. They agree, too, that the cells that make up the embryo contain the biological codes that will determine its development.[18]

The question-begging emphasis on the difference—or the absence of one—between a fetus and a baby has needlessly confused and polarized the debate, argues Ronald Dworkin.

"Self-respecting people who give opposite answers to the question of whether a fetus is a person can no more compromise, or agree to live together allowing others to make their own decisions, than people can compromise on slavery or apartheid or rape," he wrote.[19]

Dworkin offers a formulation that attempts to explain the opinion paradox on abortion and also to point a way out of the impasse, or at least to a truce in the abortion wars. The debate should begin with the recognition that embryonic human life has an intrinsic moral significance, he suggests, not with what he regards as the fallacious contention that an unborn fetus has a person's rights and interests.

"Almost everyone who opposes abortion [believes] that a fetus is a living, growing human creature and that it is intrinsically a bad thing, a kind of cosmic shame, when

"
Biologists agree that a human embryo is a living organism by the time it is implanted in the womb—that is to say, within fourteen days or so after conception.

"

American Opinion

Do you favor or oppose each of the following proposals:

	Group	Favor	Oppose	No opinion
A law requiring women seeking abortions to wait 24 hours before having the procedure:	Overall Conservative Moderate Liberal	74% 79% 74% 66%	22% 16% 23% 31%	4% 5% 3% 3%
A law requiring doctors to inform women about alternatives to abortion before the procedure:	Overall Conservative Moderate Liberal	86% 90% 89% 74%	11% 8% 10% 21%	3% 2% 1% 5%
A law requiring women under eighteen to get parental consent for any abortion:	Overall Conservative Moderate Liberal	74% 80% 76% 55%	23% 16% 22% 40%	3% 4% 2% 5%
A law requiring the husband of a married woman be notified if she decides to have an abortion:	Overall Conservative Moderate Liberal	70% 78% 68% 60%	26% 17% 30% 38%	4% 5% 2% 2%
An amendment to the Constitution banning abortion in all circumstances, except when necessary to save the life of the mother:	Overall Conservative Moderate Liberal	38% 47% 32% 27%	59% 48% 67% 72%	3% 5% 1% 1%

Source: The Gallup Poll 1996

human life at any stage is deliberately extinguished," Dworkin wrote. That said, he went on, people can believe it is wrong to end a human life and still favor choice.[20]

A Texas woman named Norma McCorvey reflects the contradictions and ambiguities that cloud the issue. She is Jane Roe, the plaintiff in *Roe v. Wade*.

"I believe in a woman's right to choose," McCorvey says. "I'm like a lot of people. I'm in the mushy middle." She continues to support abortion through the first three months of pregnancy, but not afterward. Asks McCorvey:

"Have you ever seen a second-trimester abortion? It's a baby. It's got a face and a body, and they put him in a freezer and a little container."[21]

It is "perfectly consistent" to hold such views, offers Dworkin, "and yet believe that a decision whether to end human life in early pregnancy must nevertheless be left to the pregnant woman, the person whose conscience is most directly connected to the choice and who has the greatest stake in it."[22]

Mensch and Freeman suggest that real compromise on abortion would require a public policy of restraint: one that allows abortion, with a line drawn at sixteen or twelve or even ten weeks (90 percent of abortions occur during the first twelve weeks); regulates it to a degree; and seeks ways of discouraging it. The starting point for discussion, they say, "ought to be the frank recognition that the issue is life or death."[23]

Such arguments seem more apt to strike a chord with the ambivalent middle rather than the hard irreconcilable cores of the pro-choice and pro-life movements. Obviously, it is not the majorities that favor choice but support some restrictions that keep the debate at a white heat.

All the same, a group called the Common Ground Network for Life and Choice quietly works to promote a dialogue between the two extremes. The organization, with a dozen or so chapters around the country, got its start in Washington in 1993 and now claims 1,500 members in two dozen states. It brings together pro-choice and pro-life advocates in an effort to find small areas of agreement.

Since there really is no middle ground, the group operates mostly along the margins: discussions involve teen pregnancy, birth control, sexual responsibility, adoption, and,

> **A group called the Common Ground Network for Life and Choice quietly works to promote a dialogue between the two extremes.**

sometimes, ground rules for abortion protest. But few in Common Ground believe there are any simple answers.

"I think at the beginning we may have had a giddy overestimation of what we'd accomplish," conceded Frederica Mathewes-Green, a Baltimore anti-abortion activist who belongs to the group's Washington area chapter. "If this was easy to solve, we would have solved it long ago."[24]

The Notorious "Dr. Death"

Janet Adkins, a fifty-four-year-old Oregonian, led an active, vigorous life. By 1990, though, she had entered the early phases of Alzheimer's disease. Fearing a slow, agonizing, and irreversible slide toward death, she sought out Jack Kevorkian, whose views on assisted suicide were just becoming widely known. She met Kevorkian in Pontiac, Michigan.

"Have a nice trip," Kevorkian said, attaching Mrs. Adkins to a lethal-injection suicide machine.

"Thank you," she answered.[25]

Thus began Kevorkian's career as chief practitioner and publicist of physician-assisted suicide. A rogue to many, he has been almost universally condemned by physicians, legal theorists, and ethicists. He has been tried and acquitted on charges he hastened his patients' deaths. (New criminal charges against Kevorkian were dropped in early 1997.) His medical license has been lifted. But Kevorkian's patients do not care that he scoffs at the law. To himself and some others, he is a brave and lonely crusader for the dignity of death.

"They'll have to burn me at the stake to get me to stop," Kevorkian has vowed.[26]

Kevorkian, sixty-seven years old in 1996, earned his Dr. Death sobriquet in the early 1950s, when as a University of Michigan medical student he used to haunt hospital terminal wards in search of patients who would permit him to be present at their last moments. In the 1960s, he argued controversially for lethal medical experiments on willing condemned prisoners, and for the drawing of blood from the recently dead for transfusions.

Since 1990, Kevorkian has assisted at some four dozen suicides. All his patients were suffering, but clearly all were

> " **Since 1990, Kevorkian has assisted at some four dozen suicides.** "

not terminally ill. In one of his most controversial cases, he helped to death a confused, depressed, and drug-dependent Pembroke, Massachusetts, woman who apparently suffered nothing worse than a debilitating but not life-threatening ailment known as chronic fatigue syndrome. Supporters of the right to die argue that Kevorkian's excesses make a compelling case for a thoroughgoing reform of the laws.

"We don't know whether Jack Kevorkian exceeded the limits or not," said Dr. Faye Girsh, executive director of the Hemlock Society," a right-to-die advocacy group. "But this is a good thing because it underlines what anarchy we have out there now. We have a situation now where anyone can do it for any reason, and that is not right. What we need are tightly regulated laws that permit it with safeguards."[27]

Gallup polls suggest people are divided on right-to-die issues, although the surveys have tracked gradually rising support for voluntary euthanasia over time. The results correspond with the expanding ability of medical technology to prolong life, even in dreadful circumstances.

"For centuries, death off the battlefield occurred at home or at accident scenes," wrote Franklin G. Miller and John C. Fletcher, biomedical ethicists at the University of Virginia. "In the United States and other developed nations, dying and the event of death have been rapidly transformed into a clinical event. Ordinary dying in the United States is no longer a 'natural' event, something that simply happens to us."[28]

> **Gallup polls suggest people are divided on right-to-die issues.**

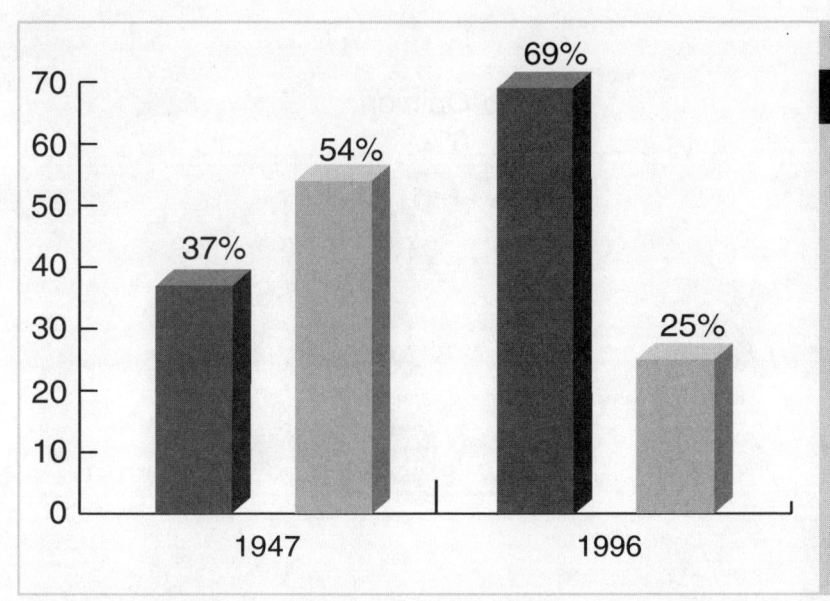

American Opinion

When a person has a disease that cannot be cured, do you think doctors should be allowed by law to *end the patient's life* by some painless means if the patient and his family request it?

("No opinion" omitted)

■ Yes   ■ No

Source: The Gallup Poll 1996

Year	Yes	No
1947	37%	54%
1996	69%	25%

In a 1996 survey, Gallup asked a right-to-die question two ways, with divergent responses.

Here is the question asked of half of the 1996 sample: "When a person has a disease that cannot be cured, do you think doctors should be allowed by law to *end the patient's life* by some painless means if the patient and his family request it?" A strong majority, 69 percent, answered yes. Twenty-five percent said no.

Here is the question asked of the other half: "When a person has a disease that cannot be cured, do you think doctors should be allowed by law to *assist the patient to commit suicide* if the patient requests it?" Only 52 percent answered yes; 42 percent of the sample said no.

Support fell off generally with mention of suicide, especially among women and among those with strong religious beliefs, according to the polltakers.

Gallup has been asking the first form of the question since 1947. In that year, 37 percent answered yes, 54 percent no. By 1973, a slight majority, 53 percent, responded in favor of a law allowing doctors to end a patient's life, rising to seven of every ten a generation later.

From Augustine to the Appellate Courts

With few exceptions, the ancient and medieval worlds condemned suicide in any form. The Church Father Saint Augustine in the fifth century judged Judas Iscariot's hang-

American Opinion

When a person has a disease that cannot be cured, do you think doctors should be allowed by law to *assist the patient to commit suicide* if the patient requests it?

- Yes 52%
- No 42%
- No Opinion 6%

Source: The Gallup Poll 1996

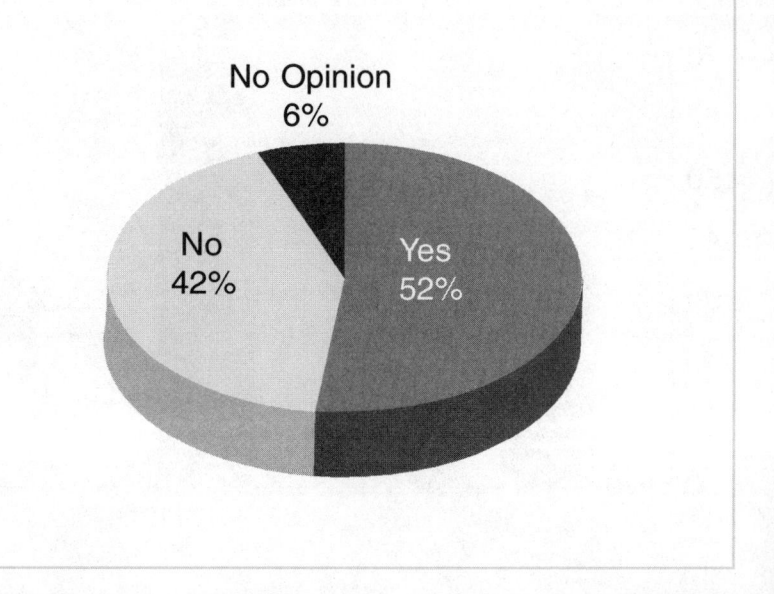

ing himself a graver sin than his betrayal of Jesus. Life was God's gift, and only God could take it back.

By the sixteenth century, some thinkers—notably the English metaphysical poet and cleric John Donne—were staking claims for suicide as a personal choice rather than a moral iniquity. In the modern era, self-killing has been erased from the criminal codes nearly everywhere.

Ethicists draw a distinction between what has come to be regarded as passive euthanasia—that is to say, allowing someone to die by forgoing treatment that would prolong life—and active forms such as physician-assisted suicide and physician-performed euthanasia.

The term derives from two Greek roots meaning "good death." Narrowly defined, euthanasia is "the act or practice of intentionally, mercifully, and painlessly causing the death of persons suffering from serious injuries, system failures, or fatal diseases."[29]

Right-to-die issues rest on shifting moral ground, where one conundrum opens into another. Court rulings in the 1990s have fairly firmly established a patient's right to refuse treatment. Where does that lead?

Ethicist Tom L. Beauchamp of Georgetown University shaped the question this way:

"If competent patients have a legal and moral right to refuse treatment that brings about their deaths, is there not a similar moral right to enlist the assistance of physicians to help patients cause their deaths by an active means? And is it not morally acceptable for physicians to assist these patients?"[30]

Federal appellate courts answered the question affirmatively in 1996, taking as a precedent the 1990 U.S. Supreme Court ruling in the case of Nancy Cruzan, a comatose woman whose family wished to withdraw treatment that kept her alive in a vegetative state.

In two physician-assisted suicide cases, U.S. Courts of Appeals in San Francisco and New York recognized no distinction between passive and active forms of euthanasia for mentally competent patients.

"We see no ethical or constitutionally recognizable difference between a doctor's pulling the plug on a respirator and his prescribing drugs which will permit a terminally ill patient to end his life," Judge Stephen Reinhardt wrote in

> **Right-to-die issues rest on shifting moral ground, where one conundrum opens into another.**

> "
> **The AMA opposes physician participation in voluntary euthanasia and in suicides.**
> "

the majority opinion.[31]

In the New York case, Judge Robert J. Miner wrote: "Physicians do not fulfill the role of 'killer' by prescribing drugs to hasten death any more than they do by disconnecting life-support systems."[32]

The issue is hardly so clear to medical ethicists. The American Medical Association supported the Cruzan family. "For over 2,000 years, the predominant responsibility of the physician has not been to preserve life at all costs but to serve the patient's needs while respecting the patient's autonomy and dignity," the AMA said in its brief in the Cruzan case.[33]

On the other hand, the AMA opposes physician participation in voluntary euthanasia and in suicides. The physicians' Hippocratic oath is clear on the point: "To please no one will I prescribe a deadly drug, nor give advice which may cause his death."

A Slippery Slope?

To a degree, physicians are caught in a legal snare, anticipating malpractice consequences when they act to end a patient's life—or when they fail to act. A wave of lawsuits in the 1990s has sought to hold doctors, nursing homes, and hospitals liable for ignoring living-will right-to-die directives. In some of the cases, plaintiffs have won substantial awards.

Most such cases turn on a theory of medical battery. "The idea is that patients have a right to refuse treatment," explained Anna Moretti, a lawyer for the advocacy group Choice in Dying, "so if the patient has expressed a wish not to have a particular treatment or procedure and the doctors and hospitals do it anyway, it's legally like an assault on the patient." The medical profession's response: No one should be able to recover damages for living.[34]

Far more compelling than fear of litigation is the "slippery slope" argument: the notion that allowing doctors to help kill patients, whether through assisting suicide or themselves administering the lethal dose, would cheapen attitudes toward life. There are concerns, too, that the powerless would be vulnerable to abuse.

"Let nobody think this is an argument about putting to

death people with terminal cancer," said Dr. Arthur Caplan, director of the Center for Bioethics at the University of Pennsylvania. "That will last about five minutes. Then it will move to, 'I don't want to be alive with Alzheimer's disease. I'm not terminally ill, but by the time I am, I will not be able to ask for help in dying.'"

Sooner or later, Caplan went on, there will be situations such as this one: "My mother always said she didn't want to be kept alive if she had Alzheimer's disease."[35]

To critics, the demise of Judith Curren of Pembroke, Massachusetts, is a clear case of a premature shove down the slippery slope. Kevorkian helped Curren to death in a Pontiac, Michigan, hotel room in August 1996. She had a history of depression and drug dependency, but no life-threatening illness.

Others say the Curren case, the Janet Adkins case, and other Kevorkian suicides underline the need to ease the tension between public law and the growing private belief that some patients should have suicide as an option. "That tension has corrupted the law and created the dangerous possibility that rogues like Kevorkian might be emboldened to help in suicides almost no one would condone," *The Boston Globe* editorialized. "Judith Curren may have been miserable and tormented, but she was not terminal. The only hurdles between her life and her death were the private scruples of Dr. Kevorkian."[36]

Dr. Girsh, of the Hemlock Society, opposes physician-assisted suicides in murky cases such as Curren's. "Let's begin with the terminally ill and see how that works in our society," she said.[37]

Notes: Abortion and Euthanasia Controversy Over the Beginning and End of Life

1. Ronald Dworkin, *Life's Dominion: An Argument About Abortion, Euthanasia, and Individual Freedom* (New York: Alfred A. Knopf, 1993), 10.
2. Dworkin, *Life's Dominion*, 4.
3. Jack Lessenberry, "Kevorkian Is Arrested and Charged in a Suicide," *The New York Times*, November 8, 1996, 19.
4. Robin West, "Taking Freedom Seriously," *Harvard Law Review* 104 (November 1990), 84-85.
5. Naomi Wolf, "Our Bodies, Our Souls," *The New Republic*, October 16, 1995, 26.
6. Wolf, "Our Bodies, Our Souls," 26.
7. Wolf, "Our Bodies, Our Souls," 33.
8. Wolf, "Our Bodies, Our Souls," 28.
9. Quoted in Dworkin, *Life's Dominion*, 39.
10. Shelley Donald Coolidge, "Clinic-Shootings Trial Shows Depth of Divide in U.S. Abortion Debate," *The Christian Science Monitor*, February 2, 1996, 3.
11. Coolidge, "Clinic-Shootings Trial Shows Depths of Divide."
12. Robert Pear, "Protests at Abortion Clinics Have Fallen, and New Federal Law Is Credited," *The New York Times*, September 24, 1996, 18.
13. Pear, "Protests at Abortion Clinics Have Fallen."
14. C. Everett Koop, "Why Defend Partial Birth Abortion?" op-ed, *The New York Times*, September 26, 1996.
15. Elizabeth Mensch and Alan Freeman, *The Politics of Virtue: Is Abortion Debatable?* (Durham, N.C.: Duke University Press, 1993), 126.
16. Melinda Henneberger, "Senate Fails to Override Veto of Ban on Type of Abortion," *The New York Times*, September 22, 1996, 20.
    Koop, "Why Defend Partial Birth Abortion?"
17. Henneberger, "Senate Fails to Override Veto."
18. Dworkin, *Life's Dominion*, 21; 51.
19. Dworkin, *Life's Dominion*, 10.
20. Dworkin, *Life's Dominion*, 13.
21. Wolf, "Our Bodies, Our Souls," 28; 29.
22. Dworkin, *Life's Dominion*, 15.
23. Mensch and Freeman, *The Politics of Virtue*, 157.
24. Ann O'Hanlon, "Agreeing to Disagree, Abortion Advocates and Foes Gather to Talk and Listen," *The Washington Post*, October 27, 1996, A20.
25. Jack Lessenberry, "Life and Dr. Death," *The Boston Globe*, August 25, 1996, D1.
26. Lessenberry, "Life and Dr. Death."
27. Lessenberry, "Life and Dr. Death."
28. James M. Humber, Robert F. Almeder and Gregg A. Kasting, eds., *Physician-Assisted Death* (Totowa, N.J.: Humana Press, 1993), 76.
29. Tom L. Beauchamp, ed., *Intending Death: The Ethics of Assisted Suicide and Euthanasia* (Upper Saddle River, N.J.: Prentice Hall, 1996), 2.
30. Beauchamp, ed., *Intending Death*, 13.

31. Linda Greenhouse, "High Court to Say If the Dying Have a Right to Suicide Help," *The New York Times*, October 2, 1996, 1.
32. Greenhouse, "High Court to Say If the Dying Have a Right to Suicide Help."
33. Linda Greenhouse, "An Issue for a Reluctant High Court," *The New York Times*, Week in Review, October 6, 1996, 3.
34. Tamar Lewin, "Ignoring 'Right to Die' Directives, Medical Community Is Being Sued," *The New York Times*, June 2, 1996, 1.
35. Gina Kolata, "Concerns Grow That Doctor-Assisted Suicide Would Leave the Powerless Vulnerable," *The New York Times*, October 20, 1996, 20.
36. "In Memory of Judith Curren," editorial, *The Boston Globe*, August 20, 1996.
37. Lessenberry, "Life and Dr. Death."

Notes: The Abortion Pill

1. Tamar Lewin, "Dispute May Delay Abortion Drug in U.S.," *The New York Times*, November 6, 1996, 16.
2. Linda Feldman, "FDA's Move on New Drug Adds Fuel to Abortion Fire," *The Christian Science Monitor*, July 22, 1996, 3.

6 Education Reform
Do America's Schools Make the Grade?

For a decade or more, dire reports of failure, neglect, and decay have been filtering out of America's classrooms. High school graduates barely read on a ninth-grade level. All but the simplest arithmetical operations seem beyond their grasp. They mix up the Monroe Doctrine with the Protestant Reformation.

Exaggeration? Do such reports, even when true, distort reality? Most people do not seem alarmed; if few would grade the public schools A+, fewer still would grade them F. According to the Gallup Organization, most say the nation's schools are doing an adequate job, despite some obvious shortcomings. Mainstream educators say this view accurately reflects conditions in the schools. And it reflects, too, an instinctive faith in public education as a defining feature of American democracy.

In Gallup's 1996 survey of attitudes toward education, more than three-quarters of respondents gave their own community's schools a passing grade: 8 percent awarded an A; 35 percent a B; and 34 percent a C. Eleven percent gave the schools a D; only 6 percent judged them to be failing. And those with the most vital interest, parents with children in the public schools, awarded even higher marks: 15 percent gave their local schools an A; 42 percent a B; and 29 percent a C. Only 9 percent gave the schools a D and 4 percent an F.

The survey found less enthusiasm for public education in the nation as a whole. Roughly half the sample, 46 per-

> "According to the Gallup Organization, most say the nation's schools are doing an adequate job, despite some obvious shortcomings."

> "Nationally, standardized achievement and aptitude test scores are flat, barely rising, or, in some areas, slightly falling."

cent, gave the schools a C. Only 1 percent thought the schools were doing A work, and 20 percent B work. A substantial minority—18 percent—gave the nation's schools a D. Five percent said they were failing entirely.

The 1996 results were consistent with Gallup's findings over a quarter century of polling. Year by year, the marks fall in the C range. The schools generally score higher in Gallup's periodic surveys of Americans' confidence in their institutions. In May 1996, the public schools ranked ahead of newspapers, Congress, organized labor, big business, and the criminal justice system.

All the same, school reformers say these provisional marks of confidence are a form of grade inflation, suggesting complacency. Nationally, standardized achievement and aptitude test scores are flat, barely rising, or, in some areas, slightly falling.[1] And the opinion surveys reveal a paradox. While respondents express satisfaction with their own schools, the overall judgment is harsher: elsewhere, so the belief goes, the public schools are in crisis.

In the landmark 1983 report *A Nation at Risk*, the U.S. Education Department warned of a national educational emergency, a "rising tide of mediocrity" engulfing America's schools.[2] The report launched an ambitious reform movement and fueled a drive to improve education that remains strong today.

A Nation at Risk recommended raising academic standards, strengthening high school graduation requirements,

American Opinion

Using the A, B, C, D, and F grading scale used by most public schools, what grade would you give to the public schools in your community? What grade would you give to the nation's public schools?

Source: The Gallup Poll for Phi Delta Kappa, 1996

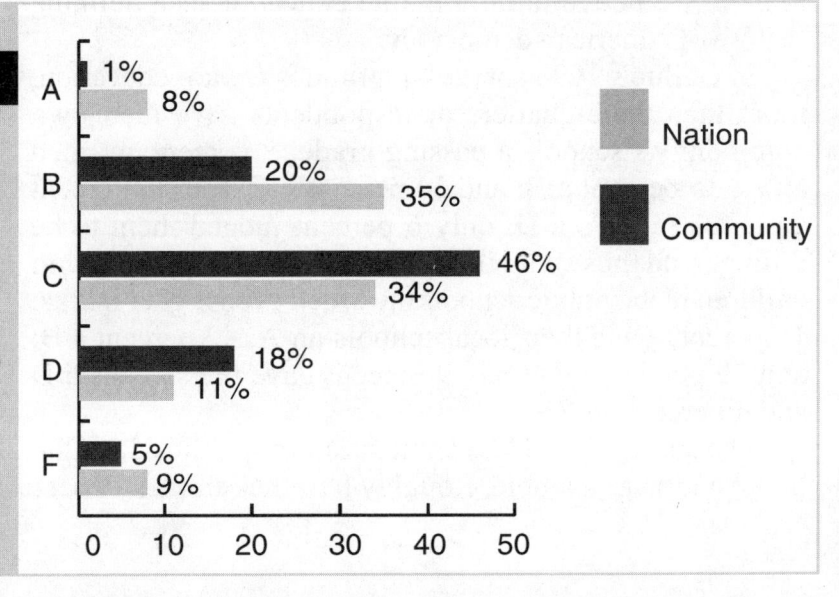

Grade	Community	Nation
A	1%	8%
B	20%	35%
C	46%	34%
D	18%	11%
F	5%	9%

lengthening the school year, and raising salaries for teachers. Most states responded with significant changes in educational policies. In the lower grades, school districts focused on improving basic reading and math skills. At the upper levels, more than forty states adopted tougher graduation requirements during the 1980s.

Reformers say, however, that fifteen years of mainstream efforts have merely slowed the rate of decline. "While our schools are not producing new adult illiterates, they are graduating an enormous number of people with mediocre skills and knowledge," education analysts Chester E. Finn Jr. and Theodor Rebarber argue.[3] Graduates score better on basic skills tests today, but the demands of an increasingly complex world discount the gains.

Finn, a former high education official in Ronald Reagan's administration, and others argue for radical approaches that would fundamentally alter power relationships in America's schools: choice, voucher, and privatization programs that would challenge the century-old public education monopoly.

How Bad Is It?

Sounding the alarm, reformers and some education analysts portray a system in a state of near-collapse.

In the nation's worst schools, "few teachers could pass the final exam in the courses they are supposed to teach," forecaster Marvin Cetron claimed in a 1991 book.[4]

"No one believes anymore that scientists are trained in science classes or politicians in civics classes or poets in English classes," wrote John Taylor Gatto, a former junior high school teacher and a New York City Teacher of the Year. "The truth is the schools don't really teach anything except how to obey orders."[5]

"Time is running out on school reform," Ernest Boyer, president of the Carnegie Foundation for the Advancement of Teaching, warned in 1993, on the ten-year anniversary of *A Nation at Risk*. "The coming decade may be our last. If we do not find a way to focus our efforts, public confidence will diminish and the structure we call public education will continue to decline."[6]

The United States spends $260 billion a year on public

"
Reformers and some education analysts portray a system in a state of near-collapse.
"

schools—a vast sum, but less per pupil than Germany, Japan, and Switzerland. As a percentage of gross national product, America invests less in public and private education than Sweden, Switzerland, Japan, Canada, Germany, France, and the United Kingdom.[7]

Americans also spend less time in school. In 1995, the National Commission on Time and Learning reported that U.S. high school students put in fewer than half the hours studying their own language, math, and science than do students in Japan, Germany, and France. The American school year averages 180 days; Japanese students are in class 240 days a year. This explains in part why the United States lags in some key measures of science achievement. A 1996 National Science Foundation study found that high school students in Japan, Germany, France, and England outperform their American counterparts on difficult advanced-placement exams in chemistry, physics, and other subjects.

In some places, the schools are failing even in the basics.

In Chicago, the authorities in September 1996 put 109 of the city's lowest-scoring public schools on probation—schools in which fewer than 15 percent of the students performed at grade level or higher on national standardized reading tests. More than 100 schools went on probation, nearly a fifth of the total. In one Chicago high school, only 2.5 percent of the students were reading at grade level.[8]

In Boston, eight of every ten students in the eleventh

American Opinion

When it comes to lengthening the school year for American students, blacks and Hispanics favor the idea more than whites do.

Source: The Gallup Poll for Phi Delta Kappa, 1996

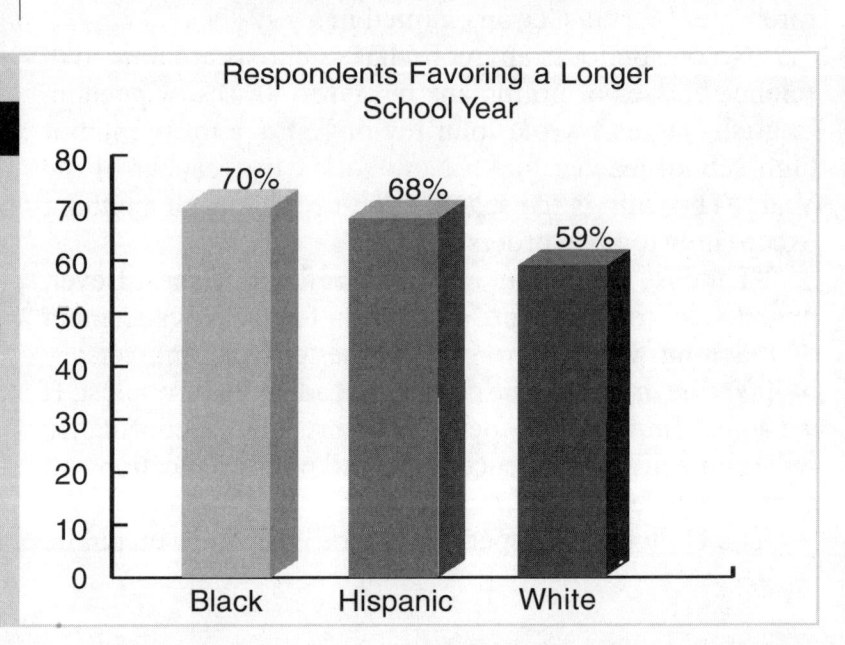

Respondents Favoring a Longer School Year

Black	Hispanic	White
70%	68%	59%

grade in 1996 scored below basic levels in math, as measured by the Stanford 9 achievement test. Four of every ten failed to reach the standard in reading. Only 24 percent of Boston eleventh-graders scored well enough to move up to the next level in reading; only 6 percent were prepared to advance in math.

The Stanford tests—given to students in grades three, five, six, seven, nine, and eleven—replaced a test that is less difficult and therefore a less honest assessment of student achievement, according to the Boston school superintendent, Thomas W. Payzant.

"This is a reality check, a tough reality check," said Payzant, who built a national reputation as a school reformer in San Diego before moving on to Boston, where poverty, parochial politics, and racial tension have corroded a once-proud school system. "The goal for so many years was just basic skills. But you can't serve students well if you lull them into thinking that a standard that is low by the judgment of the real world is okay for them."[9]

Goals 2000: Slow Progress

America's young people test poorly even in their own history. A national survey of high school seniors in 1995 found fewer than half knew the basic facts of American history. They fared even worse on interpretive questions involving historical events such as westward expansion and the civil rights movement.[10]

To a degree, achievement test results reflect the drag of poverty and scant or misspent resources. Poverty rates are higher in America than in other advanced countries, and they are climbing higher still among children. In the decade after the release of *A Nation at Risk*, the number of children living in poverty increased by four million. In the mid-1990s, one-fourth of children younger than six were growing up poor. In some cities, waves of immigrant children who don't speak English were flooding the schools.

Nationally, the 1980s reforms have achieved only modest progress, according to the National Education Goals Panel, which late in 1995 issued a report midway through the federal Goals 2000 program, a Bush administration initiative the Clinton presidency enthusiastically adopted. The

> "
> **A national survey of high school seniors in 1995 found fewer than half knew the basic facts of American history.**
> "

A Longer School Day/Year?

Would lengthening the school year dramatically improve students' performance? Some reformers think so. They say more time in school would benefit minority and disadvantaged students, too, and give working parents a safe, secure, and cost-free place to leave their children for several more weeks each summer.

In a 1996 Gallup survey, respondents evenly split on the question. Forty-nine percent favored a longer elementary school year, while 48 percent were opposed. Whites divided about 50-50, but more than six of every ten black and Hispanic respondents supported extending the year.

Gallup found greater support for lengthening the high school year, with 60 percent in favor and 37 percent opposed. Again, blacks (70 percent) and Hispanics (68 percent) were more strongly in favor of extending the year than whites (59 percent).

The American school year generally runs 180 days. For students in other industrialized countries, school is essentially full-time; in Japan, the year averages 240 days. Some reformers see a direct link between extended time in class and student achievement.

Many high schools have experimented with longer class times. In East Lyme, Connecticut, school officials said doubling the class period to eighty-five minutes led to improved performance and fewer discipline problems.[1]

Skeptics cite higher costs as an obstacle. Salaries for teachers, administrators, and other personnel would be certain to rise with a longer year. Employers who depend on teenage labor during the summer also are opposed.

Gallup didn't query students on their views. But one observer seemed certain of the response. "They know it means more time in custody," wrote *Washington Post* columnist Colman McCarthy.[2]

---

panel, an independent federal agency, monitors the goals program.

The report charted progress—or lack of it—in the eight broad areas of Goals 2000: the educational readiness of preschool children, school completion, student achievement, teacher education, math and science education, adult literacy, school safety, and parental participation. It suggested that few if any of the objectives would be met by the turn of the century. "We are at the halfway point," senior Education Department adviser Michael Cohen said, "and we have not made half the progress we need."[11] The schools actually lost ground in some categories—twelfth-grade reading, student drug use, and teacher preparedness.

In a 1996 report, the nonpartisan National Commission

on Teaching and America's Future claimed more than a quarter of newly hired teachers come to their classrooms with inadequate teaching skills or training in their subjects. The commission issued urgent recommendations for stricter teacher licensing and improved teacher education programs.[12]

America's schools are overcrowded and deteriorating physically. A record 51.7 million students were enrolled in the fall of 1996, and the school population is projected to break the record every year for the next decade. So more students are being jammed into the nation's decrepit public school facilities. One 1996 government report estimated the total cost of repairs at $112 billion. The study prompted the Clinton administration to propose an election-year $5 billion reconstruction program for crumbling schools in one hundred cities.[13]

Still, signs are encouraging in some areas, especially in the lower grades. More students were meeting national standards in math. More parents were reading to their preschool children. The number of children born with health risks was falling slightly. In Boston, younger students outperformed older ones on the 1996 Stanford test, suggesting better days ahead. Boston's third-graders reached the national average in math and scored slightly above the standard in reading.

Optimists say the successes of 1980s blunt the arguments of radical reformers who argue that only the free play of market forces—school choice, vouchers, charter schools, private, for-profit schools—can rescue American education. They say the evidence suggests a resurgence. In the words of forecaster Cetron, the nation's public schools have "begun the long climb back to excellence."[14]

There is some evidence to support this view. Eight of every ten Americans are high school graduates. One survey found that at least half the states are reporting modest gains on math achievement tests, at least at some grade levels. Average Scholastic Aptitude Tests (SAT) scores have improved even as more students sit for the exam—more than one million by the mid-1990s (41 percent of all high school graduates), including 250,000 members of minority groups. Math SAT scores in 1996 were the highest in nearly two decades.[15]

Dropout rates have declined slightly. The education gap

"
America's schools are overcrowded and deteriorating physically.
"

> "Americans expect more than schooling from the schools."

between the races continues to close, with minority test scores and high school graduation rates on a steady rise. (The Education Trust reported at the end of 1996, however, that the gap may be widening again.) Many school districts have imposed stricter attendance rules and lengthened the school day or year. Overall spending on education has increased.

California, the nation's largest school system, reported impressive gains from the 1980s reforms. In the state's 1989 comprehensive tests in reading and math, high school seniors scored a full year ahead of the seniors of 1983. Dropout rates were down, more graduates were meeting tough University of California entrance requirements, and SAT scores were up.

"Educators are being challenged on whether we have a strategy that can produce results," wrote Bill Honig, superintendent of California's 5-million-student public school system. "We do, and this nation should be discussing how best to build on this record and accelerate the pace of reform—not how to dismantle public education."[16]

Expectations: Purposes and Problems

What makes an adequate high school education? There is probably no absolute measure, but *A Nation at Risk* recommended a basic load of four years of English; three years each of math, science, and social studies; two years of a foreign language; and a half year of computers.

Americans, though, expect more than schooling from the schools—a lot more. According to Gallup's 1996 survey, they want the public school system to turn out good citizens, improve social conditions, foster cultural unity among races and ethnic groups, and lead graduates toward economic self-sufficiency.

Here are some of Gallup's findings:
- Eighty-six percent of those sampled judged it "very important" for the schools to prepare students to become responsible citizens. Twelve percent thought it "quite important." A full two-thirds agreed that America's high schools should adopt some form of community service or public service as a requirement for graduation.
- Nearly six of every ten respondents (58 percent) believed

it very important for the schools to improve social conditions. Another 28 percent thought it quite important. Only 10 percent found the issue to be "not too important."

Breaking down these results, Gallup found African-Americans and Hispanics more likely to assign a social role to education. Three-quarters of black respondents judged the question very important; 19 percent thought it quite important. Among Hispanics, the figures were 74 percent and 17 percent.

Democrats (66 percent) were more likely than Republicans (49 percent) to say it was very important for the schools to improve social conditions. Women (63 percent) were more likely than men (52 percent) to say so.

- Nearly two-thirds of all respondents, 63 percent, thought it very important for the schools to promote cultural unity. Among public school parents, the figure rose sharply—to 80 percent. Not surprisingly, blacks (83 percent) and Hispanics (76 percent) graded the unity issue very important. Again, Democrats (71 percent) were much more likely to view it that way than Republicans (50 percent); women (68 percent) more likely than men (57 percent).
- Nearly everyone agreed the schools should prepare students to become economically self-sufficient; 78 percent judged this very important and 18 percent quite important.
- Respondents differed most sharply when asked whether the schools should take responsibility for minimizing inequities in education for minorities. Fewer than half, 44 percent, regarded this form of affirmative action very important. Around a third, 32 percent, rated it quite important. Fourteen percent found it not too important; 5 percent not at all important.

More than three-quarters of black respondents, however, thought closing the gap a very important school function. Among Hispanics, the figure was 62 percent. Nearly half (49 percent) of Democrats polled thought so; among Republicans, fewer than four in every ten (37 percent) judged an egalitarian mission for the schools to be very important.

In assessing all the problems facing America's schools,

"
In assessing the problems facing America's schools, Gallup's 1996 sample rated social issues ahead of purely academic issues.
"

"Gallup polls hardly confirm a broad consensus for comprehensive school reform."

Gallup's 1996 sample rated social issues ahead of purely academic issues. Respondents cited drug use most often—16 percent said drugs caused the most problems in school. Lack of discipline came next, at 15 percent, followed by fighting and violence (14 percent), lack of money (13 percent), and overcrowding (8 percent).

Academics ranked first, though, when Gallup asked how respondents would spend a windfall of money for schools if one became available in their community. Nearly a quarter, 23 percent, said they would improve the curriculum; 15 percent would spend the money on computers and other new technology; 14 percent would hire more staff; 12 percent would refurbish school facilities; and 11 percent would raise teacher pay.

Respondents seemed to acknowledge that drugs, discipline, and violence are not, in the end, problems money can fix. Only 2 percent said they would spend the windfall on security, on tightening discipline, or on drug education.

Reform: A Long, Continuing Debate

Gallup polls hardly confirm a broad consensus for comprehensive school reform, yet reformers have been in the ascendant for fifteen years. From earliest times, when most communities made do with charity or religious schools, Americans have carried on conversations about how to improve education.

American Opinion

Although many Americans see drugs, violence, and a lack of discipline as the major problems facing American schools today, most would not spend money to increase security at their public schools.

Source: The Gallup Poll for Phi Delta Kappa 1996

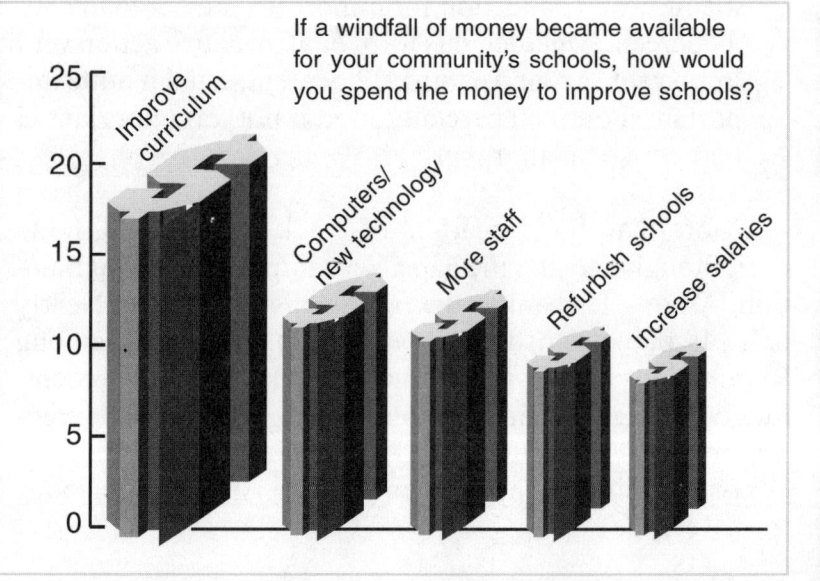

If a windfall of money became available for your community's schools, how would you spend the money to improve schools?

- Improve curriculum
- Computers/new technology
- More staff
- Refurbish schools
- Increase salaries

During the first half of the nineteenth century, reformers fought for universal public education. Massachusetts in 1852 became the first state to adopt compulsory school legislation, overriding strong, sometimes violent opposition in some localities. During the latter half of the century, progressive educators campaigned for an improved curriculum with less emphasis on rote learning, a ban on religious instruction, the addition of kindergarten, and more rigorous teacher training in state-supported "normal" schools. By century's end, public schools were the dominant form of education in America.

The modern reform era began in the late 1950s with the Soviet Union's launch of the first Sputnik satellite in 1957. To some, this event suggested the United States had fallen behind in an important competition with its superpower rival, and it revealed alarming deficiencies in Americans' scientific and technical education.

A quarter century later, *A Nation at Risk* argued that matters had gone from bad to worse. The response: an era of unprecedented change, experiment, and reform.

In the mid-1980s, the "excellence movement" sought to renew the emphasis on basic skills and to raise academic standards. Spending on schools rose substantially. Some localities extended the school day and year. Critics, however, claimed that the gains were negligible. A second wave of reform pressed for more radical approaches: fundamental restructuring of schools, with more parental and community authority; stricter assessment and accountability; and a school choice option that, in purest free-market form, would allow private and religious schools to compete as equals with the public schools, which educate about 90 percent of American children.

School Choice

In the late 1980s, Minnesota became the first state to let parents choose between public schools within a district or schools in other districts. Iowa, Arkansas, Ohio, and other states followed. In 1991, the Bush administration endorsed a wider choice plan, a voucher program that would provide government tuition money for some parents with children in private schools.

"
The modern reform era began in the late 1950s with the Soviet Union's launch of the first Sputnik satellite in 1957.
"

> " **Opponents say public/private choice and voucher programs would destroy mass public education and create staggering inequalities of opportunity.** "

The most radical reformers call for the elimination of all but the loosest political and bureaucratic controls in favor of the market. The states would set minimum standards for academics, health and safety, and teacher training. Any group that met the criteria could apply for a charter and collect a per-pupil allocation of public money. "Schools [would] compete for the support of parents and students, who in turn are free to choose among schools," write John E. Chubb and Terry M. Moe, advocates of the market approach.[17] Competition, they say, would promote efficiency and eventually lower education costs.

Opponents say public/private choice and voucher programs would destroy mass public education and create staggering inequalities of opportunity. Cult schools teaching creationism or astrology in place of science would flourish, argues Honig, the California school superintendent. Such programs, he says, lack accountability and violate the constitutional ban on government aid to religious schools. And they would almost certainly drive up education costs, says Honig, just as college tuition charges continue to rise, in spite of competition.

More damaging still, critics claim, school choice would shift public money to private institutions at a time when resources are diminishing in many places. That issue has been hotly debated in Connecticut, where the Republican governor, John G. Rowland, is a supporter of choice. "I think we're fooling ourselves if we don't deal with the real

American Opinion

While a clear majority of Americans oppose students' attending a private school at public expense, the past five years have seen an increase in those favoring the idea.

Source: The Gallup Poll for Phi Delta Kappa, 1991, 1993, 1995, 1996

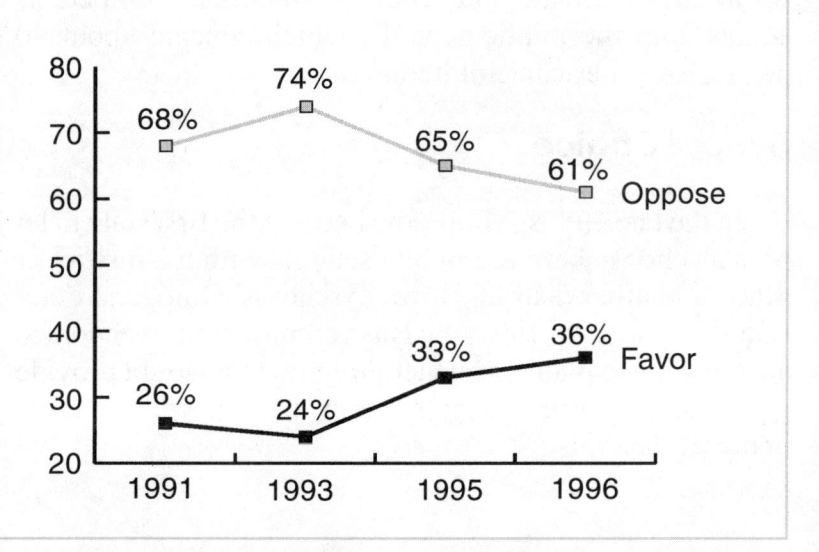

Year	Oppose	Favor
1991	68%	26%
1993	74%	24%
1995	65%	33%
1996	61%	36%

issue," said Robert Eagan, president of the Connecticut Education Association (the teachers' union), which opposes choice options. "The minute you take tax dollars from local school budgets, you're seriously affecting the programs of the children left behind."[18]

The Reagan administration first floated a voucher proposal in 1985. Milwaukee in 1990 became the first major American city to offer a voucher program. A thousand children there use vouchers now worth $4,400 a year to attend nonsectarian private schools. An independent study of standardized test results suggested the voucher students, the majority of whom are black or Hispanic, are performing better than those in Milwaukee's public schools. The city moved to expand the program, but a Wisconsin judge put everything on hold in early 1997 by ruling that tax money could not be used to send poor children to religious schools.[19]

Early in 1996, California governor Pete Wilson, a Republican, proposed a modified voucher program in which the state would pay for students from the worst public schools to attend the public, private, or religious school of their choice. Later in the year, Ohio became the first state to permit the use of government vouchers in religious schools.

In the Ohio program, the government provides $2,500 vouchers to 2,000 low- and moderate-income Cleveland children in kindergarten through third grade. There are three times as many applicants as places in the thirty-nine participating religious schools and ten nonsectarian private schools.

The Cleveland program is being challenged as unconstitutional in Ohio's Court of Appeals. As elsewhere, teacher groups are leading the opposition, claiming voucher programs drain money and good students from troubled public schools. "It allows [voucher children] to escape the problem, but it doesn't solve the problem for 70,000 other kids," observed Ron Merec, president of the Ohio Federation of Teachers.[20]

Overall support for private schools is difficult to measure. Gallup surveys indicate there is substantial interest in choice programs, though a solid majority of respondents continue to reject them.

A 1995 Public Agenda Foundation study suggests otherwise. "People think private schools do better than public

> **Teacher groups are leading the opposition, claiming voucher programs drain money and good students from troubled public schools.**

American Opinion

Do you favor or oppose allowing students and parents to choose a private school to attend at public expense?

Group	Favor	Oppose	No opinion
Overall	36%	61%	3%
Catholics	49%	50%	1%
Republicans	41%	54%	5%
Democrats	30%	64%	6%
Parents with children in a public school	39%	59%	2%

Source: The Gallup Poll for Phi Delta Kappa, 1996

schools in the areas that are more important to them: safety, order, standards, and smaller classes," the study claimed. (The Public Agenda Foundation is a nonprofit, nonpartisan education and research group.) "Moreover, if they could afford to, the majority of public school parents would send their children to private schools."[21]

In the 1996 Gallup education poll, 36 percent of those surveyed favored allowing students to choose a private school to attend at public expense. Sixty-one percent said they were opposed. Roman Catholics divided evenly, with 49 percent in favor and 50 percent opposed. Republicans (41 percent) were more likely to support school choice than Democrats (only 30 percent). Parents with children in the public schools were slightly more likely to support choice than the total sample: 39 percent were in favor, 59 percent opposed.

When Gallup broadened the question to include "any public, private, or church-related school" of a parent's choice, support rose slightly. More than four in every ten—43 percent—were in favor; 54 percent were opposed. Again, Catholics (55 percent) and Republicans (49 percent) were more likely to favor choice than Protestants (38 percent), Jews (22 percent), Democrats (37 percent), and independents (44 percent). Public school parents divided down the middle: 49 percent were in favor, 49 percent opposed.

Gallup respondents were more skeptical of a voucher system that would replace the public schools. Only a quarter favored such a system; nearly seven of every ten—69 percent—were opposed.

The Profit Motive

Some public systems have experimented with private, for-profit school management, with mixed educational results. Nor, by Gallup's measure, is privatization a hit with the public. In the 1996 survey, slightly more than a third of respondents, 34 percent, said they favored the notion of contracting out to operate the schools. Nearly six of every ten—59 percent—were opposed.

The best-known private initiative, the Edison Project, claims that 70 percent of the nation's school systems could be run at a profit. Edison operated with success in 1995-96 in four cities. The most notable failures have been the Baltimore, Maryland, and Hartford, Connecticut, projects of Educational Alternatives Inc. In both cities, disputes over payments and performance doomed EAI's ventures before they could prove their worth.

Christopher Whittle launched the Edison Project in 1991 with a goal of establishing two hundred for-profit schools by 1996. Financial considerations—development costs approached $75 million—forced a retrenchment. In its scaled-

> "Some public systems have experimented with private, for-profit school management, with mixed educational results."

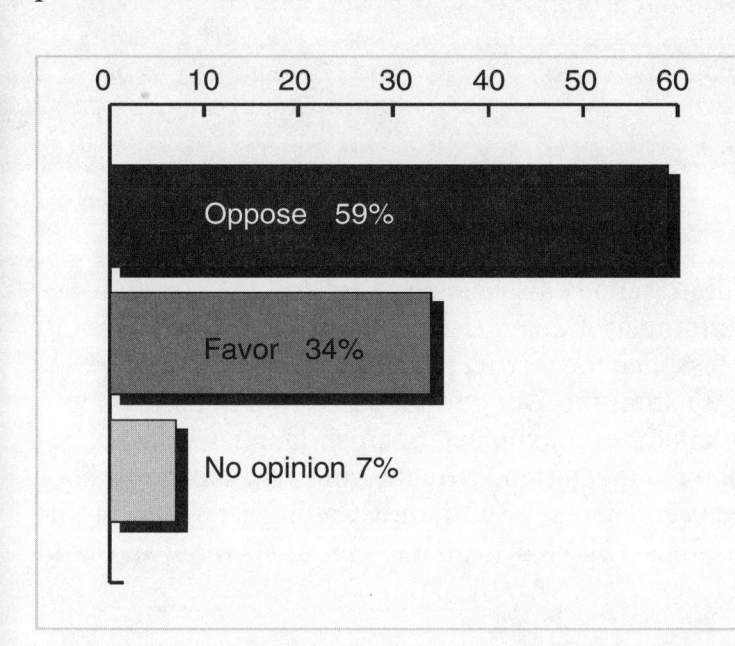

Oppose 59%
Favor 34%
No opinion 7%

American Opinion

Do you favor contracting an outside company to operate a public school?

Source: The Gallup Poll for Phi Delta Kappa, 1996

Schools, Discipline, and Violence

Children are safer at school than anywhere else. Still, parents fret about school violence and favor strict disciplinary methods to quell it, according to the Gallup Organization.

In Gallup's 1996 survey of education attitudes, nine of every ten respondents said persistent troublemakers should be expelled from school; 81 percent favored the hiring of security guards to maintain order. Close to two-thirds, 63 percent, supported a random drug-testing program for students.

A 1995 government report found that deaths from firearms on school grounds accounted for only 1 percent of all deaths among children aged five to nineteen over a two-year period. The report, from the now-defunct federal Office of Technology Assessment, covered the school years 1992–93 and 1993–94. There were about a hundred violent deaths in the schools during the period, the report said.

The findings contradict the impression of widespread carnage in America's schools. A series of highly publicized incidents of school violence prompted the U.S. Education Department in 1994 to require the states to adopt mandatory suspension policies for students caught with guns.

"We're convinced that a lot of national policy was driven not by actual data, but by fears," said Dalton Paxman, who directed the federal study. "Any child getting shot in school is a terrible thing, and we don't want to imply it's not. But we feel that children are in a safer environment than they would be out of school."

A slight majority of Gallup respondents said they favored allowing schools to prescribe uniform dress as a way of tightening discipline and curbing violence. President Clinton in 1996 ordered the Education Department to advise local public school districts on how they could legally enforce school-uniform codes.

"If it means that teenagers will stop killing each other, then our public schools should be able to require their students to wear school uniforms," the president said.

Fifty-three percent of respondents favored school uniforms; 44 percent were opposed. Blacks (66 percent), Hispanics (58 percent), and Catholics (66 percent) were more likely to support a dress code than whites (51 percent) and Protestants (48 percent), Gallup suggested.

down version, Edison managed schools in Boston; Wichita, Kansas; Mount Clemens, Michigan; and Sherman, Texas. The public school districts gave Edison the standard per pupil allotment. Edison stood to make a profit if it could spend less than the district provided.

In Wichita, the Dodge-Edison School supplies home computers for every student, Spanish-language classes beginning in kindergarten, extra tutoring, and a longer school day and year. There is a 320-family waiting list. "They promised to educate all kids, to do it to our satisfaction, and to do it for the same price we were spending," Wichita school superintendent Larry Vaughn said of Edison. "I can't think of anything they've fallen short on."[22]

Edison claimed each of its four schools operated at a profit in 1995–96, excluding start-up and development costs. The company planned to expand from four to twelve schools in 1996–97 and was negotiating with another twenty-five to thirty school districts for the 1997-98 school year.

Edison has its critics, especially in the teachers' unions. "They will get into cutting costs, and when they do it, they won't have to answer to the public," predicted Keith Welty, president of the Wichita union, a chapter of the National Education Association. "Most of what they're doing is just common sense. We just can't get the legislators to kick out the kind of money Whittle did."[23]

Educational Alternatives of Minneapolis negotiated a partnership to run twelve public schools in Baltimore in 1992, in the face of strong resistance from the American Federation of Teachers' affiliate, the Baltimore School Union. Baltimore canceled the contract with EAI in November 1995, after the firm refused a $7 million annual reduction in its $44-million-a-year contract. Hartford dissolved its partnership with EAI in January 1996, again in a dispute over money.

EAI promised its advanced teaching and management methods would produce dramatic improvements in the twelve Baltimore schools. "Baltimore has been a success, and if critics say they haven't been as successful as they promised, that's debatable," Lehman Brothers analyst Michael Moe said. "The schools that EAI took over were a disgrace, and today they're schools that work."[24] EAI claimed gains in the classroom as well as in tightening student discipline and cleaning up school facilities.

Critics noted, however, that test scores in EAI's privately run schools were comparable to those of other Baltimore schools, even though EAI spent around 11 percent more. "EAI, while proving it can repair broken windows quickly in Baltimore, has a lot to prove in the classrooms," wrote educator Stanley Elam, a skeptic on privatization. "Its so-called Testeract Way teaching strategy is essentially a collection of reforms already introduced in public education: hands-on science and math, group learning and team teach-

> "Critics noted, however, that test scores in EAI's privately run schools were comparable to those of other Baltimore schools, even though EAI spent around 11 percent more."

ing, mainstreaming special education students, individualized education plans, and well-supplied classrooms."[25]

EAI took charge of Hartford's entire poverty-blighted school system, a failing venture in which students rank last on Connecticut's standardized achievement tests despite one of the highest levels of per-capita spending in the state. The firm installed computers in several of the system's thirty-two schools, helped repair some buildings, and negotiated a teacher contract it claimed would save the city millions. But teachers' and administrators' unions were unrelentingly hostile, and the partnership broke down after only eighteen months in a bitter dispute over how much Hartford should reimburse EAI for its expenses.[26]

Public School Reform

As Stanley Elam observed, most reform schemes have been initiated—in many cases introduced—on a small scale in the public schools. In Kentucky, the entire public school system is being rebuilt, top to bottom, to a reform blueprint.

With the passage of the Kentucky Education Reform Act of 1990, the state provided more money for schools and allocated funds more equitably, set higher standards, encouraged innovative teaching methods, and improved counseling services and technology.

For the most part, the reforms are too new to have yielded any hard evidence of success, although early returns on test

American Opinion

Respondents favoring uniforms for students in public schools.

Group	Percentage
Overall (National adults)	53%
Blacks	66%
Catholics	66%
Hispanics	58%
Whites	51%
Protestants	48%

Source: The Gallup Poll for Phi Delta Kappa, 1996

scores suggest that progress is being made. According to one report, three-quarters of Kentucky schools showed gains on achievement tests between 1992 and 1994, with the most marked improvement among fourth-graders.[27]

Payzant, who now runs Boston's troubled public schools, introduced what he dubbed "controlled choice within the public sector" in San Diego when he was head of the school system there. Fifty magnet schools were open to all students in the system, subject only to the availability of space and racial balance. The initiative amounts to a sort of modified market approach, says Payzant, for if the magnet schools don't give satisfaction, they won't survive.

"They are constantly looking for ways to heighten their appeal to students and parents," he said. "If they fail to attract students, they jeopardize their magnet status and funding."[28]

Massachusetts, the cradle of American public education, seems intent on reclaiming its traditional place as a leader in the field. Charter schools—publicly funded alternatives to public education, built from the ground up—are taking root there. In Boston, the public schools have inaugurated a series of innovative pilot schools, among them the new Multicultural High School in Dorchester, with its "inquiry and project-based" curriculum.

The state's first fourteen charter schools opened in the autumn of 1995; another nine began operations in September 1996. Some urban school officials, as well as the teachers' union, opposed the charter movement, arguing that such schools would promote white flight and siphon money from struggling conventional schools. In some cases, too, facilities are barely adequate—the Lighthouse Charter School in Orleans on Cape Cod meets in a strip mall, and an Elks hall is the venue for the Marblehead Community Charter School.[29]

All the same, Massachusetts charter schools have more applicants than places. And initial reports suggest critics overstated the potential for problems. Minorities make up close to half the charter schools' enrollment, and the state has reimbursed local districts for their financial losses.

"Right now, at least, the real competition is over students, not money," *The Boston Globe* editorialized. "The unions and public school administrators have plenty of cause

> **Massachusetts, the cradle of American public education, seems intent on reclaiming its traditional place as a leader in the field.**

to worry—and to improve. That's one of the best reasons for charter schools to exist."[30]

Politics and Schools

The Reagan administration's *A Nation at Risk* helped politicize school issues in the 1980s. Generally, political, cultural, and religious conservatives are more critical of public school performance, and more skeptical of the future of public education, than those with liberal inclinations.

Conservatives tend to support broad school choice programs, including voucher systems. They see bureaucratic waste and misallocation of resources in the public schools. Some conservatives call for an emphasis on "values" education in the classroom. Liberals lean toward fixing what exists. They usually favor increased spending for schools. They emphasize the debilitating effects of poverty, violence, and broken families. And they note that it is difficult to reach a consensus on the sort of things that go into a values curriculum.

Education became a major focus of the 1996 presidential campaign, and the candidates differed sharply on several key policy issues.

Bob Dole supported more radical school-choice proposals, attacked teachers' unions as enemies of change, and called for the dismantling of the federal Education Department. Clinton acknowledged problems in public education.

> "Conservatives tend to support broad school choice programs, including voucher systems."

American Opinion

When it comes to education, the Democrats and President Clinton come out ahead of the Republicans and the Republican Congress.

Source: The Gallup Poll for Phi Delta Kappa, 1996

Which political party do you think cares more about education?

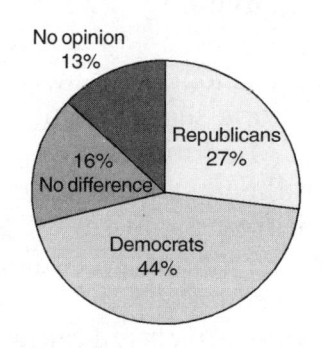

- No opinion: 13%
- Republicans: 27%
- Democrats: 44%
- No difference: 16%

Who has done more for education—President Clinton or the Republican Congress?

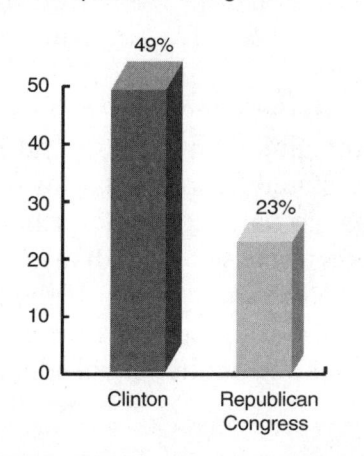

- Clinton: 49%
- Republican Congress: 23%

But his more moderate views—he supported charter schools, for example, but not vouchers for private schools—seemed more in concert with public opinion.

In Gallup surveys, Democrats "outscore" Republicans on most education issues. In the 1996 survey, Gallup asked which political party seemed more interested in improving public education. Forty-four percent chose the Democrats; 27 percent said Republicans had more interest; 16 percent discerned no difference in the parties. In breakdowns by sex, race, education, occupational group, and geographic region, the Democrats were viewed as more interested in the schools. Only parents with children in private schools leaned toward the Republicans, and those by a narrow 36 percent to 32 percent. When asked to choose between President Clinton and the Republican Congress, nearly half the sample, 49 percent, said Clinton had done more to improve public education. Only 23 percent thought the Republicans had done more for the nation's schools.

On the question that strikes closest to home, a majority of parents of public school children gave a vote of confidence to public education. "If you could send your child to any school of your choice, and cost was not a factor," Gallup asked, "would you send the child to the school he or she now attends, or to a different school?"

Fifty-eight percent said they would send their children to the same school; 41 percent would change. In an election, that result would grade as a landslide. Still, people expect more from the schools, just as they expect more from their children: As and Bs rather than Cs and Ds. And with four in every ten registering for change, the pressure for reform will doubtless continue to build.

Notes: **Education reform** Do America's Schools Make the Grade

1. Laurel Shaper Walters, "'A Nation at Risk:' + 10 years = A Nation Still at Risk," *The Christian Science Monitor*, April 26, 1993, 12.
   Peter Applebome, "10-Year Plan for Education Makes Spotty Progress," *The New York Times*, November 9, 1995, B11.
2. National Commission on Excellence in Education, *A Nation at Risk: The Imperative for Education Reform* (Washington: U.S. Government Printing Office, 1983), 5.
3. Chester E. Finn Jr. and Theodor Rebarber, "The Changing Politics of Education Reform," in Finn and Rebarber, eds., *Educational Reform in the '90s* (New York: Macmillan, 1992), 180.
4. Marvin Cetron and Margaret Gayle, *Educational Renaissance: Our Schools at the Turn of the Twenty-first Century* (New York: St. Martin's Press, 1991), 5.
5. John Taylor Gatto, "Public Education Needs Extensive Reform," in Charles P. Cozic, ed., *Education in America* (San Diego: Greenhaven Press, 1992), 18.
6. Walters, "'A Nation at Risk.'"
7. Stanley Elam, *How America Views Its Schools: The PDK/Gallup Polls, 1969–1974* (Bloomington, Ind.: Phi Delta Kappa Educational Foundation, 1995), 18.
8. Don Terry, "One-Fifth of Schools Put on Probation in Chicago," *The New York Times*, October 1, 1996, 14.
9. Karen Avenoso, "Boston students lag in tests," *The Boston Globe*, June 25, 1996, 1.
10. "Most 12th Graders Know Little American History, Survey Says," Associated Press report in *The New York Times*, November 2, 1995, 22.
11. Applebome, "10-Year Plan for Education."
12. Peter Applebome, "Education Panel Sees Deep Flaws in Training of Nation's Teachers," *The New York Times*, September 13, 1996, 1.
13. Josh Greenberg, "Schools to Enroll Record Number," *Los Angeles Times* report in *The Boston Globe*, August 22, 1996, 3.
    Brian McGrory, "Clinton to offer plan to rebuild public schools," *The Boston Globe*, July 11, 1996, 3.
14. Cetron and Gayle, *Educational Renaissance*, 5.
15. Gerald Bracey, "The Greatly Exaggerated Death of Our Schools," op-ed, *The Washington Post*, May 5, 1991.
    Karen W. Arenson, "Schools Continue to Improve, College Board Says," *The New York Times*, August 23, 1996, 16.
16. Bill Honig, "Parental School Choice Would Harm Education," in Cozic, ed., *Education in America*, 111.
17. John E. Chubb and Terry M. Moe, "Educational Choice: Why It Is Needed and How It Will Work," in Finn and Rebarber, eds., *Educational Reform*, 40.
18. Julie Miller, "Schools, Choices and Tax Dollars," *The New York Times*, Connecticut Weekly, January 21, 1996, 1.
19. "Study Shows Voucher Pupils Thriving in Private Schools," Associated Press report in *The New York Times*, August 13, 1996, 9.

20. Kimberly J. McLarin, "Ohio Paying Some Tuition for Religious Schools," *The New York Times*, August 28, 1996, B9.
21. Miller, "Schools, Choices and Tax Dollars."
22. Peter Applebome," "Grading For-Profit Schools: So Far, So Good," *The New York Times*, June 26, 1996, A1.
23. Applebome, "Grading For-Profit Schools."
24. George Judson, "Baltimore Ends Education Experiment," *The New York Times*, November 23, 1995, 16.
25. Elam, *How America Views Its Schools*, 32.
26. Rick Green, "EAI on Way Out as Board Support Collapses," *The Hartford Courant*, January 23, 1996, A1.
27. Peter Applebome, "Kentucky's Sweeping Overhaul of Education Offers Lessons Both Positive and Negative," *The New York Times*, March 25, 1996, 10.
28. Thomas W. Payzant, "An Urban Superintendent's Perspective on Education Reform," in Finn and Rebarber, eds., *Educational Reform*, 98-99.
29. Kate Zernike, "Class Struggles: Charter Schools Sometimes Forced to Fight for Space," *The Boston Globe*, June 10, 1996, 1.
30. "Good Scores for Charter Schools," editorial, *The Boston Globe*, July 19, 1996.

Notes: A Longer School Day/Year?

1. Christopher Arellano, "East Lyme High Lengthens Class Periods," *The Day*, New London, Conn., June 8, 1996.
2. Colman McCarthy, "A Longer School Year Wouldn't Improve Public Education," in Cozic, ed., *Education in America*, 40.

Notes: Schools, Discipline, and Violence

1. "Schools Are Relatively Safe, U.S. Study Says," *The New York Times*, November 19, 1995, 40.
2. Alison Mitchell, "Clinton Will Advise Schools on Uniforms," *The New York Times*, February 25, 1996, 24.

Immigration
7 Should America Leave the Welcome Mat Out?

The nativist current in America is flowing strongly in the 1990s, quickened by persistent illegal immigration and by demographers' projections that legal newcomers, most of them from Asia and Latin America, are arriving at a rate that will radically alter the substance of national life in the twenty-first century.

Immigration has become a more potent political issue in the United States than at any time since the restrictionist 1920s. Gallup Organization surveys suggest Americans are deeply concerned about the political and cultural questions immigration raises. There is broad support, for example, for making English the official language. Close to two-thirds say immigration should be a top, high, or very important priority for the Clinton administration and Congress. More than 60 percent believe the level of immigration should be decreased.

In 1994, California's Proposition 187 denied government benefits to illegal immigrants. Welfare reform legislation in 1996 cut assistance to legal immigrants. A new antiterrorism law provided for the automatic deportation of legal immigrants convicted of felonies. There were calls for a doubling of the naturalization period, to ten years. And some Republicans in 1996 campaigned for a five-year freeze on legal immigration and for repeal of the 14th Amendment's birthright guarantee of citizenship.

Such proposals, liberal opinion makers claim, seek scapegoats rather than solutions. "Get rid of immigrants,

> **"Immigration has become a more potent political issue in the United States than at any time since the restrictionist 1920s."**

> "America's immigration policies are among the most liberal in the world."

legal and illegal," *The Boston Globe* sarcastically suggested, "and the public schools will improve, the bloated welfare caseload will decrease, and crime will evaporate."[1]

Most people recognize, too, that immigrants built the nation—after all, the aboriginal Americans are a tiny minority. In a 1996 Gallup poll, respondents divided roughly down the middle on the Republicans' proposal for a moratorium on legal immigration. Fifty percent favored a five-year freeze, 46 percent were opposed.

"The Browning of America"

America's immigration policies are among the most liberal in the world. The Immigration and Nationality Act of 1965 dropped national origin quotas and eased other restrictions, touching off a great movement of peoples. Between 1968 and 1993, 16.7 million immigrants landed in the United States, 80 percent of them from Latin America and Asia. Some 593,000 immigrants entered the country legally in 1995, with more than 800,000 expected in 1996 and 1997. In every year of the 1990s, an estimated 300,000 illegal immigrants were settling more or less permanently in America.

In 1991, according to the Immigration and Naturalization Service, 1.8 million immigrants arrived, easily breaking the previous one-year record of 1.3 million in 1907. The INS estimates 12 to 13 million legal and illegal immi-

American Opinion

Do you favor or oppose a five-year moratorium on legal immigration in the United States?

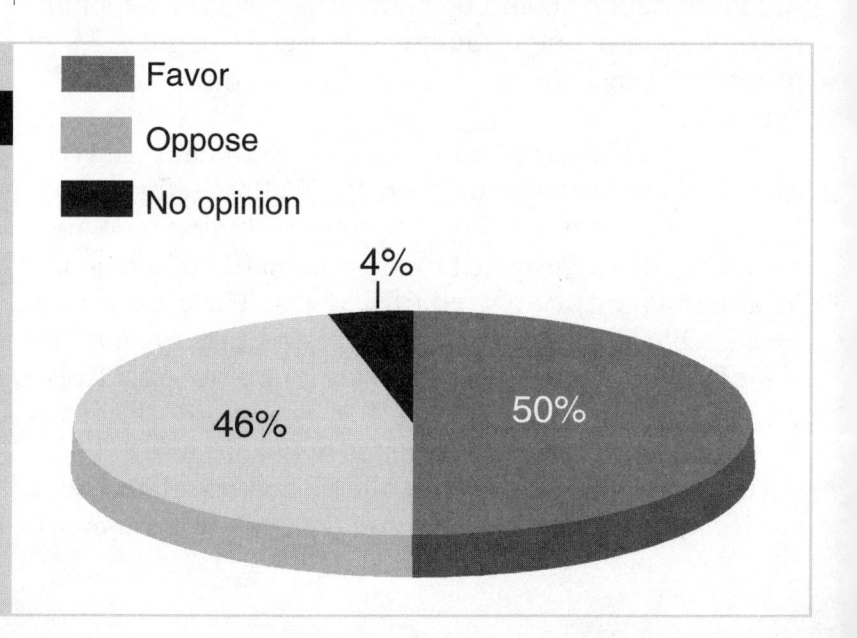

- Favor: 50%
- Oppose: 46%
- No opinion: 4%

Source: The Gallup Poll 1996

grants will take up residence the United States during the 1990s. If those projections hold, more newcomers will settle in America during the 1990s than in any other decade in the nation's history.[2]

Mass immigration already has worked substantial demographic changes. Immigrants and their offspring account for perhaps half the U.S. population growth. In New York State, 40 percent of all elementary and secondary public-school students are ethnic minorities while in California, minority students make up a majority of the public school population.[3]

Even greater change is coming. Between 2010 and 2020, Hispanics will outnumber African Americans and become the nation's largest single minority. In 1950, almost nine-tenths—89.5 percent—of Americans were white. By 2050, whites will make up 53 percent of America's population, a bare majority.[4]

According to Gallup opinion samples, many Americans find these figures alarming. In a 1992 poll, nearly seven of every ten respondents said too many Latin American immigrants were arriving in the United States. Six of every ten said too many Asians were migrating to America. Only around a third thought there were too many European immigrants. The demographic projections, obviously, have broad implications for American political, social and cultural life, and for such issues as criminal justice, health care, and education.

"Race and ethnicity are destiny in American politics," writes journalist and author Peter Brimelow, an advocate of immigration restrictions. "The racial and ethnic balance of America is being radically altered through public policy. This can only have the most profound effects. Is it what America wants?"[5]

The title of Brimelow's 1995 jeremiad, *Alien Nation: Common Sense About America's Immigration Disaster*, leaves no doubt about where he stands. Large numbers, he asserts, are drawn to America's liberal welfare state, where health, education, and other benefits are far superior to those at home.

"These are immigrants from completely different, and arguably incompatible cultural traditions. And they are coming in such numbers that their impact on America is enor-

> **Immigrants and their offspring account for perhaps half the U.S. population growth.**

> "'We've got room for people who want to come and work. We don't have room for people who are looking for a handout.'"

mous—inevitably within the foreseeable future they will transform it," Brimelow writes.[6]

Others take a sunnier view. "The U.S. was created, and continues to be defined, primarily by voluntary immigration," wrote *Time* magazine's William A. Henry III. "This process has been one of the country's great strengths, infusing it with talent and energy. The 'browning of America' offers tremendous opportunity for capitalizing anew on the merits of many peoples from many lands."[7]

Asian-Indians, for example, are the best-educated ethnic group in the United States. Japanese- and Chinese-Americans earn higher average annual incomes than whites. Collectively, Asian high school students have the highest grades and test scores of any racial group.[8]

Hardheaded economic calculations suggest, too, that without the immigrant infusion, America's labor force will become static as the nation ages. In this view, a liberal immigration policy assures a steady stream of workers to support elderly America, giving the United States a competitive edge over other older industrial nations.[9]

"We've got room for people who want to come and work," Senator Phil Gramm, a Republican from Texas, argued in opposing a 1996 measure to restrict legal immigration. "We don't have room for people who are looking for a handout."[10]

Newcomers and Nativists

The "Great Migration" of 1629 to 1640, America's founding event, brought 21,000 English Pilgrims to the Massachusetts Bay Colony. For most of the seventeenth and eighteenth centuries, the overwhelming majority of voluntary migrants were from the British Isles. At the same time, thousands were arriving involuntarily—enslaved Africans, most of them bound for the Southern colonies as agricultural laborers.

Between 1820 and 1971, the total number of foreigners to enter the United States was 45.5 million. The German states were the largest single supplier, with 15 percent of the total. Around 11 percent came from Italy, 10 percent from Ireland, 10 percent from Britain, 9 percent from the old empire of Austria-Hungary, 9 percent from Canada, 7 percent from the Russian Empire and its Soviet successor. Mexico, the Scandinavian countries, Poland, China, and the West Indies each sent less than 4 percent of the total.

The nativist movement dates from the 1850s, when the political phenomenon known as Know-Nothingism briefly flourished. Secretive, patriotic, incantatory, the American Party drew its sobriquet from the reply members were supposed to give when asked about the party and its mysteries: "I know nothing about it." Members swore to vote only for native-born Americans, to campaign for a twenty-year naturalization, and to oppose the Roman Catholic Church.

The dispute over slavery killed off the Know-Nothings, but xenophobia lived on, fueled by sharply rising numbers of more "foreign" foreigners—the Chinese in the West, and Catholic Italians and Eastern Europeans in the cities of the Atlantic and the Midwest.

America's craft and trade unions were strongly nativist. Denis Kearney and the California Workingmen's Party successfully lobbied Congress for the Chinese Exclusion Act of 1882, which prohibited the entry of Chinese into the United States.

Labor found allies in Protestant America, which resented the growing influence of the Catholic Church, and from segments of the New England intellectual elite, which argued that Italians, East Europeans, and other non-Anglo-Saxon groups should be barred because they supposedly resisted assimilation into American political and cultural life.

These new immigrants arrived in their millions—nearly 9 million during the Great Wave of 1901–1910. This influx gave new impetus to the decades-long nativist agitation and led to the passage of the nation's first sweepingly restrictive law, the openly discriminatory Immigration Act of 1924, which set strict quotas for all countries outside the Western Hemisphere. The act had such drastic effects that in 1933 only 23,000 immigrants entered the United States.

The 1965 Reforms

The restrictive system stood until 1965, when Congress set aside national quotas and made it easier for refugees and others claiming asylum to settle permanently in the

> **The nativist movement dates from the 1850s, when the political phenomenon known as Know-Nothingism briefly flourished.**

> "Asians are today America's fastest-growing racial group."

United States. In a significant departure from past practice, the 1965 act altered the preference system for immigrants, giving highest priority to family reunification and a lesser priority to people with job skills or special scientific or artistic talents.

The sponsors of the 1965 measure had no particular object in mind other than the laudatory and benevolent one of deleting explicitly racist provisions from the statutes. They saw it, too, as a sort of appendix to the epochal civil rights legislation of the period. "It was not," writes economist Vernon M. Briggs, "the product of careful design or public debate."[11] This fit of legislative absentmindedness touched off a wave of mass immigration comparable in numbers to the 1901–10 movement but quite different in kind.

"In retrospect," writes historian Otis L. Graham Jr., chairman of the Center for Immigration Studies in Washington, "it can be seen as perhaps the single most nation-changing measure of the era."[12]

Asians are today America's fastest-growing racial group. There were 9 million Americans of Asian descent in 1996, around 3 percent of the total population. Two-thirds of all U.S. Asians were born abroad.

Hispanics, the majority from Mexico, have accounted for more than 40 percent of legal immigration since 1980. They were 9 percent of the total U.S. population in 1990, up from 2.6 percent in 1950. Only 8 percent of the 1.5 million legal immigrants to the U.S. in 1990 were from northern and western Europe, the traditional source.

According to Briggs, the 1965 act and its successors replaced social and economic goals with political goals. To secure passage, Congress accommodated conservative groups such as the American Legion, which lobbied for the family priority on the largely unspoken grounds that this would preserve the old national quota system favoring immigrants from northwest Europe. Refugees from nations with which the United States had political and ideological differences—such as Vietnam, Cuba, and the Soviet Union—received preference over refugees from right-wing dictatorships allied to America.

An active lobby continues to support the existing system. "Inside the Beltway," writes Graham, "an expansive immigration policy seemed a cheap way to please special interests (in this case, ethnic, religious, and agribusiness groups), since it appeared to be one of the few federal programs that cost next to nothing. Only lately has it become clear that the economic, fiscal, and environmental costs are substantial."[13]

Obviously, family preference did not work out the way the American Legion intended. The INS today issues some 480,000 family visas a year, the cause of the so-called "chain migration" phenomenon in which tens of thousands of Third World immigrants have arrived with few or no workplace skills, limited education, and little or no English.

Critics of the system argue it should work the other way, with assessments of "human capital" characteristics rather than nepotism driving U.S. policy. As it is, skills-based immigration accounts for only around 10 percent of the total.

"Immigrants must bring in talents and skills," wrote Joseph R. Guzzardi, who teaches immigrants and refugees in Stockton, California. " 'I'm coming to be with my cousin,' which is what chain migration encourages, is not a compelling national interest."[14] Or as Peter Brimelow has it, "The immigrant would achieve the truest reunification with all his family if he returned home."[15]

The Immigrants' View

Just as their Italian, Polish, and Russian predecessors

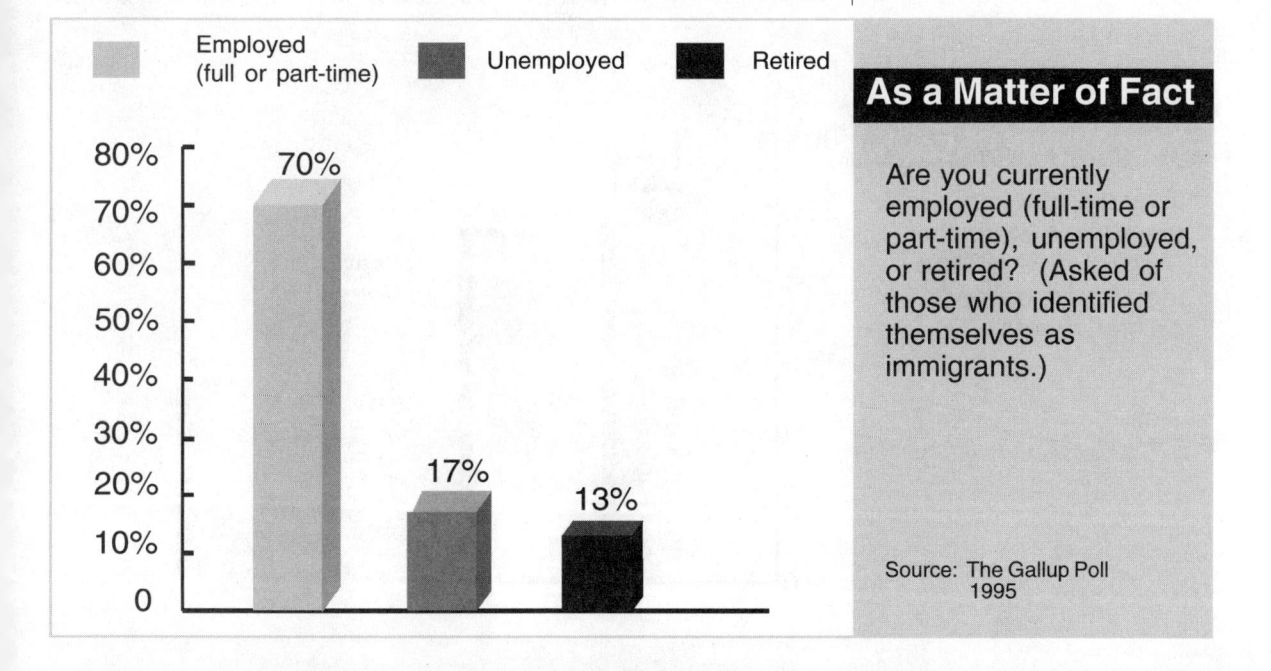

Status	Percentage
Employed (full or part-time)	70%
Unemployed	17%
Retired	13%

As a Matter of Fact

Are you currently employed (full-time or part-time), unemployed, or retired? (Asked of those who identified themselves as immigrants.)

Source: The Gallup Poll 1995

did nine decades ago, late twentieth-century immigrants come in pursuit of the American dream, according to Gallup's polltakers, who conducted a major survey of legal immigrants in May 1995.

The inquiries were in English, so the sample represented roughly three-quarters of the U.S. foreign-born population. According to the U.S. Census Bureau, around a quarter of all immigrants speak little or no English.[16]

One-third of the total sample came from Europe or the former Soviet Union. Thirty-two percent were from Latin America and the Caribbean. Another 23 percent were from the Asia/Pacific region and the Middle East. Seven percent came from Canada, and 3 percent were African in origin.

A full two-thirds of the respondents said members of their family were already settled in the United States when they arrived. Seven of every ten said they were employed full- or part-time, 17 percent said they were jobless, and 13 percent said they were retired. Sixty-nine percent of these immigrants said they mainly spoke English at home.

Most said they came to the United States either to improve their lot or to join family members already here—26 percent for better jobs, 19 percent for educational opportunities, and 23 percent for family considerations. Only 13 percent said they came for political freedom.

Nearly two-thirds said they would remain in the United States even if they could be guaranteed a comparable standard of living in their home country. Still, many in the sample

> "A full two-thirds of the respondents said members of their family were already settled in the United States when they arrived."

As a Matter of Fact

Why did you come to the United States? (Asked of those who identified themselves as immigrants.)

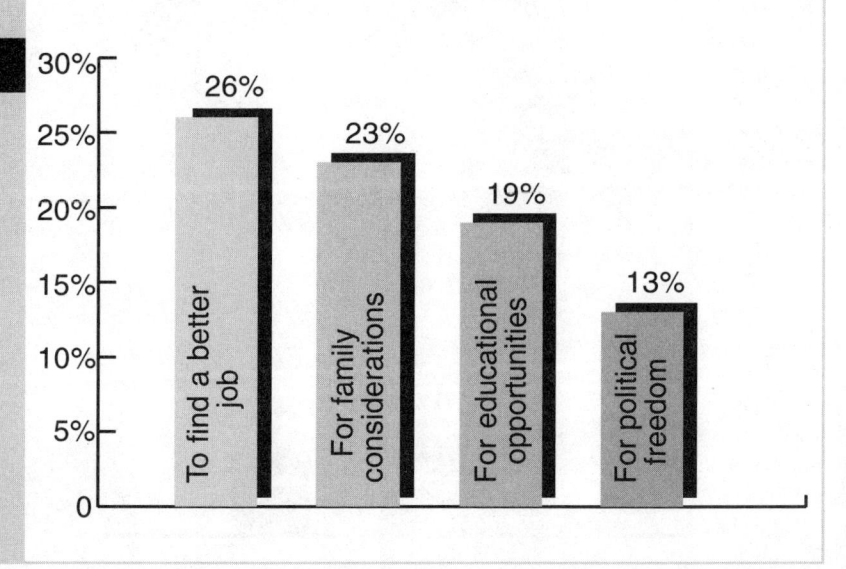

Reason	Percent
To find a better job	26%
For family considerations	23%
For educational opportunities	19%
For political freedom	13%

Source: The Gallup Poll 1995

showed ambivalence about some aspects of American life. Only around half, 54 percent, thought America was a better place than home to raise children. And only a third graded American moral values as superior to those of their home country.

More than eight of every ten in the Gallup sample said they felt welcome when they landed in the United States. Ninety percent said they felt welcome today.

Calls for Restriction

The Republican Congress in 1996 considered measures to tighten U.S. borders, particularly the 2,000-mile-long frontier with Mexico, to crack down on illegal immigrants living in this country, and to restrict some welfare and other public services even to legal immigrants.

The actions seemed to fall in line with public opinion on the issue. In the 1995 poll, for example, Gallup found that more than six of every ten respondents favored a decrease in the number of immigrants entering the country. Only 27 percent thought the flow should remain steady; 7 percent favored an increase in immigration levels.

Gallup's samples were divided on measures to curb illegal immigration. Only 35 percent favored fortifying the Mexican frontier to keep illegal immigrants out; 62 percent were opposed. An even half of respondents would deny illegal immigrants the use of schools and hospitals; 45 per-

"
Gallup's samples were divided on measures to curb illegal immigration.
"

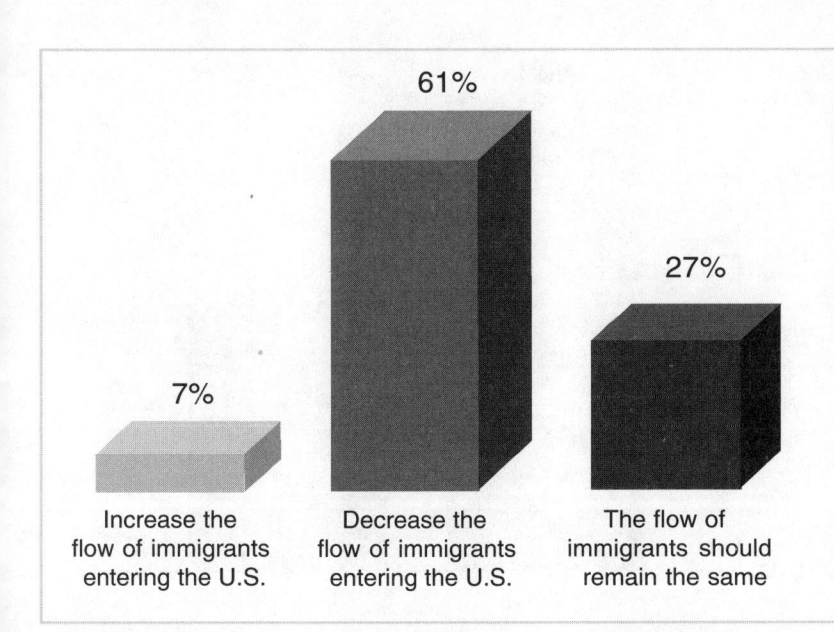

American Opinion

Should the United States increase immigration levels, decrease them, or keep the level the same?

- Increase the flow of immigrants entering the U.S.: 7%
- Decrease the flow of immigrants entering the U.S.: 61%
- The flow of immigrants should remain the same: 27%

Source: The Gallup Poll 1995

> "An estimated 300,000 to 500,000 illegals settle permanently in the United States each year."

cent were opposed. More than 60 percent favored national ID cards for citizens and legal immigrants; 37 percent were opposed.

For obvious reasons, the exact number of illegal immigrants living in the United States is unknown. Estimates range from 3.5 to 4 million, and the numbers are rising. An estimated 2 to 3 million enter the country illegally each year. (In 1993, the U.S. Border Patrol arrested 1.3 million immigrants at the frontier.) Many illegals are nomadic, crossing for seasonal work, returning home, and recrossing. An estimated 300,000 to 500,000 illegals settle permanently in the United States each year.[17]

By a landslide, Californians in 1994 approved Proposition 187, a ballot initiative that sharply reduced illegal immigrants' use of public services. The measure has been held up in the courts ever since. But in August 1996, Governor Pete Wilson, citing the new federal welfare law, moved to implement parts of Proposition 187, issuing an executive order barring illegal immigrants from a broad range of state programs.

Wilson's order covered prenatal care programs, child-abuse prevention programs, and public housing, among other California benefits. The prenatal programs alone served some 70,000 illegal immigrants a year, at a cost of $69 million, state officials estimated.[18]

Though it has been held up in the courts, Proposition 187 already has reshaped America's debate on immigration

American Opinion

Do you favor or oppose issuing national ID cards to citizens and legal immigrants?
("No opinion" omitted)

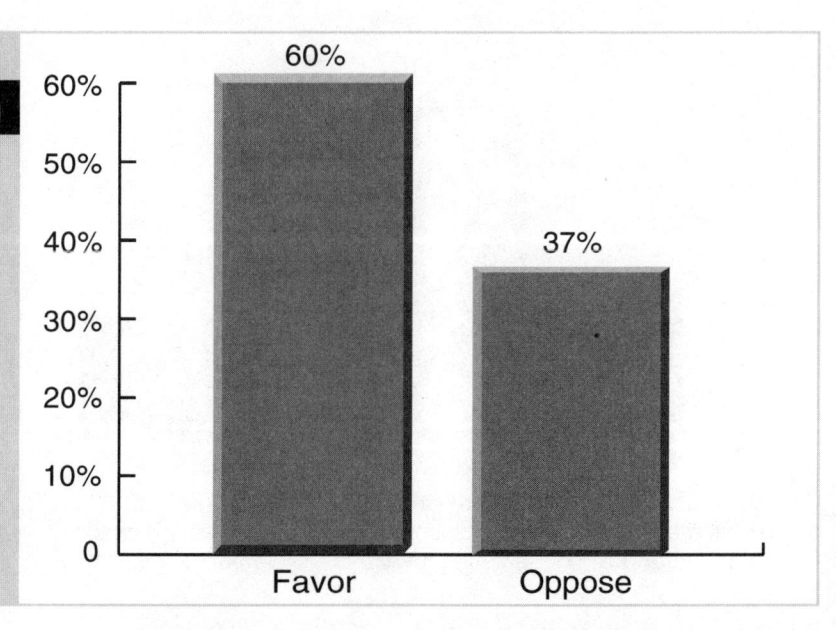

Favor	60%
Oppose	37%

Source: The Gallup Poll 1995

policy. California takes in 50 percent of all immigrants, legal and illegal. Advocates of restriction claim illegal immigrants cost the state nearly $4 billion a year. The measure would deny public schooling, nonemergency hospital care, and other benefits to illegals.[19]

Following California's lead, Congress in 1996 debated legislation that would allow states to bar the children of illegal immigrants from the public schools. The Clinton administration opposed the measure, which it claimed would throw 300,000 to 400,000 children onto the streets. "We don't want to create a farm system for gang leaders and drug dealers to recruit from," said Rahm I. Emanuel, a Clinton domestic policy adviser. Mass expulsions are unlikely anytime soon in any case, for the U.S. Supreme Court would first have to reverse a 1982 ruling that children of illegals are entitled to public education.[20]

Opponents of restrictions argue that the most effective way to curb illegal immigrants is to punish the employers who hire them. The Immigration Reform and Control Act of 1986 prohibits employers from knowingly taking on undocumented workers. But it has never been vigorously enforced.

"Politically, it is more expedient for the Republican right to target classrooms and clinics, whose clientele are children, than employers who want to hire cheap, illegal immigrant labor," the liberal commentator Robert Kuttner wrote.[21]

In a 1996 pilot program in Southern California, 234 companies checked the immigrant status of 11,000 job applicants and found that fully a quarter were not legally authorized to work in the United States.

In 1995–96, the INS carried out a campaign to search out illegal workers in New York City's garment industry. Between October 1995 and May 1996, more than 1,200 were arrested. Few were deported, though, and most soon found work in other sweatshops and factories. Some even returned within a few days to the workplaces where they had been arrested.

All the same, the INS expects that such crackdowns will gradually reduce the number of illegal workers. "If we work in an industry long enough, and impose enough serious fines, we'll get people's attention and that will provide deterrence,"

> **Opponents of restrictions argue that the most effective way to curb illegal immigrants is to punish the employers who hire them.**

Fortifying the Frontier

Trade barriers may be coming down along the U.S.-Mexico frontier, but physical obstacles to the movement of people are going up.

The influx of illegal immigrants through Mexico—mostly Mexicans and other Latin Americans but including thousands of Asians now, too—has led to a widening and hardening of the 2,000-mile-long border, which stretches from the Pacific at San Diego to the mouth of the Rio Grande in Texas. Mexico also is the leading entry point for illegal drugs into the United States.

High steel fences have gone up at major crossing points in San Diego; Nogales, Arizona; and El Paso, Texas. More than 4,000 U.S. Border Patrol agents prowl the frontier, a 50 percent increase from 1993. Army and National Guard units assist in some sectors. Congress in 1996 considered a bill that would double the strength of the Border Patrol, to 10,000 agents.

Such measures draw widespread support. But most Americans are skeptical of proposals to seal the border completely. Only around a third, 35 percent, said in a July 1995 Gallup survey that they favored building a high wall to separate the United States and Mexico. Sixty-two percent were opposed.

Critics say, too, that putting up fence and wire mocks the landmark North American Free Trade Agreement (NAFTA), which promises strengthened economic ties between the two countries.

"At the same time that the U.S. government says to Mexico, 'We are your partner,' it is taking actions that say, 'We fear you, distrust you, and reject you,'" said Rick Ufford-Chase, who directs a church-sponsored program called Borderlinks in Tucson, Arizona.[1]

Those who applaud efforts to tighten the borders say curbing illegal immigrants and the drug trade could deflect support for anti-immigrant measures such as California's Proposition 187, which denies undocumented residents education and health benefits.

---

said T. Alexander Alienikoff, the IRS executive assistant commissioner.[22]

New York's garment industry has been in decline for decades. Many factory owners say they could not survive without illegal workers, who in some cases make less than half the $7- to-$8-an-hour wage that goes to legal workers. Some foreign competitors, they point out, pay less than fifty cents an hour.

"I can't hire all legal people," factory owner Jane Lee said. "Who wants to work in this dirty job? American people? No."[23]

Gallup surveys suggest most Americans do not feel greatly threatened by immigrant workers. In a 1992 poll, 84 percent said immigrants often take jobs Americans don't want, just as Jane Lee observed. Still, many people feel a bit queasy at the thought of, say, wearing clothes made by sweatshop labor.

Said the economist Briggs: "The existence of such Third World working conditions in many cities is nothing for the nation to be proud of, regardless of whether these immigrants actually displace citizen workers in exploitative work situations."[24]

Welfare for Legal Newcomers?

Congress in 1996 debated measures that would deport legal immigrants who accepted more than one year's worth of government services during their first five years in the United States. The proscribed list included welfare, food stamps, job training, English classes, prenatal care, and college loans.

"The premise is that a legal immigrant, even though he is holding a job and paying taxes, is not entitled to the same public service as others," wrote Kuttner.[25]

Restrictionists readily accept the premise. "Americans are not obliged to finance any immigrant's transition to citizenship," columnist Jeff Jacoby asserted. "On the contrary, immigrants are obliged to prove themselves worthy of becoming Americans. How? By getting a job, staying right with the law, by learning the language—and by not becoming a public charge. Any foreigner who can't meet those requirements shouldn't bother coming. If he's already here, he should be sent back."[26]

Legal immigrants typically are sponsored, usually by a family member, sometimes by an employer. The sponsor promises that the newcomer won't become a charge on the public. The pledge, though, has not been redeemed by government agencies. Laws providing for the deportation of welfare-dependent immigrants have not been enforced. According to Brimelow, only 41 immigrants were sent home as public charges from 1961 to 1982. After that, the INS stopped reporting such deportations as a separate category.

For the first time, the 1996 welfare law states, sponsors could be forced to pay back any public benefits given to immigrants under their auspices. The new law also requires government officials to take sponsors' incomes into account

"
Congress in 1996 debated measures that would deport legal immigrants who accepted more than one year's worth of government services during their first five years in the United States.
"

> "'The more recent immigrant waves have less schooling, lower earnings, lower labor force participation, and higher poverty rates than earlier waves had at similar stages of their assimilation into the country.'"

in weighing immigrant applications for assistance.

In the 1992 Gallup poll, nearly two-thirds of respondents said they believed many immigrants wind up on welfare, causing taxes to rise for everyone else. In the 1995 survey of immigrants, only 19 percent acknowledged they had ever taken welfare, food stamps, or Medicaid benefits.

Nevertheless, recent studies suggest newcomers have gradually become more dependent than the native-born on such programs as SSI (Supplemental Social Security for the elderly poor, blind and disabled), and Medicaid. This is partly the consequence of the post-1965 flood of refugees and elderly immigrants joining families settled in the United States. Refugees don't need sponsors and are eligible for federal benefits immediately on landing.

Then, too, a high proportion of new arrivals are ill-equipped to fit into the mainstream American economy. "The more recent immigrant waves have less schooling, lower earnings, lower labor force participation, and higher poverty rates than earlier waves had at similar stages of their assimilation into the country," writes George Borjas, an economist at the University of California at San Diego.[27]

In 1970, according to Borjas, immigrants were slightly less likely to be on welfare than natives. Twenty years later, immigrants were more likely to take government assistance. Only 8.4 percent of heads of households were foreign-born in 1990, but these households accounted for 10 percent of all households on welfare. In California, 21 percent of for-

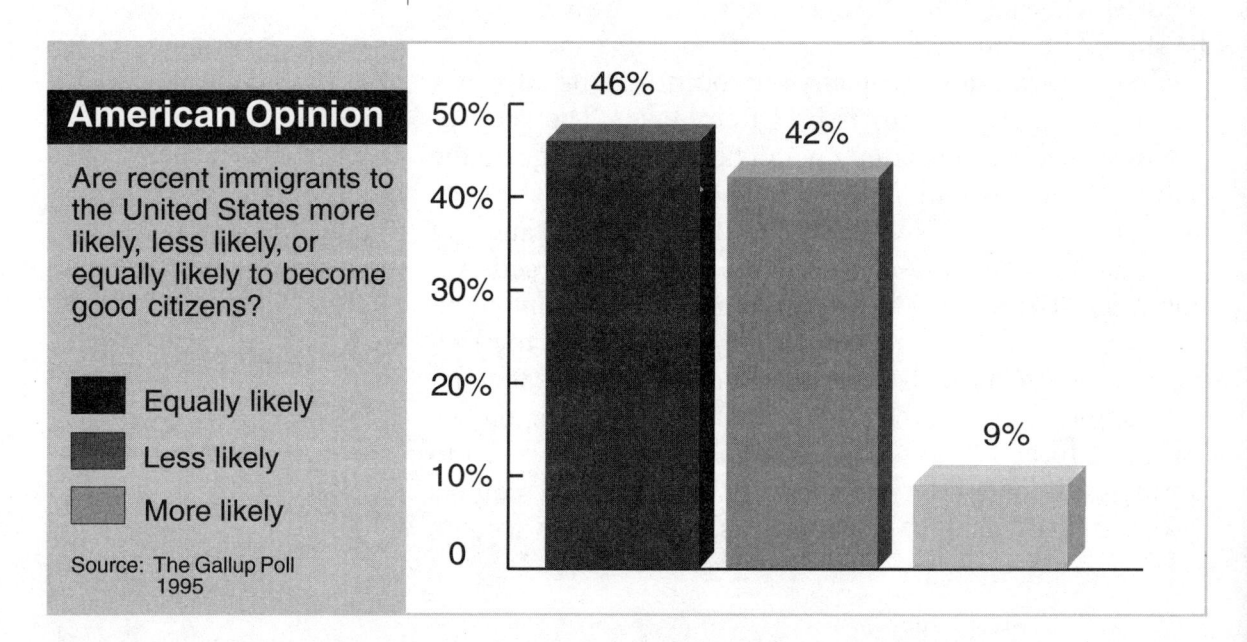

American Opinion

Are recent immigrants to the United States more likely, less likely, or equally likely to become good citizens?

- Equally likely: 46%
- Less likely: 42%
- More likely: 9%

Source: The Gallup Poll 1995

eign-born households accounted for 27 percent of households on welfare.

Some groups, Borjas found, were more likely than others to receive welfare. Four percent or fewer of households of South African, Taiwanese, or British origin were on welfare, compared to 11 percent of Ecuadorian and 12 percent of Mexican households. Borjas also determined that refugees have high rates of welfare participation—25 percent for Vietnamese immigrants and 16 percent each for those from Cuba and the Soviet Union.

An estimated 1.5 million legal newcomers receive some form of federal aid. According to a report from the General Accounting Office, the investigative arm of Congress, 25 percent of elderly SSI recipients are legal immigrants.

"The impact of this introduction to the welfare state seems to be both profound and long-lasting," said Borjas.[28]

Critics of restrictions say a shut-off of federal aid would merely shift the burden to states and localities. California, Texas, and New York would be particularly hard hit. "The immigrants will still get health care," observed Christine Burch of the National Association of Public Hospitals. "But it will be the responsibility of local government or, in the case of private hospitals, it will come out of their charity budgets."[29]

To some, federal assistance programs are the essential means of moving immigrants into the economic mainstream.

"Latinos with green cards are able to move out of pov-

" **An estimated 1.5 million legal newcomers receive some form of federal aid.** "

American Opinion

Should immigration in the United States be halted until the economy improves, should it be reduced, or should it remain the same?

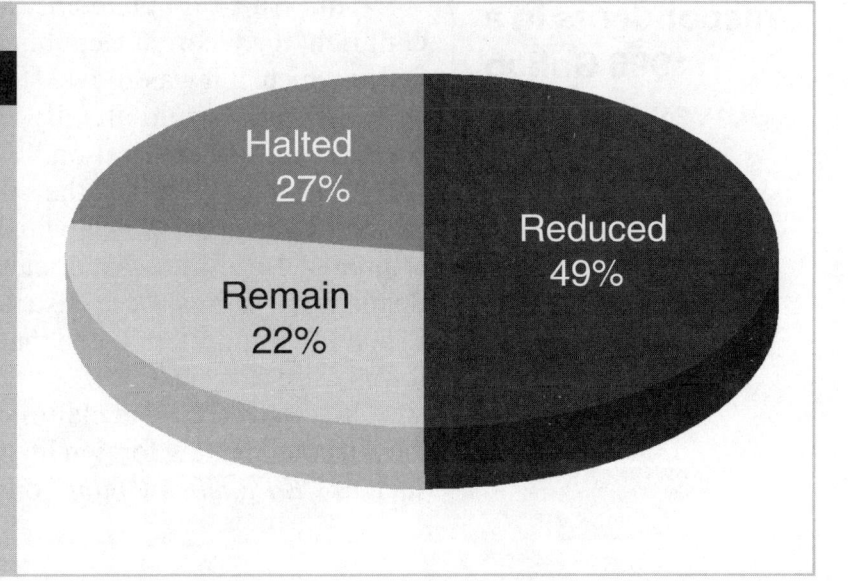

- Halted 27%
- Reduced 49%
- Remain 22%

Source: The Gallup Poll 1993

erty into a higher standard of living, but they can't do it if they can't learn English, if their babies aren't born healthy, if they can't join job training programs, and if they can't go to college," said Lori M. Kaplan, director of the Latin American Youth Center in Washington, D.C.

"This isn't a handout," she went on. "Learning Windows 95 so you can get a decent job is not welfare."[30]

Those who call for a harder line say such programs shouldn't be necessary in the first place.

"We're admitting too many immigrants who are too poor and too poorly educated," said Dan Stein, director of the American Immigration Forum. "It's very difficult to understand why poor immigrants who need all this training should be admitted at all."[31]

The Language Issue

More than eight of every ten respondents in a 1996 Gallup survey said they supported a law making English the official language of the United States. In a vote that divided along partisan lines, the House of Representatives in August 1996 approved such a measure. Republicans were strongly in favor; Democrats were generally opposed.

Proponents said the government had gone too far to accommodate foreigners with documents, ballots, and other material in languages other than English. Ninety-seven percent of Americans speak English; around 1 percent of all government documents are in languages other than English.

"This isn't bilingualism," said House Speaker Newt Gingrich, the Georgia Republican. "This is a level of confusion which, if it was allowed to develop for another twenty or thirty years, would literally lead, I think, to the decay of core parts of our civilization."[32]

Among other things, the bill would prohibit the printing of IRS tax forms in Spanish, the first language of an estimated 14 million Americans. In 1994, some 550,000 Spanish tax forms were distributed, at a cost of around $150,000. Supporters noted that fewer than 1,000 Spanish forms were returned.

They also scoffed at claims opponents put forward that the bill could outlaw foreign literary expressions or latinities such as *"E Pluribus Unum"* on coins.

> "More than eight of every ten respondents in a 1996 Gallup survey said they supported a law making English the official language of the United States."

Beyond the Melting Pot?

The political debate has two edges, both sharp.

One aspect is restrictionist. "We've carried this 'Give me your tired, your poor' to an extreme," said Betty Fine Collins, a Republican activist from Alabama who supports the party's calls for a tough new immigration policy. Opponents of restrictions, mostly Democrats, cite the nation's history of welcoming immigrants, and the strengths that diversity brings.[33]

The other involves a complex, sometimes confused set of attitudes, assumptions, and beliefs about what it means to be an American. Assimilationists argue that it is vitally important to transmit a sense of common history and a set of accepted cultural and political values to immigrants. Otherwise, the nation would gradually come apart.

"Obviously, the future of America can't be sustained if people keep only to their own ways and remain perpetual outsiders," observed the late Allan Bloom, the political philosopher whose book *The Closing of the American Mind* (1987) denounced cultural relativism, which regards all cultures as equal. "The society has got to turn them into Americans. There are natural fears that today's immigrants may be too much of a cultural stretch for a nation based on Western values."[34]

Multiculturalists counter that America is in a constant state of redefinition, that there is nothing sacred or timeless or immutable about the majority culture.

The cultural historian Lawrence Levine answered Bloom in a 1996 book titled, appropriately enough, *The Opening of the American Mind*.

"What I tried to show in this book is that the genius of America has been its ability to renew its essential spirit by admitting a constant infusion of different peoples who demand that the ideals and principles embodied in the Constitution be put into practice," Levine said.[35]

In the multiculturalists' phrase, immigrants should celebrate their diversity. "My grandparents came from Lebanon. I don't identify with the Pilgrims on a personal level," said Donna Shalala, the former University of Wisconsin chancellor now secretary of health and human services in the Clinton administration.[36]

> "**Assimilationists argue that it is vitally important to transmit a sense of common history and a set of accepted cultural and political values to immigrants.**"

As Shalala suggests, the membership list of the Mayflower Society is comparatively short. That misses the point, multiculturalism's critics say. You don't need to be a descendant of a Plymouth Plantation colonist or a First Family of Virginia to qualify for American nationality.

Then, too, conservatives say, multiculturalism is as apt to foster conflict as tolerance under a bright rainbow. On some college campuses, for example, the prevailing emphasis on racial or ethnic identity seems to breed separatism and resentment.

"There are many in my generation who see more of the commonalities and don't cling to this idea of Asian-American," said Lance Izumi, a Japanese American who was a Republican speechwriter and is now a fellow of the Pacific Research Institute in San Francisco. "But how many of these third-generation Vietnamese- and Korean-Americans will feel the same as I do now if they had it beaten into their heads that the majority culture is the enemy?"[37]

A majority of immigrants in Gallup's sample agreed the United States ought to encourage newcomers to give up aspects of their own culture in the cause of assimilation. Twenty-seven percent said immigrants should maintain their home culture; 10 percent believed the United States should encourage both equally.

In 1908, during the height of the Great Wave of "new" immigration, the English-born Zionist playwright Israel Zangwill coined the term "melting pot" to describe the process of becoming an American. Nine decades later, according to Gallup, the great majority of immigrants still respond to the notion. Fully three-quarters agreed the United States remains a melting pot, where people from beyond combine into a unified American culture.

Immigration 143

Notes: Immigration Should America Leave the Welcome Mat Out?

1. "Congressional xenophobia," editorial, *The Boston Globe,* August 21, 1996.
2. Peter Brimelow, *Alien Nation: Common Sense about America's Immigration Disaster* (New York: Random House, 1995), 5.
   Vernon M. Briggs Jr., *Mass Immigration and the National Interest* (Armonk, N.Y.: M.E. Sharpe Inc., 1992), 4.
3. William A. Henry III, "Beyond the Melting Pot," *Time*, April 9, 1990, 28–29.
4. Brimelow, *Alien Nation*, 62–66.
5. Brimelow, *Alien Nation*, xvii.
6. Brimelow, *Alien Nation*, 56.
7. Henry, "Beyond the Melting Pot," 31.
8. Norimitsu Onishi, "New Sense of Race Arises Among Asian Americans," *The New York Times*, June 30, 1996, 1.
9. "The Upside of America's Population Upsurge," *Business Week*, August 9, 1993, 20.
10. Eric Schmitt, "Senate Bars Plans to Cut Immigration to the U.S.," *The New York Times*, April 26, 1996, 26.
11. Briggs, *Mass Immigration*, 3.
12. Otis L. Graham Jr., "Tracing Liberal Woes to '65 Immigration Act," op-ed, *The Christian Science Monitor*, December 28, 1995.
13. Graham, "Tracing Liberal Woes."
14. Joseph R. Guzzardi, op-ed in *The Boston Globe*, June 6, 1996.
15. Brimelow, *Alien Nation*, 80.
16. Lydia Saad, "As Immigrants Tell It," *The Public Perspective*, August/September 1995, 9.
17. Brimelow, *Alien Nation*, 26–27.
18. Tim Golden, "California Governor Acts to End State Aid for Illegal Immigrants," *The New York Times*, August 28, 1996, 1.
19. Scott Armstrong, "California's SOS Initiative Sizzles," *The Christian Science Monitor*, August 23, 1994, 3.
20. Eric Schmitt, "Immigration Overhaul Moves Toward Vote," *The New York Times*, August 2, 1996, 12.
21. Robert Kuttner, "Beating up on immigrants," *The Boston Globe*, Op-ed, June 3, 1996.
22. Celia Dugger, "A Tattered Crackdown on Illegal Workers," *The New York Times*, June 3, 1996, 1.
23. Dugger, "A Tattered Crackdown."
24. Briggs, *Mass Immigration*, 12.
25. Kuttner, "Beating up on immigrants."
26. Jeff Jacoby, "No aid for immigrants," *The Boston Globe*, Op-ed, June 6, 1996.
27. George Borjas, *Friends and Strangers: The Impact of Immigration on the U.S. Economy* (New York: Basic Books, 1990), 20.
28. David R. Francis, "Legal Immigrants Major Welfare Users," *The Christian Science Monitor*, November 29, 1994, 8.

29. Tim Golden, "If Immigrants Lose U.S. Aid, Local Budgets May Feel Pain," *The New York Times*, July 29, 1996, 1.
30. Eric Schmitt, "Provisions on Legal Immigrants Jeopardize Bill on Illegal Aliens," *The New York Times*, May 28, 1996, 1.
31. Schmitt, "Provisions for Legal Immigrants."
32. Eric Schmitt, "House Approves Measure on Official U.S. Language," *The New York Times*, August 2, 1996, 10.
33. Anthony Lewis, "Give me your rich ...," Op-ed, *The New York Times*, August 12, 1996.
34. Henry, "Beyond the Melting Pot," 31.
35. William Honan, "Curriculum and Culture: New Round Is opened in Scholarly Fistfight," *The New York Times*, August 21, 1996, B7.
36. Henry, "Beyond the Melting Pot," 31.
37. Onishi, "New Sense of Race Arises."

Notes: Fortifying the Frontier

1. Howard LaFranchi, "America Puts up Chain Links Along a Once-Friendly Border," *The Christian Science Monitor*, February 13, 1996, 1.

8 Crime and Punishment
Anxiety Up, Crime Down

America's violent world has become measurably less so. For the first time in a decade, crime trends point consistently downward. Experts are uncertain of what the reports presage, or whether the nation may be about to break free of a thirty-year pattern of high crime rates. For now, though, the streets seem safer and people feel a bit more secure.

Overall, violent crime fell 9 percent in 1996. Murder, armed robbery, rape, and other violent crimes were down 14.5 percent in New York City, 4 percent in Los Angeles, and 2 percent in Detroit and Dallas. Even the rate of juvenile crime, soaring upward through the 1980s and early 1990s, fell slightly, and for the second consecutive year.

Gallup Organization surveys reflect the calming influence of the statistics. In a July 1996 poll, 71 percent of Gallup's sample thought, wrongly, that crime had gone up in the United States over the past year. In 1992, though, 89 percent thought the previous twelve months had seen an increase. Nine of every ten in the survey said they felt safe and secure at home at night. And for the first time since 1989, fewer than half, 46 percent, thought crime had increased in their neighborhood.

Still, anxiety about violent crime remains high. Isolated macabre events strike deeper chords than abstract trends, however favorable. "One good solid murder of a baby or a

> **Overall, violent crime fell 9 percent in 1996.**

> "Gallup surveys in 1995 and 1996 placed crime near the top of the list of problems Americans regard as most important."

rape-murder of a seven-year-old girl will outweigh a ton of statistics," remarked Stanford law professor Lawrence M. Friedman, a historian of crime.[1]

Gallup surveys in 1995 and 1996 placed crime near the top of the list of problems Americans regard as most important. On Gallup's 1-to-10 "seriousness index" of September 1995, 81 percent of respondents rated crime an 8 or higher—the highest ranking of any problem, exceeding drug abuse, health care, jobs and the economy, the budget deficit, welfare, and education.

"People have always been concerned about crime," wrote Friedman in his book *Crime and Punishment in American History*. "But there is reason to believe people are more upset about crime today than ever before—more worried, more fearful. They are most afraid of sudden violence or theft by strangers; they feel the cities are jungles; they are afraid to walk the streets at night."[2]

It's Down, but Why?

Two government reports in 1996 documented what crime experts regard as a statistically significant fall in crime rates.

The FBI's annual report showed a 4 percent drop in major crimes in 1995, the fourth consecutive decrease in this index. The report, compiled from police records from around the country, surveys eight serious crimes: murder, rape, robbery, assault, burglary, larceny, car theft, and arson. Of the eight, only one went up: larceny, and that by only 1 percent.

Crime rates were down in every region of the country. Homicides fell 8 percent, with striking decreases in some of America's murder capitals: in New York City, 1,170 killings in 1995, down from 1,561 in 1994; in Detroit, 475 killings, down from 541; in Houston, 316 killings, down from 375.[3]

The second study, the Department of Justice's survey of crime victims, reported a 9 percent overall decrease in violent crime in 1995. Analysts say the two reports combined offer persuasive evidence that America has become, at least temporarily, a safer place.

"The striking thing is not just that there has been a decline but the magnitude of the decline," said criminologist Alfred Blumenstein, of Carnegie Mellon University in Pittsburgh.[4]

Politicians manipulated crime issues for their own purposes in 1996. Bill Clinton attributed the lull to his policies, particularly the 1994 ban on some types of assault weapons and federal funding for 100,000 new police officers. With exceptionally bad timing, Bob Dole's luckless campaign stepped up its accusations of Clinton administration softness on crime just when the press and television were trumpeting some of the most encouraging crime news in years.

To most analysts, crime is a local problem. Federal anticrime efforts are for the most part irrelevant or ineffective. America's legal system assigns primary responsibility for most forms of crime to states and localities. Friedman goes further: "Fluctuations in the crime rate are largely independent of changes in the criminal justice system."[5]

Political obfuscation to one side, crime statistics are tricky to interpret, and crime patterns difficult to discern. And it is all but impossible to accurately measure any single cause for a rise or fall in the crime rate.

In part, demographics explains the decrease. The Baby Boom generation (roughly, those thirty-two to fifty) is aging, and Baby Boomer criminals' most productive years are behind them. Like athletes, violent criminals operate at their peak between the ages of fifteen and thirty-five.

> "Federal anticrime efforts are for the most part irrelevant or ineffective."

American Opinion

Is there more or less crime in the United States than there was a year ago?

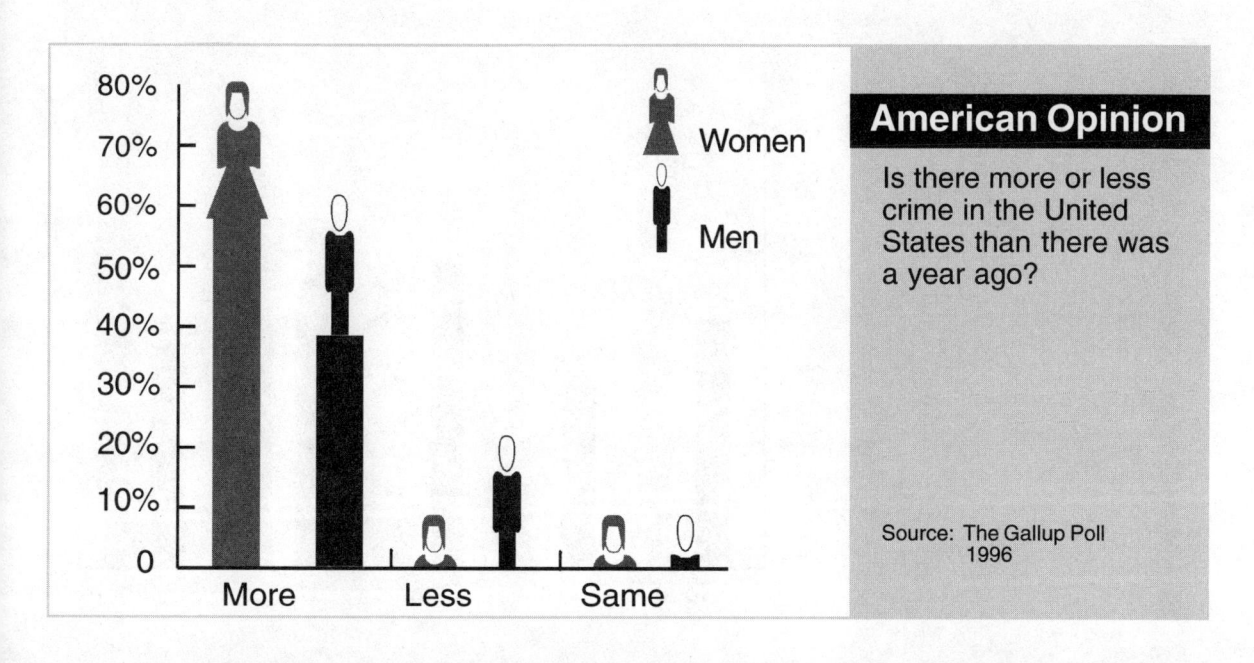

Source: The Gallup Poll 1996

> "**In many cities, more aggressive police tactics have shown results, especially against the drug trade.**"

In many cities, more aggressive police tactics have shown results, especially against the drug trade. Innovative prevention programs and tougher enforcement of gun laws also have had an impact, though it is more difficult to quantify.

And more of the nation's criminals are in prison for longer stretches. The inmate population has tripled since 1980. At the end of 1995, there were 1.6 million men and women in prison or jail—one of every 167 Americans. Another 5.3 million were on probation or parole.

Chances are, the 1994 Clinton crime package has had little or no effect on crime trends. Fewer than a third of the promised 100,000 police officers were hired, trained, and on the beat at the end of 1996. Funding for this key element of the legislation comes slowly, spread over several years, and in small packets. For one example, in September 1996, two years after the bill's passage, Boston received a $3 million grant to hire forty new officers.[6]

"When push comes to shove, nobody has an ability to explain the increases any better than the decreases," observed Franklin E. Zimring, director of the Earl Warren Legal Institute at the University of California at Berkeley. "Criminologists are like weathermen without a satellite. We can only tell you about yesterday's crime rate."[7]

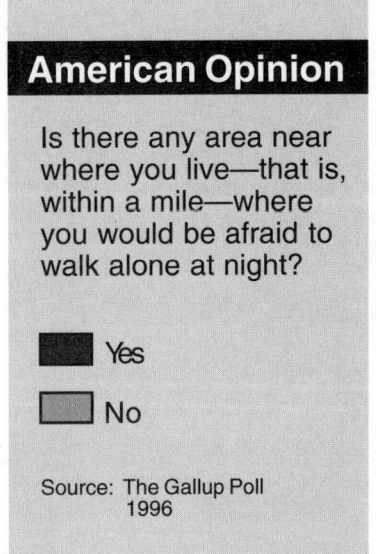

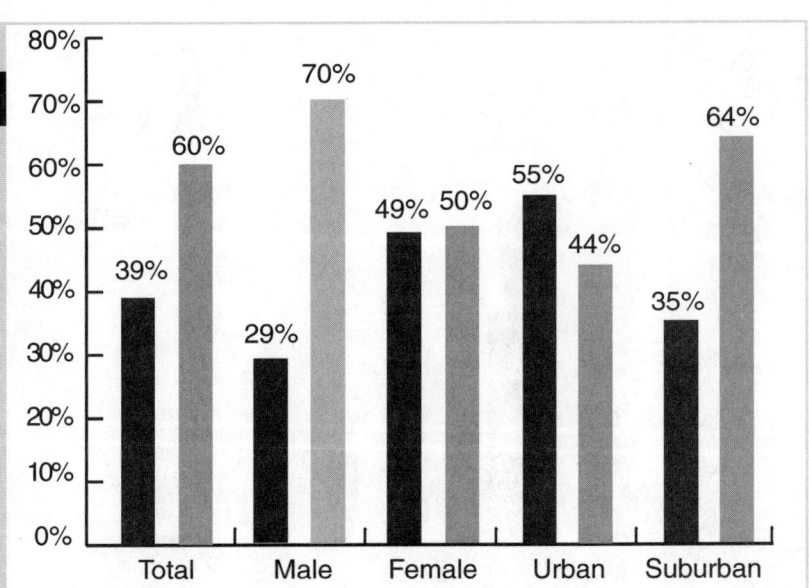

American Opinion

Is there any area near where you live—that is, within a mile—where you would be afraid to walk alone at night?

■ Yes
□ No

Source: The Gallup Poll 1996

	Yes	No
Total	39%	60%
Male	29%	70%
Female	49%	50%
Urban	55%	44%
Suburban	35%	64%

Gallup's Measure

The political debate over crime and crime fighting—Clinton's 1994 package, the Republican congressional response, the 1996 presidential campaign—fastened public attention on the issue as never before.

By Gallup's measure, interest reached historic heights in 1994 and 1995. In surveys between 1976 and 1993, crime rarely graded at the top of Gallup's "most important problem" list for more than 5 or 6 percent of the sample. By June 1994, eight of every ten were telling polltakers they regarded crime as "a very serious threat to Americans' rights and freedoms." Two months later, as Congress debated the Clinton crime measure, 52 percent ranked crime as America's most important problem.

In January 1995, after the president signed the crime bill into law and memories of the debate had faded, only 27 percent put crime at the head of the list. Even so, Americans' concern about crime remained at levels five or six times greater than the historical norm.

Women, the surveys suggested, are more fearful of crime than men. Nearly half of the women, 49 percent, in a 1996 poll thought crime had increased in their area; 42 percent of men thought so. Again, more women (49 percent) than men (29 percent) said there were areas close to home—within a mile—where they would be afraid to walk alone at night.

> "**Women, the surveys suggested, are more fearful of crime than men.**"

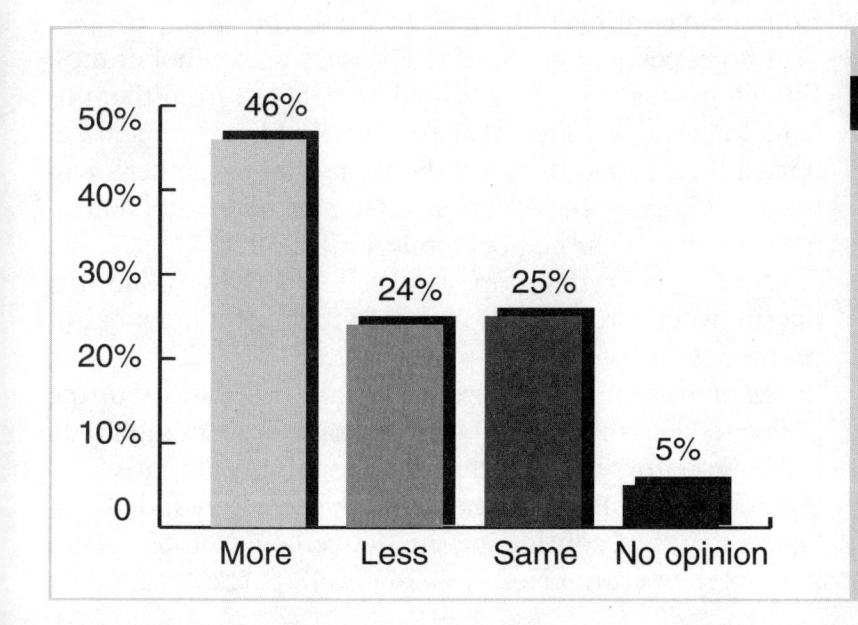

American Opinion

Is there more or less crime in your area than there was a year ago?

Response	Percent
More	46%
Less	24%
Same	25%
No opinion	5%

Source: The Gallup Poll 1996

American Opinion	Is there more or less crime in your area than there was a year ago?*		
Breakdown by Population Groups	More	Less	Same
GENDER			
Male	42%	26%	27%
Female	49%	22%	23%
RACE			
White	46%	23%	26%
Black	46%	29%	19%
REGION			
East	40%	31%	25%
West	51%	25%	20%
POLITICS			
Republican	51%	20%	24%
Democrat	41%	28%	25%

* "No Opinion" Omitted   Source: The Gallup Poll, 1996

Small percentages of respondents told Gallup they had been the victims of major crimes during the previous year. Four percent said they had been physically or sexually assaulted or mugged; 4 percent said their house or apartment had been burgled; 1 percent said money had been stolen from them by force or by threat of force.

Larger percentages reported brushes with minor crimes. Fifteen percent said money had been taken from them or from another member of their household; 18 percent reported their property or another household member's had been vandalized; 14 percent said their car or another household member's car had been burglarized.

Adding everything up, a July 1995 survey found that one in every three adults was the victim of a personal or property crime within the previous year.

Many respondents were skeptical of the ability of the police to keep their neighborhoods safe, even though they hold law-enforcement authorities in high esteem. In a September 1995 poll, just half said they had a "great deal" or "quite a lot" of confidence the police could protect them from violent crime. Nearly as many, 48 percent, said they

Crime and Americans: The Victims

Within the past 12 months:	Has Happened	Has Not Happened
Has money or property been taken from you personally by physical force or by threat of force?	1%	99%
Has your house or apartment been broken into?	4%	96%
Has a car been stolen from you or other household members?	4%	96%
Have you been personally assualted physically, mugged or sexually assaulted?	4%	96%
Has a car owned by you or other household members been broken into?	14%	86%
Has money or property been stolen from you or other household members?	15%	85%
Has property belonging to you or other household members been vandalized?	18%	85%

Source: The Gallup Poll, 1996

had "not very much" confidence or "none at all."

The Next Generation of Criminals

Juvenile violent crime fell slightly overall in 1995, and the juvenile homicide rate dropped for the second straight year. Nevertheless, the long-term trend is ominous. According to a 1995 Justice Department report, the arrest rate for children ten to seventeen shot up 100 percent between 1983 and 1992. Juvenile homicides involving handguns increased fivefold between 1984 and 1993.

Demographers project that the population of teenagers will rise 1 percent a year for the next fifteen years. The surveys, Attorney General Janet Reno said in 1995, are thus "a road map to the next generation of crime." Some 2.7 million juveniles were arrested in 1994. Males twelve to twenty-four make up 8 percent of the population. But they account for a quarter of all homicide victims and nearly half of all murderers.[8]

Still more recent reports suggest that programs to deter juvenile crime may be having some impact. Boston and New York City, for example, have launched aggressive programs to take guns out of the hands of juveniles. The 1995 report, issued in mid-1996, showed violent crimes by young people down by 2.9 percent.

In one social worker's view, the cumulative horrific effects of violent crime and punishment may finally be making a lasting impression on the young. "I think some of the glamour of being a thug, of walking around with a gun, is being removed, because people thirteen, fourteen, and fifteen years old have seen so many of their friends or relatives being killed or going to prison," said Geoffrey Canada, who heads a school and neighborhood program for New York City youth.[9]

Rising juvenile crime has prompted most states to overhaul their juvenile justice systems. More child criminals are being tried in adult courts, where they receive longer sentences and serve them under harsher conditions.

Gallup surveys show strong support for tougher penalties for juvenile offenders. In a 1994 poll, 60 percent favored the death sentence for child murderers. (In 1957, only 11 percent favored execution for juvenile killers.) Half the

> "More recent reports suggest that programs to deter juvenile crime may be having some impact."

sample said first-time juvenile offenders should face the same punishment as adult first-timers. And 80 percent said repeat juvenile criminals should be dealt with as harshly as adult repeaters. Only around a third said there should be more emphasis on rehabilitating rather than punishing young criminals.

English common law traditionally held that children younger than seven could not be charged with a crime, and that children seven to fourteen were protected by a "presumption of infancy"—the notion that there can be no criminal intent in the young.

This view has governed approaches to older child criminals. The reformer Jane Addams established the first juvenile court in Chicago, in 1899. Proceedings were confidential, punishments discretionary. The guiding principle was that children could be reformed, rehabilitated, and set on a law-respecting course to adulthood.

With the juvenile crime epidemic, that principle has been abandoned in many states. "The thinking behind the juvenile court, that everything has to be done in the best interest of the child, is from a bygone era," said Patricia L. West, director of the Virginia Department of Juvenile Justice.[10] Virginia and other states now require accused killers fourteen and older to be tried as adults. Other laws expand judges' authority to transfer juveniles to adult court for armed robbery, burglary, and other serious crimes.

Critics say such responses ignore what they contend are the underlying causes of juvenile crime—poverty, fractured families, lack of opportunity. They say treating child criminals as grown-ups merely lowers the age of adulthood. It does nothing to correct the failures of society that create young felons. Critics note, too, that violent child criminals do not automatically grow into repeat felons, and that their cases should thus be treated with subtlety. "You've got hardcore fourteen-year-olds and seventeen-year-olds that would never do this again. Discretion is what judges are paid to exercise," said David Kopel, an expert on violence with the Independence Institute of Golden, Colorado.[11]

More often, the authorities respond to the epidemic by meeting violent crime with harsh punishment. California now prosecutes as adults three-quarters of teenagers charged with murder.

"
California now prosecutes as adults three-quarters of teenagers charged with murder.
"

"I'm not interested in legislating out childhood," said Los Angeles County District Attorney Gil Garcetti. "My concern is that juvenile crime has been rising unacceptably fast, and kids learn they can get away with it because there is no real punishment for the first few crimes."[12]

No one can say with certainty if tougher approaches deter juvenile crime. "Jailing youths with adult felons under spartan conditions will merely produce more street gladiators," criminologist John DiIulio Jr. predicts.[13] He and others argue that the problem begins in childhood. Children who suffer from neglect and abuse are far more likely to become delinquent. For many at-risk children, the answer is a responsible adult presence for protection, supervision, and guidance.

Florida tried 7,000 youths in adult courts in 1995, more than all other states combined. A preliminary study found youths punished as adults there had higher rates of relapse,

American Opinion

Most Americans favor giving juvenile offenders the same punishment as that given to adult offenders, no matter what the crime.

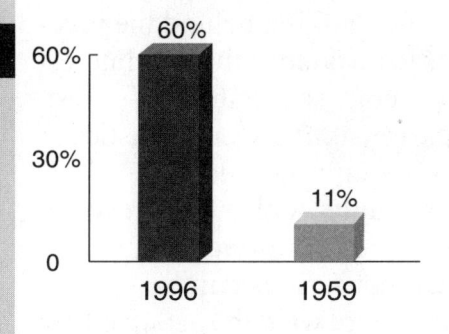

Source: The Gallup Poll 1959, 1996

Respondents favoring the death sentence for juvenile murderers.
- 1996: 60%
- 1959: 11%

Respondents who feel first-time juvenile offenders should receive the same punishment as adult first-time offenders.
- Yes: 80%
- No: 20%

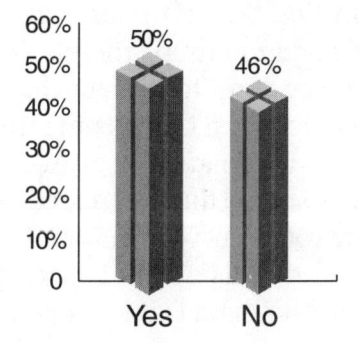

Should repeat juvenile criminals be dealt with as harshly as adult repeat offenders?
- Yes: 50%
- No: 46%

with more serious crimes, than teens who served time in juvenile institutions.

Some Programs That Work

In some big cities, gun control and curfew programs appear to have reduced juvenile crime.

In Boston, a pilot program tracks black-market gun sales to children. (It is illegal under federal law and in most states to sell handguns to juveniles.) Coupled with aggressive police tactics, the computer tracking program scored a remarkable initial success: no young people in Boston were killed by gunfire during the first six months of 1996.[14]

In a Clinton administration initiative, police chiefs and prosecutors from Boston and sixteen other cities agreed to provide information on every gun they seize from a juvenile. The data are fed into a Bureau of Alcohol, Tobacco and Firearms computer. Gun sellers, when identified, are prosecuted.

"This allows us to isolate the small number of dealers who are a faucet of firearms to minors," said James Alan Fox, a criminologist at Northeastern University in Boston. "We will never become a gun-free America for kids, but that doesn't mean we shouldn't try."[15]

In New York City, authorities traced 4,000 seized guns to one store in Alabama. Thirty-five people were arrested for importing the handguns into the city and selling them there, according to the ATF.

Curfew programs for teens appear to be working in several cities. They are politically popular, too; both Clinton and Dole called for teen curfews during the 1996 campaign. Still, analysts suggest they are at best a short-term solution, and that they tend to miss the mark anyway because most juvenile crime occurs after school, from 3 to 6 P.M. "The problem with curfew laws is that most kids, the good, the bad, and the tired, are asleep at midnight," notes Fox.[16]

The Justice Department says some form of curfew is in effect in 150 or so of America's 200 largest cities. Dallas, in May 1994, imposed a curfew for all children seventeen and younger. The Dallas police say violent juvenile crime there is down 30 percent.

"These figures tell us that the curfew works," police

> **The Justice Department says some form of curfew is in effect in 150 or so of America's 200 largest cities.**

Fewer Claim Gun Ownership

A Gallup survey in 1996 suggests that gun possession in America may be on the decline. Either that, or poll respondents have become reluctant to admit they keep firearms at home.

"Do you have a gun in your home?" Gallup asked in July 1996. Thirty-eight percent of the sample answered yes, down from 51 percent in 1993, the highest figure Gallup has recorded. A clear majority of the 1996 sample, 60 percent, answered no.

From 1959 until 1996, affirmative replies held fairly steady, averaging out in the mid-40s, with a low of 40 percent in 1983.

Ten percent of the 1996 respondents who owned guns claimed membership in the National Rifle Association, which aggressively opposes new restrictions on firearms.

The NRA waged a highly visible and often roughhouse campaign against government gun regulations in 1994 and 1995. The lobby opposed the Clinton administration's 1994 ban on some types of assault weapons and threatened to "clean Clinton's clock" at the polls in 1996. And gun lobbyists launched scathing attacks on federal police agencies, culminating in a widely publicized NRA fund raising letter that characterized Bureau of Alcohol, Tobacco and Firearms agents as "jackbooted government thugs."

The NRA failed to overturn the assault-weapons ban, not surprising in light of opinion surveys that showed overwhelming support for the measure. And the lobby substantially toned down its overheated rhetoric in 1996.

In the 1996 survey, around a third of gun owners, 35 percent, said the NRA reflects their views about guns always or most of the time. Another third told Gallup the lobby sometimes reflects their views. Twenty-two percent said the NRA never spoke for them.

---

spokesman Jim Chandler said. "Fewer kids on the streets mean fewer crimes and fewer victims."[17]

The American Civil Liberties Union has challenged curfews as a violation of children's freedom of speech and assembly. The courts, however, have generally upheld curfew ordinances.

Guns, Police, and Prisons

There are no solutions to crime, only more or less effective strategies for containing it. During the 1990s, the most insistent voices have called for deterrence and punishment: more police, tougher laws, longer sentences, more prisons.

Opinion seems to favor the sterner approach. Gallup surveys have tracked rising support for the death penalty, more spending on police and prisons, longer sentences for repeat felons, and other tough crime-control measures.

Gallup samples also strongly support two 1994 gun-control measures, the assault-weapons ban and the Brady Law, which requires background checks for gun purchases and a five-day wait for a permit. In a 1995 survey, respondents thought America's gun laws should be even further strengthened.

The United States already has more firearms laws than any other country, and more firearms, too—an estimated 220 million guns of all types in citizens' hands, according to the ATF. Firearms claim 35,000 lives a year by design or accident. Guns are used in two-thirds of all homicides in the United States.[18]

In Massachusetts, state officials tried in 1996 to use the state's consumer protection laws to ban the sale of the cheap, often defective handguns known as "Saturday night specials." A joint Boston Police-ATF study found that these handguns account for seven of every ten firearms traced in U.S. crimes.[19]

A new Texas law, on the other hand, seems to encourage citizens to rove about armed. The measure, which took effect in January 1996, allows Texans to carry concealed weapons, the better to defend themselves against criminals. Other states are considering similar legislation, with a strong prod from the National Rifle Association, the powerful gun lobby that opposes almost all restrictions on firearms. Advocate Jim Wilson summarized the argument for concealed weapons in the magazine *Shooting Times*:

"An armed society is a polite society," wrote Wilson. Gun owners "treat others with respect, tolerance, and consideration. And they expect to be treated the same way in return. The handguns that they pack are for those who just don't get the message until they look down the gun bore and get a glimpse of those pearly gates."[20]

Initial studies suggested the 1994 Brady law denied gun permits to at least 45,000 felons in its first year. Presumably, the law prevented at least some crimes those felons might have committed.[21] In the short term, though, police, courts, and prisons probably have had a greater impact on crime rates.

In New York City, beat cops began to take greater notice of minor crimes, on the theory that major crime sus-

> **"The United States already has more firearms laws than any other country."**

> "Along with Russia, America has the highest incarceration rate in the world."

pects would be caught in the net. The city's falling murder rate suggests these tactics may be paying off. During the first six months of 1996, in fact, no murders were reported in Central Park.

New York police also targeted the drug trade in 1996. A few hundred drug organizations are suspected of causing most of the city's crime. Disrupt those organizations, police believed, and crime rates would go down.

The department assigned 1,200 additional officers in 1996 to high-crime neighborhoods in Manhattan, Brooklyn, and the Bronx. Federal authorities, patrol officers, detectives, and narcotics investigators worked in teams to break up neighborhood drug organizations, attacking middle- and upper-level dealers together with the usual street-level suspects.

The police claimed dramatic results, though they expected many bankrupt dealers to reorganize eventually and reappear in new locales. "Drug organizations are like cockroaches," Police Commissioner Howard Safir said. "We need to spray them constantly." In a few months, police identified and put out of business more than fifty drug organizations. Not coincidentally, crime rates in the fourteen target precincts fell 20 percent in the first half of 1996, close to double the overall rate of decline.[22]

One consequence of the war on drugs, in New York City and elsewhere, is a sharp upward spike in America's prison population. Along with Russia, America has the highest incarceration rate in the world.

As a Matter of Fact

This question, asked of those who said they own at least one gun, shows that the majority of American gun owners have more than one gun in their homes.

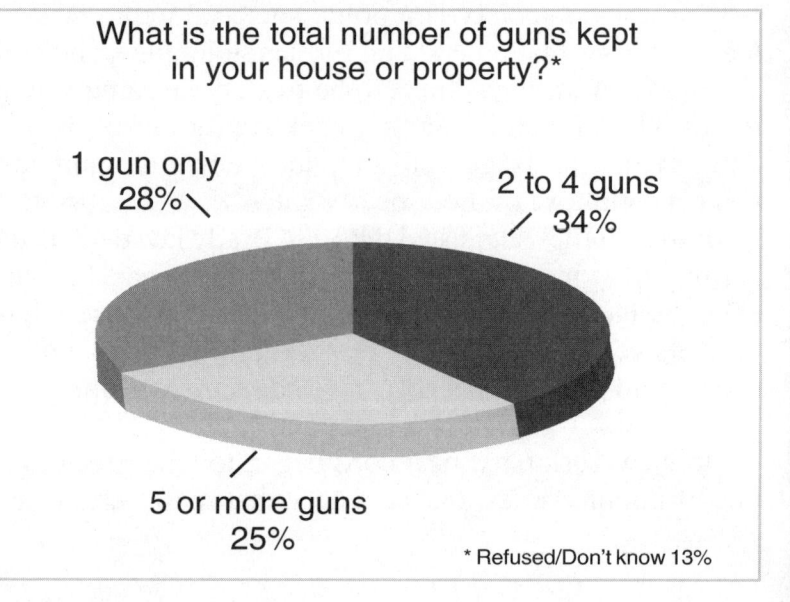

Source: The Gallup Poll 1996

What is the total number of guns kept in your house or property?*

- 1 gun only: 28%
- 2 to 4 guns: 34%
- 5 or more guns: 25%

* Refused/Don't know 13%

Jails and prisons serve four purposes: incapacitation, deterrence, retribution or expiation, and reformation. Obviously, an imprisoned felon can do little or no harm to anyone on the outside. Experts disagree on prison's deterrent effect; most believe the threat of punishment has scant influence on criminal behavior. Clearly prisons satisfy society's urge for retribution. They are unpleasant places in which to be shut up for ten years or so. As for reformation, few would argue that prisons turn out improved citizens, or even comparatively docile ones. "It is hard to train for freedom in a cage," prison historians Norval Morris and David J. Rothman write.[23]

At $40 billion to $50 billion a year, prisons and jails are massively expensive to operate. Estimates for keeping one felon behind bars for a year range from $25,000 to $33,000. For the first time, California in 1996 spent more to build and run prisons than it spent on its public university system.

Is punishment or rehabilitation more cost-effective? "The real question is where will you produce the most crime reduction for a dollar spent," Urban Institute analyst Jeffrey Roth said. "This is not a liberal-versus-conservative question. It is a bang-for-your-buck question." Some studies suggest prisons, though expensive, may yield a net savings from crimes averted. Other surveys project savings in preventing "high-risk" young people from becoming career criminals—$1.5 million to $2 million a year, according to one.[24]

Gallup surveys generally suggest a preference for crime prevention over deterrence, though support for social solutions has fallen in recent years. In an August 1994 poll, a bare majority, 51 percent, favored spending on social and economic programs over spending on prisons and law enforcement. Only a few years earlier, though, two-thirds favored the social approach. The opinion trend is in line with 1990s policy on crime and punishment.

"We send people to prison at a faster clip than any serious country on earth," writes commentator David Nyhan. "The cost has doubled in just five years, to $1 billion a week. Average cost per inmate per year in the jug? Try $33,334.

"Today we are giving the equivalent of a $33,000 scholarship to more than 1.5 million of the worst types of people. We cut back on teachers, welfare, medical care for the poor.

> **Estimates for keeping one felon behind bars for a year range from $25,000 to $33,000.**

> "In roughly half the states with three-strikes laws, prosecutors have obtained only a handful of convictions."

We lay off doctors and nurses, social workers, and counselors. But we hire prison guards to beat the band."[25]

Three Strikes

State and federal three-strikes laws aim not to deter but to punish, and to remove career criminals permanently from circulation. In late 1996, some twenty-four states had repeat-offender laws on the books.

Critics say such laws are cosmetic, costly, and discriminatory. More often than not, they are used against middle-aged criminals who are nearing the end of their violent lives. One study estimated the federal three-strikes law would cost the government an additional $700,000 over the lifetime of each prisoner older than fifty. And three-strikes laws fall most heavily on poor people, who are unable to afford a high-quality legal defense.

"You have to ask yourself, 'Where is three strikes coming from?' If you had a great demand for it from prosecutors and judges, that would be one thing," said University of Wisconsin law professor Walter Dickey, author of the first national study of three-strikes effects. "But when the people pressing for it are mostly politicians, that tells me it's driven by political opportunity and emotion."[26]

Three-strikes statutes have been rarely used, two 1996 studies showed, and have had only a marginal influence on crime rates. In roughly half the states with three-strikes laws, prosecutors have obtained only a handful of convictions. In part this is because many states have long imposed stiffer penalties for career felons. Massachusetts, for example, has had a repeat-offender law since the 1870s. On the federal level, prosecutors have rarely found occasion to use the 1994 three-strikes law. As of September 1996, only nine career criminals had been sentenced under it.

The exception is California. There an estimated 17,000 felons have been sentenced under the repeat offender law, and the authorities say the crime rate is falling as a result. California's crime index has dropped 13 percent since the law went onto the books in 1994, according to Governor Pete Wilson's office.

Most of the sentences—some 14,000—were actually second-strike offenses, though, in which the usual term is

Fighting Terror

The Clinton administration pressed for new, tougher antiterror legislation in the aftermath of the Oklahoma City bombing in April 1995. One year later, Congress passed the Antiterrorism and Effective Death Penalty Act, which authorized $1 billion to fight terror in the United States.

Intensive lobbying from an unlikely coalition of civil libertarians and gun advocates stripped the final bill of two key provisions: expanded federal wiretapping authority and a requirement for chemical markers in the most common types of explosives.

The National Rifle Association led the fight against the chemical markers, called taggants, that make explosives easier to trace after a blast. NRA lobbyists argued that the markers would make explosives unstable and therefore dangerous—a claim that a history of safe and effective use in Switzerland belies. Mandatory use of taggants has helped Swiss police solve more than 500 explosives cases since 1985.[1]

The Clinton White House proposed another round of actions against terror after the unexplained explosion and crash of a TWA jetliner and the Atlanta Olympics bombing in July 1996. The plan sought an additional $1 billion for airline and airport security and other measures, including an updated study of chemical taggants for explosives.

Gallup surveys suggest Americans are skeptical of the government's ability to counter terrorism. And in polling in the wake of the Oklahoma City attack, the great majority—83 percent—said they planned no change in their habits or activities to reduce their chances of becoming a victim of terror.

---

doubled. And of the third-strike sentences, 85 percent were for nonviolent crimes, according to Dickey's study for the Campaign for an Effective Crime Policy, a national coalition of criminal justice officials.

California prosecutors, wary of court challenges, were reluctant from the start to file third-strike charges, which carry an automatic sentence of twenty-five years to life. And in fact a June 1996 state Supreme Court ruling restored to judges the discretionary authority to disregard previous convictions and impose lesser terms.[27]

Unlike California's, Washington State's three-strikes law—the nation's first, approved in 1993—targets certain violent crimes: murder, armed robbery, rape, kidnapping. Each strike must fall into one of those categories of violent felonies. The law has been applied only fifty-three times. And Washington authorities have been modest about making claims for the law's effectiveness as a deterrent. "Crimi-

> "Opinion in recent years has flowed strongly toward support for the death penalty."

nals don't think about what kind of punishment they are going to get before they act," observed Chase Riveland, secretary of the state's Department of Corrections. "I don't get a lot of rational people coming in here."[28]

The Death Penalty

Opinion in recent years has flowed strongly toward support for the death penalty. In 1936, a Gallup survey found 62 percent of respondents favored capital punishment for killers. By 1966, support had declined to 42 percent. Over the next three decades, though, sentiment for the death penalty rose with the crime rate. In a 1995 poll, more than three-quarters, 77 percent, favored the death penalty for murderers.

Support for capital punishment is strong and steady across gender, age, education, and income groups, according to Gallup. Whites, however, are more likely to favor the death penalty than blacks and other minorities; Republicans and independents are more strongly in favor than Democrats. A majority of respondents believe the death penalty should be extended to crimes other than murder. And most say they would continue to support capital punishment even if they knew for certain that some wrongly accused defendants would die.

In *Furman v. Georgia* in 1972, the U.S. Supreme Court invalidated every death penalty law in the United States.

American Opinion

Support for the death penalty has reached its highest level in sixty years. By 1996, over three-quarters of Americans supported the death penalty for murder.

Source: The Gallup Poll 1936, 1966, 1996

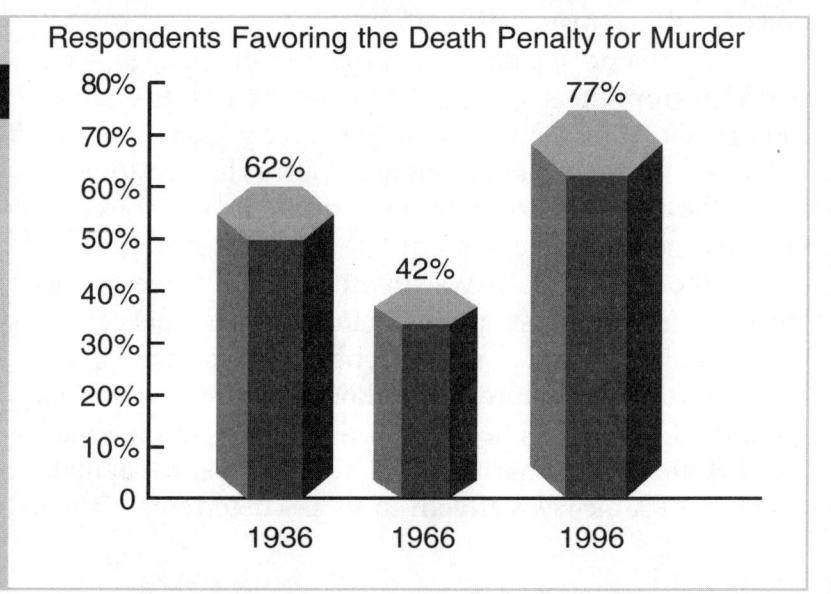

Respondents Favoring the Death Penalty for Murder

Year	Percent
1936	62%
1966	42%
1996	77%

Almost overnight, Georgia and other states wrote new legislation to meet the court's constitutional tests. The high court eventually accepted a redrawn Georgia statute that obligated judges to consider aggravating circumstances, such as premeditation or a prior murder conviction, and mitigating circumstances, such as mental problems or the influence of alcohol or drugs, before passing a capital sentence.

The Georgia law inaugurated an era of seemingly endless appeals from America's death rows. Retrials, appeals, writs of *habeas corpus*, stays, and other legal maneuvers extended the average wait between condemnation and execution to nearly eight years. California reinstated the death penalty in 1977 but provided no work for the state's executioner until 1992.

A June 1996 Supreme Court ruling in another Georgia case may speed the journey from death row to the execution room. The court rejected a Georgia inmate's claim that a new federal law designed to curb frivolous and expensive appeals eroded the judiciary's authority. The ruling brings judgment day closer for 3,000 convicted killers on U.S. death rows.[29]

The Anti-terrorism and Effective Death Penalty Act of 1996 restricted death row inmates' ability to file *habeas corpus* petitions. It gave convicts only one year in which to file such appeals, and it limited them to one appeal. Inmates rebuffed on the first try must now obtain permission from a three-judge panel to proceed with further appeals.

The new law doubtless will curb the costs of capital punishment. Still, whatever its merits as a deterrent, the death penalty is unlikely ever to be a bargain. Even life in prison may be cheaper. In a 1993 study of North Carolina murder trials, Philip J. Cook and Donna B. Slawson found that it cost double the amount to try, convict, sentence, and execute a killer as to secure a first-degree murder conviction with a prison term of twenty years to life.

"Common sense says that it's cheaper to supply a few jolts of electricity than to shell out the equivalent of tuition at Harvard for incarceration for the next twenty years," Cook and Slawson wrote. "But when all the costs are weighed, just the opposite is true."[30]

In the end, for most supporters of the death penalty, eye-

> "A June 1996 Supreme Court ruling in another Georgia case may speed the journey from death row to the execution room."

for-an-eye justice is more important than cost or even deterrence. "I don't look at it as a money saver or money waster or whatever," New York state legislator Anthony S. Seminerio said. "I don't care if it costs more. I don't care, as long as the guy pays with his life."[31]

Crime Around the Corner

Given the trends, it seemed surprising that the Republican presidential challenger fastened on the crime issue during the post–Labor Day stages of the 1996 campaign. Clinton parried Dole's attacks with FBI reports of falling crime rates and with claims, sometimes exaggerated, for the effectiveness of his 1994 anticrime and gun-control legislation. Throughout 1996, Clinton outscored Dole on crime issues in Gallup's samples.

All the same, part of the rationale for Dole's approach lies in the trend of opinion on crime. In politics, perception and reality are not always aligned. As Lawrence Friedman noted, one grisly murder overreported on the local TV news trumps sheaves of government statistics.

Tellingly, Gallup respondents consistently see crime as a greater problem elsewhere than in their own neighborhoods. In the face of three years of reported crime decreases, more than seven in every ten in the 1996 sample still thought crime was worsening in the United States. But fewer than half believed that to be the case at home. "Drugs and crime are sort of good-weather concerns in American politics," the criminologist Franklin Zimring observed. "Violence around the corner is something we always have to worry about when we don't have any more pressing problems in the immediate vicinity."[32]

Notes: Crime and Punishment Anxiety Up, Crime Down

1. Tim Golden, "Crime Rates May Be Down, but the Problem Stays Hot with Politicians, and Voters, *The New York Times*, September 22, 1996, 26.
2. Lawrence M. Friedman, *Crime and Punishment in American History* (New York: Basic Books, 1993), x.
3. Fox Butterfield, "Major Crimes Fell in '95, Early Data by FBI Indicate," *The New York Times*, May 6, 1996, 1.
4. Fox Butterfield, "A Large Drop in Violent Crime Is Reported," *The New York Times*, September 18, 1996, 14.
5. Butterfield, "Major Crimes Fell in '95."
6. Meg Vaillancourt, "Boston to get U.S. funds for 40 officers," *The Boston Globe*, September 25, 1996, A9.
7. Butterfield, "Major Crimes Fell in '95."
8. Fox Butterfield, "Grim Forecast Is Offered on Rising Juvenile Crime," *The New York Times*, September 8, 1995, 16.
   John DiIulio Jr., "Stop Crime Where It Starts," op-ed, *The New York Times*, July 23, 1996.
9. Fox Butterfield, "After 10 Years, Juvenile Crime Begins to Drop," *The New York Times*, August 9, 1996, 1.
10. Fox Butterfield, "States Revamping Laws on Juveniles as Felonies Soar," *The New York Times*, May 12, 1996, 1.
11. Robert Marquand, "Justice Trend: Violent Teens Get Their Day in Adult Court," *The Christian Science Monitor*, February 14, 1996, 1.
12. Butterfield, "States Revamping Laws on Juveniles."
13. DiIulio, "Stop Crime Where It Starts."
14. Scott Baldauf and Christina Nifong, "Cities to Track Guns in Youth-Crime Fight," *The Christian Science Monitor*, July 9, 1996, 3.
15. Baldauf and Nifong, "Cities to Track Guns."
16. Fox Butterfield, "Success Reported for Curfews, but Doubts Persist," *The New York Times*, June 3, 1996, 1.
17. Butterfield, "Successes Reported for Curfews."
18. Franklin E. Zimring and Gordon Hawkins, *The Citizen's Guide to Gun Control* (New York: Macmillan, 1992), 146.
19. "Better Gun Control," *The Christian Science Monitor*, August 22, 1996, 20.
20. Sam Howe Verhovek, "Why Not Unconcealed Guns?," *The New York Times*, The Week in Review, September 3, 1995, 1.
21. Fox Butterfield, "Handgun Laws Deter Felons, Studies Show," *The New York Times*, March 12, 1995, 23.
22. Clifford Krauss, "As Police Hit Drug Rings, Neighbors See the Results," *The New York Times*, August 26, 1996, 1.
23. Norval Morris and David J. Rothman, eds., *The Oxford History of the Prison: The Practice of Punishment in Western Society* (New York: Oxford University Press, 1995), x.

24. Fox Butterfield, "Prison: Where the Money Is," *The New York Times*, The Week in Review, June 2, 1996, 16.
25. David Nyhan, "Our lock-'em-up attitude is breaking the bank," op-ed, *The Boston Globe*, July 12, 1996.
26. William Claiborne, "California Only State Applying `Three Strikes' Law Extensively," *The Washington Post*, September 10, 1996, A3.
27. Adam Pertman, "Ruling deals blow to 3-strikes law," *The Boston Globe*, June 21, 1996, A3.
28. Fox Butterfield, "Three Strikes Rarely Invoked in Courtrooms," *The New York Times*, September 10, 1996, 1.
29. Richard Carelli, "Justices uphold limit to death row appeals," Associated Press report in *The Boston Globe*, June 29, 1996, 1.
30. Sam Howe Verhovek, "Across the U.S., Executions Are Neither Swift Nor Cheap," *The New York Times*, February 22, 1995, 1.
31. Verhovek, "Across the U.S."
32. Golden, "Crime Rate May Be Down, but the Problem Stays Hot."

Notes: Fighting Terror

1. Michael Kramer, "Without a Clue," *Time*, August 12, 1996, 27.

Welfare Reform
9 Will It Break the Dependency Cycle?

A flourish of the presidential pen ended the sixty-year guarantee of aid for America's poor in 1996. With the signing of the Personal Responsibility and Work Opportunity Act, the nation crossed into unfamiliar, potentially hostile social territory, hoping that enough jobs could be found to get millions of Americans off welfare and onto payrolls.

The law, in President Clinton's words, aims to "make welfare what it was meant to be: a second chance, not a way of life." It replaces the main federal cash-assistance program, Aid to Families with Dependent Children, with block grants the states are to spend largely as they choose. The states will need to spend cleverly, for federal welfare aid levels are to fall by $55 billion over six years.[1]

AFDC delivered monthly cash benefits to 12.8 million people in 1996, more than 8 million of them children. The new law requires most of the 4.4 million adults on welfare, most of them single women, to find work within two years and places a lifetime five-year limit on public assistance.

The states are supposed to have their new welfare plans in place by July 1, 1997. By the end of 1996, more than half had submitted their proposals for Washington's approval. The overhaul will be carried out in slow motion, in stages over several years, and no sudden disruptions are likely. Advocates of the poor are challenging some of the law's allegedly punitive aspects and future legislation will probably amend it in some details. In fact, the administration in late

> "AFDC delivered monthly cash benefits to 12.8 million people in 1996, more than 8 million of them children."

> "One in every four children 12 or younger is hungry or on the edge of hunger."

1996 said it would try to restore around a quarter of the $55 billion spending cut. All the same, the new system breaks sharply with the past.

"The nation is embarking on a vast domestic social experiment," *Newsweek's* Jonathan Alter wrote. "The new law is not conservative; it's radical. It throws the dice on the future without knowing the consequences."[2]

Work or the Streets?

The law's champions see 2 million Americans moving from the spiritual narcotic of the dole to the dignity of work. They see a historic opportunity to disrupt the numbing cycle of poverty and dependency and to strengthen families.

A Congressional Budget Office study forecasts a 30- to- 40-percent drop in the welfare rolls. Optimists anticipate a double benefit for the government: savings on welfare programs, plus tax revenues from the newly self-sufficient. Still, the short-term effects could be damaging. America's child poverty rates already are among the highest in the industrial world. One in every four children twelve or younger is hungry or on the edge of hunger. The Urban Institute predicts the overhaul will throw more than a million children into poverty.

"If you think things can't be worse, just you wait until there are a third of a million children in the streets," warned Daniel Patrick Moynihan, the Democratic senior senator from New York and an expert on welfare policy. "That's what you're talking about—children on grates, because there is no money in the states and cities to care for them.

"It is a social risk that no sane person would take, and I mean that."[3]

Close to half the promised federal welfare savings, $24 billion, comes from cuts in the food stamp program, which helps 25 million poor people. Barring legal immigrants from most welfare programs accounts for another big chunk of savings.[4]

Some welfare reform advocates say it's impossible to save money *and* reduce caseloads, that saving money has nothing to do with fixing welfare. It's cheaper, they say, for the government to distribute benefit checks than to make honest efforts to train people, give them options for caring for their children, and put them to useful work. Wisconsin's innovative welfare-reform programs have cut rolls there by more than 40 percent since 1987. At the same time, though, state spending on welfare has actually gone up.

"You can't just pass a bill and assume you'll save money the next day," Wisconsin governor Tommy Thompson explained. "How can you ask a welfare mom to get a job if she has to give up the medical insurance she gets on welfare, if she has no training or a bus ticket to get there, if she can't find a safe place to leave her children?"[5]

The System Nobody Loved

Nearly everyone agreed the old welfare system had broken down. The debate turned on whether it should be repaired or scrapped. Senator Joseph I. Lieberman, a Connecticut Democrat, offered this précis of its flaws:

"Welfare makes it feasible for a man to father a child without worrying about being a parent. It makes it possible for a young woman (too often a teenage girl) to have a child, move away from home, get an apartment and survive—without working. It makes it easier for millions of families to get by, but virtually impossible for them to get ahead."[6]

Gallup Organization surveys in the mid-1990s strongly suggested the half-century-old consensus on welfare had collapsed. Nearly three-quarters (71 percent) of a December 1972 Gallup sample favored maintaining or increasing existing levels of welfare spending. Only one-quarter thought it should be reduced or ended altogether. By 1994, only 48 percent thought welfare spending should remain steady or increase. An overwhelming 90 percent in the 1994 poll believed the welfare system to be in crisis.

Gallup tracked a rising interest in welfare issues during 1994 and 1995 as Congress debated welfare reform. In a 1995 poll, 12 percent of the sample judged welfare the nation's most pressing problem—the first time ever it had reached double digits in Gallup's periodic rankings of critical issues. In a July 1996 survey, welfare continued to rank near the top of the list of most important issues (at 7 percent), trailing only crime, the economy, and the budget deficit.

Still, the surveys found no broad agreement on what

"**Nearly everyone agreed the old welfare system had broken down.**"

ought to be done to fix the system. Most respondents favored tough policies to force people off public assistance. In a 1994 survey, 58 percent said people who had not found a job after two years should be denied benefits, and 62 percent favored a lifetime five-year limit. In 1996, nearly three quarters of the sample (71 percent) favored a cutoff after two years. And a majority favored denying welfare benefits to new immigrants. At the same time, respondents tended to oppose cutbacks that might harm children. More than three-quarters of a 1994 sample said the children of recipients dropped from the rolls should continue to receive government aid.

Is the Personal Responsibility and Work Opportunity Act what Americans had in mind when they told polltakers they supported welfare reform? Do they wish legal immigrants to be denied benefits? What if Senator Moynihan is right and children really are driven into the streets?

"There is harsh talk about work instead of welfare, but no talk of where to find it," wrote the Harvard social scientist William Julius Wilson. In many urban neighborhoods, Wilson noted, a majority of adults today do not have work.[7] Economic growth tends to reach the blighted districts of large cities late, if it arrives at all. And should the economy falter, Moynihan's direst predictions may be realized.

"A child could very well have to go to foster care," Louisiana social worker Vera Blakes said. "Parents will say, 'I have a six-year education, and I can't find a job. I can't

American Opinion

Are you for or against cutting off federal welfare benefits to people who had not found a job or become self-sufficient after two years?

- For
- Against
- No opinion

For: 71%
Against: 24%
No opinion: 5%

Source: The Gallup Poll 1996

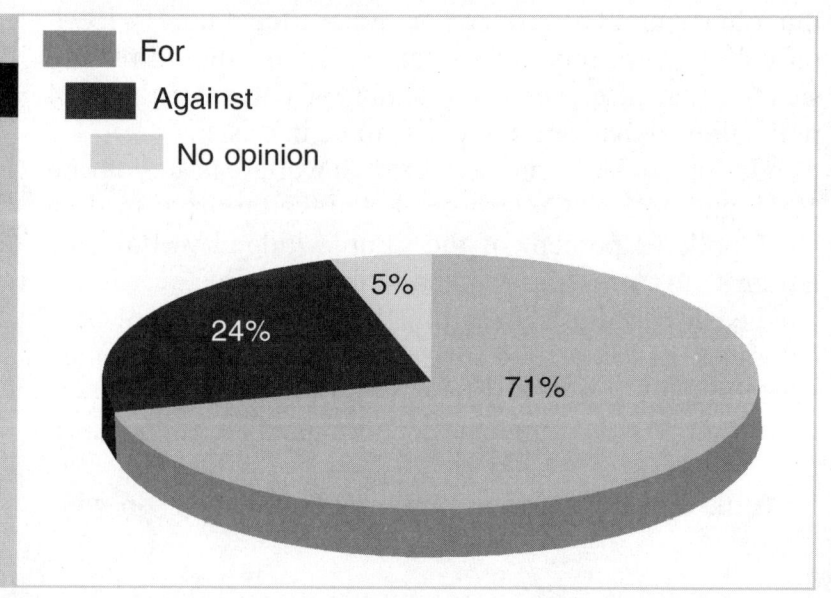

afford to care for this child.' It takes a lot to give up a child. But imagine a child with no place to sleep. It sounds like Charles Dickens, but people will have to make those decisions."[8]

Generally, Gallup surveys suggested Americans supported the 1996 legislation and were optimistic about its long-term impact. Early in the year, nearly two-thirds, 64 percent, said they favored the Republican approach—making deep cuts and shifting authority for welfare programs to the states. At year's end, more than half, 54 percent, believed the new law would improve the welfare system. Around a third, 31 percent, expected the system to fail.

Here are some of the specifics of the act:

- Able-bodied adults must find work within two years of first taking welfare or lose their benefits. States that fail to move 20 percent of their caseloads to work by the end of 1997 and 50 percent by 2002 face cuts in their federal block grants. States must maintain welfare spending at 80 percent of 1994 levels or risk losing federal aid.
- The five-year lifetime limit on benefits applies to most recipients. The states may exempt up to 20 percent of their caseloads as hardships, however, and single women who can't find day care for their children younger than six can't be penalized. Senator William V. Roth, a Delaware Republican, estimated a typical welfare family receives $50,000 in tax-free benefits over five years—enough time, he said, "to finish a high school degree or learn a skill through vocational training."[9]
- Stricter standards apply for the Supplemental Social Security Income program (SSI) for disabled children. An estimated 300,000 children could lose their benefits, according to a Congressional Budget Office estimate.
- Most legal immigrants are barred from the food stamp and SSI programs. Future legal immigrants are to be ineligible for most federal benefits and social services during their first five years in the United States. A CBO study estimated 500,000 noncitizens will eventually be dropped from the SSI program for the elderly poor and the disabled.
- The federal government will pay out annual $20 mil-

"**Gallup surveys suggested Americans supported the 1996 legislation and were optimistic about its likely long-term impact.**"

> ### As a Matter of Fact
>
> **Provisions of New Welfare Bill**
>
> - Federal entitlement to welfare is ended. Welfare is limited to five years. Able-bodied adults are required to work after two years.
> - Hardship exemptions are allowed for up to 20 percent of each state's caseload.
> - Aid to Families with Dependent Children is replaced with block grants to states, which will run their own programs.
> - Medicaid is continued as an entitlement to families on welfare and coverage is continued for one year for people who leave welfare to go to work.
> - States may deny Medicaid to any adult who loses welfare benefits for not meeting work requirements.
> - Restrictions on children's eligibility for Supplemental Security Income disability are tightened.
> - Cash aid and food stamps are denied to anyone convicted of felony drug charges. Pregnant women and adults in drug treatment
>
> (Continued on page 173)

lion cash bonuses to each of the five states that show the largest drop in illegitimate births each year from 1999 to 2002. Women who refuse to help identify the fathers of their children are to lose 25 percent of their benefits. Unmarried teen mothers are eligible for benefits only if they stay at home and attend school.

Welfare as We Knew It

With an assist from a strong economy, ten years of effort to reform the old system began to show results in 1995 and 1996. The average welfare caseload dropped 9 percent nationwide in 1996, when 4.4 million families were on welfare. A number of states reported impressive decreases: In Maryland, the rolls were down 26 percent; in Wisconsin, 24 percent; in Indiana, 21 percent; in Louisiana, 15 percent.[10] And a good thing, too, suggested welfare's critics. Hardly anyone in 1996 could be found to put in a good word for the old federal entitlement system.

The Social Security Act of 1935, the New Deal response to the mass social and economic deprivation of the Great Depression, established the principle of federal responsibility for the poor. One provision guaranteed federal cash payments to widows and orphans, an entitlement that evolved into the main federal welfare program, Aid to Families with Dependent Children.

Before it passed into history on October 1, 1996, AFDC paid monthly cash benefits ranging from $187 in Mississippi to $655 in Vermont. AFDC families could also tap into other assistance programs: food stamps, free school lunches, housing assistance, and Medicaid, the health insurance program for the poor. Food stamps and Medicaid remained federal responsibilities under the 1996 overhaul.[11]

Even in combination, though, the various programs provide for only the necessities of life. Moreover, the value of cash benefits has eroded substantially over time. In constant dollars, the monthly benefit declined from $676 in 1970 to $373 in 1993.

Manda Seefield, a 26-year-old high school dropout, is raising two young children in a rusting house trailer in the Mississippi River Valley town of Coal Valley, Illinois. She scrapes along on a $365-a-month government check. The father of her children owes $22,000 in uncollectable child support.

On welfare for long stretches of the past six years, Ms. Seefield, the subject of a profile in *The New York Times*, has worked only intermittently. Her children (a boy, six, and a girl, four) are not in robust health. The sorts of jobs she qualifies for—hotel maid, convenience store clerk—rarely offer medical insurance. She could not get along without Medicaid.

"They think we have this easy life," she says of those who call for welfare cuts. "They ought to come down to my level once. See what it's like to take care of kids on this kind of money. See what it's like to run into obstacles everywhere you turn."[12]

In fact, Gallup polling suggests a high level of public support for programs to help welfare mothers find and keep work. A 1994 survey found overwhelming approval, 90 percent or higher, for job-training programs that teach welfare recipients new skills and for child-care subsidies for working welfare parents or for welfare parents who are looking for work. Two-thirds supported transportation subsidies to help people on welfare get to work or to a job interview.

Though theoretical support for such programs may be strong, practical assistance, in the form of public funds, is often weak. Over time, dependency becomes an all-but-permanent condition for many poor families. The government estimates that as many as 70 percent of recipients leave the rolls within two years, but that fully half return later. Nationally, the average cumulative time on welfare is six years.[13] Critics interpret such figures as evidence that the entitlement system creates a helpless class and encourages welfare as a way of life.

In a 1994 study, social scientists Mary Jo Bane and David T. Ellwood characterized the typical welfare recipient as a never-married mother in her twenties or thirties with one or two children. Like Manda Seefield, she has a sketchy education, no specific job training or skills, and little or no experience in the job market. The old system offered little incentive to help her achieve self-sufficiency.

In fact, the odds were weighted heavily against a typical recipient breaking out of the welfare bind. The system ac-

would be exempted, and family members could still get benefits. (States could reject or modify this.)
- States are required to deduct at least one-quarter of the benefits for aid applicants who do not help determine the fathers of their children.
- Non-citizens who are not military veterans, or who have not worked and paid taxes in the United States for at least 10 years, are barred from any SSI or food stamp benefits. Future legal immigrants who are not citizens would also be barred from receiving most federal benefits for their first five years in the country.
- Illegal immigrants are excluded from most federal means-tested benefits, other than in emergencies and cases of communicable diseases.
- Students are eligible for school lunch programs as long as they are eligiblfor free public education.

Source: The Associated Press 1996

tually discouraged work. Bane and Ellwood calculated that a single mother in Illinois would need to earn close to twice the then-minimum wage of $4.25 an hour (it rose to $5.15 in 1996), with medical benefits and affordable day care, to be materially better off working than on welfare. And even if $8-an-hour jobs were plentiful in the inner-city slums and blighted rural areas where most welfare recipients live, she would have to be taught the skills to qualify for one. "Welfare as we know it is structured so that those who work are no better off than if they had remained on welfare," Bane and Ellwood concluded.[14]

(Bane and Ellwood are reform-minded Harvard professors who joined the Clinton administration to work on welfare reform in 1993. Both sides cited their research in the congressional welfare debates of 1995 and 1996. Though they were critical of the old system, Bane and Ellwood broke with the president over his decision to sign the 1996 welfare overhaul.)

Cause or Corrective?

AFDC began taking on its contemporary shape in 1962, with passage of a series of Social Security amendments that eased eligibility requirements and led to a steady increase in welfare caseloads. By the end of the decade, the familiar system was in place. One set of welfare officers determined an applicant's eligibility. Another set wrote and distributed the checks.

Caseloads continued to rise, doubling between 1967 and 1972. Job-training programs, built into the system as early as 1967, were ineffective. The Work Incentive Program, for example, required dependents to enroll in work or training programs. By 1986, WIP had registered 1.6 million AFDC recipients, yet only 220,000 people were actually getting any job training, and only about 130,000 WIN alumni managed to work their way off welfare.

The Family Support Act of 1988 sought to restore the emphasis on work, child care, education, and training. It also gave the states more flexibility in testing new approaches. Inadequate funding doomed this reform effort. The federal government met only about 60 percent of the costs of the new programs, and in the recessionary late eight-

"
'Welfare as we know it is structured so that those who work are no better off than if they had remained on welfare.'
"

ies, few states could afford to increase their welfare spending. Even the most effective state programs reached only about 15 percent of the adult welfare population.

So the eligibility technicians and disbursement officers went about their bureaucratic business. "We'd just give them this application and say, 'Go for it,'" Maryland social worker Janice Hicks observed.[15] The checks went out monthly to applicants as long as they met the eligibility test and followed the rules.

To conservative critics, entitlement and social ills are cause and effect. Since the early 1960s, the percentage of children on AFDC has tripled. The birthrate for unmarried teens has tripled. In New York City, half of all births, an even 50 percent, are out of wedlock. The *rate* of illegitimate births dropped 4 percent in 1995—the first decrease in sixteen years, the federal Centers for Disease Control and Prevention reported. Even so, 1.2 million babies were born out of wedlock that year. In 1970, 10.4 million children lived in poverty; by 1993, the number had risen to 15.7 million.

"This catastrophe wasn't caused by war or plague or depression," Jeff Jacoby wrote in *The Boston Globe*. "It was caused by welfare as we came to know it—by a well-intentioned, hideously misguided government policy of rewarding self-destructive behavior and paying good money for making bad choices."[16]

Over the years, a powerful coalition of Democratic poli-

" **In New York City, half of all births, an even 50 percent, are out of wedlock.** "

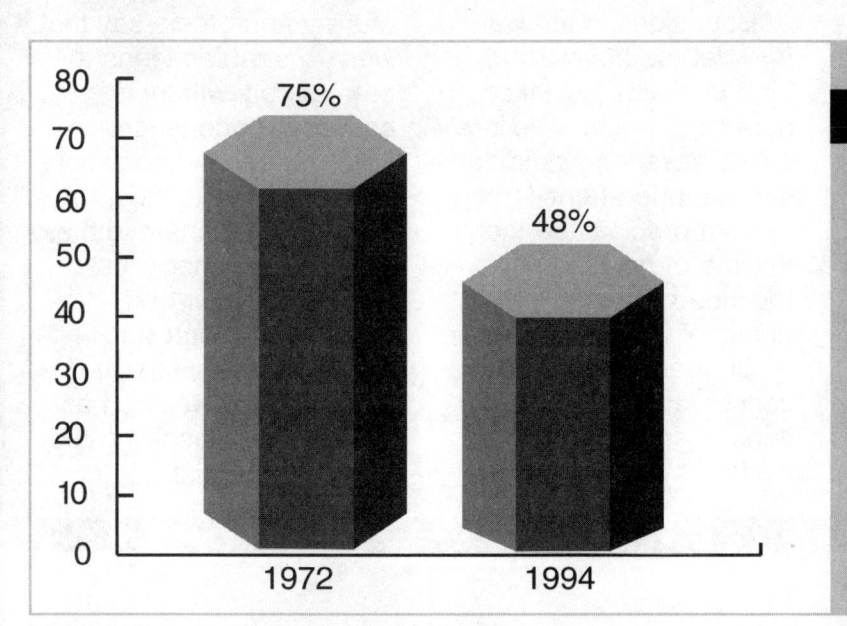

American Opinion

A comparison between 1972 and 1994 of respondents who favored maintaining or increasing existing levels of welfare spending.

1972: 75%
1994: 48%

Source: The Gallup Poll 1972, 1994

ticians and antipoverty groups closed ranks to protect the entitlement system. Moynihan, a long-time welfare reformer cast as a defender of the entitlement in 1996, lobbied for a restructuring of welfare when few in his own Democratic Party cared to listen.

"For years, whenever the critics said, correctly, that the welfare system was doing more harm than good, and suggested that it be rethought, its defenders screamed 'racism' and 'slavefare,' " Moynihan said on the eve of Clinton's signing of the 1996 law. "They did that until there was no public support left at all. Now they are stunned at what they are getting."[17]

The Politics of Welfare

The coalition began to break up during the 1992 campaign, with candidate Clinton's pledge to "end welfare as we know it." The Republicans who took over Congress in

Illegitimacy Rates: Fact or Illusion?

Close to 30 percent of American babies are born to single mothers. But there were indications in 1996 that the long-term trend toward out of wedlock birth has slowed, and possibly even begun to move slowly in the other direction.

In 1995, according to the federal Centers for Disease Control and Prevention, the number of illegitimate births declined 4 percent, the first overall decrease in sixteen years. The largest drop: out-of-wedlock births to black teenagers. They were down 9 percent from 1994. Overall, the rate for teenagers fell for the fourth consecutive year, for a total 8 percent drop since 1991.[1]

Both sides in the welfare debate have used birth statistics to make polemical points. Welfare's critics have long claimed the old federal entitlement system precipitated the decline of families and touched off a near-epidemic of illegitimate births.

Charles Murray, the conservative political thinker, argued that the welfare system was the main cause of the rise in births to single mothers, and that birth trends—if not reversed—would lead to a large, dispossessed, and volatile underclass. Murray and others say that welfare enables teens to prematurely win their economic independence from parents by the simple act of bearing a child, which entitles them to their own welfare check and sometimes their own apartment. Moreover, conservatives warn, the availability of welfare has the effect of absolving the

(Continued on page 177)

the midterm elections of 1994 moved swiftly to hold President Clinton to the promise.

Welfare experts Bane and Ellwood helped draft Clinton's original reform proposal, which called for a two-year time limit on benefits and for $10 billion in new spending over five years to help move people from welfare to work. But the Democrats had made little progress on the issue when they lost their congressional majority, and the ascendant Republicans pushed through a plan of their own that ended the entitlement, cut spending, and turned over responsibility for welfare to the states.

Clinton vetoed two Republican welfare bills as unduly harsh. But on the third pass, Congress agreed to soften some provisions and break out Medicaid as a separate issue, thus sparing it major changes. After a bitter internal debate within the administration, the president announced he would sign the measure—and would try in 1997 to force alterations that would soften its impact.

fathers from the responsibility of supporting their children or marrying the mother. In pre-AFDC days, "shotgun marriages" were directed by economics as much as by morality.

Many social scientists dismiss such claims. While it is true, says Harvard's William Julius Wilson, that the out-of-wedlock birth rate for teens has nearly doubled since 1975, the actual value of Aid to Families with Dependent Children, food stamps, and Medicaid benefits, adjusted for inflation, has fallen during the same period.[2]

Around two-thirds of all black births are to single mothers. Murray and others have argued that the rate of such births has risen dramatically as a result of the welfare entitlement.[3]

But *New Yorker* writer Michael Lind counters that the claim is based largely on a statistical mirage.

The proportion of illegitimate births among black women rose from 23 percent in 1960 to 62 percent in the early 1990s. According to Lind, most of the increase—four-fifths, he says, citing U.S. government data—is the result of married, working black women having fewer children. The rising proportion of out-of-wedlock births, black and white, is almost wholly a result of decisions on the part of intact families to have fewer children, he says.[4]

Lind labels the widely accepted notion that welfare has caused an epidemic of illegitimacy a hoax. "Conservatives have sacrificed both honesty and accuracy in order to cynically manipulate the paranoid fantasies of white middle-class voters about being out-bred by a supposedly lazy, overpaid black underclass," Lind says.[5]

> "'This is not reform, it is punishment.'"

Liberals accused Clinton of betraying the poor to redeem his 1992 vow and advance his re-election prospects. In a clever burlesque, *Atlanta Constitution* cartoonist Mike Luckovich pictures the president holding a piece of paper labeled "Welfare Reform" and explaining matters to a solemn-looking group of five children. "This bill will hurt you," he tells them. "I feel your pain, but signing it helps my re-election effort. Do you feel my joy?"

Advocates of the poor made the same point more soberly. "The premise is that the behavior of certain adults can be changed by making the lives of their children as wretched as possible," said Moynihan. "This is not reform, it is punishment," *The New York Times* editorialized. "A moment of shame," charged Marian Wright Edelman, president of the Children's Defense Fund.[18] Her husband, Health and Human Services assistant secretary Peter B. Edelman, resigned in protest, along with HHS reformer Mary Jo Bane.

"The welfare legislation is in no way a reform measure," columnist Bob Herbert wrote. "It is a form of officially sanctioned brutality aimed at the usual suspects—the poor, the black and the brown, the very young, the uneducated, immigrants. Somebody has to be the scapegoat and they're it."[19]

Conservatives challenged such responses as gross exaggerations.

"This isn't the end of the world," wrote the *Boston Globe's* Jacoby. "It isn't the end of welfare. It is barely the end of welfare as we know it. For all the keening and hysterics, [the law] will make only modest changes. An unmarried woman who decides to have children she can't support will still collect free money from the government. She'll still get food stamps. She'll still be covered by Medicaid. She'll still be able to avoid work for up to two years—longer if she can't find day care. She'll still be able to shield the identity of her children's father(s) without forfeiting most of her benefits."[20]

The State Experiments

The states—notably, Wisconsin, Michigan, and Ohio—have led the way in the welfare overhaul. Waivers of federal regulations allowed states to experiment with work

American Opinion

Are you for or against cutting off federal welfare benefits to people who had not found a job or become self-sufficient after two years?

Breakdown by Population Group	For	Against	No Opinion
Overall	71%	24%	5%
Male	72%	24%	4%
Female	71%	23%	6%
East	70%	26%	4%
West	74%	21%	5%
White	74%	21%	5%
Non-white	53%	42%	5%
Black	44%	49%	7%
18–29 Years Old	73%	26%	1%
30–49 Years Old	73%	22%	5%
50–64 Years Old	65%	23%	12%
Urban	66%	29%	5%
Suburban	71%	23%	6%
Rural	78%	17%	5%

Source: The Gallup Poll, 1996

rules, time limits, and other changes. The Clinton administration granted most states's requests for waivers, which for the time being are to remain in effect even when they come into conflict with provisions of the welfare law.

Wisconsin's reform program, dubbed W2, combines tough eligibility standards and time limits with expanded child care and job-training programs. It replaces the entitlement with wage subsidies for single parents who work and increases spending for child care and transitional community-service jobs.

A pilot version, the "Work Not Welfare" program in Fond du Lac County, Wisconsin, reported a 50 percent drop in caseloads during an eighteen-month period in 1995–96. Jobs were found for many former dependents, though county authorities attributed part of the caseload decrease to recipients who dropped off the rolls when they learned they'd have to work for their benefits.[21]

Wisconsin's reform has been a lightning rod, drawing praise from the mainstream and criticism from advocates of the poor. Some initiatives appear to work. Others, such as a program linking aid and school attendance, have accomplished little. And though Wisconsin tripled spending on child care, one study forecast demand for services to rise 1,700 percent.

"W2 would force women into the work force when their babies are twelve weeks old, despite the fact that decent infant care is so hard to find," claimed the National Center for the Early Childhood Work Force, a Washington advocacy group.[22]

Social service groups and some religious organizations have opposed the Wisconsin changes, charging they strip income from families who can't comply with the work requirements. And even well-disposed observers conceded the program is expensive, almost certainly beyond the reach of poorer states. It clashes, too, with the budget-cutting obsessions of many politicians.

All the same, Wisconsin has scored more hits than misses. "It is not punitive," commentator Thomas Oliphant said of the state's reform program. "It has a safety net, it has clear potential to help young mothers enter the larger economic culture, and it invests in their success."[23]

Maryland, Ohio, Kentucky, and Florida are close behind Wisconsin in the van of the welfare overhaul.

A pilot program in Anne Arundel County, Maryland, requires applicants to go for ten job interviews a week—and prove it—and to accept any job on offer. In return, the county welfare office provides vouchers for day care and transportation and coaching in interview techniques.

An Ohio program rewards teenage parents who stay in school with extra cash each month. "It's pretty simple," explained Mike Dawson, an aide to Governor George Voinovich, a Republican. "If you stay in school, you get 62 bucks more. If you don't, you get 62 bucks less."[24] An initial study reported an increase in high school graduation rates for those in the program.

Kentucky will offer "relocation assistance" for dependents moving within the state in search of work and help poor people fill out job applications and prepare for interviews. The state also will extend tax credits to employers who hire people off welfare.

Florida's $1 billion restructuring of welfare, launched on October 1, 1996, is tougher than the new federal law. It cuts benefits after two years, bars families from getting assistance for more than twenty-four months out of a sixty-month period, and sets a lifetime four-year aid limit. The law penalizes parents for having more children, reducing aid levels after the birth of a second child. It also ends direct payments for teen mothers, who are now required to live at home or with a legal guardian.

The overhaul affects 560,000 poor families in Florida and will require the creation of 160,000 jobs for those who will lose welfare assistance. There is no evidence yet that enough jobs will be available for dependents soon to be cast adrift.

"I have to be really skeptical about it," said Virginia Foy, a Florida children's advocate. "There are many more needs than there is money. We're all nervous."[25]

Where Are the Jobs?

So everything depends on work. Without it, people will suffer or the federal government will again take up the burden of responsibility for the poor. In William Julius Wilson's view, the crisis of dependency grew out of the absence of jobs in America's cities, not out of federal government policies that created a helpless class, and still less out of the moral failings of the poor.

"High neighborhood joblessness has a far more devastating effect than high neighborhood poverty," Wilson writes. "A neighborhood in which people are poor but employed is different from a neighborhood in which people are poor and jobless. Many of today's problems in the inner cities—crime, family dissolution, welfare—are fundamentally a consequence of the disappearance of work."[26]

In the mainly African-American Chicago community of North Lawndale, for example, Western Electric and International Harvester factories employed more than 55,000 people in 1960. Harvester closed in the late sixties; the Western Electric plant shut down for good in 1984. When jobs go and nothing replaces them, neighborhoods wither.

"
'Many of today's problems in the inner cities—crime, family dissolution, welfare—are fundamentally a consequence of the disappearance of work.'
"

> "**New York State in 1996 launched the largest public jobs program since the New Deal.**"

"You could walk out of the house and get a job," one black Chicagoan told Wilson. "Maybe not what you want, but you could get a job. Now, you can't find anything."[27]

Wilson proposes major education, training and childcare initiatives, and the introduction of a massive public jobs program modeled on the Works Progress Administration of the New Deal. Like others, though, he recognizes that the short-term costs of such programs far exceed the costs of cash welfare.

The notion of government jobs draws considerable support, according to Gallup's surveys, at least in areas where employment is scarce. In one poll, 60 percent favored publicly funded jobs; 37 percent were opposed.

To meet the new welfare-law requirements, New York State in 1996 launched the largest public jobs program since the New Deal. Within two years, 100,000 dependents, mostly single mothers, are to go to work for cities and other state and local agencies in return for their benefits.

The new workers will answer telephones and do other clerical tasks, clean parks and courthouses, and supervise school lunchrooms. The cost will approach $1 billion a year, including day care. State officials estimate the bill for day care alone at $540 a month for each worker. A family of three cashed a $577-a-month check in New York in 1996.

New York City established a workfare program early in 1995. The nation's largest, it employed 34,000 welfare recipients in 1996. The program is expensive, supporters concede, but at least people are working and the city is cleaner.

Not all those employed on workfare jobs are grateful, however. Some say the tasks are menial and lead nowhere. Pat Wiley picks up trash along the walkways of Prospect Park in Brooklyn.

"We're not stupid people who never had a job," she said of herself and others on her work crew. "I was never a bum. I don't want welfare. What am I learning. Learning to clean up? I learned that in my back yard when I was four years old."[28]

The early history of a modest public-private initiative in Kansas City, Missouri, suggests some of the difficulties of moving people from welfare to work. Eighty women were hired in 1995 and 1996 as home aides for disabled and elderly people. After seventeen months, only twenty-five women remained on the job. The hirees lacked job skills, missed work frequently, and resisted following their bosses' directions.

"As single mothers, they are on their own and think of themselves as authority figures," explained Deborah Washam, president of Community Home Health Care in Kansas City. "They won't take routine supervision at work."[29]

Few prospective employers are in a position to teach communications and other skills to entry-level new hires, let alone negotiate with them over their duties every day. Some business leaders recognize—along with Wisconsin governor Thompson, New York senator Moynihan, William Julius Wilson, and others—that genuine reform carries a high price.

"Business is not in the business of providing jobs for welfare recipients," said Robert T. Jones, president of the National Alliance of Business. It's up to the states, he went on, to prepare people for work.[30]

For years, state and local governments pressed Washington for more flexibility on welfare. With the Personal Responsibility and Work Act, the realities of moving people from welfare to work began to penetrate statehouses from Maine to California. In the weeks following President Clinton's August 22, 1996, signing of the bill, the states flooded the much-maligned Health and Human Services bureaucracy with questions and requests for clarifications. The response: You're on your own. You'll have to work things out for yourselves.

"States are like the dog that ran after the car and finally caught it," one federal welfare official remarked. "Now they're not sure what to do with it. It's amazing what happens when you wish for something and actually get it."[31]

Notes: **Welfare Reform** Will It Break the Dependency Cycle?

1. Francis X. Clines, "Clinton Signs Bill Cutting Welfare; States in New Role," *The New York Times*, August 23, 1996, 1.
2. Jonathan Alter, "Washington Washes Its Hands," *Newsweek*, August 12, 1996, 43.
3. R. W. Apple Jr., "His Battle Now Lost, Moynihan Still Cries Out," *The New York Times*, August 2, 1996, 16.
4. Peter Grier, "Welfare Reform Stamps Varied Imprint on States," *The Christian Science Monitor*, August 2, 1996, 1.
5. Alter, "Washington Washes Its Hands," 44.
6. Joseph I. Lieberman, "Welfare as We Know It," op-ed, *The New York Times*, July 25, 1996.
7. William Julius Wilson, "Work," *The New York Times Magazine*, August 18, 1996, 27.
8. Peter T. Kilborn, "With Welfare Overhaul Now Law, States Grapple with Consequences," *The New York Times*, August 23, 1996, 22.
9. Robert Pear, "Senate Approves Sweeping Change in Welfare Policy," *The New York Times*, July 24, 1996, 1.
10. Robert Pear, "Most States Find Welfare Targets Well Within Reach," *The New York Times*, September 23, 1996, 1.
11. George J. Church, "Ripping Up Welfare," *Time*, August 12, 1996, 21.
12. Dirk Johnson, "One Mother's Ordeal With Life on Welfare," *The New York Times*, July 31, 1996, 10.
13. Johnson, "One Woman's Ordeal."
14. Mary Jo Bane and David T. Ellwood, *Welfare Realities: From Rhetoric to Reform* (Cambridge: Harvard University Press, 1994), 136.
15. Church, "Ripping Up Welfare," 21.
16. Jeff Jacoby, "Welfare Catastrophe? No it's a Modest Reform," op-ed, *The Boston Globe*, August 7, 1996.
17. Apple, "His Battle Now Lost."
18. Alter, "Washington Washes Its Hands."
    Clines, "Clinton Signs Bill Cutting Welfare."
    "A Sad Day for Poor Children," editorial in *The New York Times*, August 1, 1996.
19. Bob Herbert, "The Mouths of Babes," op-ed, *The New York Times*, July 22, 1996.
20. Jacoby, "Welfare Catastrophe?"
21. Church, "Ripping Up Welfare," 21.
22. Claudia Wayne and Marcy Whitebook, "The Coming Child-Care Debacle," op-ed, *The Christian Science Monitor*, August 30, 1996.
23. Thomas Oliphant, "Clinton's Welfare Move Scores Points in Policy and Politics," *The Boston Globe*, op-ed, May 21, 1996.
24. Dirk Johnson, "Wisconsin Welfare Effort on Schools Is a Failure," *The New York Times*, May 19, 1996, 20.
25. "Floridians Face Sweeping Changes in Welfare Oct. 1," Reuters dispatch in *The Boston Globe*, September 16, 1996, A7.
26. Wilson, "Work," 28.

27. Wilson, "Work," 28–29.
28. David Firestone, "New York Girding for Surge in Workfare Jobs," *The New York Times*, August 13, 1996, 1.
29. Jon Nordheimer, "Welfare-to-Work Plans Show Success Is Difficult to Achieve," *The New York Times*, September 1, 1996, 1.
30. Nordheimer, "Welfare-to-Work Plans."
31. Robert Pear, "State Welfare Chiefs Ask for More U.S. Guidance," *The New York Times*, September 10, 1996, 16.

Notes: Illegitimacy Rates: Fact or Illusion

1. Lauran Neergaard, "Fewer Babies Born to Unwed Mothers," Associated Press report in *The Boston Globe*, October 5, 1996, A3.
2. William Julius Wilson, "Work," *The New York Times Magazine*, August 18, 1996, 31.
3. Jason DeParle, "Abolishment of Welfare: An Idea Becomes a Cause," *The New York Times*, April 22, 1994, 14.
4. Michael Lind, "A 'Crisis' of Illegitimacy? Try Hoax Instead," *The Boston Globe*, August 11, 1996, D1.
5. Lind, A 'Crisis' of Illegitimacy?"

10 Affirmative Action
Does It Widen or Narrow the Racial Divide?

Few issues divide Americans as deeply as race. And nowhere in the discussion of race is the gap broader than in perceptions of discrimination and the validity of government programs to remedy it. To most people, these issues are etched sharply in black and white.

If attitudes toward affirmative action are a measure of racial strain, black and white relations could be building to a crisis in the United States. Gallup Organization surveys show a fundamental divergence on the question of preferences. They have come under attack in the courts, in the Congress, and in state legislatures. In California, with 12 percent of the American electorate, voters emphatically rejected affirmative action in 1996—a verdict that is almost certain to encourage efforts to overturn antibias programs for minorities and women nationwide.

Proposition 209 bars discrimination against, or granting preferential treatment to, anyone in public employment, education, and contracting. Invoking Martin Luther King Jr., supporters presented 209 as color-blind, a way of assuring that people are judged on their ability rather than the hue of their skin. Whites voted for it overwhelmingly; blacks and Hispanics were overwhelmingly opposed. Although the words "affirmative action" never appeared on the ballot, it was clear to nearly everyone that such programs were the central issue.

The Gallup Organization's national surveys mirror Californians' racial fault lines. In a survey in late November

"
If attitudes toward affirmative action are a measure of racial strain, black and white relations could be building to a crisis in the United States.

"

1996, more than six of every ten respondents said they favored the racial component of the California initiative. Around a third, 35 percent, opposed it.

In a separate poll, minorities strongly favored aggressive affirmative action, while a majority of whites opposed it. And in a July 1996 survey, blacks were far more likely than whites to regard discrimination as a "very serious" problem in their home communities. Nearly a quarter of black respondents felt that way, compared with only 7 percent of whites.

The aftershocks of the California initiative, it seemed clear, would be felt into 1997 and beyond.

"This is no longer just some idea out in California," said Georgia state legislator Earl Ehrhart, a Republican who favors ending affirmative-action programs. "It's something that was actually passed by the people in the most populous state in the nation. So that puts it right into the middle of the radar screen."[1]

Few defenders of preference were inclined to understate the importance of the California vote. "At a minimum, it sends a very bad message that our country will continue down the road of division, of opposing women's progress and of racial animosity," lamented Connie Rice, of the NAACP's Legal Defense Fund.[2]

Signs of Progress

If the assault on affirmative action, the rash of church burnings in the South, and the Texaco discrimination scandal troubled African Americans in the mid-1990s, there were grounds for optimism, too. By a number of indicators, many of America's 33.5 million blacks were recording substantial material gains.

Black incomes were up; poverty levels were down. In 1995, for the first time since the Census Bureau began keeping track, in 1959, the poverty rate for all blacks fell below 30 percent. Median income for black households rose 3.6 percent, compared with a rate of only 2.2 percent for white households.

The income gap between blacks and whites closed a bit. Blacks were the only group whose median incomes, adjusted for inflation, increased during the 1990s. In 1989,

> "
> **By a number of indicators, many of America's 33.5 million blacks were recording substantial material gains.**
> "

black households earned 79 percent as much as white households. In 1995, blacks earned 87 percent as much.

For the first time, the proportion of young black adults (aged twenty-five to twenty-nine) who had completed high school reached that of young white adults. Scores on national education tests were rising faster for blacks than for whites, though blacks still were scoring lower across the board than whites.

Life expectancy for black males rose to 65.4 years, the highest level since 1984. The birthrate for black teenagers had fallen 17 percent since 1991. Overall, black out-of-wedlock births decreased from 70.4 percent to 69.5 percent, the first decline since 1969.[3]

"In the heat of the political debate and atmosphere of the last year or so, very few people have been paying serious attention. And yet when you do, you see that by virtually every measure of well-being, African-Americans have been on a significant uptrend during the nineties," observed Milton Morris, of the Joint Center for Political and Economic Studies, which tracks issues affecting blacks.[4]

Some analysts recommend caution, however, in interpreting the data. Black married couples recorded the biggest income gains, but most black households are headed by single women. Some economists suggest the figures look better than they should in some categories because the 800,000 black adults in federal and state prisons and local jails were not counted. Others note that an economic slump could rapidly erode the gains. There are unknown factors, too, such as the impact of the 1996 welfare legislation that aims to substantially reduce welfare rolls.

In any event, such statistics cut either way. Both sides in the debate, which is in one aspect an argument about the role of government, could cite reports of material gains among blacks to support their case.

Affirmative action has helped to narrow the gap between whites and blacks, say advocates of activist government, but the gap remains. The programs they support range from voluntary initiatives such as employer outreach and education to mandatory preferential programs for minorities and women, including hiring and promotion guarantees and government-contract set-asides.

Such programs are in place at all levels of government

"
'By virtually every measure of well-being, African-Americans have been on a significant uptrend during the '90s.'

"

> "Gallup opinion surveys suggest most whites question the fairness of race and gender preferences."

and in many private enterprises and educational institutions. The federal Small Business Administration, the Defense Department, and the Transportation Department reserve contracts for minority-owned firms. States set aside federal funds for highway construction and other projects. State-funded universities and most private institutions practice affirmative action in admissions, hiring, and promotion.

Gallup opinion surveys suggest most whites question the fairness of race and gender preferences. In a 1995 poll, two-thirds of whites opposed hiring quotas for minorities and women. (Two-thirds of blacks favored such quotas.) Fair or not, though, preferential programs seem to have opened up educational and professional opportunities for minorities. The number of blacks in managerial positions, for instance, has doubled during the affirmative-action era.

"There has been a stunning increase in the number of middle-class blacks and the number of blacks going to college or business or trade schools," noted Hugh B. Price of the National Urban League. "Our talent bank is exponentially fuller than it was twenty or thirty years ago."[5]

Partisans of less government involvement argue that affirmative action has done its work and can be scaled back or even eliminated.

"[They] would like to have you believe that there is equality and therefore we can't give anybody a break anymore," Stanford economist Martin Carnoy said. "But there are tremendous labor market imperfections. They would

American Opinion

Would you favor a national bill similar to California's Proposition 209, which bars discrimination against or granting preferential treatment to anyone in public employment, education, and contracting?

- Favor: 61%
- Oppose: 35%
- No opinion: 4%

Source: The Gallup Poll 1996

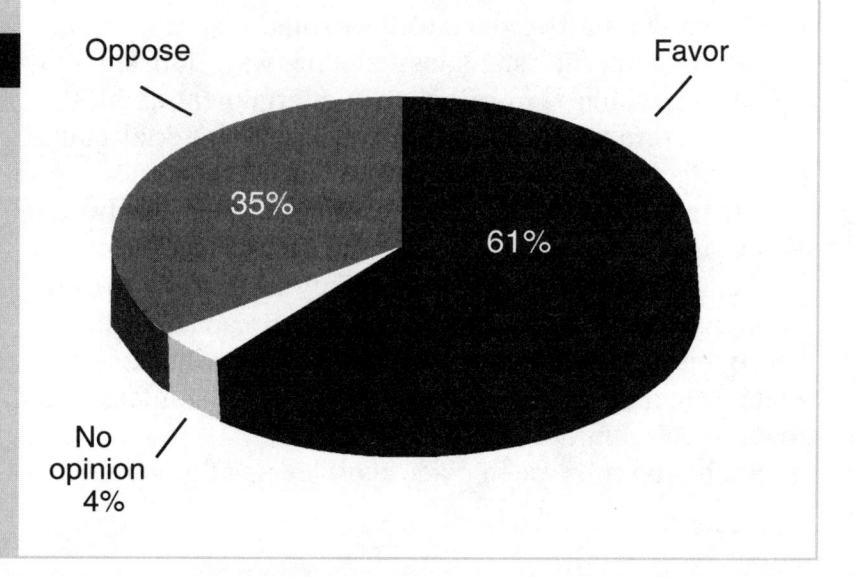

have you believe this is now a world of merit. If you ease up on employers, they tend to fall into old, bad habits."[6]

Opponents of affirmative action say the preference system breeds resentment among whites and devalues the gains minorities achieve by their own efforts. Ward Connerly, a Sacramento businessman and one of two African-American members of the University of California Board of Regents, led the campaign to end race-conscious affirmative action in the 150,000-student, nine-campus University of California system. "The purpose of affirmative action has been noble, perhaps even necessary until now," said the Louisiana-born Connerly. "But the happy face we have put on these practices to achieve diversity has become to me morally offensive."[7]

Some beneficiaries of affirmative action say, too, that the preference extracts a price. "I got into law school because I am black," wrote Yale constitutional law scholar Stephen L. Carter.[8] He argues that those who advance by this means carry a heavy psychological burden. Could they have succeeded without it? All too often their colleagues doubt them—and they doubt themselves.

In any case, Carter suggests that preference programs choose the wrong targets.

"Among those training for business and professional careers, the benefits of affirmative action fall to those least in need of them," he wrote. "We should be concentrating on constructive dialogue about how to solve the problems of the real and continuing victims of the nation's legacy of racial oppression: the millions of struggling black Americans for whom affirmative action and entry into the professions are stunningly irrelevant."[9]

From Kennedy to Clinton

Hobart Taylor Jr., a young black Detroit lawyer, coined the term in 1961, in the early weeks of the Kennedy administration: In an executive order he helped write, he called for "affirmative action" to assure jobs went to applicants without regard to race or color.

The term at first carried no connotation of preference, and President Kennedy remained cool to the idea of preferences. "I think we ought not to begin the quota system," he

" **Opponents of affirmative action say the preference system breeds resentment among whites and devalues the gains minorities achieve by their own efforts.** "

said in 1963. "We should look over the employment rolls, look over areas where we are hiring people and at least make sure we are giving everyone a fair chance. But not hard and fast quotas."[10]

The landmark Civil Rights Act of 1964 made job discrimination illegal and established an Equal Employment Opportunity Commission to review complaints. Southern Democrats and some of their conservative Republican allies sought to block the measure, claiming it would discriminate against whites. "I know what will happen if the bill is passed," Mississippi Senator James O. Eastland warned. "I know what will happen if there is a choice between hiring a white man or hiring a Negro, both having equal qualifications. I know who will get the job. It will not be the white man."[11]

To outflank Eastland, the bill's authors dropped enforcement powers that would have given the commission authority to go after discrimination in the workplace. Civil rights groups recognized another weakness: Color-blind programs that relied on persuasion and good faith failed to take into account inequities in background, education, and training, still less the nation's long, grim history of race and gender discrimination.

In September 1965, after a summer of violent racial insurgency in Los Angeles and other cities, President Lyndon B. Johnson reached for a remedy. His Executive Order 11246, the founding document of affirmative action, gave

American Opinion

The support, according to race, for expanding affirmative-action programs.

Source: The Gallup Poll 1996

Black: 66%
White: 35%

the U.S. Department of Labor the authority and the resources to force employers to aggressively search out minority candidates.

From this starting point, a series of court rulings and executive orders built a system of race-conscious affirmative action. In 1966, Johnson introduced the Philadelphia Plan, one of the first preference programs. It mandated the hiring of minorities in federal construction jobs. In 1971, the Supreme Court defined discrimination not only as the denial of an individual's rights but as the sum of the unequal effects of racist employment practices.

In its best-known ruling, the high court ordered the University of California at Davis to admit a *white* medical school applicant who claimed he had been a victim of reverse discrimination. The court went on, though, to say colleges and universities could make race a positive factor in admissions—an authorization of race-conscious preference.

The Reagan administration launched the first systematic challenge to affirmative action in the 1980s, arguing broadly that discrimination must be proved, not assumed as a legacy of the racist past. America, the Reaganites said, should assure equal opportunity, not equality of outcome.

In June 1995, the Supreme Court shook the foundations of thirty years of affirmative action policy, ruling in a Colorado case that any federal program that classifies persons by race is constitutional only if it is tailored narrowly to achieve a compelling government interest. In a 5-to-4 decision, the court said in *Adarand Constructors v. Pena* that the government must show evidence of specific discrimination to justify programs that set aside contracts for minority-owned firms.

In the Colorado case, a white contractor lost a highway construction job to a Hispanic firm even though the minority company had submitted a higher bid.

"Whenever the government treats any person unequally because of his or her race, that person has suffered an injury that falls squarely within the language and spirit of the Constitution's guarantee of equal protection," Justice Sandra Day O'Connor wrote in the court's majority opinion.[12]

In response, the Clinton administration ordered federal agencies to shut down any programs that enforced quotas, gave preference to unqualified persons and businesses, or

> **The Reagan Administration launched the first systematic challenge to affirmative action in the 1980s.**

used reverse discrimination to reach their minority hiring, promotion, or contracting goals.

Gallup: The Racial Chasm

In an extensive 1995 survey, Gallup found what it called a clear racial fault line on affirmative action. White men, white women, black men, and black women have substantially different perceptions of specific elements of affirmative action, and especially on government imposed remedies for discrimination. Black women showed the firmest support for aggressive programs, white men the least.

Surprisingly, though, the same poll showed considerable support for the *principle* of affirmative action. "There is no broad consensus for eliminating affirmative action programs," Gallup noted in a special report on the issue, "although there is even less support for expanding them."

Blacks were far more likely than whites to favor remedial programs such as quotas and contract set-asides. Blacks supported expanding affirmative action; whites wanted no change or a reduction. Majorities of Democrats supported most affirmative-action programs; majorities of Republicans opposed them.

Respondents overwhelmingly believed affirmative-action programs were needed when they were introduced in the mid-1960s, but they were ambivalent about the need today. Levels of support varied widely, depending on the program. Voluntary measures drew nearly unanimous approval: Remedial programs were far less popular, especially among whites.

Nearly three-quarters of the 1995 sample agreed companies ought to make a particular effort to find and hire qualified minorities and women. Eight of every ten favored job-training programs. But fewer than half thought businesses should fill job openings with minorities instead of equally qualified white applicants. Fewer than half believed the government should reserve contracts for minorities and women, and two-thirds opposed setting aside scholarships for minorities.

Clear majorities rejected racial-quota systems for businesses and schools. Close to two-thirds opposed job quotas and nearly six of every ten opposed college admission quo-

> " **White men, white women, black men, and black women have substantially different perceptions of specific elements of affirmative action.** "

tas. More than eight of every ten opposed promotions for minorities who are less qualified than whites.

Two-thirds of black respondents supported the expansion of affirmative-action programs, compared with only a quarter of whites. Three-quarters of blacks said black men endure major discrimination at work; fewer than half the white respondents agreed.

The California Initiative

Legislators in twenty-six states introduced measures to repeal or roll back affirmative action in 1995. Not a single one passed. Approval in 1996 of Proposition 209—formally, the California Civil Rights Initiative—will doubtless encourage opponents of such programs to try again.

"We can point to California now and we've got liberals on the defensive, where they've got to defend sexist and racist programs," said David Jaye, a Michigan Republican legislator whose bill to ban affirmative action failed in 1995. Jaye said he would reintroduce the bill in 1997.[13]

In fact, California had moved aggressively to dismantle affirmative action well before Proposition 209 came to a vote. In June 1995, Republican governor Pete Wilson issued an executive order abolishing some state government preference programs. Then, at Wilson's urging, the University of California Regents voted to bar affirmative action in university admissions, hiring, and contracting.

> " Two-thirds of black respondents supported the expansion of affirmative-action programs, compared with only a quarter of whites. "

American Opinion

In general, do you think we need to increase, keep the same, or decrease affirmative-action programs in this country?
("No opinion" omitted)

■ Decrease
□ Keep the same
■ Increase

Category	Increase	Keep the same	Decrease
Overall	31%	26%	36%
White	26%	26%	41%
Black	65%	26%	6%
Men	27%	24%	43%
Women	35%	28%	30%

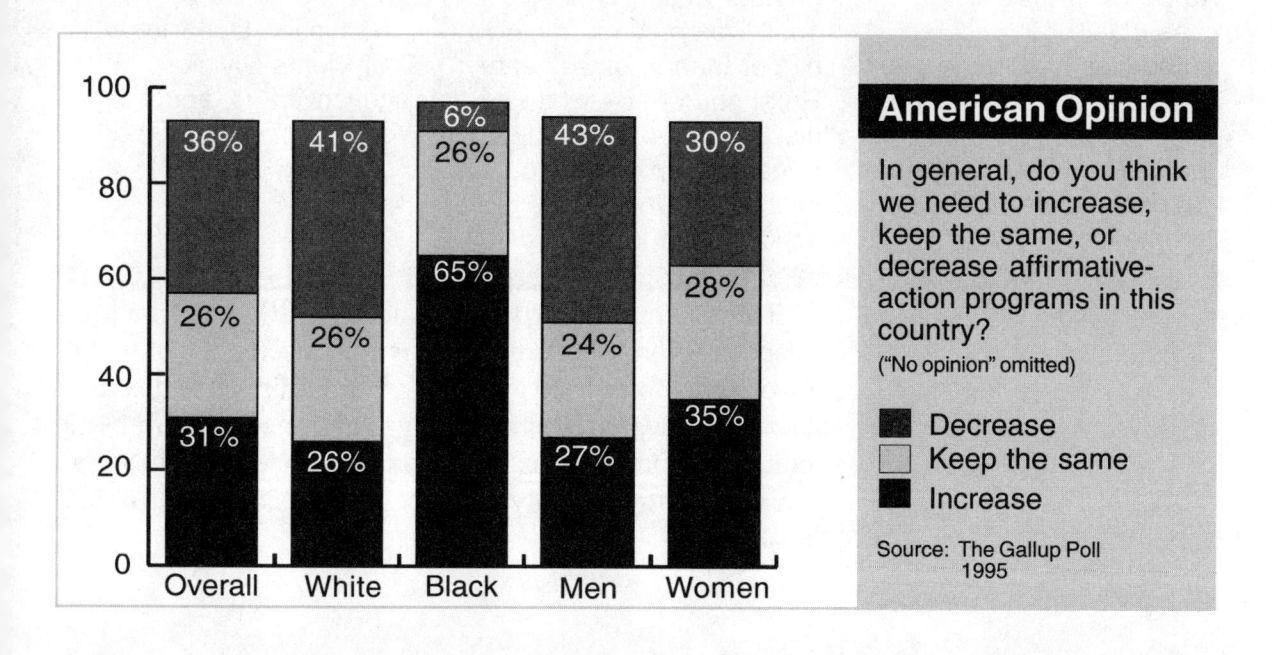

Source: The Gallup Poll 1995

The Church Arsons

A wave of arson attacks on black churches began to be reported in January 1995. For most people, black and white, the attacks are an expression of racial hatred. For a substantial minority of African Americans, they are further evidence of a persistent racism in American society.

In a 1996 Gallup survey, 42 percent of black respondents agreed the arsons "reflect the fact that American society is basically racist." Only 24 percent of white respondents agreed.

Two-thirds of the whites in Gallup's sample said the burnings were isolated incidents that did not reflect on society generally. Fewer than half the blacks, 48 percent, agreed.

As of late 1996, U.S. authorities had made 120 arrests in the arson cases. In some, though not all, of the incidents, investigators suspect racial hostility as the motive.

Some observers have suggested the racial element has been overemphasized—that some attacks were acts of teenage vandalism and that in others crime or revenge may have been the motive. Still others were the acts of deranged persons, and in some cases those arrested for burning black churches were themselves African-Americans.

Commentators noted, too, that white churches have been attacked as frequently as black ones. In fact, more white than black churches were torched between January 1995 and June 1996 —75 white churches and 73 black churches.[1] Insurance industry and arson experts also pointed out that the number of church fires in 1995 was only marginally higher than in other years. Rural churches—white and black—had suffered high rates of suspicious fires over many decades, according to insurance investigators, because their isolation made them easy targets for vandals and arsonists. "The story that has been told of the black-church burnings is more a myth than a lie—a large fiction spun out of a smaller truth," journalist Michael Kelly wrote in The New Yorker in July 1996.[2]

Civil rights groups say the figures are misleading, if for no other reason than that there are many more white than black churches—six times as many. Still, proving a racial connection can be difficult.

"There is a large class of cases where we suspect that racial hostility or religious bigotry is driving these fires, but we're not confident that we can show that beyond a reasonable doubt in a court of law," said Deval Patrick, the former head of the U.S. Justice Department's Civil Rights Division. "But race is with us, and it is with us in the context of the attacks on the black churches."[3]

The assumption driving Proposition 209 was that preference programs had created a disfranchised class of whites and other nonpreferred groups—victims of reverse discrimination. Whites, and particularly white males, were being denied jobs, promotions, contracts, and places in California's elite universities simply because of their skin color or gender.

The University of California's 8,000-point admissions system awarded an automatic 300-point bonus to blacks, American Indians, and Mexican-Americans. Connerly and other opponents charged this gave an unmerited advantage to the children of well-to-do minorities or noncitizens.

"Now, I don't find any moral defense for giving a higher-income Chicano a preference over a lower-income Chinese, especially if the Chinese has a higher academic performance," said Connerly. "What we do is harmful to people who are not part of preferred groups."[14]

Connerly offered the example of a white San Diego couple who sued to obtain university admissions records to learn why their son had been denied a place in a UC medical school. The couple presented the results at a session of the Regents' finance committee. "My mouth fell open," recalled Connerly. "They showed you had a better chance to win the California lottery than to be admitted as a white or Asian with a 4.0 grade average over another minority with a 3.2 average."[15]

From 1984 to 1994, white undergraduate enrollment at all UC campuses fell from 70 percent of the total to 49 percent. Hispanic enrollment during the period nearly doubled, from 7 percent to 13 percent. Asian enrollment grew from 16 percent to 29 percent. Black enrollment remained steady at 4 percent.

Qualified applicants were not refused undergraduate admission to the UC system, though the preference system meant some were denied places at the campuses of their first choice, Berkeley and UCLA. Nor were unqualified students being let in. According to Connerly, 16 percent of black students were admitted by exception in 1994, compared with only 2 percent of whites. But UC sets high standards. One study showed that black students at Berkeley had a mean grade point average in high school of 3.43 out of 4.0. Hispanics had a GPA of 3.65, whites had 3.86, and Asians had a near-perfect 3.95.[16]

A 1996 Berkeley study projected that without affirmative action freshman enrollment of blacks would drop 46 to 62 percent and Latino enrollment would drop 43 to 59 percent. The Asian freshman class would go up 12 to 24 percent while white freshman enrollment would rise 6 to 10 percent.[17]

> "**'What we do is harmful to people who are not part of preferred groups.'**"

As it happened, the effects of affirmative action on white men's hiring and promotion chances were difficult to document. One analyst, an opponent of Proposition 209, said there is little or no evidence that affirmative-action programs were enabling minorities and women to seize jobs from whites.

"With all of the right-wing think tanks and the resources at their disposal, you'd think there would be tons of data," said David Oppenheimer, a law professor at Golden Gate University. "They have none. That shows you how hollow this debate is."[18]

Supporters of preference refused to accept defeat in California. Hardly had the votes been counted on November 5, 1996, before the American Civil Liberties Union filed suit to block Proposition 209. Before month's end, a federal judge had issued an order barring enforcement of the proposition, and in December the Clinton administration decided to contest its constitutionality. "This is California, land of lawyers," noted Jennifer Nelson, a spokeswoman for the advocacy group Yes on 209. "There is nothing that is not challenged in court." In fact, a 1978 ballot initiative requires an appellate-court ruling before state agencies can eliminate affirmative-action programs.[19]

All the same, UC moved at once to advise some 50,000 applicants for admission that candidates would henceforth be evaluated without regard to race or gender. But California cities found themselves in a quandary: Should they dis-

American Opinion

Respondents who regard discrimination as a "very serious" problem in their home community.

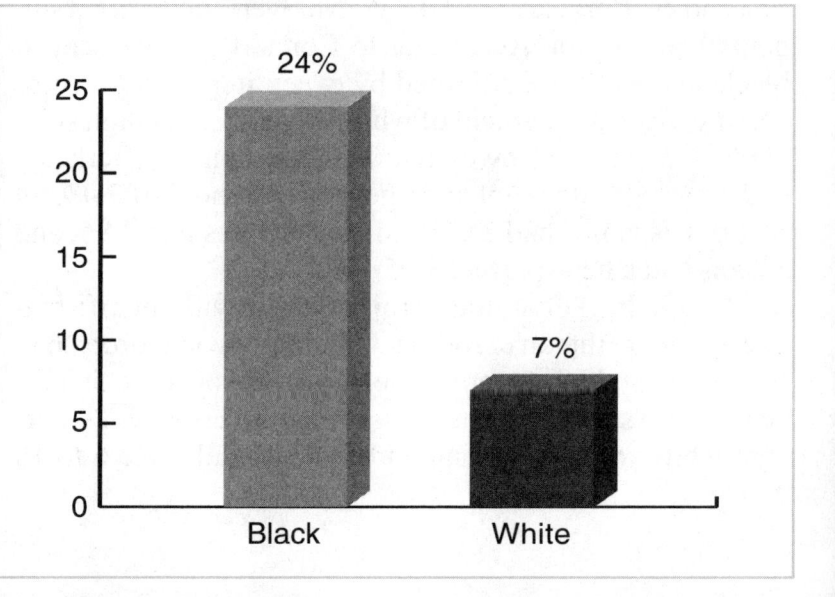

Black: 24%
White: 7%

Source: The Gallup Poll 1996

mantle their contracting programs at once, or wait for the courts to lay down the law?

"If we continue to enforce the program as it currently exists, we will undoubtedly face legal action by nonminority contractors," said Scott Emblaidge, the San Francisco deputy city attorney. "If we were to abandon it under Prop. 209, we will undoubtedly face legal action by minority contractors."[20]

Broadly, the courts have validated preference, subject to strict criteria. Supporters of affirmative action vowed to put up strong legal and political defenses wherever such programs are challenged. "We're determined to have the last word on the issue," said Kathy Spillan of Stop Prop 209. "No matter what happens, this is the beginning of a nationwide battle."[21]

Rollbacks in Massachusetts

The expectation of court challenges led Massachusetts to scale back its affirmative-action policies—some of the nation's most aggressive—in 1996.

When thirteen-year-old Julia McLaughlin, who is white, applied to the elite Boston Latin School in 1995, the school turned her down even though she outscored 103 black and Hispanic applicants on the entrance exam. Her father filed suit to overturn the Boston school committee's rigid affirmative-action policies.

The school committee reserved 35 percent of the places in Boston's three exam schools for minorities. Under threat of the suit, the committee in the summer of 1996 agreed to drop the existing racial-quota system—and to admit Julia McLaughlin.

Fittingly, the McLaughlin case came before U.S. District Judge W. Arthur Garrity, whose 1974 order for the desegregation of Boston's schools touched off a decade of near-civil war in parts of the city. The ruling led, too, to the exam schools' strict racial-quota system. Opponents of affirmative action hoped Garrity would come full circle and decide the constitutionality of the exam schools' policy. Instead, he declared the issue moot. Since Boston Latin had offered a place to the McLaughlin girl, she had nothing more at stake in the case, the judge said.

> **"Supporters of affirmative action vowed to put up strong legal and political defenses wherever such programs are challenged."**

"What a profile in courage," political commentator Jon Keller remarked. "Twenty-two years after imposing a 'solution' to Boston's segregated schools that nearly killed the city, the Julia McLaughlin case offered Garrity a chance to clean up his own mess. But at the moment of truth, Garrity blinked."[22]

Even so, the Boston school committee thoroughly overhauled its preference programs, instructing exam school admissions directors to offer places to half the applicants on merit alone. The rest would be let in according to the percentage of their racial group in the applicant pool. The effect will be to reduce the black population at Boston Latin from 24 percent to 15 percent and the Hispanic population from 11 percent to 7 percent. The white population will rise from 43 percent to 54 percent.[23]

In another rollback, Massachusetts substantially scaled back what may have been the nation's most ambitious affirmative-action program, dropping a minority-contract goal for a Boston-area public housing reconstruction project from 80 percent to 30 percent.

The $200 million federal-state project will rebuild ten crumbling housing complexes in Dorchester and Roxbury. Ninety-nine percent of the residents are minorities. The state replaced the 80 percent goal for minority contractors with an 80 percent goal of hiring firms with a record of working in Boston's minority neighborhoods.

Housing officials acknowledged the chilling effects of legal and political challenges to affirmative action.

"If we get sued and lose, that could shut down the whole project for good," said Stephen D. Pierce, director of the Massachusetts Housing Finance Authority.[24] One minority contractor agreed. "There's $200 million out there; any minority company worth its salt is going to get some work," said John B. Cruz, owner of a Roxbury construction company. "We just want the damn program to start."[25]

Republicans and Democrats

President Clinton put up a partial defense of affirmative action in 1995. "The job of ending discrimination is not over," he said. "We should have a simple slogan: Mend it, but don't end it."[26]

> "'The job of ending discrimination is not over. We should have a simple slogan: Mend it, but don't end it.'"

The issue, however, had little or no impact on the 1996 presidential campaign. In one of his last acts as Senate majority leader, Bob Dole, Clinton's Republican opponent, proposed legislation to outlaw affirmative action on the federal level. The bill went nowhere, and Dole did not press the matter until late in the race, when he endorsed the California initiative and pronounced thirty years of affirmative-action programs a failure.

Proposition 209 won; Dole lost. Are the state legislatures and the Republican Congress likely to revisit the issue? Certainly most observers expect the pressure on affirmative action to mount during the late 1990s. California voters' repudiation of affirmative action seems to guarantee that.

"A lot of people wound up waiting to see what would happen in California," Brenda A. Trolin of the National Conference of State Legislatures said in explanation of the 1996 lull. "It was almost like, 'This is a road map to see how we handle this issue.'"[27]

Congress could dismantle or at least cut back the politically fragile set-aside programs. The Small Business Administration alone disburses nearly $6 billion a year worth of preference contracts. Affirmative-action programs in employment may be safe for now. They have benefited white women more than minorities and thus have a larger and more powerful political constituency.

Supporters of preference are counting on Clinton to keep his promise to fix abuses while preserving the core of affirmative action. To most supporters, such abuses as exist have been exaggerated for partisan effect. "Affirmative-action faces a sort of opposition by slander, the notion that all affirmative-action is some form of bean counting or that it's a compromise of quality," said Deval Patrick, who resigned as chief of the Justice Department's Civil Rights Division at the end of 1996. "That has absolutely nothing to do with the way affirmative action is supposed to be done and the way the courts have upheld it."[28]

Notes: Affirmative Action Does It Widen or Narrow the Racial Divide?

1. Sam Howe Verhovek, "Vote in California Is Motivating Foes of Anti-Bias Plans," *The New York Times*, November 10, 1996, 1.
2. Adam Pertman, "Affirmative Action at Crossroads," *The Boston Globe*, October 5, 1996, 1.
3. Figures for black income and other gains were drawn from Steven A. Holmes, "Quality of Life Is Up for Many Blacks, Data Say," *The New York Times*, November 18, 1996, 1.
4. Holmes, "Quality of Life Is Up for Many Blacks."
5. Steven A. Holmes, "As Affirmative Action Ebbs, A Sense of Uncertainty Rises," *The New York Times*, July 6, 1995, 1.
6. Derrick Z. Jackson, "Facts Favor Affirmative Action," op-ed, *The Boston Globe*, October 30, 1996.
7. Daniel B. Wood, "Why a Man Who Knows Racism Fights Affirmative Action," *The Christian Science Monitor*, March 1, 1996, 1.
8. Stephen L. Carter, *Reflections of an Affirmative Action Baby* (New York: Basic Books, 1991), 5.
9. Carter, *Reflections of an Affirmative Action Baby*, 72.
10. Herman Belz, *Equality Transformed: A Quarter-Century of Affirmative Action* (New Brunswick, N.J.: Transaction Books, 1991), 22.
11. Nicholas Lemann, "Taking Affirmative Action Apart," *The New York Times Magazine*, June 11, 1995, 40.
12. Steven A. Holmes, "Justices Cast New Doubts on Minority Preferences," *The New York Times*, June 13, 1995, 1.
13. Verhovek, "Vote in California Is Motivating Foes."
14. Wood, "Why a Man Who Knows Racism Fights Affirmative Action."
15. Wood, "Why a Man Who Knows Racism Fights Affirmative Action."
16. George Will, "Powell is Out of Step with Civil Rights Advocates on Racial Preferences," syndicated column in *The Boston Globe*, July 15, 1996.
    William H. Honan, "College Admission Policy Change Heightens Debate on Impact," *The New York Times*, July 22, 1995, 7.
17. Jackson, "Facts Favor Affirmative Action."
18. Jackson, "Facts Favor Affirmative Action."
19. B. Drummond Ayres Jr., "U.S. Judge Blocks Voters' Initiative on Job Preference," *The New York Times*, November 28, 1996, 1.
    Judith Havemann, "Limit on Affirmative Action Wins in California," *The Washington Post*, November 6, 1996, B12.
20. Daniel B. Wood, "Affirmative-Action Rollback Sifts Through a Legal Sieve," *The Christian Science Monitor*, November 12, 1996, 3.
21. Verhovek, "Vote in California Is Motivating Foes."
22. Jon Keller, "It's Time for the Annual Turkey Awards," op-ed, *The Boston Globe*, November 25, 1996.
23. Karen Avenoso, "Garrity Dismisses Boston Latin Suit," *The Boston Globe*, November 20, 1996, 1.

24. Michael Grunwald, "Goal is Cut for Minority Contracts," *The Boston Globe,* October 11, 1996, 1.
25. Grunwald, "Goal is Cut for Minority Contracts."
26. Todd S. Purdum, "President Shows Fervent Support for Goals of Affirmative Action," *The New York Times*, July 20, 1995, 1.
27. Verhovek, "Vote in California Is Motivating Foes of Anti-Bias Plans."
28. "Serenely Against the Tide," *U.S. News & World Report*, November 25, 1996, 45.

Notes: The Church Arsons

1. Robert Marquand, "Church Fire Phenomenon Goes Beyond Racial Lines," *The Christian Science Monitor*, July 10, 1996, 1.
2. Marquand, "Church Fire Phenomenon Goes Beyond Racial Lines."
3. "Serenely Against the Tide," *U.S. News & World Report*, November 25, 1996, 45.

11 Israel, the Arabs, and the U.S.
Americans Give Israel Cautious Support

Americans have shown scant interest in, and still less understanding of, the long and tortured clench of Jews and Arabs in Palestine. Over the half century the Gallup Organization has tracked opinion on Israel, American views have warmed on occasion from indifference to a mild sympathy for Israel. Rarely, though, have Americans expressed more than marginal support for the Arab cause. Nor have they favored any form of direct U.S. military role in the region, either to defend the Israeli state, by turns besieged and expansionist, or as peacekeepers, to break the endless cycle of outrage and reprisal.

Levels of American knowledge of the region and concern with its problems have been modest at best. In June 1996, Gallup asked whether respondents "would happen to know" the name of the newly elected prime minister of Israel. Only 16 percent answered Benjamin Netanyahu, the leader of the conservative Likud Party. Three percent offered other names; 81 percent did not hazard a guess.

In September 1995, polltakers wanted to know how much respondents had seen and heard about the peace agreement between Israel and the Palestine Liberation Organization (PLO). Twenty-seven percent said they'd heard a "moderate" amount, 36 percent said only "a little," and 26 percent said "nothing at all." By contrast, 58 percent had heard "a great deal" and 19 percent a "moderate" amount about the double-murder trial, then in progress, of the one-time football star and minor celebrity O.J. Simpson.

"**Americans have shown scant interest in, still less understanding of, the long and tortured clench of Jews and Arabs in Palestine.**"

> "Since the 1970s, successive U.S. administrations have sought to negotiate peace between the Israelis and the Arabs."

For American policymakers, however, few conflicts have been of more absorbing interest than that in the Middle East. The United States inherited the "Palestine problem" from the exhausted British in the aftermath of World War II. Ever since, the United States has been a reliable ally of Israel, though in recent years it has consistently opposed Israeli settlement of Gaza and the West Bank, territories the Jewish state won on the battlefields of 1967.

At the same time, America's leaders have recognized the oil-rich region as of vital concern to American security and have labored to maintain alliances with Israel's Arab enemies, suppliers of much of the West's oil.

Since the 1970s, successive U.S. administrations have sought to negotiate peace between the Israelis and the Arabs. Carter, Reagan, Bush, and finally Clinton administration diplomacy managed to contain hostilities to a comparatively small area on the rim of the Arab world—Israel's frontiers and southern Lebanon. Egypt, Jordan, and Israel have made peace; Syria and Israel maintain an uneasy truce. So far, though, no initiative has produced a durable settlement that assures Israel's security and satisfies the Palestinian aspiration for a homeland. Peace has been a chimera for Israeli Jews and Palestinian Arabs alike.

The United States helped negotiate the 1993 Oslo accords in which Israel bartered land for peace and the Palestinians won an offer of autonomy they believed would lead to statehood. The Clinton administration invested heavily

As a Matter of Fact

Would you happen to know the name of the newly elected prime minister of Israel?

- Benjamin Netanyahu: 16%
- Don't know: 81%
- Other: 3%

Source: The Gallup Poll 1996

in the outcome. But events in 1995 and 1996 threatened to unravel it all: the assassination of Israeli prime minister Yitzhak Rabin in November 1995, a renewed Palestinian terror offensive early in 1996, and a conservative backlash in Israel that led to the May 1996 election of Netanyahu, who had campaigned on a pledge of slowing down the implementation of the Oslo accords and, to some critics, seemed bent on undermining them entirely.

The troubles turned on the extraordinarily sensitive questions of the Jewish settlements in the territories and of Israeli control over Jerusalem. To the Palestinians, and to much of international opinion, Israeli government moves in late 1996 to restore economic aid to Jewish West Bank settlers and to authorize new Jewish housing projects in Jerusalem were provocations. To Israel, the Palestinians were pressing for more, far more, than Oslo meant to deliver.

Tension mounted and violence flared in Gaza and the West Bank in the autumn of 1996, delaying the cession of Hebron, the traditional burial place of the patriarch Abraham and sacred to Jews and Arabs alike, to the semiautonomous Palestinian Authority. Early in '97, with prodding from the Americans and King Hussein of Jordan, the two sides resolved the immediate dispute over Hebron and negotiated an agreement to push back the staged Israeli withdrawal from most of the West Bank by about a year, to mid-1998.[1]

During the autumn crisis, Benjamin Netanyahu and PLO Chairman Yasser Arafat, the two paramount leaders, grew increasingly mutually suspicious and distrustful. Arafat especially seemed to have lost his faith in Israel's good intentions. The leaders' public statements emphasized the depth and bitterness of the dispute.

"Don't they understand where they are dragging this region? In the end, it will be impossible to stop the downward flight," Arafat said in December 1996. "After the dead are laid to rest, we will be standing in the same place."[2]

Netanyahu, defiant, accused the PLO and its allies of trying to negotiate through terror. "I'd like to remind you that for a hundred years of Zionist settlement there was always resistance to settlement," he said. "The reason the settlements were successful is because we were able to overcome this resistance. We are under an attack aimed at us all."[3]

> **Netanyahu accused the PLO and its allies of trying to negotiate through terror.**

> "Rival claims on the ancient city of Jerusalem, rigidly segregated today into Jewish and Arab districts, are at the core of the conflict."

Comparatively minor disputes disrupted the Hebron negotiations and fueled the autumn outbreaks. The two sides had not yet approached the most difficult issues—Jerusalem and the problem of refugees. If Israel and the PLO were at an impasse on the terms of the Israeli pullout from Hebron, where 500 Jewish settlers live in fortified enclaves amid 160,000 Arabs, how were they ever to settle the far more volatile question of Jerusalem? The Oslo agreement left this issue for the last of the seven stages to peace, but already in 1996 it threatened to wreck the process.

Rival claims on the ancient city, rigidly segregated today into Jewish and Arab districts, are at the center of the conflict. "When you separate all trivia from substance, this [Jerusalem] is the core of the Jewish existence," said Jerusalem's mayor, Ehud Olmert. "This is everything that constitutes the *raison d'etre* of our existence."[4]

The Arabs are entirely as passionate. Palestinians want East Jerusalem for the capital of their state. The Dome of the Rock in Jerusalem has become the most prominent symbol of Palestinian nationhood. For the religious, the Dome and the neighboring Al Aksa Mosque are sacred shrines—the two together constitute the third-holiest place in all of Islam.

"This is a place for Muslims, only Muslims," Sheik Mohammed Hussein, director of the mosque, said of the plateau known to Jews as the Temple Mount and to Muslims as Haram al-Sharif—the noble sanctuary. "There is no temple here, only Al Aksa Mosque and the Dome of the Rock. It is not a matter of assumption, or history or archeology. It is a matter of religion and belief. There is no place for argument."[5]

In September 1996, an Israeli excavation near the Muslim shrines touched off violent outbreaks among Palestinians. The dig, a tunnel exit from an archeological site, did not seem significant in itself. It did, however, take on enormous importance as a symbol of who controls Jerusalem. Arafat called the work "a crime against our holy places."[6] Israeli hard-liners, including Mayor Olmert, dismissed Palestinian objections. They said they would rule the City of David as they saw fit.

In mid-October, Arafat suggested U.S. peacekeeping troops might be needed to quell the outbreaks, in which more than seventy Palestinians and Israelis were killed, and restore calm to the troubled areas. The suggestion seemed to surprise American policymakers. It hung in the air for a time, then dissolved. Arafat said no more about it.

American opinion has been clear on the matter of military involvement from the start: no U.S. forces in Palestine. Gallup first asked the question—whether the United States should send soldiers to maintain peace there—in January 1946. An overwhelming 83 percent answered no. Only 13 percent thought the Americans should take on a military role.

Broadly, Americans have tended to favor the Israelis, according to Gallup. In a 1991 poll, 64 percent said their sympathies were with the Israelis and only 7 percent were sympathetic to the Palestinians. In November 1996, though, with the Oslo process imperiled, only 38 percent were sympathetic to Israel. Palestinian support had doubled to 15 percent; 27 percent, registered no opinion.

From Haifa to the Holocaust

It is perhaps the longest-running, most intractable conflict in the modern world. Arabs and Jews have struggled in Palestine since the last quarter of the nineteenth century, when antisemitism in Europe gave rise to the Lovers of Zion, whose program called for Jewish settlements and an eventual Jewish homeland in the Land of Israel. The original Zionist group, a party of fourteen, landed at Haifa, on the Mediterranean, on July 7, 1882. There were stirrings of opposition from the outset, and later that year the Ottoman overlords of Palestine moved to restrict Jewish immigration. The Zionists persisted, and by 1903 around 10,000 Jews, some of them fleeing savage pogroms in Russia, had settled in the region. For Zionists, this meant a return to the Biblical homeland—the ultimate end of two thousand years of Jewish history.[7] Mythically, Jews and Arabs share a common origin. Both peoples regard themselves as descendants of the patriarch Abraham—the Arabs from Ishmael, Abraham's first son born of Hagar, handmaiden of Sarah; the Jews from Isaac, son of Abraham and Sarah.

With the destruction of the Temple in 586 B.C., the Jews of Biblical Judea were banished to Babylon. In due course,

> **American opinion has been clear from the start: No U.S. forces in Palestine.**

> **Though religion is an element of the conflict, much of it is secular.**

the Persians restored the region to the Jews, and they lived there under a succession of nominal suzerains until the Romans in, A.D. 70, burned the second Temple and touched off the Diaspora.

According to Islamic belief, the Prophet Muhammad, born in A.D. 570, carried God's final revelations to mankind. When his Arabian adherents swept through the Middle East and North Africa in the seventh and eighth centuries, Arabic became the language of Islam and Islam the religion of the region. And Muslims ruled Jerusalem from 1187, when they drove out the Crusaders, until a British imperial army captured the city from the Ottoman Turks in December 1917.

Arabs and Jews alike regard themselves as more than a religion or an ethnic group or a cultural tradition. They regard themselves as a people. Though religion is an element of the conflict, much of it is secular. Many of the issues dividing Jews and Arabs—territory, economic self-determination, security—are negotiable matters on the face of it. But negotiation and compromise have never been a feature of Arab-Jewish relations.

Beginning in 1904, the second wave of Jewish immigration led to the establishment of agricultural kibbutzes and cooperative villages, among them Tel Aviv, a garden suburb (established in 1909) of the ancient port of Jaffa. The Turks continued intermittently to choke off the Jewish influx, Jews were given second-class citizenship and the Arab *fellahin*—landless peasants the Jewish settlers often displaced—broke into occasional violent protest. Still, by the beginning of World War I in 1914, around 90,000 Jews were settled in Palestine, 13 percent of the region's population.[8]

War destroyed the Turkish empire. A British army under General Edmund Allenby, with insurgent Arabs on its eastern flank (and their British adviser/admirer T. E. Lawrence, in his flowing robes), marched northward from Egypt, swept over the Judean hills, and entered Jerusalem on December 9, 1917.

Allenby's capture of the city inaugurated a confused and murky era of British rule. In November 1917, as the imperial army approached Jerusalem, the British government's Balfour Declaration "viewed with favor" a Jewish homeland in Palestine. At the same time, the British were giving their wartime Arab allies assurances of independence.

The League of Nations assigned the British a mandate over Palestine in 1921. Much as the Ottomans had done, the British over the next two decades followed a fits-and-starts policy of allowing, then restricting, Jewish immigration and land sales. Hitler's rise in Germany created unprecedented migratory pressures in the mid-1930s. By 1936, the Jewish population of Palestine had reached 400,000, 30 percent of the total.

The Arab response: rebellion. From 1936 to 1939, Arab groups launched periodic violent outbreaks—arsons, bombings, assassinations—against Jewish settlers and British imperial police and military forces. As a defensive measure, the British allowed the Jewish underground militia Haganah, forerunner of the Israeli Army, to operate openly.

The British finally quelled the uprising in 1939 with what amounted to a repudiation of the Balfour Doctrine. A government white paper decreed that Palestine would become an associated state of the British Empire within ten years and that it would be an *Arab* state. Jewish immigration and land sales were to be strictly regulated, and after five years Arab consent would be required for any immigration at all.[9]

In 1945, the remnants of European Jewry—the approximately one million survivors of the Holocaust, out of a prewar European Jewish population of 7 million—sought a safe haven in Palestine. The British, disavowing any obligation, humanitarian or otherwise, to Germany's victims, continued their 1939 policy of restricting the inflow of Jews into the mandate.

The Arabs made their position uncompromisingly clear: They were not responsible for the Holocaust (though the mufti of Jerusalem had struck a wartime agreement with the Axis powers that would have led to the extermination of Palestinian Jews), and if the West felt bound to make some recompense, that should not be at Arab expense.[10]

"To draw the boldest outlines of the past is to make Israel's basic case," David K. Shipler wrote in his 1986 study *Arab and Jew*. "To sketch the present is to see the Arabs' plight."[11]

> **In 1945, the remnants of European Jewry sought a safe haven in Palestine.**

Enter the Americans

Immediate postwar U.S. concerns about the Middle East involved oil and the potential of Soviet penetration. Like their British counterparts, American diplomats were cool to the claims of the Holocaust survivors. President Harry Truman, however, acting more or less on his own, pressured the reluctant British to admit 100,000 Jewish displaced persons to Palestine.

Truman pressed, too, for a partition plan that would divide the region into Jewish and Arab substates. In October 1946, he announced U.S. backing for such a plan, even though public opinion in America, by Gallup's measure, endorsed a policy of noninvolvement. In a February 1947 poll, only 27 percent thought the United States should "try to do anything" about the Palestinian situation. Sixty-one percent said the United States should do nothing at all; only 3 percent believed America should work for a settlement through the newly established United Nations.

Truman persisted, partly as a matter of conviction, partly as a response to the intense lobbying of American Jewish organizations. The British—weakened, drained of resources, stretched thin, their imperial vocation fading—gave in finally. In February 1947, the British handed Palestine over to the United Nations—one of the world organization's first major tests.

The U.N. solution, approved in a General Assembly vote

American Opinion

Is your overall opinion of Israel very favorable, mostly favorable, mostly unfavorable, or very unfavorable?

Response	Percentage
Very favorable	17%
Mostly favorable	45%
Mostly unfavorable	18%
Very unfavorable	11%
No opinion	9%

Source: The Gallup Poll 1996

of November 19, 1947, called for a partition that gave more land to the Jews (650,000 population) than to the Arabs (1.27 million population). The Jewish Agency accepted the plan; the Arab League rejected it, refusing to countenance a Jewish state in the midst of what they thought of as Arab territory. The British, meanwhile, prepared to withdraw their 80,000-man garrison from Palestine by May 1948.

The British departed on schedule, on May 14, 1948. No sooner had the color guard at the King David Hotel in Jerusalem hauled down the Union Jack than the Jewish Agency, acting as the provisional government, issued a decree establishing the state of Israel. The next day Arab forces attacked, vowing to "drive the Jews into the sea." The 1948 war ended in an Israeli victory that, among other things, created a displaced, floating Arab population of some 700,000 and set the stage for forty years of uninterrupted conflict.

By supporting partition, the United States had done much to assure the creation of Israel. But American opinion remained noncommittal on the issue of the new nation's survival. In July 1948, with Israel under heavy Arab military pressure, Gallup polltakers asked whether "the Jews in Palestine" should be permitted to buy arms and war material from the United States. Fewer than one-quarter, 23 percent, answered yes; 62 percent said no.

From Suez to the '73 War

Americans still did not favor becoming involved when the Suez Canal crisis boiled over in 1955 and 1956. Several factors combined to ignite the crisis: the rise of Pan-Arab leader Gamal Abdel Nasser in Egypt, Israel's concern over the fragile 1949 frontiers, the U.S.–Soviet rivalry, and Britain's waning but still vital imperial instincts, which flared when Nasser moved to nationalize the Suez Canal.

On October 29, 1956, Israeli parachute troops floated down on the central Sinai, opening the Suez War. When Egypt moved to counter the assault, the British and French announced that they would land at Port Said to protect the canal. British and French warplanes attacked Egyptian air bases.

British indecision and delay gave the United States,

"
By supporting partition, the United States had done much to assure the creation of Israel.

"

> "Decisive victory in the '67 war gave Israel defensible borders, but also an inassimilable, suppressed, and politically volatile population of 1.3 million Palestinians in Gaza and the West Bank."

which had not been informed of the British–French–Israeli scheme, time to apply diplomatic pressure and turn back the offensive. The Americans coerced the British into accepting a ceasefire on November 6–7. By then, though, while their allies dithered, the Israelis had overrun the entire Sinai Peninsula.

American opinion strongly favored neutrality in the Suez crisis. Only around a quarter in a September 1956 Gallup survey thought the United States should help in the event the British and French went to war over the canal. The surveys showed still less support for Israel. In a November poll, only 10 percent approved of Israeli actions in the conflict.

Paradoxically, the outcome of the Suez Crisis drove the United States and Israel into closer alliance. By 1967, America had replaced France as the major supplier of modern weapons to Israel. Weapons, however, did not guarantee security. Paramilitary forces of the PLO (founded 1964) carried out hit-and-run raids along Israel's borders. In the north, the Syrians diverted the Jordan River headwaters to dry up Israeli irrigation schemes and shelled Jewish settlements from the Golan Heights. Then, in mid-May, Egyptian forces crossed the Suez Canal and expelled U.N. peacekeepers from the Sinai, Gaza, and Sharm al-Sheik, the strategic height that commands Israel's outlet to the Red Sea.

The Israelis responded with a powerful land, sea, and air assault. In six climactic days in June 1967, Israeli armed forces overwhelmed the Arab alliance of Syria, Jordan, and Egypt; seized the Old City of Jerusalem and the West Bank, Gaza, and the Golan Heights; and pushed columns of putty-colored tanks across the Sinai to the banks of the Suez Canal.

From Camp David to Oslo

Decisive victory in the '67 war gave Israel defensible borders, but also an inassimilable, suppressed, and politically volatile population of 1.3 million Palestinians in Gaza and the West Bank. The war also increased the influence of the PLO. In reaction to the existence of Israel and to the neglect of their Arab allies, Palestinians began to plan for their own state, independent of Jordan, Egypt and Syria.

Most Favored Nations

Hands down, Canada and Great Britain grade as America's favorite foreign countries over four decades of Gallup organization surveys.

America's northern neighbor scored consistently in the 90 percent range in polling from 1953 through 1996. Britain, the closest of U.S. allies during two world wars and the Cold War, won 80–90 percent favorable ratings. America's southern partner in free trade, Mexico, generally rated in the 60s, though in 1993, with controversies over immigration, loan repayments and trade, the figure fell to a low of 43 percent. Gallup respondents were generally friendly to France, the other major Western European ally of the U.S. during most of the 20th century. Scores ranged in the 60s and 70s to a high for the period of 79 percent.

In 1953, with memories of World War II still vivid, Germany received only a 54 percent favorable rating. By the 1990s, though, the reliable, U.S.-friendly Germans were scoring in the 70 percent range.

Ratings of Russia, America's long-term Cold War rival, rose from a negligible 1 percent in 1953, the year of Stalin's death, to a post-*glasnost* high of 66 percent in 1991.

A harsh communist regime and disputes over trade and human rights generally depressed China's ratings. Approval levels were in the 30 percent range during the 1990s, though these were up substantially from a low of 5 percent in 1967, during the Cultural Revolution of 1966–69.

In the Middle East, Israel's ratings ranged from a low of 49 percent during the Suez Crisis of 1956 to a high of 79 percent at the end of the Gulf War with Iraq in 1991. Egypt's approvals ranged in the 30s and 40s to a Gulf War high of 66 percent.

Syria, suspected of supporting terrorism over the years, scored only a 23 percent approval rating in 1991. Iraq, America's enemy during the Gulf War, earned a paltry rating that year of 7 percent.

The Palestinians pushed their way to the front as the overriding issue in the Arab-Israeli conflict.[12]

The United Nations, which had created Israel, veered sharply toward the Arab view and recognized Palestinians' right to self-determination. U.N. Resolution 242 rejected the notion of territorial acquisition by conflict. With its implicit suggestion that Israel could exchange land for peace, the resolution formed the basis for later efforts to reach a permanent settlement.

Egypt failed in its 1973 bid to retake the Sinai by force —the short, sharp, bloody conflict the Israelis call the Yom Kippur War. Still, the Israelis had been hard-pressed in the initial phase, and Egypt's improved military performance restored national confidence and gave President Anwar al-

> "As the Arab nations and Israel carried on their blood feud, the Palestinians became more insistent in their demand for nationhood."

Sadat, Nasser's successor, an opening to reach for a separate peace. The Camp David accords of 1979 brought peace between Israel and Egypt; and the Egyptians regained the Sinai in the bargain.

Israel, however, gave little indication it was prepared to negotiate away the Golan Heights, Gaza, and the West Bank —the nearer territories it had won by force of arms in 1967. On the contrary, the Israelis planted close to 150 settlements in the occupied lands. By 1996, 145,000 Jews were settled in the territories.

The PLO, Saudi Arabia, Jordan, and Syria rejected the Camp David settlement. In many ways, the conflict deepened and grew fiercer. Lebanon was drawn in beginning in the mid-1970s, and a bloody civil war culminating in the Israeli invasion of 1982 nearly destroyed the country. Syria and Iraq remained implacably hostile, sponsoring periodic terror offensives that seemed to draw the entire world into the conflict.

And all along—through the wars of 1948, 1956, 1967, 1973, and 1982—the Palestinian problem festered. "The struggles generated a new subculture of Arabs divorced from their own land," Shipler wrote. "Palestinians found themselves scattered and rejected in the Arab world at large, excluded from full participation in the Arab countries where many settled, and confined to squalid refugee camps, often by the venal politics of their own leaders." As the Arab nations and Israel carried on their blood feud, the Palestinians became more insistent in their demand for nationhood.[13]

Through all these developments, American opinion remained aloof. In June 1967, at the time of the Six-Day War, a majority, 53 percent, told Gallup polltakers the United States should steer clear of the troubles in the Middle East. Only 12 percent thought the United States should help Israel. A year later, only around a quarter, 24 percent, said the United States ought to supply Israel with arms and war material should another full-scale war break out. And only 9 percent thought U.S troops should be sent to help the Israelis.

Americans were pessimistic, too, about the prospects for long-term peace. In January 1979, Gallup asked whether the Camp David agreement would bring lasting peace between Israel and Egypt. Only 24 percent thought it would;

55 percent thought it would not; 21 percent were too confused by the tangle of Middle East politics to venture an opinion.

A 1990 Gallup survey suggested that the passage of eleven years of Middle East history had left Americans no more hopeful. During the Reagan years, Cold War preoccupations brought the United States and Israel into closer alliance. In the Reagan view, the Israelis were useful allies against Soviet-backed regimes in Iraq and Syria; U.S. policymakers, too, viewed the PLO as Soviet-dominated. American policy made it easier for Israel to pursue a hard line on the question of the territories.

At the same time, the spontaneous Palestinian uprising known as the Intifada (1987–1990) focused world attention on Israel and the plight of the Arabs as never before. The Israeli reaction to the insurgency, widely viewed as harsh, led to U.N. condemnations and, in 1988, to a PLO declaration of independence for a Palestinian state in Gaza and the West Bank.

Yasser Arafat shrewdly seized on the Intifada to put further pressure on Israel (and the United States) to negotiate directly with the PLO. He also made important concessions that led him into trouble with more radical Arabs. In 1990, he issued statements implicitly recognizing Israel's right to exist and explicitly condemning terrorism.

"Enough is enough. Enough is enough. Enough is enough," Arafat said.[14]

Oslo and the Troubles of 1996

The Oslo agreements of September 1993 made permanent peace at least theoretically possible. From January to August of that year, Israeli and PLO representatives met in secret in the Norwegian capital. On September 9, 1993, Arafat signed a letter recognizing Israel; Rabin, the Israeli prime minister, signed a letter recognizing the PLO as the representative of the Palestinian people. "The time has come to take a risk for peace," Rabin told the Knesset, the Israeli parliament.[15]

The accords were signed in Washington on September 13. The remarkable image of Arafat and Rabin clasping hands, unthinkable only a few years earlier, gave cause for

> **The Oslo agreements of September 1993 made permanent peace at least theoretically possible.**

> "Even well-intentioned Palestinians and Israelis disagree on the meaning and potential of the Oslo accords."

hope that a century of conflict might be nearing an end, that the 3.5 million Jews and 2 million Arabs in the lands of the Palestinian mandate could learn to live amicably together.

That may be an overly optimistic view, however. Americans certainly think so. When Gallup asked in a 1994 poll how likely it was that the Israeli/PLO accords would lead to a lasting peace, only 3 percent of respondents thought it very likely. Close to 60 percent took the view that the chances for Middle East peace were not too likely or somewhat likely.

Even well-intentioned Palestinians and Israelis disagree on the meaning and potential of the Oslo accords. To Israel, they are transitional and will not necessarily lead to the establishment of a Palestinian state. The Palestinians regard the Oslo process as having a certain ending in Arab sovereignty over Gaza and the West Bank.

When he first learned of it, Netanyahu called the Oslo agreement "the start of Israel's destruction." During the election campaign, he opposed the return of the Golan Heights to Syria and the establishment of a Palestinian state. Netanyahu's rise thus stirred deep doubts among the Palestinian leadership that the Israelis were willing to make the necessary sacrifices for peace—the renunciation of lands holy to Jews and as necessary as life to Arabs.

The processes of history forged this modern obsession with a few thousand square miles of broken hills and dry valleys. As Shipler notes, the old distinction between nomadic Arab desert tribes and sedentary town-dwelling Jews has largely disappeared. "In its place, a passion for the land —as divinely given, as a mystical force, as a symbol of peoplehood and nationality, as a place of origin and security—now governs the conflict and fuels the violence between the two peoples," he wrote.[16]

Divisions among Israeli Jews have grown more desperate and bitter in the wake of the movement toward peace, the Rabin assassination, and the advent of the hawkish Likud party—so much so that in one survey more than 40 percent of Israelis feared their country was headed for civil war. As it happens, many observers see Jewish Israel as two countries: a liberal/secular society with a longing for accommodation and reconciliation, at odds with a deeply nationalist/religious society that has no desire at all to live on terms of equality with Arabs.

"Two peoples are living side by side, speaking two languages in the same tongue, reacting differently to the same events," the author Yizhar Smilansky wrote on the anniversary of a religious fanatic's killing of Rabin.[17]

The Israeli journalist Daniel Ben-Simon had this to say of the divide, perhaps unbridgeable, among Israeli Jews: "For the religious, Rabin represents the Jew who wants to be a non-Jew. His peace vision was part of this, part of the bigger vision of what Israel should be. Should it be part of the international community, part of the Middle East, or something apart?"[18]

So the difficulties over Hebron, the expansion of the settlements and the timetable for an Israeli withdrawal were the outward signs of serious inward disturbances. The outcome seemed to lie more with Israel than with the Palestinians. Which vision, secular or religious, will prevail?

"I have strong emotions about the parts of the Land of Israel that are heavily populated by Palestinians," said Ehud Barak, a former Israeli army chief of staff, an opposition Labor Party leader and an advocate of accord. "It has to do with the roots of our civilization. But in reality, it's clear that we cannot hold all this territory. Toward the end of the twentieth century, we cannot have messianic dreams."[19]

The stubborn strength of those dreams threatens to fracture Israel and spoil the chance for a settlement. The secular nation recognizes that the dream is the enemy of peace, and that the Palestinians will not simply disappear.

"Whatever happens in war or diplomacy, whatever territory is won or lost, whatever accommodations or compromises are finally made," wrote Shipler, "the future guarantees that Arabs and Jews will remain close neighbors in this weary land, entangled in each other's fears. They will not escape from one another. They will not find peace in treaties, or in victories. They will find it, if at all, by looking into each other's eyes."[20]

Notes: Israel, the Arabs, and the U.S. Americans Give Israel Cautious Support

1. Serge Schmemann, "Israel–PLO Deal Reported on 1998 West Bank Pullout, Easing Way to Hebron Pact," *The New York Times*, January 13, 1997, 1.
2. Serge Schmemann, "Moving to Defuse Split, Netanyahu and Arafat Talk," *The New York Times*, December 16, 1996, 1.
3. Schmemann, "Moving to Defuse Split, Netanyahu and Arafat Talk."
4. Serge Schmemann, "Rival Claims on Jerusalem Lie at Heart of Palestinian-Israeli Hostility," *The New York Times*, October 27, 1996, 14.
5. Schmemann, "Rival Claims on Jerusalem."
6. Alan Cooperman, "Bullets not stones," *U.S. News & World Report*, October 7, 1996, 44.
7. Ian J. Bickerton and Carla L. Klausner, *A Concise History of the Arab-Israeli Conflict* (Englewood, N.J.: Prentice Hall, second edition, 1995), 23.
8. Bickerton and Klausner, *A Concise History of the Arab-Israeli Conflict*, 23.
9. Bickerton and Klausner, *A Concise History of the Arab-Israeli Conflict*, 54.
10. Bickerton and Klausner, *A Concise History of the Arab-Israeli Conflict*, 68.
11. David K. Shipler, *Arab and Jew: Wounded Spirits in a Promised Land* (New York: Times Books, 1986), 10.
12. Bickerton and Klausner, *A Concise History of the Arab-Israeli Conflict*, 152–53.
13. Shipler, *Arab and Jew*, 9.
14. Bickerton and Klausner, *A Concise History of the Arab-Israeli Conflict*, 222.
15. Bickerton and Klausner, *A Concise History of the Arab-Israeli Conflict*, 270.
16. Shipler, *Arab and Jew*, 8.
17. Joel Greenberg, "Rabin's Death Still Divides Israel," *The New York Times*, The Week in Review, November 10, 1996, 3.
18. Ethan Bronner, "After Rabin, rifts not healed," *The Boston Globe*, October 24, 1996, 1.
19. Anthony Lewis, "No Messianic Dreams," op-ed, *The New York Times*, December 19, 1996.
20. Shipler, *Arab and Jew*, 16.

Campaign Reform
12 Can We Cut Spending Without Curbing Free Speech?

Americans are of two minds about politics and politicians. They mistrust the leaders they elect and at the same time expect great things of them. The commanding role of money and the candidates' brazen flouting of the spirit of campaign-finance laws fill them with disgust, yet they rarely turn offenders out of office. Fewer than half the voters troubled even to register their choices in the 1996 presidential election, the lowest rate of participation since Calvin Coolidge defeated John Davis in 1924. And they blamed the candidates and the journalists who cover them for their lack of interest.

Only around half the respondents in a post-1996 election Gallup Organization survey said they were very satisfied (14 percent) or somewhat satisfied (40 percent) with the conduct of the presidential campaign. A sizable minority were somewhat dissatisfied (26 percent) or very dissatisfied (19 percent).

They complained about the tiresome, dispiriting barrage of political advertisements on television. They called for an overhaul of regulations that govern campaign finances. Strong majorities favored strict limits on the amounts the candidates can collect and spend to wage an election campaign.

For their part, some political leaders and campaign consultants found fault with the electorate. If a country gets the leaders it deserves, perhaps that is because it creates the voters it deserves. In the aftermath of the 1996 campaign,

> "**Americans mistrust the leaders they elect and at the same time expect great things of them.**"

> "'What you see more and more, particularly in this whole Baby Boomer group, is that their interest in politics is only triggered to the extent it has an impact in their own family and immediate surroundings.'"

politicians complained of self-absorbed, inattentive, petulant, and above all ill-informed voters who griped about government intrusion at one moment and seemed to expect the presidential candidates to take up the matter of stop signs on Main Street at the next.

Talk-show callers confused Social Security with Medicare. They objected to high levels of taxation but were at a loss to distinguish among federal, state, local, and Social Security levies. One Harvard survey showed that most people thought the United States spends more on foreign aid, which consumes a minuscule 2 percent of the budget, than on Medicare, which accounts for 13 percent.

Voters may say they want their leaders to confront large questions and articulate a clear, compelling vision of the nation's future. To many observers, though, the reality is otherwise: In 1996 people responded, when they responded at all, to such issues as teenage smoking and electronic chips that deny children access to sexually explicit or violent programs on television.

"What you see more and more, particularly in this whole Baby Boomer group, is that their interest in politics is only triggered to the extent it has an impact in their own family and immediate surroundings," said William Carrick, a California political consultant who advised the Clinton campaign. "Are the voters totally disinterested? I don't think so. On the other extreme, are they sitting in front of the TV set every night trying to figure these things out? No."[1]

American Opinion

Were you very satisfied, somewhat satisfied, somewhat dissatisfied, or very dissatisfied with the conduct of the presidential campaign in 1996?

Response	Percent
Very satisfied	14%
Somewhat satisfied	40%
Somewhat dissatisfied	26%
Very dissatisfied	19%

Source: The Gallup Poll 1996

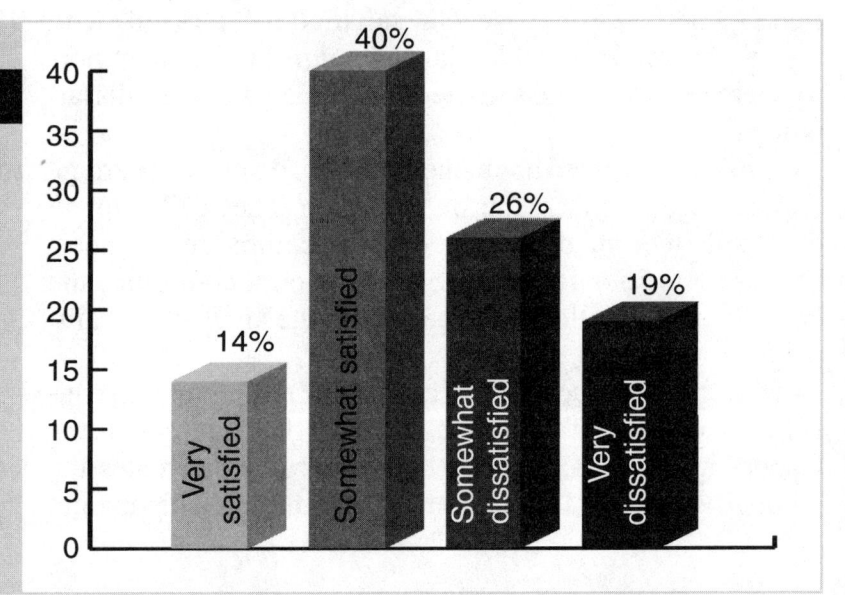

Former Tennessee governor Lamar Alexander, a failed Republican presidential candidate, learned early on in his campaign that the people who showed up for his events were preoccupied with issues close to home. In Mount Dora, Florida, in 1995, for example, voters wanted to talk about violence in their public schools because an eighth-grader had just been shot in one of them.

"We talked a long time about what to do about that," recalled Alexander. "We talked through what we could do and really decided there wasn't anything Washington could do. The responsibility was right there in Mount Dora."[2]

A General Discontent

Post-1996 election surveys suggested a considerable degree of voter disappointment with the candidates—as noted, only around half the Gallup sample thought the campaign measured up. The press came out slightly ahead of the politicians. Fifty-six percent of respondents said they were very satisfied or somewhat satisfied with the news media's performance during the campaign. A substantial minority, 42 percent, however, were somewhat dissatisfied or very dissatisfied.

Those attitudes may help explain the lowest rate of voter participation in 72 years. Turnout fell from 55 percent in 1992 to 49 percent in 1996, even though the voting population had become older and better educated and 5 million new voters had been added to the rolls.

What accounts for the public's apathy and dissatisfaction? Possible reasons, suggested Curtis Gans of the Committee for the Study of the American Electorate, were the 1990s fashion of antigovernment demagoguery, the rightward shift of the Republican Party, a Democratic drift away from traditional liberal causes and constituencies, and the savagery of political attack ads.[3]

A general sense of well-being among the electorate and the absence of compelling issues may have been part of the answer. By most measures, the economy performed well in 1995 and 1996. Inflation and unemployment were low, growth steady if unspectacular. Voters may be more likely to act when pressing issues are at stake. In the view of some, nothing really important needed to be settled in 1996.

"
Voters may be more likely to act when pressing issues are at stake.
"

> "The citizens' group Common Cause, which advocates strict limits on political finances, estimated total expenditures for the '96 campaign cycle at an astonishing $2 billion."

As it turned out, both major-party candidates avoided discussions of difficult, complex, divisive issues such as welfare, abortion, and affirmative action. President Clinton emphasized his family-leave initiative and other feel-good issues. Republican challenger Bob Dole dwelled on character, claiming himself to be the better man, promised a large tax cut that most voters figured the country could not afford, and, toward the end, sought to gain ground with an assault on questionable Democratic campaign financing practices, particularly the solicitation of money from foreign sources.

To a degree, the commentator George Will suggested, "nonvoting is the way contented people express passive consent to current conditions. And nonvoting is a sensible way for people who feel soiled by contemporary campaigning to express disgust."[4]

Voter ignorance, if that is not too strong a term, is another matter.

"It's a problem with deep roots," said Marvin "Mickey" Edwards, a former Oklahoma congressman at Harvard's Kennedy School of Government. "The public schools do a bad job of teaching American history and politics. The media does a bad job of giving the voters information. Where can you go to get a good, general, fair, and objective telling of what's on the table?"[5]

Money and Politics

"Money is the mother's milk of politics," the California Democratic politician Jesse Unruh said in 1962.[6] True then, truer now—and the sums expended on political campaigns in the 1990s would make Unruh gasp.

In 1972, all candidates for Congress together spent a total of $77.3 million on their campaigns. In the 1996 races, congressional candidates ran through an estimated $800 million while the presidential contenders spent another $800 million. The citizens' group Common Cause, which advocates strict limits on political finances, estimated total expenditures for the 1996 campaign cycle at an astonishing $2 billion—three times as much as the 1992 campaign.

Though Democratic fund-raising practices drew more

unwanted attention in 1996, the Republicans easily outraised and outspent their rivals. As of November 25, 1996, the Republican National Committee had disbursed $168 million for the year—nearly twice the $87 million the Democratic National Committee had allocated. During the two-year cycle, the RNC outspent the DNC by $226 million to $130 million.[7]

The totals do not include so-called soft money, funds solicited from corporations, labor unions, and other special interests for general "party-building" work. The Republicans spent at least $111 million in soft money in 1995–96. The Democrats were slower to report; as of September 30, 1996, they had spent $76 million, a figure certain to rise in the final accounting.[8] And this excludes expenditures by special-interest groups—such as trade unions and business associations—or issue ads, phone banks, and get-out-the-vote efforts.

Where does all the swag come from? Tens of thousands of individuals contributed sums ranging upward to the legal limit of $1,000 for one candidate. Candidates for office—billionaires Ross Perot, an independent, and Steve Forbes, a Republican, to name two—tapped their personal fortunes without limit. Political action committees, or PACs, and special interests poured in millions to both parties.

One analyst sought an explanation for the political parties' impressive ability to raise money in America's tradition of voluntarism. "The ease with which a little persuasion can coax money from Americans for a worthy purpose has no parallel in the rest of the world, nor is there any parallel to the extensive and thriving American fund raising industry," wrote Frank J. Sorauf.[9] This willingness to pay to further a cause has made American politics so expensive a proposition that candidates actually calculate the cost of a single vote, just as manufacturers figure the unit cost of the articles they produce.

Special interests are the largest contributors. They seem, too, to expect the most in return—in access, in legislation, in favors.

U.S. businesses, by far the largest single source of campaign largesse, contribute millions. Philip Morris, the tobacco conglomerate, gave $2.2 million to the Republicans; the Association of Trial Lawyers raised more than $1.5

"
Though Democratic fund-raising practices drew more unwanted attention in 1996, the Republicans easily outraised and outspent their rivals.
"

million for the Democrats. Foreign firms with American subsidiaries lavished funds on both major parties—Joseph Seagram & Sons, the Canadian distiller, gave in excess of $1 million, roughly 60 percent of it to the Republicans, 40 percent to the Democrats. "We have a political system paid for by Wall Street, not Main Street—and also by Tobacco Road," observed Ellen Miller, executive director of the Center for Responsive Politics, which tracks campaign spending.[10]

Labor unions rake off a mandatory percentage for politics from members' dues. Though business raises $7 for every $1 labor collects, according to the center, the AFL-CIO managed to spend $35 million in a controversial (and unsuccessful) campaign to return a Democratic majority to Congress in 1996.

Over time, the influence of big money in American politics gave rise to a confusing patchwork system of regulation that claims some control over contributions but none at all on expenditures, which have come under First Amendment protection as a form of free speech. So spending,

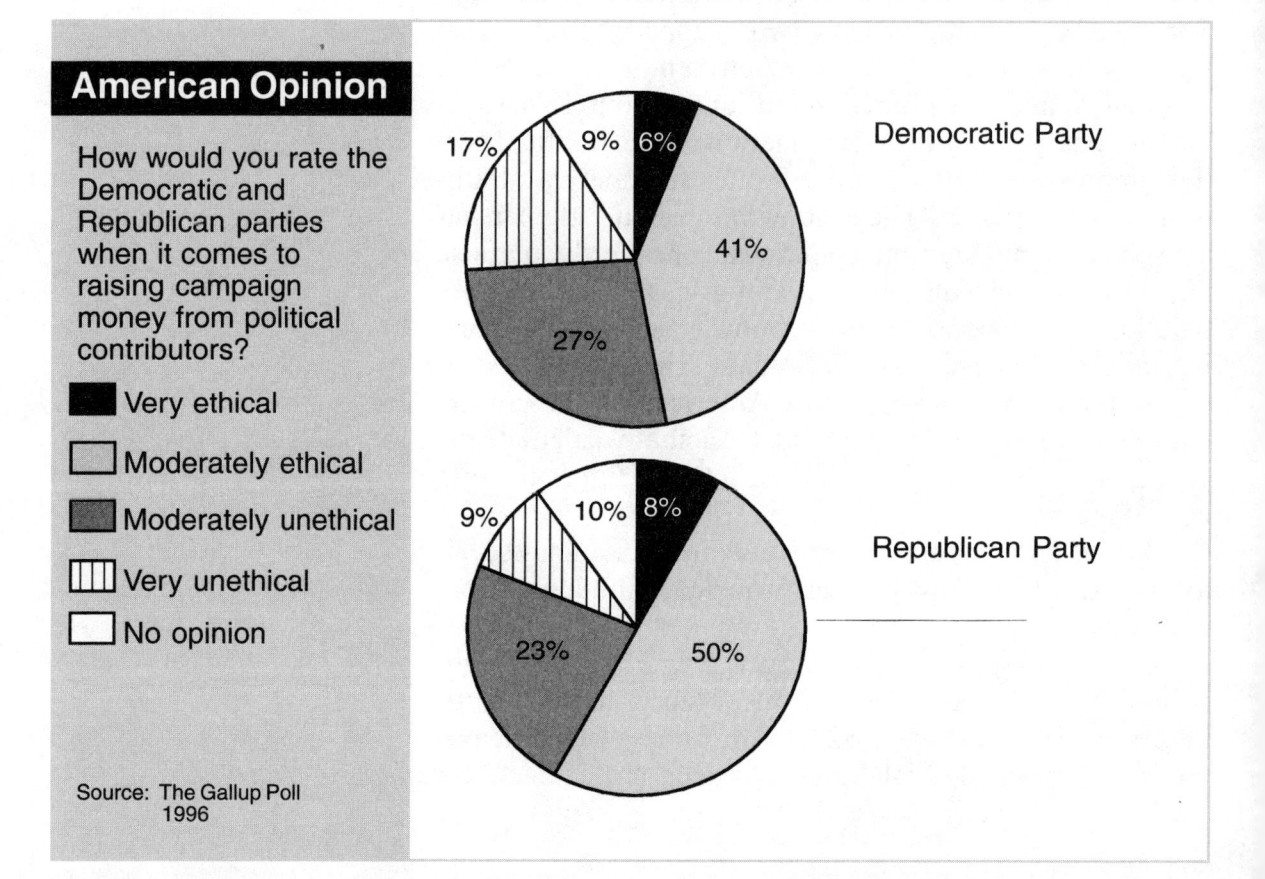

American Opinion

How would you rate the Democratic and Republican parties when it comes to raising campaign money from political contributors?

- ■ Very ethical
- □ Moderately ethical
- ▨ Moderately unethical
- ▥ Very unethical
- □ No opinion

Democratic Party
- 6% Very ethical
- 41% Moderately ethical
- 27% Moderately unethical
- 9% Very unethical
- 17% No opinion

Republican Party
- 8% Very ethical
- 50% Moderately ethical
- 23% Moderately unethical
- 10% Very unethical
- 9% No opinion

Source: The Gallup Poll 1996

mostly on television advertising spots, rises with each campaign cycle, while politicians labor under an ever-increasing pressure to pull off something spectacular in the way of cash plunder.

"People with the stomach to follow such business have long known that politicians' need for fantastically expensive TV campaign money has reduced government to a bazaar and political office to a perpetual fund-raising racket," the satirist Russell Baker wrote toward the end of the 1996 campaign.[11]

Clearly, the system feeds Americans' cynicism about politics. In an October 1996 Gallup survey, hardly anyone gave the two major parties more than perfunctory credit for honesty. Fewer than 10 percent judged the Democrats and Republicans "very ethical" in their approach to raising campaign funds. Forty-four percent regarded Democratic fund-raising practices as moderately unethical or very unethical; 32 percent felt that way about the Republicans. "There is no ethical high horse for either party to get on," the former Common Cause president Fred Wertheimer observed.[12]

The Watergate Reforms

Post-Watergate legislation in 1974 put a $1,000 limit on individual campaign contributions and established a public fund for presidential elections. A 1979 law allowed political parties to collect unlimited amounts from corporations, unions, and other special interests for party building and voter mobilization. This soft money can be used for what is called issue advocacy but is actually a thinly disguised pitch for the (unnamed) representative of one cause or another—it was in 1996, to the unprecedented total of more than $200 million.

In the afterglow of the Nixon scandals, the 1974 reformers tried to do more: They set strict limits on campaign spending. An unlikely alliance of conservatives, big-money interests, and civil libertarians formed to challenge the law. In January 1976, in *Buckley v. Valeo*, the U.S. Supreme Court struck down all limits on campaign spending as a violation of First Amendment free-speech rights. The court also voided limits on candidates' use of their personal wealth and on independent contributions from people or organiza-

"
'There is no ethical high horse for either party to get on.'
"

> "Gallup surveys suggest broad support for reforms."

tions with no direct ties to a campaign.[13]

The 1976 ruling and successive court rulings wrecked the reform effort. With no cap on spending, contributions could be funneled with relative ease through various loopholes in the law.

In 1996, an AFL-CIO advertising campaign targeted Republican congressional candidates on the basis of issue advocacy—the ads fell within the letter of the law because they did not explicitly urge viewers to choose a particular Democrat over a particular Republican. And in any case, the high court in June 1996 ruled that limiting issue advocacy is a violation of free speech, and that First Amendment freedoms outweigh any risk of corrupting the political process with money.

"We are not aware of any special dangers of corruption associated with political parties that tip the constitutional balance in a different direction," Justice Stephen Breyer wrote in the majority opinion.[14]

The Republicans, naturally, used identical tactics, and neither party bothered to keep up much of a pretense that ads bought with soft money were independent of the campaigns. Bob Dole had this lighthearted comment about one of the Republican ads: "It never says that I am running for president, though I hope that is fairly obvious, since I am the only one in the picture."[15]

Gallup surveys suggest broad support for reforms. In the 1996 post election poll, two-thirds favored capping the amount a candidate for president or for the Congress could contribute to his own campaign; 71 percent favored further limits on the amount individuals can donate; 76 percent favored limiting organized labor's contributions; and 81 percent were in favor of limiting political contributions from corporations.

In an October 1996 poll, nearly two-thirds of the sample, 65 percent, thought it a good idea for the federal government to provide a fixed amount for presidential and congressional campaigns and to ban all private contributions. That represented essentially no change from the immediate post-Watergate era; when Gallup asked the question in 1974, 67 percent favored such a system.

Evidently, though, support for a good idea does not automatically lead to support for a major change in policy. In the post-election poll, only 43 percent favored "establishing a new campaign system where federal campaigns are [fully] funded by the government, and all contributions from individuals and private groups are banned." Fifty-two percent opposed this near-revolutionary approach to American campaign finance.

The Foreign Connection

Reformers say now is the time to strike, in the wake of Democrats' troubles with suspect contributions from overseas corporations and alleged influence peddling involving the Lippo Group, the Indonesian financial giant.

"I predicted a major scandal would be the catalyst," said Senator John McCain, the Arizona Republican who advocates campaign reform. "I do not underestimate the challenge here, but I do believe there is widespread distaste and anger about the present system."[16]

Whether the Democratic National Committee's dealings with the Lippo Group grade as a scandal is a matter of opinion. Democratic fund-raiser John Huang, a former Lippo executive, collected some $2.5 million for the Democrats in 1995 and 1996, some of it from what appeared to be out-of-bounds foreign sources. The Democrats returned more than $1 million of Huang's haul, but questions persisted.

McCain and other Republicans pressed for the Justice Department to appoint a special prosecutor to investigate

"**Whether the Democratic National Committee's dealings with the Lippo Group grade as a scandal is a matter of opinion.**"

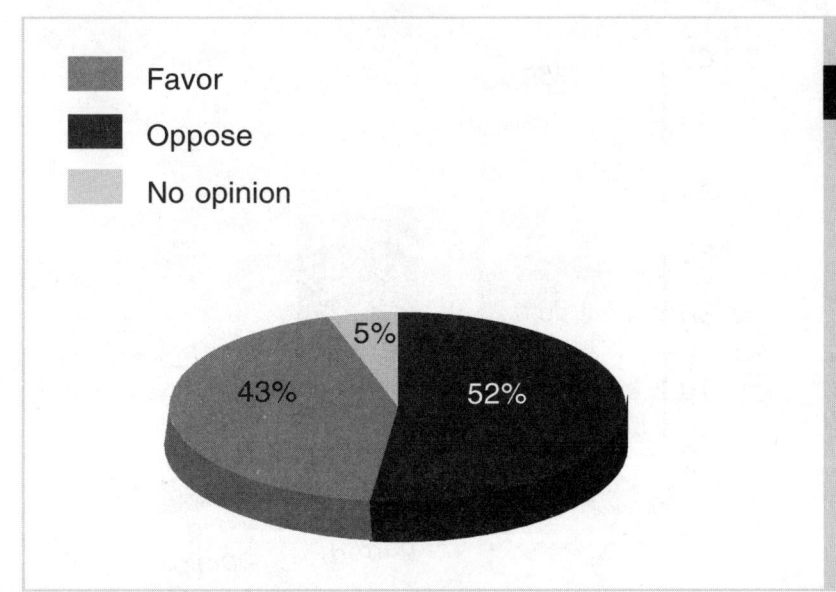

- Favor
- Oppose
- No opinion

Favor: 43%
Oppose: 52%
No opinion: 5%

American Opinion

Do you favor or oppose establishing a new campaign system where federal campaigns are funded by the government and all contributions from individuals and private groups are banned?

Source: The Gallup Poll 1996

> **Federal law prohibits political donations from foreign companies and foreign nationals.**

the Democrats' fund-raising practices. In late November 1996, however, Justice declined, saying the department had no evidence to suggest high Clinton administration officials had engaged in illegal activities. A review would continue, a department spokesman said, and the question could be reopened if the evidence warranted it.[17]

Federal law prohibits political donations from foreign companies and foreign nationals. U.S. subsidiaries of foreign firms and legal alien residents are allowed to contribute, however. The Gallup post-election survey showed a mixed verdict on foreign contributions: Fifty-five percent of the sample said legally resident noncitizens should be barred from donating to U.S. campaigns; 41 percent said they should be allowed to contribute.

Nonpartisan reformers say both parties share in the guilt, if guilt there be, for both have accepted many thousands of dollars from U.S. subsidiaries of foreign companies. And both parties surely acknowledge the unspoken assumption that contributors get *something* for their money, even if it's only the prestige of a dinner at the White House or a brief meeting with a senior congressional leader.

"The magnitude and the blatantness and the shamelessness of the interests giving money, and their cavalier attitudes, have brought us to a crescendo of sleaziness," said Common Cause president Ann McBride. "The stage is set for reform."[18]

Political fund-raisers of both parties say they operate

American Opinion

Should legally resident noncitizens be barred from donating money to U.S. election campaigns?

Response	Percent
Barred	55%
Not barred	41%
No opinion	4%

Source: The Gallup Poll 1996

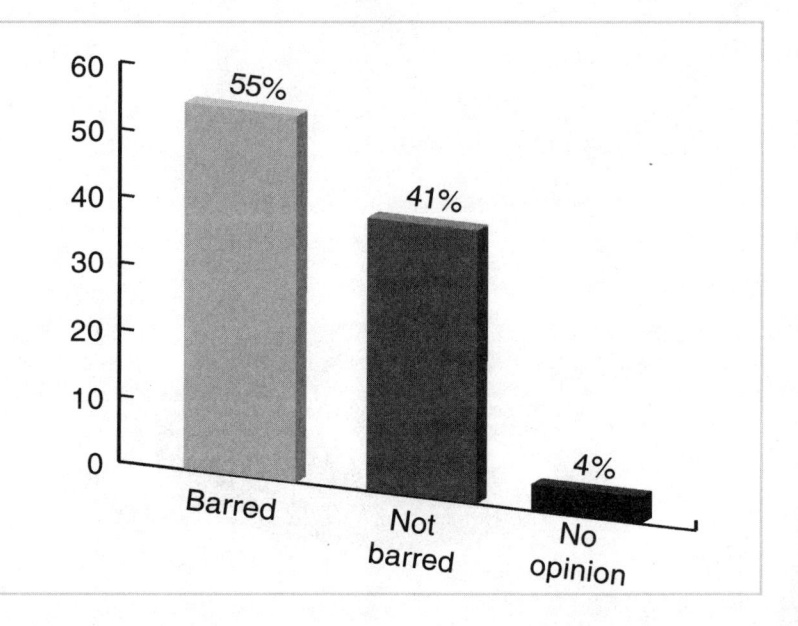

within the letter of the law. They say, too, that it is difficult in an increasingly interconnected world to police every donation and track every source. It's often practically impossible to determine what is foreign and what is domestic. Ford, a U.S. company, owns 50 percent of Saab, a Swedish company. Should the Swedish concern, which makes high-performance aircraft and upscale cars, be barred from contributing to American political parties?

For the most part, the political parties are expected to police themselves. How aggressive are they likely to be? Besides, in diverse America, a foreign-sounding last name on a contributors list is hardly sufficient grounds for a Federal Elections Commission probe. "Just having a name that is not Smith or Jones is not enough to trigger anything," said Trevor Potter, a former FEC chairman. "The FEC has no system to process this."[19]

Nor, as it happens, do the Democrats and Republicans, though critics charge that is often simply an excuse for looking the other way. The backgrounds of most large donors, those in the $50,000 and up category, for instance, probably would be well-known to party officials. Perhaps, say the politicians; perhaps not.

"If you made a contribution to the Republican National Committee and you were laundering foreign money, would I know that? Probably not," said Howard Leach," the Republican Party finance chairman. "I can't look at your bank account and see where the money comes from. We try to determine the source, but if someone is trying to launder money, no one can help on that."[20]

The Drive for Reform

Reform gained momentum at the state level in 1996. In the November balloting, six states passed initiatives limiting special-interest money in elections. Maine voters approved a voluntary system in which candidates for state office can either take public money for their campaigns or raise funds privately. Colorado voters approved a measure that sets voluntary spending caps, bans corporate contributions, and establishes a $100 limit for individual contributions for legislative races and $500 for statewide races.[21]

In Washington, McCain and a Democratic colleague,

> "
> **In the November balloting, six states passed initiatives limiting special-interest money in elections.**
> "

The FEC and the Christian Coalition

The Federal Election Commission took one of America's most powerful political-action organizations to court in 1996, challenging the conservative Christian Coalition's claim of nonpartisanship and accusing the group of acting illegally to promote several Republican candidacies in the 1990s.

In a civil suit filed in July 1996, the FEC, which enforces the nation's patchwork of federal laws governing campaign activities, charged that the 1.7-million-member coalition's voter guides, distributed by the millions in churches, were clearly partisan political literature. The FEC also alleged that the Christian group had illegally donated to some Republican campaigns. The suit claimed the coalition actively worked for the campaigns of former President George Bush, House Speaker Newt Gingrich, Senator Jesse Helms, and failed Senate candidate Oliver North—all Republicans.

"The FEC is recognizing the obvious: the Christian Coalition's deceptive voter guides and aggressive campaigns are designed to help elect right-wing Republicans to public office," said Carole Shields, president of the liberal advocacy group People for the American Way.[1]

The Christian Coalition dismissed the lawsuit as baseless. "The courts will affirm that people of faith have every right to be involved as citizens and voters," Ralph Reed, the coalition's executive director, predicted at the time of the filing.[2]

Nonprofit organizations that establish political action committees, or PACs, must file spending reports and accept federal limits on political spending and contributions. The Christian Coalition has argued that it is exempt from the law because its activities are educational rather than political.

Some campaign finance reformers would sharply curtail the activities of PACs of all kinds, a notion that has gained considerable public support. In a post-1996 election Gallup survey, a majority of respondents, 55 percent, said PACs should be barred from contributing money to political campaigns. More than a third, 38 percent, said the election laws should continue to allow PAC contributions.

Senator Russell Feingold of Wisconsin, promised to reintroduce their campaign-finance reform bill early in the 1997 congressional session. The McCain-Feingold measure, which foundered in the Senate in mid-1996, would ban soft money donations and contributions from political action committees. And it would provide free or discounted television air time to candidates who observed voluntary campaign spending limits.

Reform's fiercest Senate opponent is Senator Mitch McConnell, a Kentucky Republican. McConnell needs only 41 votes for a filibuster that would effectively kill the bill.

McConnell and his allies say citizens have a right to spend what they want on politics or anything else. They say, too, that the chief effect of finance reform would be to fill Congress with millionaires. With McCain's bill in force, nobody from the middle class could afford to campaign.

Others question McCain's targeting of the pervasive and powerful PACs, which after all were an outgrowth of the first burst of campaign reform after Watergate, an effort to substitute many small contributors for the fabled "fat cats" of American political history—the shadowy, powerful purchasers of executive influence, legislative favors, and ambassadorships. "PACs are not the political equivalent of the devil," said Curtis Gans. "They represent our pluralism, and any desire to get rid of PACs would be an unconstitutional infringement on their right to organize."[22]

As Gans suggested, the courts have been even less friendly to campaign finance reform than politicians committed to the existing system. Some advocates of reform believe that real change will require a constitutional amendment that would allow Congress to limit campaign spending—"to make it clear," in the words of one reformer, the outgoing Senator Bill Bradley, "that money does not equal free speech."[23] According to Bradley, the McCain-Feingold measure is well intentioned but weak. "Incremental reforms are bound to fail because they are not radical enough to change the role of special-interest money in our political system," wrote Bradley, who left the Senate voluntarily early in 1997. "The piecemeal rules now in place prove that money in politics is like ants in the kitchen: Without closing all the holes, there is always a way in."[24]

The challenge, a difficult one, is to construct a formula that would reduce the costs of campaigning and the power of money in political life while at the same time protecting freedom of political speech.

"The values at stake here could not be more important," wrote political commentator David S. Broder. "Freedom of political expression is at the heart of the First Amendment, and no sensible person wants to see a government agency regulating the content or format of campaign pamphlets or ads. The question is whether the volume of such messages can be constrained without seriously impairing the rights of individuals or groups of all kinds to have their say."[25]

> "'The piecemeal rules now in place prove that money in politics is like ants in the kitchen: Without closing all the holes, there is always a way in.'"

The Media, Politics, and the Public

In Gallup's post-election poll, respondents said they were generally satisfied with the amount of information they were able to get about the candidates, and a majority thought the press, television, and radio did a satisfactory job of covering the campaign. Two-thirds, though, were dissatisfied with the political advertisements they saw on television.

Politicians were somewhat less generous than Gallup's sample. The once and perhaps future Republican presidential contender Lamar Alexander blamed the media for building unreasonable expectations among the electorate. "The voters are going to be waiting a long time if they're waiting for the perfect candidate, because no one who goes through the media process these days is going to come out looking perfect," said Alexander, whose plaid-shirt campaign failed to catch fire with Republican primary voters in early 1996.[26]

Some candidates questioned whether the universal late twentieth-century practice of campaigning almost entirely through television advertisements might need rethinking. The TV onslaught alienated many voters; two-thirds told Gallup they were dissatisfied with the season's political fare. Others simply tuned it out, lengthening the already substantial distance that separates politicians from their constituents.

In a New Hampshire congressional district, Democrat Deborah Arnesen lost to Republican incumbent Charles Bass in a campaign that rival liberal and conservative political-action groups managed to dominate through TV ads that had little connection to the living, breathing candidates or the voters who were supposed to choose between them. "The voices that were lost were mine and Charlie's," Arnesen lamented.[27]

At the same time, the television networks cut back substantially on their *news* coverage of the campaign. By one accounting, the networks generated 40 percent less coverage of politics in 1996 than in 1992.

Perhaps that was just as well, say some critics, given journalists' ingrained habit of discerning phantom trends and even of fabricating entire subgroups of voters endowed with the strength to determine the outcome of elections. "The news media ought to be embarrassed about inventing

> "In Gallup's post-election poll, respondents said they were generally satisfied with the amount of information they were able to get about the candidates."

the 'soccer moms' phenomenon," commentator John Leo offered. "These married, college-educated suburban moms with school-age children turned out not to be a juggernaut at all but only 4 to 5 percent of the electorate. The 'angry white males' of 1994 were a newsroom construct too, and journalists are now struggling to explain how this huge, maddened mob could have disappeared in only two years. The simplest explanation is that the bloc of AWMs never really existed."[28]

In some quarters, the press took a tougher view of its 1996 performance than the public, the academics, or even the politicians. Lewis Wolfson, a communications professor at American University, in Washington, gave journalists a solid B to B-plus for their coverage of the presidential campaign. Others agreed that taking the good with the bad, the press turned in a creditable performance in 1996.

As sometimes happens, it was a lapsed journalist, an apostate, who offered one of the sharpest critiques, as well as a proposal he believed might restore some measure of balance and proportion to the process.

As a reporter for *The Washington Post* in 1988, Paul Taylor stunned Democratic presidential candidate Gary Hart with a question that some believe radically altered the tone and nature of American political journalism. He asked Hart whether he had ever committed adultery. Hart answered that he did not feel bound to answer, and he thereby doomed his campaign.

" **By one accounting, the networks generated 40 percent less coverage of politics in 1996 than in 1992.** "

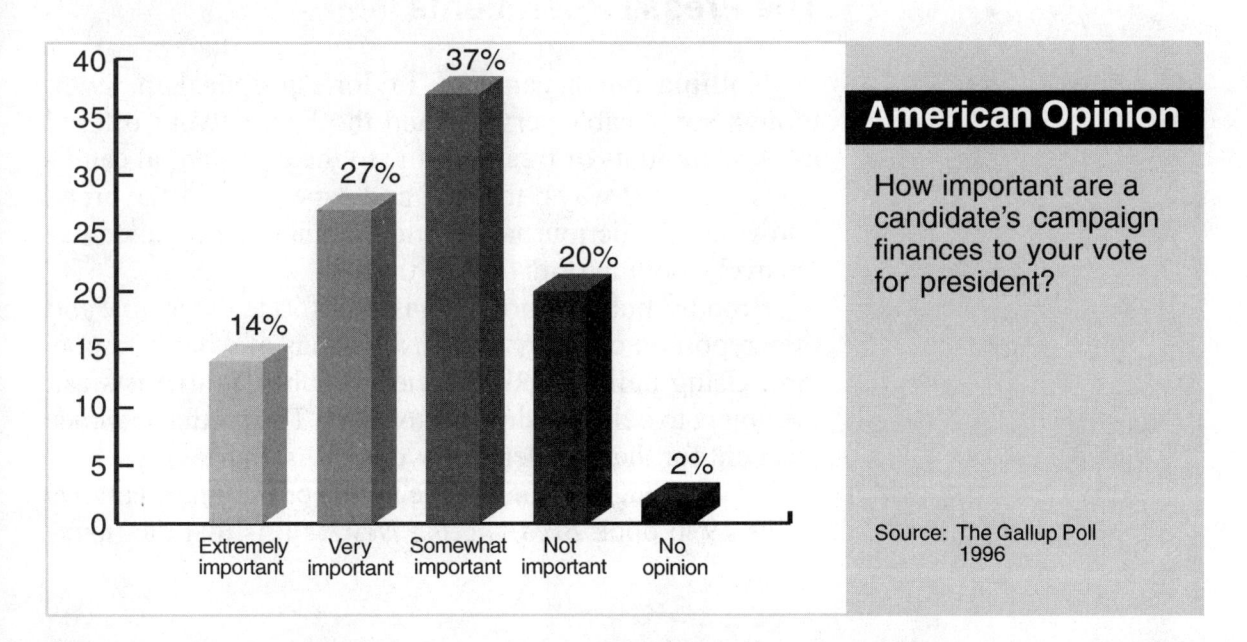

American Opinion

How important are a candidate's campaign finances to your vote for president?

Response	Percent
Extremely important	14%
Very important	27%
Somewhat important	37%
Not important	20%
No opinion	2%

Source: The Gallup Poll 1996

> "'At the end of an American campaign, people want to take a shower, not go into the voting booth.'"

Thus Taylor introduced a new trend in political coverage. Before the Hart episode, the tendency of journalists, if not biographers, had been to overlook the sexual escapades of politicians: Franklin D. Roosevelt, Warren Harding, and John F. Kennedy come to mind. After Hart, private lives were in bounds and in fashion. No love affair could be exempt, however deeply buried in a candidate's past. In 1996, a report even surfaced that Bob Dole, of all people, had conducted an amorous conversation with a Washington lady. That was back in the 1960s, but the comparative antiquity of the event did not deter Taylor's old paper from investigating it. True, *The Post* never published the story, but it traveled anyway.

In 1996, a disheartened Taylor left *The Post*, deciding journalism had become part of the problem of voter cynicism and lack of interest, rather than part of the cure. "At the end of an American campaign, people want to take a shower, not go into the voting booth," Taylor said. Too much political reporting, especially in the elite national newspapers, had taken on an air of all-knowing smugness, exasperating to the voter and debilitating to the nation's public life.[29] "Increasingly," he said, journalism "takes on this edge, this attitude, this smirk, this swagger."[30]

Taylor's prescription: free TV air time, lots of it, for the candidates, with the aim of removing the artificial barrier—journalism—that separates politicians from voters.

The Press Experiments

Nothing much came of Taylor's proposal in 1996, though some cable services and the Fox network offered modest amounts of free TV time to the presidential candidates. In other ways, though, and especially in the arena known as public journalism, the media experimented extensively, both in print and on the air.

Broadly, public journalism is an effort to determine and then report on ordinary citizens' notions of what is important. Using polling and interviews, public journalists ask the voters to help decide what to cover. The media becomes an agent for their readers, viewers, or listeners.

"If anything is clear," wrote media critic James Fallows in his 1996 book *Breaking the News*, "it is that the main-

American Opinion

It has been suggested that the federal government provide a fixed amount of money for the election campaigns of candidates for the presidency and for Congress, and that all private contributions be prohibited. Do you think this is a good idea or a poor idea?

	Good idea	Poor idea	No opinion
Overall	65%	27%	8%
Men	69%	24%	7%
Women	62%	28%	10%
East	65%	26%	9%
Midwest	75%	19%	6%
South	58%	31%	11%
West	65%	29%	6%
Republican	62%	26%	12%
Democrat	62%	31%	7%

Source: The Gallup Poll, 1996

stream press is pathetically out of touch with what people want to hear."[31]

In September 1996, the Public Broadcasting System sponsored an hour-long debate among the congressional leadership. Before and after the debate, some seventy PBS affiliates broadcast debates involving local House and Senate candidates. The goal, PBS explained, was to engage citizens more directly in the political process.

In the best-known of such experiments, a group of North Carolina newspapers, television stations, and radio outlets collaborated on coverage of 1996 statewide races there, including the Jesse Helms–Harvey Gantt U.S. Senate rematch. The group prepared a series of special reports on crime, drugs, taxes and spending, education and health care, and tracked the candidates' views on these issues, which poll

> "'We cover the campaign that's there. We don't invent the campaign.'"

ing had identified as uppermost in citizens' minds.

The journalists proceeded even though from the outset Helms declined to cooperate, refusing to sit for the long interviews on issues the group had settled on. The presidential candidates provided written answers to the public journalists' questions. The effort received mixed reviews.

"This philosophy says it is up to the poll to determine what should be covered and what should not be covered," said Jim Andrews, the campaign manager for Gantt, a Democrat who lost his bid to unseat longtime Republican Senator Helms. "Part of the job of the candidate is to talk about something he feels is important."[32]

"The candidates are having more trouble getting their message out except through paid advertising," Rob Christensen, a columnist for the Charlotte *News & Observer*, one of the participating newspapers, said toward the close of the campaign. "I don't know of any candidate or campaign manager who likes it. We're not writing about the issues they want to talk about."[33]

One veteran television journalist had a brief answer for media reformers who complained about the vacuity and dullness of mainstream reporting on the 1996 political year. "We cover the campaign that's there," said Hal Bruno of ABC News. "We don't invent the campaign."[34]

The Prospects for Action

Between the courts' First Amendment preoccupations and opposition in Congress, what are the chances for even mild reform of the McCain–Feingold sort? Will the public swallow its distaste for the existing system as the memory of the $2 billion campaign of 1996 fades? Will politicians listen, now that the threat of voter reprisal is two, four, or even six years distant?

"This is the best opportunity since Watergate to have some real finance reform," said Common Cause's Ann McBride.[35]

Others, however, argue that Congress lacks the political will and the Clinton administration the political commitment to the cause to make real reform happen.

Bill Bradley, the former New Jersey senator who favors a constitutional amendment that would permit sweeping limits on campaign spending, believes it is up to the voters to force change, by evicting reform-resistant politicians from office if necessary. Perhaps it's asking too much to expect the president and Congress to voluntarily suppress their appetites for the political millions available to them every election cycle. "A successful push for reform will need aggressive forces outside the Beltway," wrote Bradley. "And it will depend on whether concerned citizens will hold newly elected officials to their pledges for reform."[36]

Notes: Campaign Reform Can We Cut Spending Without Curbing Free Speech?

1. Peter S. Canellos, "It's Their Turn: Candidates Gripe About the Voters," *The Boston Globe*, December 3, 1996, 1.
2. Canellos, "It's Their Turn."
3. George Will, "Why Is Voter Participation Falling Despite All Our Efforts?," syndicated column in *The Boston Globe*, November 1, 1996.
4. Will, "Why Is Voter Participation Falling?"
5. Canellos, "It's Their Turn."
6. Frank J. Sorauf, *Money in American Elections* (Glenview, Ill.: Scott, Foresman and Company, 1988), 4.
7. Janet Hook and Sara Fritz, "Post-Election Reports Show GOP Outspent Democrats," *Los Angeles Times* report in *The Boston Globe*, December 7, 1996, A3.
8. Hook and Fritz, "Post-election Reports Show GOP Outspent Democrats."
9. Sorauf, *Money in American Elections*, 5.
10. Leslie Wayne, "Business Is Biggest Campaign Spender," *The New York Times*, October 18, 1996, 1.
11. Russell Baker, "Gulling the Rubes," op-ed, *The New York Times*, October 26, 1996.
12. Leslie Wayne, "Tough Task in Campaigns: Policing Foreign Donations," *The New York Times*, October 17, 1996, 1.
13. Sorauf, *Money in American Politics*, 40.
14. Warren Richey, "Campaign Finance Reformers Face Big Hurdles: High Court," *The Christian Science Monitor*, October 23, 1996, 3.
15. E.J. Dionne Jr., "Blowing up Campaign Reform," syndicated column in *The Boston Globe*, October 18, 1996.
16. Edward T. Pound and Bruce B. Auster, "The Jolly Green Giant," *U.S. News & World Report*, December 2, 1996, 30.
17. David Johnston, "Justice Dept. Says No to Prosecutor on Campaign Cash," *The New York Times*, November 30, 1996, 1.
18. Jane Fritsch, "Excesses of '96 Race Make Finance Reform a Top Issue," *The New York Times*, November 1, 1996, B10.
19. Wayne, "Tough Task in Campaigns."
20. Wayne, "Tough Task in Campaigns."
21. Warren Richey, "Washington, Take Note: States Pass Campaign Finance Reform," *The Christian Science Monitor*, November 12, 1996, 3.
22. Richey, "Campaign Finance Reformers Face Big Hurdle."
23. Bill Bradley, "Congress Won't Act. Will You?," op-ed in *The New York Times*, November 11, 1996.
24. Bradley, "Congress Won't Act."
25. David S. Broder, "Campaign Finance: No Easy Fixes," op-ed in *The Washington Post*, December 1, 1996.
26. Canellos, "It's Their Turn."
27. Canellos, "It's Their Turn."

28. John Leo, "A Great Story Never Told," *U.S. News & World Report*, December 2, 1996, 24.
29. Peter S. Canellos, "Taking the Edge off Political Coverage," *The Boston Globe*, May 13, 1996, A3.
30. Canellos, "Taking the Edge off Political Coverage."
31. James Bennet, "North Carolina Media Try to Lead Politics to Issues," *The New York Times*, September 24, 1996, 1.
32. Bennet, "North Carolina Media Try to Lead Politics to Issues."
33. Bennet, "North Carolina Media Try to Lead Politics to Issues."
34. Canellos, "Taking the Edge off Political Coverage."
35. Michael Rezendes, "Campaign Reform Flounders," *The Boston Globe*, November 15, 1996, 1.
36. Bradley, "Congress Won't Act."

Notes: The FEC and the Christian Coalition

1. Richard L. Berke, "Federal Election Commission Sues Christian Group on Political Aid," *The New York Times*, July 31, 1996, 1.
2. Berke, "Federal Election Commission Sues Christian Group."

13 The 1996 Election
Americans Stay the Course

By Frank Newport, Lydia K. Saad,
and David W. Moore
Editors, The Gallup Poll

If the question in this year's presidential race was "Why re-elect Bill Clinton?" Americans' answer seems to have been "Why not?" The election of 1996 was a classic example of a referendum on the incumbent. No obvious foreign or domestic crisis drew attention away from the Clinton record, the Clinton agenda, or Bill Clinton himself, and the president was able to convince enough Americans—on the basis of his record, his agenda, and the defense of his own character—that he deserved a second term. The Republican challenger, Bob Dole, attempted to generate opposition to Clinton on several fronts—taxes, foreign affairs, drugs, and character—but never to much effect.

Falling just short of majority support, Bill Clinton won the 1996 national popular vote by eight percentage points over Bob Dole, 49 percent to 41 percent, with Reform Party candidate Ross Perot receiving 8 percent. Clinton won in the Electoral College more decisively: 379 to 159. Clinton thus became the first Democrat to earn a second term since Lyndon Johnson in 1964, and the first Democrat to be elected twice since Franklin Delano Roosevelt over fifty years ago.

The same electorate that kept a Democrat in the White House put Republicans back in charge of Congress by a razor-thin margin. Gallup researchers estimate that 50.3 percent of all votes cast nationally in congressional races in 1996 went to Republican candidates while Democrats received 49.7 percent of the vote. The resulting party split in

> "The election of 1996 was a classic example of a referendum on the incumbent."

House seats gave Republicans a slightly greater advantage than the popular vote, as they won 227 (52 percent) of the 435 congressional seats, compared with the Democrats' 207 (48 percent). The GOP also picked up two Senate seats, to increase their majority to 55 seats to the Democrats' 45.

Chronology of the Clinton-Dole Race

Bill Clinton appeared much more vulnerable in 1995 than he turned out to be in 1996. Victorious in the 1994 congressional elections, Republicans had a good year in 1995, and Bob Dole benefited. Dole's high profile as majority leader in the new Republican-led Senate earned him widespread recognition and largely favorable ratings from the public. Except for two brief periods, one after his State of the Union Address in January, the other after the terrorist

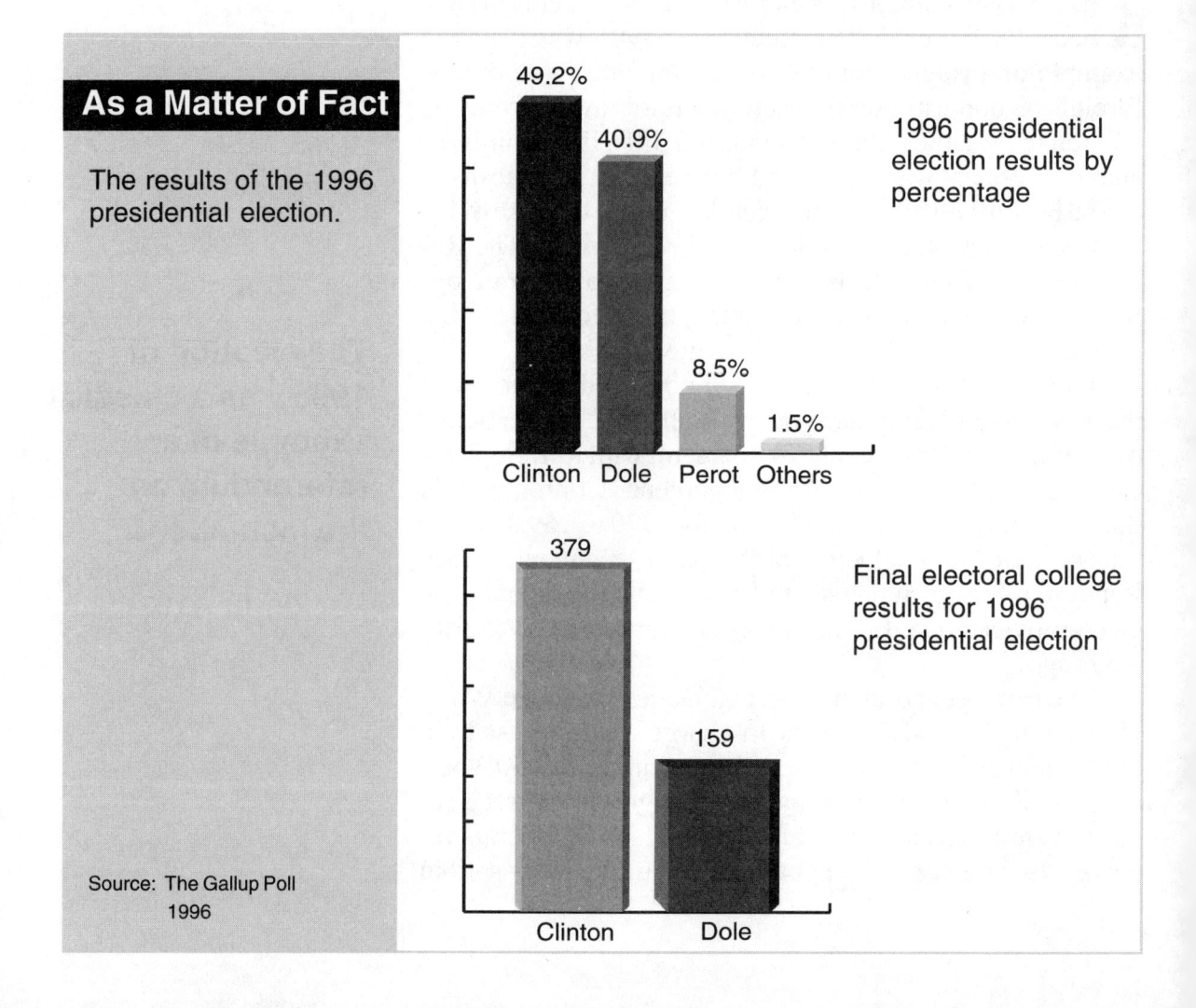

As a Matter of Fact

The results of the 1996 presidential election.

1996 presidential election results by percentage

- Clinton: 49.2%
- Dole: 40.9%
- Perot: 8.5%
- Others: 1.5%

Final electoral college results for 1996 presidential election

- Clinton: 379
- Dole: 159

Source: The Gallup Poll 1996

bombing of a federal building in Oklahoma City in April, President Clinton's approval rating in 1995 was consistently under 50 percent, the level usually considered necessary for an incumbent to achieve if he hopes to be re-elected. In fact, Bob Dole ran even or ahead of Clinton in seven out of eight Gallup trial heats taken between February and August of 1995.

All of this changed dramatically in the fall of 1995, when the Republicans in Congress took on President Clinton over the budget and set out on a course that resulted in a partial shutdown of the federal government in November. Public displeasure with this dispute was evident as early as September. Americans preferred compromise over dogmatism in budget negotiations and held Republicans mostly responsible for the standoff. Throughout this period, Gallup chronicled an increase in voter support for Clinton against Dole in two-way test elections. The Clinton-Dole race changed from a dead heat in August to a 7-point lead for Clinton in September, a 10-point lead in November, and a 16-point lead by December 1995.

By the tail end of the government shutdown in early January of 1996, negative publicity over the budget finally appeared to have some negative impact on Clinton, particularly when it was Bob Dole who brought a budget compromise to the negotiating table around New Year's. Clinton's approval rating slipped 9 points in January (to 42 percent from December's 51 percent), and he was back in a

"
Bob Dole ran even or ahead of Clinton in seven out of eight Gallup trial heats taken between February and August of 1995.
"

American Opinion

A comparison between President Clinton's approval rating for a ten-month period in 1995 and 1996.

☐ 1996
■ 1995

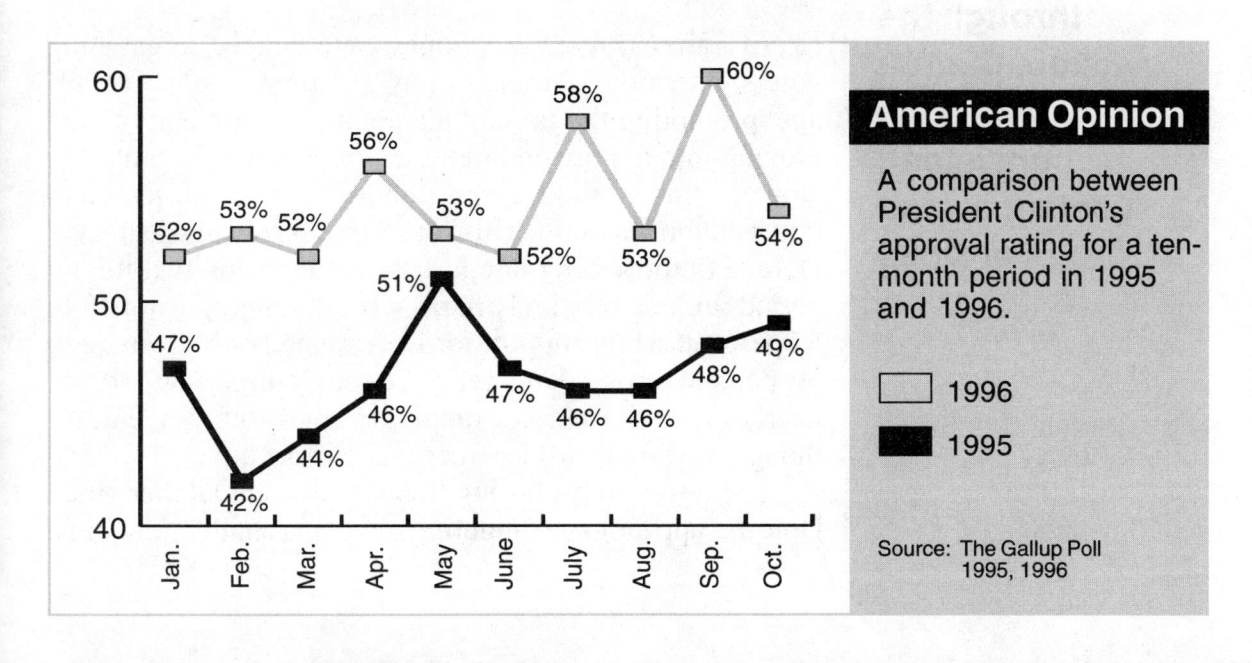

Source: The Gallup Poll 1995, 1996

stiff horse race with Dole. In late January, however—after a budget agreement was reached, and shortly after Clinton's State of the Union address—Gallup recorded another turnaround in Clinton's position against Dole, with the president going from a one-percentage-point deficit to a 12-point lead, essentially back where he was during the height of the government shutdown late in 1995.

Once back in this commanding position, Clinton never looked back. Across all of the test elections taken by Gallup between March and Labor Day of 1996, Clinton led Dole by an average of 14 points (with Ross Perot dropping gradually from 16 to 6 points). The gap between Clinton and Dole grew tighter around the time of the Republican National Convention in mid-August, when Dole managed to cut Clinton's lead down to 7 points, but rebounded to a 21-point lead for Clinton after the Democratic National Convention at the end of August.

When all was said and done, the publicity surrounding the Republican primary season from February through June, Dole's ultimate winning of the nomination, Dole's selection of Jack Kemp as his running mate, and Dole's announcement of a 15 percent tax-cut proposal did nothing to change the fundamental positioning of the race leading up to the traditional beginning of the "campaign in earnest" on Labor Day.

The Final Chapter

At Labor Day, Dole's hopes were pegged to catching voters' attention, chipping away at Clinton's positive image, promoting the tax-cut plan, gaining momentum, and moving into a more competitive position by November 5. None of this worked. From Labor Day through the election, Clinton maintained his consistent, substantial lead over Dole. Clinton's voter support throughout this two-month period fell in a relatively narrow band, ranging from 48 to 57 percent, while support for Dole ranged only from 32 to 39 percent. Ross Perot received single-digit support for nearly the entire period, ranging from 4 to 9 percent, although he did reach 11 percent for a short time.

There were days during September and October when Dole *did* appear to be mounting more of a challenge against

> "From Labor Day through the election, Clinton maintained his consistent, substantial lead over Dole."

Clinton. Toward the end of the month of September, for example, Dole knocked Clinton's support down into the upper 40s and Dole's percentage of the vote increased to the high 30s. This tightening of the race was coincident with an apparently effective Dole television spot featuring a 1992 videotape of Bill Clinton on MTV talking about his past use of marijuana. This Dole surge, however, like several others, petered out, and Clinton soon regained his wider lead.

In the last days of the campaign, Gallup polling showed another slight tightening, with Dole picking up 2 to 3 points of support and Clinton's lead slipping. Some political analysts linked this shrinkage in Clinton's lead to news reports about the controversial flow of Indonesian and other foreign money to the Clinton campaign. Dole was also hitting harder at Clinton's alleged character deficiencies as the race came to a close. Gallup's final poll, taken November 3 and 4, 1996, showed 48 percent of likely voters ready to vote for Bill Clinton, 40 percent for Bob Dole and 6 percent for Ross Perot, with another 6 percent undecided. After making assumptions about how the undecided voters would ultimately break, Gallup's final estimate of the vote was 52 percent for Clinton, 41 percent for Dole and 7 percent for Perot. These estimates closely approximated the final election tally of 49 percent for Clinton, 41 percent for Dole, and 8 percent for Perot.

Ross Perot's Reform Party candidacy met with the same

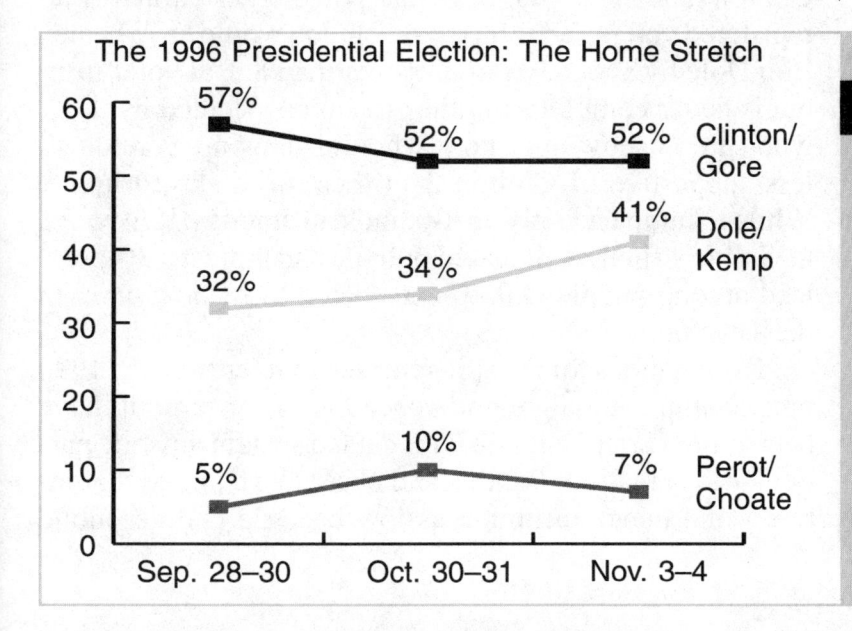

The 1996 Presidential Election: The Home Stretch

Date	Clinton/Gore	Dole/Kemp	Perot/Choate
Sep. 28–30	57%	32%	5%
Oct. 30–31	52%	34%	10%
Nov. 3–4	52%	41%	7%

American Opinion

Gallup's tracking of the three major presidential tickets during the last months of the 1996 presidential race.

Source: The Gallup Poll 1996

> "Voter turnout in 1996 was the lowest in modern history."

frustration as Dole's throughout the year. Perot was never able to generate the same level of interest in the 1996 campaign as he had in 1992. In 1996, Perot's percentage of the trial-heat vote rarely reached double-digit figures. Perot to some degree was "old news" in 1996, and the fact that he was excluded from the two presidential debates sponsored by the Commission on Presidential Debates in October of 1996 deprived the maverick Texas billionaire of the opportunity for wider exposure of his views and for increased legitimization of his candidacy.

Turnout Smacks of Voter Apathy

Voter turnout in 1996 was the lowest in modern history, and interest in the election was the lowest in the annals of Gallup's pre-election polls. Just 77 percent of all registered voters said they had given the campaign a great deal of thought in 1996, compared to 90 percent in 1992, and over 80 percent in several previous elections.

Since 1972 (when the voting age was lowered from twenty-one to eighteen years), voter turnout—measured as the percent of adults aged eighteen and over who vote in presidential elections—has varied between 50 percent and 55 percent. In 1996, turnout dropped below that range, with just under half of eligible national adults showing up at the polls.

In the end, the low voter turnout helped stave off a Clinton landslide. Gallup's final poll suggested that if all registered voters had turned out, Clinton would have beaten Bob Dole by about 16 points rather than 8. But voter turnout is never complete and the election is decided by those who care to show up. Those who did show up were much less supportive of Clinton than those who stayed home. While Clinton had only an 8-point lead among *likely voters* in Gallup's final unallocated poll, he had almost a 30-point lead among people Gallup considered to be *nonvoters* in the same poll.

Explanations for the apparent lack of interest in the 1996 presidential campaign, and hence the lower turnout, have been quite varied, with no hard data to sustain any one particular explanation. Pundits and observers claimed that interest and hence turnout was low because (1) the public was relatively satisfied with the ways things were going in the country, particularly in terms of the economy, and therefore had less reason to look to the presidential contest as a remedy for pressing problems; (2) the office of president may be less important to voters and hence the perceived importance of a presidential vote was lower than it had been previously; (3) the excitement generated by Ross Perot's candidacy in 1992 was missing in 1996; (4) the campaign itself was lackluster, with an incumbent who was attempting to make no waves, and a challenger who generated little excitement; (5) there were few exciting senatorial and gubernatorial races in large states to generate interest in voting "down ticket"; (6) the fact that an incumbent in the polls appeared to be moving fairly easily to re-election caused a lack of interest in the campaign.

Why Clinton Won

One of the more remarkable aspects of the 1996 presidential election was its basic stability. Every Gallup poll taken between February of 1996 and the election on November 5 showed Clinton ahead of Bob Dole, and it has been pointed out that not a single poll taken by any organization showed Dole leading Clinton in the fall 1996 campaign. In retrospect, this stability suggests that the general political environment in 1996 made it difficult, if not impossible, for Bob Dole, or perhaps even Colin Powell, if he had been a candidate, to convince Americans to reject President Clinton's bid for a second term.

Four basic aspects of public opinion measured by Gallup in 1996 seem to be among the most important factors in setting the stage for the re-election of Bill Clinton: (1) general satisfaction with the country, (2) specific satisfaction with the economy, (3) approval of the way Clinton handled his job as president, and (4) favorable attitudes toward Clinton personally.

1. General Satisfaction with the Country

The public was more satisfied with the general state of the nation in 1996 than at any other time in the Clinton presidency. Throughout the year, about four in ten Americans

> **One of the more remarkable aspects of the 1996 presidential election was its basic stability.**

> "Historically, it seems clear that the collective mood of the country is an important indicator of the political health of an incumbent president."

said they were satisfied with the general state of the nation, while roughly six in ten were dissatisfied. In 1993, satisfaction with the United States averaged 28 percent; in 1994 it was 33 percent; and in 1995 only 31 percent.

Historically, it seems clear that the collective mood of the country is an important indicator of the political health of an incumbent president, and thus his re-election chances. Since 1979, when Gallup first asked Americans whether or not they were "satisfied or dissatisfied with the way things are going in the U.S.," three incumbent presidents have sought re-election. In the case of the two who failed, Jimmy Carter in 1980 and George Bush in 1992, satisfaction levels in the year or two preceding their re-election were extremely low. Heading into 1980, public satisfaction was only 12 percent, and in 1992 it ranged from 14 to 22 percent. When Ronald Reagan was seeking re-election in 1984, however, fully 50 percent of Americans were satisfied with the direction of the country.

On this dimension, Bill Clinton's situation in 1996 most closely resembled that of Reagan. Across the six satisfaction measures taken by Gallup after the Congress passed a budget agreement in January of 1996, the average satisfaction rating was 39 percent and it never dipped below 37 percent after that. The highest level of satisfaction all year, 45 percent, was recorded near Labor Day, although it fell back to 39 percent just before the election. These ratings may seem low in the absolute sense, but they represented a substantial improvement for the Clinton presidency compared with the initial years of his term, and were, as noted, higher in historical terms than was the case for either Carter or Bush.

No single issue or problem dominated the minds of American voters in 1996, providing another indication of voter contentment. In 1992, more than 40 percent of Americans cited the economy as the most important problem facing the country. Another quarter of the public mentioned unemployment, specifically, as the major problem. Throughout all of 1996, however, no single issue emerged with more than 25 percent of responses to Gallup's question about the nation's most important problem. As of July 1996, the highest single concern cited by Americans was crime, mentioned by 25 percent of all respondents, followed by welfare at 16 percent, the budget deficit at 12 percent, and the economy, in general, at 11 percent.

This dispersion of public concern shielded Clinton from campaign attacks on any specific issue. Unlike 1992, when the economy was a raw issue to use against Bush, Dole and Perot faced the formidable challenge of having to convince Americans that crime, or drugs, or the economy was a critical problem, even before they could argue that they were the better candidate to deal with that issue.

2. Specific Satisfaction with the Economy

While Americans were hardly elated over the state of the nation's economy in 1996, their perceptions of it were extremely positive on a relative basis, particularly compared with 1992. In October of 1992, close to half of voters (43 percent) condemned the economy as "poor" and only 11 percent thought it was "good." (Less than 1 percent gave it the highest rating, "excellent.") In October 1996, these figures were nearly reversed: 47 percent rated it good or excellent and only 13 percent considered it poor.

The impact of the public's different perceptions of the economy on the eve of Bill Clinton's re-election bid in 1996 versus that of George Bush four years earlier probably cannot be overemphasized. In Bush's case, the ratings probably devastated his political aspirations. In Clinton's case they gave voters a powerful reason to support him for "four more years."

But it took Clinton over three years to get to this enviable position. The low economic ratings of 1992 were carried into the first part of Clinton's term. In 1993, barely 15 percent of Americans considered economic conditions to be "excellent" or "good," while about half thought they were "only fair" and more than a third considered conditions to be "poor." Positive evaluations gradually increased between 1994 and 1995, however, from about one-quarter of the public to one-third. And by October of 1996, close to half of all Americans were solidly positive about the nation's economy, giving Clinton perhaps the most significant credential an incumbent president can have when he asks the American people for a second term.

Not only were current ratings of the economy better in

> **While Americans were hardly elated over the state of the nation's economy in 1996, their perceptions of it were extremely positive on a relative basis.**

> "Bill Clinton's job-approval ratings were not auspiciously high for most of his first term, averaging 47% for the first three years."

1996 than in 1992, but the outlook for the future was much more upbeat. As George Bush was seeking re-election in 1992, over 60 percent of those interviewed also said that economic conditions in the country were getting worse; less than one-third felt conditions were improving. In 1996, by contrast, economic optimists consistently outnumbered pessimists, with 50 percent of Americans saying in October that the economy was getting better, and only 38 percent saying it was getting worse.

3. Approval of the Way Clinton Handled His Job as President

Since the days of Franklin Roosevelt, Gallup's presidential job-approval measure has served as an important indicator of an incumbent president's re-election strength. The question "Do you approve or disapprove of the way the president is handling his job as president?" provides a useful historic index for evaluating public confidence in the president between elections. All recent presidents running for re-election with approval ratings in the year of their re-election that averaged 50 percent or better won their bids for a second term. All but one president with ratings under that level went on to lose.

Of the six incumbent presidents re-elected since World War II, five had approval ratings in their election year that averaged over 50 percent: Dwight Eisenhower, 71 percent; Lyndon Johnson, 75 percent; Richard Nixon, 56 percent; Ronald Reagan, 54 percent; and Bill Clinton, 54 percent. The sixth, Harry Truman, was the exception. His average pre-election approval rating in 1948 was well below 50 percent, and his last rating, in June of his re-election year, was 39 percent. Nevertheless, Truman won with 50 percent of the vote.

The three incumbent presidents who did *not* get re-elected all had job-approval ratings in their last year that averaged *less than* 50 percent: Gerald Ford, 47 percent; Jimmy Carter, 39 percent; and George Bush, 38 percent.

Bill Clinton's job-approval ratings were not auspiciously high for most of his first term, averaging 47 percent for the first three years. Even at the start of election year, in January of 1996, only 42 to 46 percent of Americans approved of the job he was doing. But Americans' evaluation of Clinton turned positive by the end of January and rose to the middle 50s by March. It never fell below 50 percent for the rest of the year. The fact that his rating held above 50 percent throughout the spring provided a strong clue that the election was his to lose. Additionally, for two weeks after the Democratic National Convention in Chicago (spanning a brief military confrontation between the United States and Iraq), Clinton's approval rating was recorded at 60 percent, the highest of his entire term.

The Dole campaign made every effort to hammer away at the public's positive perception of Clinton's performance in office but was ultimately unsuccessful. A majority of Americans acknowledged that if elected, Dole would make a good president, but an even higher percentage made this judgment about Clinton. And by Labor Day, nearly two-thirds of Americans said they considered Clinton's presidency in his first term to be a "success."

4. Favorable Atitude Toward Clinton Personally

Throughout the 1996 campaign, the percentage of Americans who had a favorable personal impression of Clinton ranged from 54 to 63 percent, while only 33 to 40 percent had an unfavorable impression. As is the case with most presidents, opinions about Clinton as a man tended to be slightly more positive than his job-approval ratings as president. Clinton's average job-approval rating in 1996 was 54 percent; his average favorable rating was 59 percent.

In fact, Clinton enjoyed high favorability ratings for most of his first term. The only times when the public generally viewed the president unfavorably were during the two months leading up to the midterm congressional elections in 1994, and at two rather rocky points in 1993, his first year in office.

The public also tended to have favorable opinions of Bob Dole, but not quite as high as their opinions of Clinton. Dole's favorable ratings ranged from 44 to 58 percent in 1996 and his unfavorables from 35 to 45 percent. Dole was a generally popular, well-liked candidate, but was matched against an equally or even better-liked incumbent.

Of the three leading candidates, the one who generated

> "Of the three leading candidates, the one who generated the most unfavorable public reaction in the 1996 campaign was Ross Perot."

> "The character issue has dogged Bill Clinton since 1992."

the most unfavorable public reaction in the 1996 campaign was Ross Perot. Most Americans liked Perot when he first came on the scene four years ago, and at one point in 1992 he led George Bush and Clinton in Gallup's trial heat presidential polls. Since that time, Perot has had a volatile run with public opinion, his stock plummeting when he dropped out of the presidential race in July of 1992, zooming back up after his strong performance in the presidential debates, dropping back down again after he took on the Clinton administration over the North Atlantic Free Trade Agreement in 1993, and remaining low for most of Clinton's first term.

Throughout 1996, only about 30 to 40 percent of the public held a favorable impression of Perot, while well over half viewed him unfavorably.

The Character Issue

The character issue has dogged Bill Clinton since 1992, when questions about infidelity, his draft status during the Vietnam War, and past use of marijuana became issues in the campaign. Since then, new charges or revelations have inevitably renewed discussion about the earlier ones, never allowing the president to escape discussions of his honesty and trustworthiness.

American Opinion

Percent saying each phrase applies to Bill Clinton or Bob Dole

	Clinton	Dole
Cares about the needs of people like you	63%	50%
Can get things done	62%	55%
Shares your values	54%	49%
Has a clear plan for solving the country's problems	46%	35%
Honest and trustworthy	46%	66%

Source: The Gallup Poll, 1996

The cumulative effect has been a persistent weakness in Clinton's character ratings. Of all the leadership qualities Gallup measured in 1996, public perceptions that Clinton is "honest and trustworthy" were among the lowest, and the character dimension was one of the few areas where Dole received higher ratings than Clinton.

In a late October poll, voters picked Dole over Clinton by a solid margin, 46 percent to 34 percent when asked to choose which one of the three candidates would provide the "best moral leadership for the country." Similarly, Bob Dole beat Bill Clinton in the same poll by a 37 percent to 31 percent margin as the candidate who can be "trusted more to keep his promises."

Why didn't this character weakness more seriously hurt Clinton's candidacy? For one thing, a Gallup poll experiment in mid-October suggested that Americans may demand a lower standard of honesty in their president than might be expected. Gallup posed two different questions. One question asked Americans if Bill Clinton was "honest," to which the public split 46 percent yes to 46 percent no—hardly a ringing endorsement. Another group of Americans, however, were asked whether Bill Clinton was "honest enough to be president," and here the majority said yes, by a 55 percent to 40 percent margin. In other words, Clinton appears to have met the minimal threshold for honesty and integrity required by the public to occupy the office of the president, even though he is not generally seen as an honest individual.

> **In a late October poll, voters picked Dole over Clinton by a solid margin when asked to choose which one of the three candidates would provide the 'best moral leadership for the country.'**

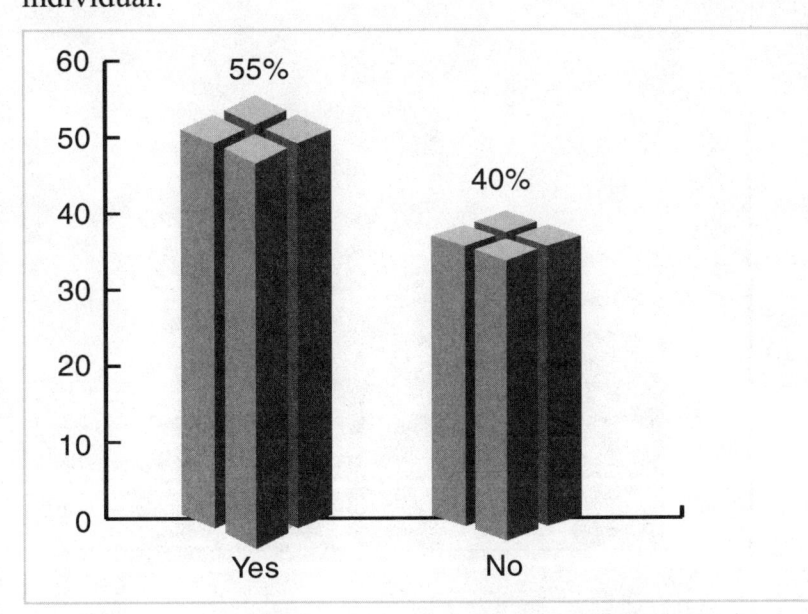

American Opinion

Is Bill Clinton honest enough to be president of the United States?

Yes: 55%
No: 40%

Source: The Gallup Poll 1996

> "Polling shows that most of Clinton's actual voters believed he was 'honest and trustworthy.'"

A separate Gallup poll underscored that moral virtue in a candidate for presidency was less important to the voting public in 1996 than a president's position on the issues or his ability to manage the government. Asked which of the three dimensions was most important in their assessment of a president, only 21 percent of those interviewed in the October survey picked moral values; 25 percent picked positions on issues, while 45 percent picked management abilities in government. Asked to compare Clinton and Dole, Dole was picked by most voters as being more moral, but Clinton was far and away preferred on the other two.

As it turns out, however, polling shows that most of Clinton's actual voters believed he was "honest and trustworthy." Those who were voting for him seemed to give him the benefit of the doubt, if not an enthusiastic endorsement, on the question of his integrity. Those voting against him, however—whether Dole or Perot voters—solidly denounced his integrity. It appeared that Clinton had just enough voters who granted him an "honest" label to carry him to victory.

Anatomy of the Vote for Clinton

Clinton handily won re-election in 1996 by virtue of particularly high support from three key groups of Americans: women, Catholics, and blacks. Had the election been

American Opinion

Which one of the following characteristics is the most important to you in rating how a president is handling his job?

Characteristic	Percentage
Moral values	21%
Position on the issues	25%
Ability to manage the government	45%
All equally	5%
No opinion	4%

Source: The Gallup Poll 1996

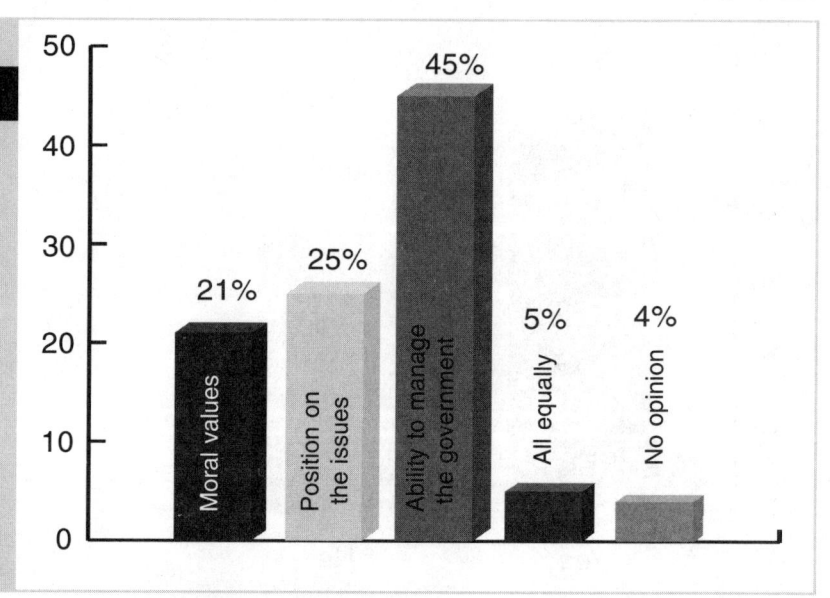

left up to only men or only whites, Gallup polls indicate that Dole had a good chance of winning. If only Protestants (constituting about six in ten Americans) had voted, Clinton would have lost to Dole by only about 2 points.

Overall, most of the groups that formed the bedrock of Clinton's campaign—women, low-income voters, minorities, and Catholics—represent the largely traditional base of the Democratic Party. In 1996, Clinton also added young people—who were not a particularly strong constituency for him in 1992—to his coalition of supporters. Gallup polling shows that while Bill Clinton beat Bob Dole among each major age group in the electorate, he performed especially well among young voters. Clinton enjoyed a 24-percentage-point lead over Dole among voters between the ages of eighteen and twenty-nine years. His lead fell to 7 points among middle-aged voters, and dropped to only five points among voters fifty and older.

The Gender Gap

Perhaps the most celebrated demographic difference in support for the presidential candidates in 1996 was the "gender gap." According to Gallup's final pre-election poll, Clinton beat Dole among women by 15 percentage points, 53 percent to 38 percent, but he led Dole among men by only one point, 45 percent to 44 percent. The difference between Clinton's 15-point lead among women and his 1-point lead among men resulted in a net gender difference, or "gap," of 14 points. This pro-Clinton tendency among women (or anti-Clinton tendency among men) took hold early on in the campaign and persisted throughout 1996, with women consistently preferring Clinton over Dole by a double-digit margin and men closely split between the two candidates.

The gender gap first emerged as a national political phenomenon in 1980, when the difference between men's and women's support for Ronald Reagan against Jimmy Carter was 10 points—with women more supportive of Carter than men. In 1984, the Reagan-Mondale gender gap expanded to 18 points, the highest on record. In 1988 and 1992, with Bush at the top of the Republican ticket, the gender gap shrank substantially: in 1988, it was 8 points, and in 1992,

"
Clinton did not strongly appeal to *all* women in 1996, but specifically to *lower income* women.

"

> "Catholics and Protestants have historically had very different voting patterns."

only 4 points; 1996 thus represented a revival of the 1980s-level gender gap.

Clinton did not strongly appeal to *all* women in 1996, but specifically to *lower income* women, suggesting a possible basis for the gap. Women living in households making $50,000 or more in annual income split their vote for Clinton and Dole, 45 percent to 45 percent. Women with household incomes between $30,000 and $50,000 went only slightly in favor of Clinton, 49 percent to 45 percent. Women in households earning less than $30,000, however, voted overwhelmingly for Clinton, 63 percent to 28 percent. The vote differences among men of various income levels was substantial, but not as great as among women.

The Religion Factor

At 24 points, the religion gap in 1996 was even larger than the gender gap. Protestants gave Dole a 2-point edge, 46 percent to 44 percent; Catholics, (representing over one-quarter of Americans), overwhelmingly supported Clinton, 55 percent to 33 percent—a 22-point margin.

Although less so in recent years, Catholics and Protestants have historically had very different voting patterns, with Catholics solidly in the Democratic camp and Protestants tending to vote Republican. In 1952 and 1956, for example, a majority of Catholics supported Adlai Stevenson, while most Protestants backed Dwight Eisenhower. Similarly in 1976, the Catholic vote favored Jimmy Carter, while Protestants' favored Gerald Ford. The largest religion gap ever recorded was in 1960, when John F. Kennedy became the first Catholic presidential candidate. In that election, 78 percent of Catholics voted for Kennedy and 62 percent of Protestants supported Richard Nixon.

In fact, there have only been two elections since Gallup polls began in which a majority of Catholics and Protestants supported the same candidate: 1964, when Lyndon Johnson beat Barry Goldwater, and 1984, when Reagan defeated Walter Mondale.

Race

In almost every election since Gallup presidential polling began, blacks and whites have thrown their support behind different candidates, with most blacks voting for the Democratic candidate and a majority of whites voting for the Republican. The only clear exception was 1964, when a majority of both whites and blacks supported LBJ over Goldwater. In the 1996 election, Gallup found whites evenly split, at 45 percent for Clinton and 45 percent for Dole, while 92 percent of blacks favored Clinton.

The Fight for Control of Congress

In 1996, Republicans maintained majority control in both the U.S. Senate and House, actually picking up two seats in the Senate, but losing eight seats in the House. In the Senate, the Republicans now have a 55-to-45 advantage, and in the House their margin is 227 to 207.

This was the first election since the years of the Great Depression in which the Republicans were able to retain majority control of the House for a second consecutive term. In 1994, the GOP won control for the first time since 1952, when Eisenhower ushered in a new Republican House and Senate. But in 1954, two years after the 1952 GOP win, Democrats regained control of the House. The only other Republican victory since 1930 was in 1946, but that also lasted just one term.

Unlike the presidential race, the contest for majority control of the House was competitive all year long, with the results of the Gallup "generic ballot"—a question that asks voters which party's candidate they will support in their congressional district—fluctuating between a Republican and a Democratic advantage. In its final poll, Gallup showed a one-point advantage for Republicans among likely voters, and in fact they won the overall national vote by just over half a percentage point.

No doubt the advantages of incumbency helped freshman Republicans hold on to the seats they were awarded in 1994, when the Democrats lost control of Congress. The normal advantages of incumbency, however, may have been buoyed in 1996 by general public satisfaction with the country and with the policies of the Republican-controlled Congress.

Although Americans disliked the Republican House

> "This was the first election since the years of the Great Depression in which the Republicans were able to retain majority control of the House for a second consecutive term."

> "Republicans were seriously wounded after their budget confrontation with Clinton late in 1995."

Speaker, Newt Gingrich, they generally favored the Republicans' policies. Speaker Gingrich consistently registered as the most unpopular major political leader in the country, with well over half of the public saying they had an unfavorable view of him, prompting many congressional Democrats across the country to gear their campaigns as much against Gingrich as against their actual opponent. In spite of Gingrich, Americans were relatively approving of Congress in 1996. Not only did a large majority say that their own representative in Congress deserved to be re-elected, but over half also felt that *most* members deserved another term. This endorsement represented a near-reversal of 1992 attitudes after the check overdraft scandals, and was significantly more approving than in 1994, just before Americans voted out many incumbent Democrats.

A possibly pivotal event in the Republicans keeping control of the House may have been their passage of the *Personal Responsibility and Work Opportunity Act* in August of 1996—otherwise known as welfare reform. Immediately after the measure passed in Congress, Americans' approval of the way Congress was handling its job shot up 9 points, and opinion about whether the Republican Congress had been a "success" or a "failure" turned decidedly positive. This positive reaction to welfare reform was no doubt an important reason why the bill was quickly signed into law by President Clinton.

To be sure, Republicans were seriously wounded after their budget confrontation with Clinton late in 1995. For much of the year, they were in a defensive mode, trying to combat the Democrats drumbeat that the Republicans were radical and "too extreme." In May of 1996, several months after the budget confrontation, more Americans said the Republican Congress had been a failure than said it had been a success. But by the end of August, the picture was much brighter.

In the final days before the election, with Clinton's victory seemingly a foregone conclusion, many Republican congressional candidates campaigned on the theme that the country needed a "balance" to President Clinton, and that a return of the Democratic Congress would bring with it a return to big government. A post-election Gallup poll suggests this last-minute strategy may have been the final key

American Opinion

Regarding the 1996 elections, please say whether you were very satisfied, somewhat satisfied, somewhat dissatisfied, or very dissatisfied with each of the following:

	Very satisfied	Somewhat satisfied	Somewhat dissatisfied	Very dissatisfied	No opinion
The amount of information you were able to get about the presidential candidates.	26%	41%	19%	12%	2%
The amount of information you were able to get about the congressional candidates in your district.	22%	43%	17%	14%	4%
The way the news media covered the presidential campaign.	22%	34%	19%	23%	2%
The way the congressional campaign in your district was conducted.	19%	45%	18%	12%	6%
The way the presidential campaign was conducted.	14%	40%	26%	19%	1%
The political advertisements you saw on television.	8%	21%	25%	42%	4%
The campaign finance laws that govern the way the candidates and political parties raise money.	7%	26%	22%	36%	9%

Source: The Gallup Poll, 1996

to the narrow Republican victory in the House. One in six voters who voted for a Republican after having voted for Clinton said they did so to provide "balance" to their Clinton vote. While the number of such party switchers is small, the net effect would have been more than enough to provide the GOP its margin of victory.

Final Thoughts

In retrospect, Gallup trial-heat surveys throughout 1996

> "One key to the success or failure of Clinton's second term may be the level of cooperation between the President and the Republican Congress."

give a sense of inevitability about Clinton's re-election, but they also indicated just how vulnerable the Republican majority was in Congress.

For Clinton, his consistently high approval ratings in 1996 represented wholesale improvement over the first three years of his administration, when he was in and out of trouble with public opinion. Most of the stars were lined up appropriately in the re-election firmament for Bill Clinton in 1996. The economy was perceived as doing well, the voters approved of Clinton's job performance and liked him personally. Bob Dole's economic tax package did not excite voters, and Clinton's vulnerability—his character—did not appear to be a defining issue for enough voters to seriously wound his candidacy.

For the Republicans in Congress, 1996 was a constant struggle as they fought against Clinton's coattails to keep a majority of voters on their side.

One key to the success or failure of Clinton's second term may be the level of cooperation between the president and the Republican Congress. After the apparent disgust registered by the public over the 1995 government shutdowns, the two branches of government adopted a much more cooperative mode of operation in 1996. They passed a budget and other legislation, and promised after the November 5 election to work harder at working together for the next few years. Gallup polling after the election registered some public optimism that there will be greater cooperation in Washington. Whether these good intentions take root or go wildly astray, the Gallup Poll will be there to measure Americans reaction to what happens in 1997, and in politics for the foreseeable future.

INDEX

abortion(s) and abortion rights vii, xviii, 25, 77-91, 224; abortion rights 78, 83, 86; access 87; clinics 87; laws 87; legal 83; opponents 85; pill 86, 87; protest 91; services 80; *(see also* partial birth abortion)
addict(s) 60; cocaine 72; hard-core 60, 72
adolescent(s)—*see* teens
advertisements, political 221, 223, 234
advertisers, advertising 41, 42, 49, 54; campaign 228; paid 238; television 227
affirmative action vii, 109, 187-203, 224
AFL-CIO 226, 228
African Americans 109, 127, 181, 188, 189, 196; black(s) 106, 109, 113, 116, 162, 177, 178, 182, 187-189, 191, 195-197, 200, 258, 261;
Aid to Families with Dependent Children (AFDC) 167, 172, 174, 175, 177
AIDS 2, 11, 13, 67;
alcohol(ism) 25, 51-53, 56, 57, 68, 163; abuse 40; ban 55; beverages 55; breath test 55; consumption 51, 52
AMA—*see* American Medical Association
America vii, 29, 60, 64, 111, 125, 127, 133, 141, 146, 212, 215, 231
American(s) ix, xx, xi, xiv, xix,xxi, 21, 22, 24, 39, 40, 49, 51, 54, 56, 60, 63, 64, 66, 77, 78, 84, 104, 105, 107, 108, 110, 111, 120, 125, 127, 136, 140-142, 148, 156, 158, 161, 167, 168, 170, 171, 187, 209, 211, 213, 216, 218, 221, 225, 227, 243, 245, 249-254, 262
American Civil Liberties Union 156, 198
American: democracy 101; dream 132; history 105, 226; politics 228
American Federation of Labor/Congress of Industrial Organizations—*see* AFL-CIO
American Medical Association (AMA) 96
antipornography ordinance 33
antiterrorism and Effective Death Penalty Act of 1996 125, 161, 163
arabs 205, 206, 208, 209, 211, 212, 212, 216, 217, 218, 220
arafat, Yasser 207, 208, 209, 217
armed Forces (US) 2, 3, 7, 9
Asia(ns) 40, 125-127, 130, 136, 197
assault weapon(s) 147, 156; ban 156, 157
ATF—*see* Bureau of Alcohol, Tobacco and Firearms
atlanta Olympics bombing 161

B

baby boomer(s) 72-73, 147, 224
Balfour Doctrine 210, 211

beer(s) 51, 52, 53, 54, 55, 57
benefits 171; medical 174; tax-free 171
Bennett, William J. 13, 60, 69, 70, 71
birth(s): blacks 177; defects 57; control 91; illegitimate 172, 175, 176, 177
birthrate 176, 189; out-of-wedlock 175, 176, 177, 189; statistics 176; trends 176
block grants, federal 171, 172
Boston 104-105, 107, 115, 118, 119, 148, 152, 155
Bradley, Senator Bill 233, 239
Brady bill, Law 157
Breyer, Justice Stephen 228
Brimelow, Peter 127-128, 131, 137
British 206, 210, 211, 212, 213, 214; Empire 211; Isles 128 (*see also* United Kingdom)
Buckley v. Valeo 227-228
budget 262; agreement 250; deficit 146, 169, 251; federal 245
Bureau of Alcohol, Tobacco and Firearms (ATF) 155, 156, 157
Bush, President George 60, 69, 70, 72, 105, 111, 206, 232, 250, 251, 252, 254, 257

C

California 67, 108, 127, 133, 135, 139, 153, 159, 160, 161, 163, 187, 188, 195, 198, 201
California Civil Rights—*see* Proposition 209
Camp David Accords of 1979 215, 216
campaign: contributions 227; finances(ing) 221, 224, 229; finance laws 221; finance reform bill 232; reform 221-241; spending 226, 227, 239
Canada 128, 132, 215
capital punishment—*see* death penalty
Carter, President Jimmy 206, 250, 252, 257, 258
casino(s) 19, 20, 21, 22, 24, 25, 26, 27, 30, 31; gambling 24, 25, 36; Indian 19
Catholics—*see* Roman Catholics
Centers for Disease Control and Prevention 40,41, 48, 175, 176
Central Intelligence Agency (CIA) 8
character issue 254-256
charter schools 119, 120
child-abuse prevention programs 134
child care 174, 179; initiatives 182
children 41, 42, 79, 154, 168, 169, 170, 171, 172, 175, 177, 178, 197; disabled 171; unborn 85
Christian Coalition 12, 232
church(es), 234; black 196; burnings 188
CIA—*see* Central Intelligence Agency
cigarette(s) 40, 43; advertising 41, 44;

makers 49; packs 46; cigars 40, 43
civil rights 2, 4, 9; groups 192; laws, legislation 3, 130; movement 105; protection 3
Civil Rights Act of 1964 192
Clinton, President Bill xii, xix, xxi, 3, 9, 11, 12, 20, 41, 62, 69, 72, 73, 88, 105, 107, 116, 120, 121, 125, 135, 142, 147, 148, 149, 155, 156, 161, 164, 167, 174, 177, 178, 179, 183, 193, 198, 200, 201, 206, 207,222, 224, 230, 238, 243-262
Clinton-Dole Race 244-246
cocaine 44, 59, 64, 66, 67, 68, 70 *(see also* addicts, cocaine; crack cocaine, drugs)
college admission quotas 194-195
Colombia(n) 64, 70; drug cartels 62
Columbia University 73; Center on Addiction and Substance Abuse 72
computer(s) xiv, xvi, xx, 108, 110, 116, 118
Congress—*see* U.S. Congress
Congressional Budget Office (CBO) 168,171
Connecticut 25, 28, 31, 32, 34, 36, 47, 112;
conservative(s) 2, 69, 120, 142, 177, 178, 229
crack 60, 67; cocaine 64; epidemic 62
crime(s) vii, 25, 27, 30, 31, 33, 59, 126, 145-166, 169, 181, 196, 237, 250, 251; bill 149; index 160; juvenile 145, 152, 154, 155; organized 21, 23, ; personal or property 150; prevention 159; rate(s) 19, 145, 146, 147, 148, 158, 160, 162; wave 31
criminal(s) 148; behavior 159; career 160; child 152, 153; juvenile 153

D

day care 171, 174, 178, 180, 182
death(s) and dying 77, 78, 93, 116; dignity of 62; row(s) 163; sentence 152
death penalty xx, 69, 156, 162-154;
Defense of Marriage Act 10, 11, 12
Democrat(s), Democratic Party xxii, 10, 35, 60, 62, 109, 114, 120, 121, 140, 141, 162, 192, 194, 223, 224, 225, 226, 227, 228, 229, 230, 231, 235, 236, 243, 244, 258, 259, 262
Democratic National Committee 229, 246, 253
discrimination 3, 187, 188, 192, 193, 194; gender 192; job 192; race 192
Dodge-Edison School 115-117
Dole, Senator Robert (Bob) 12, 36, 60, 120, 147, 155, 164, 201, 224, 228, 236, 243, 244, 245, 246-248, 249, 251, 253, 255, 256, 257, 258, 259, 262

drinkers, drinking 39, 51, 56, 57, 72
Drug Abuse Resistance Education (DARE) 72
drug(s) 33, 44, 45, 109, 110, 163, 238, 245, 253; abuse 59, 69, 70, 146; addicts, hardcore 60; adolescent or teen 60, 61, 62; agents 70; antidrug activities 63; antidrug programs 59; strategy 63; dealers 69, 71; dependency 97; education 63; hard 67; illegal 60, 62, 73, 136; illicit 59, 60; kingpins 66; laws 63; legalization of 59; offenders 63, 69; organizations 158; possession 60; possession laws 67; prevention and treatment programs 60, 61, 62; problem 64, 71; psychoactive 67; sellers 63; smuggling 60; supply, reduction of 63; trade 136, 148, 153; traffickers, trafficking 63, 70, 71; treatment 172; use 59, 109; war on 59-75
drunk driving 51-52; arrests 55

E
Eastland, Senator James O. 192
economy 23, 146, 169, 170, 223, 249, 250, 251-252, 262
Eduation Alternatives Inc. (EAI) 115, 117-118
education vii, xix, 71, 72, 83, 108-111, 120, 127, 136, 146, 162, 173, 174, 182, 189, 192, 238; public 173; reform 101-123
Egypt(ians) 206, 210, 213, 214, 215, 216
Eisenhower, President Dwight 252, 258, 259
Elders, Jocelyn 84, 86
Election 1996 245-265 (see also presidential campaign)
elections, congress ix, (1994) 255; presidential viii, ix, xi
Empower America 13
English 105, 107, 125, 131, 132, 137, 140; common law 153; Pilgrims 128
entitlements 172, 173, 175, 176, 177 (see also welfare)
euthanasia 77, 84, 89, 96; physician performed 95

F
families, 168, 169, 172, 176; broken 120
family: dissolution 181; entertainment 26; leave initiative 224; preference 131; priority 130; reunification 130
Federal Elections Commission (FEC) 231, 232
Feingold, Senator Russell 231-232
felons 153, 154, 156, 157, 159, 160
felony(ies) 31, 161, 172
firearm(s)—see gun(s)
Florida 20, 47, 154, 180, 181

food stamp(s) xvi, 30, 133, 137, 168, 172, 173, 177, 178
Food and Drug Administraton (FDA) 40, 42, 44
Ford, President Gerald 252, 258
Foxwoods Casino 32-34
France 86, 87, 214, 215
free speech 6, 221, 226, 228, 233 (see also U. S. Constitution, First Amendment)
Freud, Sigmund 14, 15, 16
Furman v. Georgia 162

G
Gallup (poll) viii, xx, xi, xii, xiii, xiv, xv, xvi, xvii, xviii, xix, xx, xxi, xxii, 3, 6, 7, 8, 10, 15, 21, 24, 39, 40, 44, 45, 46, 49,51, 53, 54, 59, 63-64, 67, 78, 79, 81, 82, 83, 84, 87, 88, 93, 94, 101, 102, 106, 108, 109, 110, 113, 114, 115, 116, 120, 121, 125, 126, 127, 132, 133, 136, 137, 138, 140, 142, 145, 146, 149, 152, 156, 161, 164, 169, 171, 173, 182, 187, 190, 194, 196, 205, 209, 212, 213, 215, 216, 218, 221, 223, 227, 228, 230, 232, 233, 243, 245, 246, 247, 248, 249, 250, 252, 254, 255, 256, 257, 259, 262
gamblers 27, 31, 33; addicted 28
gambling and gaming 19-38 ; centers 31; compulsive 28; halls 33; legal 19, 23; lobby 25; resort casino 22; riverboat 20
gay(s), lesbian(s) and homosexual(s) 1, 3, 2, 4, 6, 7, 9, 11, 12, 13, 15, 16; acts 9; activists, 9; baiting 12; civil rights protection of 1; clergy 7; clubs 6; couples 10, 12; employees 12; equality 13 in the military 3; marriage(s) 10, 11, 12, 13; rights v, 1-18; activists 2, 4, 6; advocates 9; agenda 1, 3, 15; issues 2, 15; unions 11, 13 gay rights: leaders 1, 13; lobby 3
Gaza, Israel 206, 207, 214, 215, 217, 218
gender xx, xxi, 2, 54, 162, 196, 198; gap 257-258; preferences 190
Gingrich, House Speaker Newt 140, 232, 260
Golan Heights, Israel 214, 216, 218
GOP—see Republicans
government, federal 28, 44, 77, 171, 174, 181, 228; shutdowns 262
Gramm, Senator Phil 128, 130
Great Britain—see United Kingdom
Great Depression 50, 259
gun(s) 116, 152, 155, 156, 157; advocates 161; handguns 152, 155, 157; laws 148, 157; lobbyists 156, 157; permits 157; possession 156; sellers 155 (see also firearms, handguns, weapons)
gun control xviii, 155; legislation 164;

H
Haifa, Israel 209
Harvard University 224; Medical School 57
health 127; benefits 136; care 59, 127, 139, 146, 238; coverage 12; reform xx; system, overall of xviii; insurance 12, 29
Hebron, Israel 207, 208, 219
Helms, Senator Jesse 237, 238
heroin 66, 68 (see also drugs)
high school: education 107; graduate 101, 107; students 104
Hispanic(s) 106, 109, 113, 116, 127, 130, 140, 187, 200
Holocaust 209, 211, 212
homicide(s) 146, 157; rate, juvenile 152; victims 152
Household Survey 64, 68
Huang, John 231
human immunodeficiency virus (HIV) 11

I
immigrants, immigration vii, 125-144, 70, 178; European 127; illegal 125, 126, 133, 134, 173; Jewish 211; Latin American 127; legal 125, 128, 130, 133, 137, 139, 168, 170, 171, 173; mass 130; newcomers 125, 138, 142; policy 128; Third World 131; workers 137
Immigration and Naturalization Service (INS) 126, 131, 135, 137
Indian(s) 20, 29; affairs 29; American 197; casino gamblin 20; pueblos 29; reservation 28; tribes 19, 28
Indian Gaming Regulatory Act (1988) 25, 32
insurance, medical 173
intifada (1987-1990) 217
Iraq 215, 216, 217, 255
Islam 208, 210
Israel 205, 206, 207, 208, 209, 213, 214, 215, 216, 217, 219; Land of 219
Israeli/PLO accords 218
Israeli(s) 209, 213, 215, 216, 218; Jews 206, 219
Israeli Wars of 1948, 1956, 1967, 1973, 1982 216
Italians, Italy 126, 129, 131

J
Japan 104, 106
Jerusalem, Israel 207, 208-209, 210, 213; Old City of 214
Jewish 8; Agency 212, 213; immigration 209; Jewish settlements, 207, 208
Jews 205, 209, 210, 211, 212, 213, 218, 220
job(s) 23, 25, 31, 35, 137, 146, 179, 181, 182; approval rating xvi, 252, 253;

Index

community service 179; discrimination 3, 13; opportunity 1; performance 262; quotas 194; training programs 173, 174, 179, 194

Johnson, President Lyndon B. 192-193, 243, 252, 258

journalists (ism) viii, 221, 235, 236, 238; public 236, 238

juvenile(s) 152, 155; court 153; crime epidemic 153; justice system 152; killers 152; offenders 152

K

Kemp, Jack 246
Kennedy, President John F. 191-192, 236, 258
Kevorkian, Dr. Jack 78, 92-93, 97
King, Martin Luther, Jr. 187
Koop, C. Everett 86, 88

L

labor: organized 102; sweatshop 137; unions 226 (*see also* AFL-CIO)
Las Vegas (Nevada) 19, 20, 22, 24, 27, 31
Latin America(ns) 125, 126, 136
Latinos—*see* Hispanics
law(s) 230, 232; enforcement 159; agents 61; authorities 39; officers 71
Lebanon 141-142, 206, 216
Ledyard (Connecticut) 32, 33, 34
liberal(s) 69, 120, 178, 195
Life Legal Defense Foundation of Napa, California 85
liquor 52, 54, 55, 57; hard 54
Los Angeles 62, 66, 145, 192
lottery 20, 23, 24; ticket 19, 22
lung cancer and disease 39, 47, 68

M

magnet schools 119
marijuana 60, 66, 67, 68, 73, 248, 254 (*see also* drugs)
marriage 1, 8, 11, 12, 13, shot-gun 176
Mashantucket Pequot(s) 25, 32-33, 36
Massachusetts 20, 21, 36, 47, 49, 52, 110, 119, 157, 160, 199-200; Bay Colony 128; Housing Finace Authority 200
McCaffrey, Barry R. 61, 67, 70
McCain, Senator John 229, 231
McCain-Feingold measure 232-233, 238
McCorvey, Norma 91
Medicaid & Medicare 46, 47, 87, 138, 159, 172, 173, 177, 178, 224
men 4, 10, 21, 40, 51, 54, 57, 83, 84, 85, 109, 148, 149, 152, 257; black 194, 195; white 194

mental: disorder 14; health 80; illness 69
Mexico 64, 66, 129, 130, 133, 134, 136, 215
Middle East 132, 206, 210, 211, 215, 216, 218, 219
military, the—*see* armed forces
minorities, minority 3, 4, 109, 119, 162, 187, 188, 189, 190, 191, 193, 194, 195, 199, 200, 201, 221
Mohegan Sun casino 34, 35
money; laundering 70, 231; soft 225, 227, 228, 232; special interest 231
mother(s), single 174, 176, 182, 183
Moynihan, Senator Daniel Patrick 168, 170, 176, 178, 183
multiculturalism 141-142
murder(s) 77, 85, 145, 146, 152, 153, 157, 161, 162, 164; rate 39, 157
Muslims 208, 210

N

Nation at Risk, A (report) 102, 103, 105, 107, 111, 119
National Guard 70, 136
National Rifle Association (NRA) 156, 157, 161
National Urban League 190
Navy, United States 70 (*see also* Armed Forces, U.S.)
Netanyahu, Prime Minister Benjamin 205, 207, 218
New Deal 50, 172
New Hampshire 24, 52, 236
New Orleans (Louisiana) 20, 24
New York 24, 35, 54, 127, 139, 168, 182
New York City (NY) 31, 66, 145, 146, 152, 155, 157, 158, 175, 182
New Yorker, The 177, 196
New York Times 173, 178
nicotine 42, 44, 45, 47, 49
Nixon, President Richard M. 227, 252, 258
North American Free Trade Agreement (NAFTA) 136, 256
NRA—*see* National Rifle Association

O

O'Connor, Justice Sandra Day 193
Ohio 52, 111, 113, 178, 180; Federation of Teachers 113
Oklahoma City 247; City bombing 161
Oslo accords (1993) 206, 207, 208, 217

P

PACs—*see* political action committees
Palestine 205, 209, 210, 211, 212-213; mandate 218; problem 206, 216
Palestine Liberation Organization (PLO) 205,
208, 214, 216, 217
Palestinian(s) 207, 208, 209, 214, 216, 218, 219; Arabs 206; Authority 207; Uprising 217 parents, single 179
partial birth: abortion(s) 81, 86, 88; procedure 88-89 (*see also* abortion)
Pequots—*see* Mashantucket Pequots
Perot, Ross 225, 243, 246, 247, 248, 249, 251, 254, 256
Persian Gulf, War of (1990 & 1991) xxi
Personal Responsibility and Work Opportunity Act 167, 170, 183, 261
Philip Morris 42, 43, 225
Planned Parenthood v. Casey 87
PLO—*see* Palestinian Liberation Organization
police 156, 158; officers 72,
political action committees (PACs) 225, 232, 233, 234
political parties xxii, 227, 231 (*see also* specific party)
politicians and politics viii, 222, 223, 224, 227 233, 236
poverty and the poor 69, 105, 120, 138, 140, 153, 167, 168, 172, 173, 175, 180, 181, 188; elderly 17; rates 168
Powell, Colin 249
Presidential Campaign (1996) 59, 88, 120, 155, 164, 221, 223, 227, 235, 246, 248, 249, 250, 253, 254; (1992) 176, 254
prison(s) 60, 148, 156, 157, 158, 159, 189; prisoners 92, 160
private schools 111, 113, 114, 120, 121;
pro-choice movement 78, 81, 82, 83, 85, 91
pro-life movement 81, 83, 84, 85, 91
prohibition(ists) 54, 55, 56
Proposition 187 (California) 125, 134, 135, 136
Proposition 209 (California) 187-188, 195, 196, 198, 201; Yes on 209 198
Protestant(s) 9, 54, 78, 114, 116, 257, 258
public xxii; assistance 167, 170; choice 112; citizens 3; education 101, 103, 110, 112, 117, 119, 120, 121,135; funds 176; opinion v, vii, viii, xv, xviii, xx, 19, 120, 133, 256, 264; schools 102, 103-104, 107, 111, 113, 119, 120, 223, 224; system 108; service 108 (*see also* community service)

Q

Quaker(s) 11
quotas, national 129
quota system 191

R

Rabin, Prime Minister Yitzhak 207, 217, 219

race(s) xx, xxi, 2, 54, 107, 121, 127, 187, 196, 198, 258-259; preferences 190
racial-quota systems 194, 199
racism 176, 196
rape 89, 145, 146, 161
Reagan, President Ronald 5, 103, 113, 119, 193, 206, 217, 250, 252, 257, 258
Reform Party 243, 247
refugees 129, 130, 138, 208
religion 9, 54, 82, 258; wars of 78
religious: affiliation xix; belief 8-9, 54
Republican(s) (GOP) vii, xxii, 10, 35, 60, 62, 72, 109, 113, 114, 120, 121, 135, 140, 162, 171, 176, 177, 180, 188, 192, 194, 246
right to die 93; issues 93, 95; question 93
robbery 146; armed 145, 161
Roe v. Wade 78, 86-91
Roman Catholics 114, 116, 256, 257, 258
Roosevelt, President Franklin D. xix, 236, 243, 252
Roth, Senator William V. 171
Rowland, Governor John G. 112
Russia 129, 131, 158, 209, 215

S

Salvi, John 85
same-sex marriage(s) 1, 2, 3, 10, 11, 12, 13
sampling: biases xx; frame xiii; probability x; theory xv; validity x
Saturday night specials (guns) 157 *(see also* firearms, guns, weapons)
school(s) 2, 101, 104; choice 111, 112, 114; cult 112; day 106, 116; lunch programs 172, 173; prayer 25; -uniform codes 116; year 106, 116
scores, aptitude test 102, 107, 108; standardized achievement 102
Seminole Tribe of Florida v. Florida 28
sex 121; education 3
sexual: orientation 3, 6,9; self-control 8
Simpson, O. J. 205
Sinai Peninsula 213-214, 215
slavery 8, 89, 129
slots, slot machines 19, 20, 26, 27, 28, 31, 34
smoking v, 39, 43, 44, 45, 46, 57, 72; related deaths 46; -related illnesses 46; teenage 222 *(see also* tobacco)
social: costs 39; ills 60, 175; issues 109; problems 30; scientists 177; studies 108
Social Security 48, 133, 224 amendments 174
Soviet Union 130, 132, 139
subsidies, child care 173; wage 179
Suez Canal 213; crisis 214, 215
suicide(s) 94, 95, 96, 97; assisted 77; cases 95; physician-assisted 78, 92, 95 97

Supplemental Social Security (SSI) 138, 139, 171, 172, 173
Syria(ns) 206, 214, 216, 218

T

taxation, taxes 137, 138, 224, 245, 240; credits 181; property 30; revenues 168
teen(s), teenagers and adolescents 59, 63, 72, 73, 116, 152, 153, 154, 155, 176, 177, 189; blacks 176; curfew(s) 155; mothers 172; parents 180; pregnancy 91
television (TV) xi, 41, 49, 54, 64, 147, 221, 222, 232, 234, 236
terror, terrorism, terrorists 85, 161, 215; bombing 244-245
Thompson, Governor Tommy 169, 183
three-strikes 160-162
tobacco 20, 39, 40, 42, 44, 50, 53; chewing 40; companies 46, 47; tobacco industry 41, 47, 48; litigation 46; lobby 48; regulation 44; -related deaths 43; -related illnesses 40 *(see also* smoking)
Tobacco Institute 41, 47
Truman, President Harry S. 212, 252

U

unemployment 29, 30, 250
United Kingdom 104
United Nations 212, 214
University of California 73, 108, 191, 193, 195, 197
University of Pennsylvania, Center for Bioethics 96
U.S. vii, xiii, xiv, xviii, 10, 20, 29, 55, 64, 66, 70, 78, 84, 87, 93, 103, 104, 111, 125, 127, 128, 129, 130, 132, 133, 134, 136, 137, 138, 140, 142, 145, 157, 164, 173, 187, 205, 206, 209, 212, 213, 214, 215, 217, 222, 250, 253
U.S. Congress vii, xxii, 61, 72, 78, 87, 88, 89, 102, 121, 125, 129, 133, 136, 137, 140, 149, 169, 176, 177, 187, 201, 224, 226, 228, 233, 238, 239, 243, 244, 245, 250, 259-262,
U.S. Constitution 12, 42, 78, 89, 141; 18th Amendment 55; First Amendment 226, 227, 228, 233-234, 238; 14th Amendment 125; 21st Amendment 55
U.S. Deaprtment of Education 102, 116, 120
U.S. Department of Health and Human Services 178, 183
U.S. Department of Justice 146, 152, 155, 231, 232; Civil Rights Division 196, 201
U.S. Senate 88, 232, 233, 244, 259
U.S. Supreme Court 4, 6, 10, 20, 25, 28, 78, 86, 89, 162, 163, 193, 227

V

Vietnam, Vietnam War xix, 130, 256
violence 85, 110, 116, 120, 146, 164, 223; school 116
voter(s), voting 221, 222, 223, 224, 234, 236; age 248; apathy 248; disappointment 223; guides 232, ignorance 223; non- 248; participation 223; turnout 248
voucher(s) 120; program(s) 111, 112, 113; proposal 113; system 114, 120

W

Wall Street Journal 35
Washington, DC 20, 140, 183, 217, 223, 231
Washington Post 48, 62-63, 106, 235-236
Watergate 227, 233, 238
weapons—*see* guns
Weld, William 21
welfare xviii, 30, 59, 126, 138, 139, 146, 159, 167, 168, 169, 170, 171, 173, 174, 175, 176, 177, 178, 181, 182, 183, 224, 250; legislation 189; reform 167-186, 261; rolls 189 *(see also* entitlements, government assistance)
West Bank, Israel 206, 207, 208, 214, 215, 217, 218
white flight 119
White House Office of National Drug Control Policy 60, 67
white(s) 106, 116, 127, 128, 162, 177, 187, 188, 189, 190, 191, 192, 195, 196, 197, 200, 259, 261
Wilson, Governor Pete 113, 134, 135, 160, 195
Wilson, William Julius 170, 177, 181-182, 183
woman, women 3, 4, 10, 21, 40, 43, 51, 52, 54, 56, 57, 77, 79, 81, 82, 83, 84, 85, 87, 88, 94, 109, 148, 149, 172, 180, 183, 187, 189, 190, 256, 257, 258; black 177, 194; single 167, 171, 189; unmarried 178; white 194, 201
work 168, 174, 177, 178, 180, 181; rules 178-179
Work Incentive Program(s) (WIP) 174
Works Progress Administration (New Deal) 182
World War II 24, 43, 206, 215
Wynn, Stephen 27, 31, 35

Y

Yom Kippur War 215

Z

Zimbabwe 7, 50; Harare 7
Zionists 209